THE COMPLETE EDITION
AMERICA'S HISTORY
LAND OF LIBERTY

BY VIVIAN BERNSTEIN

CONSULTANTS

Dr. James E. Davis
Social Science Education Consortium
Lafayette, Colorado

Richard Jankowski
Social Studies Department Chairman
West Hills Middle School
Bloomfield Hills School District
Bloomfield, Michigan

Karen Tindel Wiggins
Director of Social Studies
Richardson Independent School District
Richardson, Texas

STECK-VAUGHN®
COMPANY
ELEMENTARY • SECONDARY • ADULT • LIBRARY

ABOUT THE AUTHOR

Vivian Bernstein is the author of *World History and You*, *America's Story*, *World Geography and You*, *American Government*, *Decisions for Health*, and *Life Skills for Today*. Bernstein is active with professional organizations in social studies, education, and reading. She gives presentations to school faculties and professional groups about content area reading. She received her Master of Arts degree from New York University and was a teacher in the New York City Public School System for a number of years.

STAFF CREDITS

Executive Editor: Diane Sharpe

Senior Editor: Martin S. Saiewitz

Senior Design Manager: Pamela Heaney

Photo Editor: Margie Foster

Electronic Production: Jill Klinger

Electronic Specialist: Alan Klemp

ACKNOWLEDGMENTS

pp. 20–21 Excerpt from *The Log of Christopher Columbus* by Christopher Columbus; translated by Robert H. Fuson. Copyright © 1987. Reprinted by permission of the McGraw-Hill Companies; p. 333 Excerpt from *The Grapes of Wrath* by John Steinbeck. Copyright 1939, renewed © 1967 by John Steinbeck. Used by permission of Viking Penguin, a division of Penguin Books USA Inc.; pp. 358–359 Excerpt from *In Search of Light: The Broadcasts of Edward R. Murrow* by Edward R. Murrow. Copyright © 1967 by the Estate of Edward R. Murrow. Reprinted by permission of Alfred A. Knopf, Inc.; pp. 386–387 Reprinted with the permission of Pocket Books, a Division of Simon & Schuster from *Warriors Don't Cry* by Melba Pattillo Beals. Copyright ©1994, 1995 by Melba Beals.; pp. 444–445 Reprinted from *Barrios and Borderlands* by Heyck Denis and Lynn Day, (1994) with permission from the publisher Routledge.

Cartography: GeoSystems, Inc.

Charts, Graphs, and Tables: Chuck Joseph, Chuck Mackey

Cover Photography: (Eagle) © Daniel J. Cox/Tony Stone Images, (Flag) © Superstock

Photo Credits: (KEY: C=Corbis; CB=Corbis-Bettmann; CP=Culver Pictures; GC=The Granger Collection; NP=National Portrait Gallery, Smithsonian Institution; NW=North Wind Picture Archive; SS=Superstock) Unit opener medals, unit opener time lines, chapter opener books, chapter opener frames, biography frames, biography notebooks, Voices from the Past frames, map caption globes, skills page flag, p. 228, p. 402 Images © 1996 PhotoDisc, Inc.; pp. 2–3 St. Augustine Historical Society; p. 4 GC; pp. 5, 6 © SS; p. 8 NW; p. 9 GC; p. 10 (left) NW, (center) © SS; p. 14 GC; p. 15 (both) NW; p. 16 © SS; p. 19 GC; p. 20 NW; pp. 22, 25, 26, 27, 28 GC; p. 30 New York Historical Society; pp. 31, 35, 37, 38, 39, 40, 43 GC; p. 44 © SS; p. 45 Colonial Williamsburg Foundation; pp. 47, 49 © SS; p. 50 GC; pp. 56–57 © Charles D. Winters/Stock Boston; p. 58 GC; p. 60 © Photri; pp. 61, 63 NW; p. 64 © SS; p. 68 GC; p. 69 (both) NW; p. 71 (top) © Daniel J. Cox/Tony Stone Images, (bottom) GC; p. 72 GC; p. 73 (center) © SS, (right) NW; p. 74 Courtesy, Museum of Fine Arts, Boston, Gift of Joseph W., William B., and Edward H.R. Revere; p. 78 © SS; p. 79 GC; p. 80 © SS; p. 81 NW; p. 82 © SS; p. 85 NP/Art Resource; p. 86 GC; p. 96 Abby Aldrich Rockefeller Folk Art Center, Williamsburg, VA; p. 97 GC; p. 98 (both) Independence Hall National Historic Park; p. 101 GC; p. 102 AP/Wide World; p. 103 NP; pp. 136–137 Lafayette College; p. 138 (all) Mt. Vernon Ladies Association; pp. 139, 140 GC; p. 141 The National Archives of the United States by Herman Viola, photographer, Jonathan Wallen; continued on page 502.

ISBN 0-8172-6337-3

Copyright © 1997 Steck-Vaughn Company

1 2 3 4 5 6 7 8 9 VHP 00 99 98 97 96

ONTENTS

To the Reader

You are about to read an exciting story about American history, and it is different from the story of all other nations. *America's History: Land of Liberty* begins thousands of years ago with Native Americans who lived throughout the Americas. Then a few hundred years ago, people from Europe explored and settled these continents. After the United States became independent from Great Britain, more land and then more states became part of the nation.

The nation grew larger and stronger, but it was almost destroyed during the bitter Civil War between the North and the South. Find out how Americans rebuilt the South after the Civil War and reunited the nation. Discover how millions of immigrants from many nations made the United States their home during the past one hundred years. Learn how the United States became a world power and succeeded in defeating its enemies during World Wars I and II. Explore how the United States has become the most powerful and important nation in the world today.

As you explore your nation's past, use *America's History: Land of Liberty* to become a stronger social studies student. You will need a social studies notebook for assignments and writing activities. Begin by mastering new vocabulary words for each chapter and reviewing vocabulary from earlier chapters. Locate new places on a map and understand the ways geography can affect history. Read each chapter carefully. A second reading will improve your comprehension and recall. By working carefully on end-of-chapter activities, you will improve your vocabulary, critical thinking, writing, and social studies skills.

As you study American history, you will learn how many kinds of Americans built your nation. Think about the ways events of the past have created the nation that you are a part of today. An understanding of America's triumphs and mistakes in the past can help you work for a better future. As you journey through American history, remember that the story of the United States is your story, too!

Vivian Bernstein

Unit 1

AMERICA'S EARLY YEARS

Would you travel through dangerous, unknown land to find gold and become rich? Imagine being told that somewhere in North America there are seven cities where jewels cover the houses and gold covers the streets. During the 1500s, people from Spain explored North America as they searched for the seven cities of gold. Although they never found the seven cities of gold, the Spanish did build an empire.

As you read Unit 1, you will learn how Europeans explored and settled America and changed the lives of the Native Americans who had been living there.

The Maya begin their empire in Central America.
A.D. 300

1492
Columbus reaches the Americas.

| 300 | 1200 | 1300 | 1400 |

A.D. 300
Africans begin the Empire of Ghana.

1200
Africans build the great Empire of Mali.

1271
Marco Polo begins his travels to Asia.

1455
Gutenberg invents the printing press.

1497
Da Gama sails around Africa to Asia.

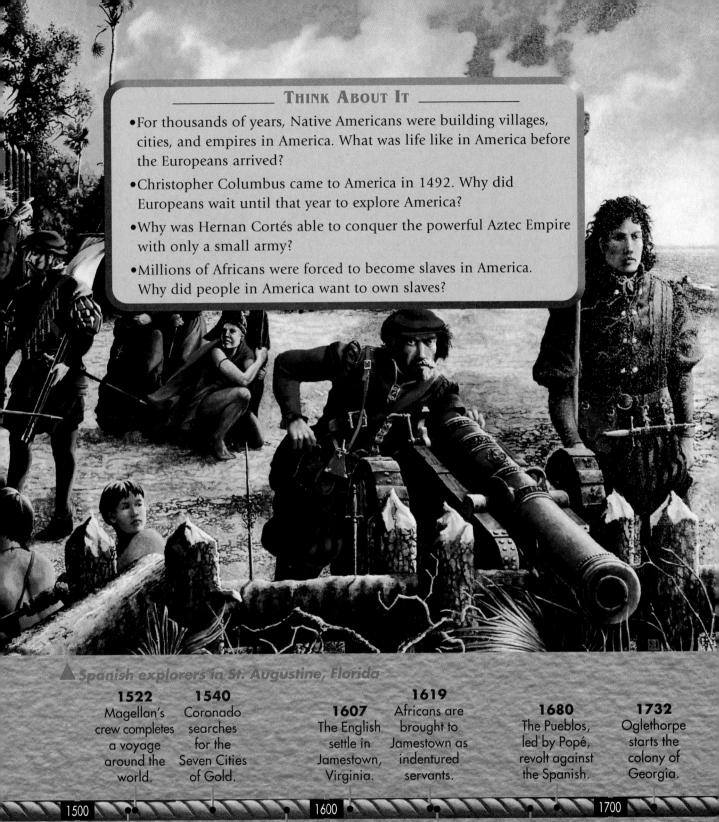

THINK ABOUT IT

- For thousands of years, Native Americans were building villages, cities, and empires in America. What was life like in America before the Europeans arrived?

- Christopher Columbus came to America in 1492. Why did Europeans wait until that year to explore America?

- Why was Hernan Cortés able to conquer the powerful Aztec Empire with only a small army?

- Millions of Africans were forced to become slaves in America. Why did people in America want to own slaves?

▲ *Spanish explorers in St. Augustine, Florida*

1522
Magellan's crew completes a voyage around the world.

1540
Coronado searches for the Seven Cities of Gold.

1607
The English settle in Jamestown, Virginia.

1619
Africans are brought to Jamestown as indentured servants.

1680
The Pueblos, led by Popé, revolt against the Spanish.

1732
Oglethorpe starts the colony of Georgia.

1500   1600   1700

1521
Cortés conquers the Aztec Empire.

1588
The English defeat the Spanish Armada.

1620
The Pilgrims settle in Plymouth, Massachusetts.

1664
The English win New Netherlands from the Dutch.

Chapter 1

EARLIEST PEOPLE OF THE AMERICAS

◀ *Mask of the Aztec god Quetzalcoatl*

People

Native Americans •
Pueblos • Mound Builders •
Iroquois • Maya• Aztec •
Inca • Hiawatha •
Tadodaho • Peacemaker

Places

Bering Sea • Mississippi
River • Rocky Mountains •
Great Plains • Ohio River
Mexico • Tenochtitlan •
Andes Mountains • Peru

New Vocabulary

archaeologists • artifacts •
gatherers • culture •
irrigation canals • totem
poles • survive • tepees •
confederation •
civilization • pyramids •
human sacrifices •
empire • terraces

Focus on Main Ideas

1. What is known about the first Americans?
2. How did Native American life differ in the Southwest, the Northwest, the Great Plains, and east of the Mississippi River?
3. What kinds of civilizations did Native Americans build in Mexico, Central America, and South America?

Imagine what America was like 50,000 years ago. It was a time called the Ice Age. The climate was much colder than it is today, and most of North America was covered with huge sheets of ice. Fifty thousand years ago, people had not yet come to America.

The First Americans

Archaeologists believe that people first came to America between 20,000 and 50,000 years ago. People walked across a land bridge from Asia to North America. This land bridge was located where the Bering Sea is today. For several thousand years, groups of Asians continued to cross this land bridge. As time passed, Earth's climate became warmer and the Ice Age ended. As the huge sheets of ice that had covered North America melted, the level of the sea became higher. Finally the land bridge disappeared under the Bering Sea.

The first Americans did not have a writing system, so they left no books about their lives. Without written records no one really knows exactly how these people lived. But archaeologists have found bones from people who lived in America thousands of years ago. They have also found tools that these early people made. By studying bones, tools, and other **artifacts**, archaeologists have learned a lot about the earliest Americans.

The earliest Americans fished and hunted for food. These early people were also **gatherers**. They gathered wild berries, nuts, and plant roots for food. They moved from place to place as they hunted and gathered food. Their lives changed when they learned to plant seeds and grow their own food. Once they learned how to farm, they stayed in one place. As time passed these first Americans, or Native Americans, settled throughout North and South America. Their **culture**—how they lived, how they dressed, what they ate, and the language they spoke—often depended on where they lived.

Native Americans West of the Mississippi River

Hundreds of years ago, the Pueblo built large apartment houses along the sides of steep cliffs. The Pueblo also lived in villages of stone buildings. The land where they lived is now the southwestern part of the United States. Parts of the Southwest do not get enough rain to grow crops. In order to grow crops, the Pueblo built **irrigation canals** that carried river water to their farms. The Pueblo worked hard to

Some Pueblo were cliff dwellers. They built apartments into cliffs like the one pictured here in Colorado. Some of the buildings were more than four stories tall. For safety, none of the doors were on the first floor. If the Pueblo were attacked, they pulled their ladders into the upper floors.

Totem poles were used by several Native American groups in the Northwest. Each part of the totem could represent a different person or event in a family's history.

grow corn and beans for food. Religion was an important part of Pueblo life. The people did religious dances so there would be rain and crops.

Getting food was easier for Native Americans who lived in what is today the Pacific Northwest of the United States. Native Americans who lived in forests near the Pacific Ocean always had plenty of food. There were fish from the oceans and the rivers. They also ate nuts and wild berries from the forests. They ate meat from the animals that they hunted. Native Americans of the Northwest were not farmers because it was easy for them to find food.

The people of the Northwest used the trees in the forest in many ways. They built wooden homes and put tall wooden

totem poles in front of their homes. Trees from the forest were also made into long canoes. They used their canoes to fish in the ocean and the rivers and to travel when trading with other nations. Even their clothing was made from trees. Native Americans took the bark off trees, made it very soft, and then made the bark into clothing.

Life was far more difficult for the Native Americans who lived on the plains between the Rocky Mountains and the Mississippi River. The flat land of the Great Plains had few trees and not much rain. It was terribly hot in the summer and very cold in the winter. Since it was difficult to be farmers on this dry, flat land, Native Americans hunted buffalo to **survive**. Millions of buffalo lived on the Great Plains. Native Americans ate buffalo meat, made clothes out of buffalo skin, and made tools from buffalo bones. Even their homes, which were tents called **tepees**, were made of buffalo skins and bones.

To hunt buffalo Native Americans moved from place to place to follow the herds. Since the Native Americans did not have horses, they hunted by walking and running after the buffalo. They used bows and arrows and long spears to kill the buffalo. It was hard, dangerous work.

Native Americans East of the Mississippi River

Many forests covered the land that was east of the Mississippi River. Native Americans who lived near the Ohio and Mississippi rivers built huge mounds, or hills of dirt, that were sometimes fifty feet high. These Native Americans have been called Mound Builders. Temples were built at the top of some mounds. Important people who had died were buried inside the mounds. Archaeologists have found pots, bowls, and pearls in some mounds. Since the pearls came from the Pacific Ocean, which was thousands of miles away, archaeologists believe the Mound Builders were excellent traders. By the late 1500s, the Mound Builders were replaced by other Native American groups.

One group that replaced the Mound Builders was the Iroquois. They settled in the eastern forests. The Iroquois hunted animals in the forests. They were also farmers. To clear the land, they chopped down the trees. Then they burned the tree stumps. After the trees were gone, they planted corn, beans, and squash. These crops were so important that the Iroquois called them the "Three Sisters."

The Iroquois lived in homes called longhouses. As many as twenty families would live together in a longhouse. Each family had its own small apartment in the longhouse. All of the families were related to each other. The oldest woman in the longhouse became the leader of all the families in the house.

There were many different Iroquois nations, and they often had wars with each other. People of one nation were often attacked by another nation. After many years of war, five Iroquois nations joined together in a **confederation** to have peace. They formed the Iroquois Confederation

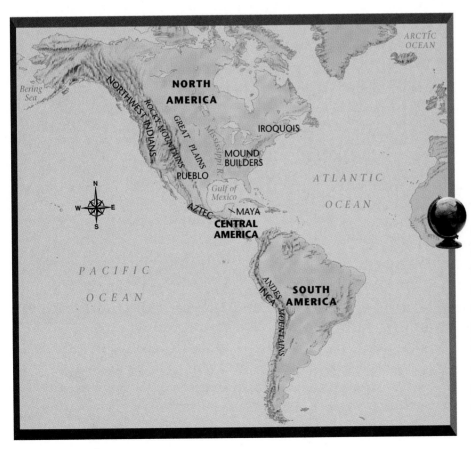

Several Native American Cultures Hundreds of different Native American cultures developed throughout North and South America. Which Native American group lived in the Andes Mountains?

of Five Nations. All five nations sent chiefs to represent them at council meetings. The chiefs were chosen by women. At Council meetings laws were made and problems between nations were solved. The five nations remained independent, but they worked together for peace. When the United States became a free nation, it used the Iroquois's ideas about government to help plan the new American government.

Native Americans of Mexico, Central America, and South America

Thick rain forests cover parts of Mexico and Central America. The weather in the rain forests is always hot and rainy. In these rain forests, people called the Maya built an amazing **civilization**. Between the years A.D. 300 and 900, the Maya built many beautiful cities. They studied math and invented a calendar. They were the first Native Americans to develop a system of writing. They used many small pictures to write their language.

The Maya built huge **pyramids** where they buried their dead kings. Temples were built on top of some pyramids. The Maya prayed to many different gods in these temples. The sun god was the most important Mayan god. The Maya believed they had to make **human sacrifices** to the

Native Americans grew corn, beans, squash, potatoes, and many other types of products. The Iroquois cleared land in the eastern forests for their fields. Besides raising corn, the Iroquois also fished, hunted, and gathered to get food.

sun god so that the sun would continue to shine. This means they killed people as a sacrifice to the sun god. About the year 900, the Maya left their cities and their civilization ended. No one knows why this happened. But people from ancient Mayan families still live in Mexico and Central America today.

The Aztec were Native Americans who built a great civilization in Mexico. The Aztec conquered and ruled a large **empire**. Perhaps eleven million people lived in this empire. Like the Maya, the Aztec developed a system for writing their language.

The Aztec were great builders. They built huge pyramids and temples. Their capital, Tenochtitlan, was built on an island in a lake. Bridges connected the city to the mainland. Large temples, houses, and government buildings were built in the city. Tenochtitlan was larger and cleaner than any city in Europe at that time.

The Aztec believed in many gods, but the sun god and the war god were the most important ones. The Aztec believed these gods needed human sacrifices. The Aztec sacrificed thousands of people each year. They went to war in order to capture people whom they could sacrifice.

The Inca were Native Americans who built an empire that extended through the Andes Mountains of South America. Their capital was in the country that is now Peru. People everywhere in the Inca Empire spoke the same language and obeyed the same king. The Inca built roads to connect cities throughout the empire. They also built bridges across deep valleys. Although they lived in very tall mountains, they learned how to grow food by making

The Aztec capital of Tenochtitlan in the Valley of Mexico was the center of an empire. More than 100,000 people lived in this city.

terraces on the sides of the mountains. They built irrigation canals to carry water to their farms. The Inca took care of their people, and poor people were not allowed to go hungry.

By the year 1492, millions of Native Americans were living throughout North, Central, and South America. They spoke hundreds of languages and had developed many different cultures. Until 1492 no one in Europe knew about the land we call America or the Native Americans who lived there. But in the year 1492, people from Europe began exploring America. As more and more people from Europe came to America, Native American life changed forever. Read on to learn what happened to Native Americans as people from Europe explored and settled America.

BIOGRAPHY

Hiawatha

Hiawatha was an Iroquois who helped bring peace to the five Iroquois nations.

For many years people from one Iroquois nation were often attacked and killed by people from another nation. Attacks among the five nations—Mohawk, Oneida, Cayuga, Seneca, and Onondaga—happened so often that it became unsafe to work on a farm or to hunt in the woods. One young Iroquois man, Hiawatha, believed the Iroquois should stop fighting and work together for peace. When Tadodaho, the leader of the Onondaga nation, heard

Hiawatha's ideas about peace, he became so angry that he had all of Hiawatha's daughters killed.

Symbol of the Confederation of Five Nations

Hiawatha was filled with grief after his daughters were killed. He was so unhappy that he left his home and went to live alone in a small house in the forest. One day he met a man from another Indian nation who also spoke about peace. His people called him Peacemaker. Hiawatha and Peacemaker decided to travel together to the different Iroquois nations to convince them to join a confederation that would work for peace. Since Hiawatha was an excellent speaker and Peacemaker was a poor one, the two men decided that Hiawatha would speak to the leaders of the nations. Hiawatha convinced four Iroquois nations to accept peace, but he wanted the Onondaga nation to join the Confederation, too. So Hiawatha faced his old enemy Tadodaho and spoke softly to him about peace. Tadodaho listened and agreed that the Onondaga nation would join the Confederation of Five Nations. The confederation kept peace among the Iroquois for about 300 years.

In Your Own Words

Write a paragraph in the journal section of your social studies notebook that explains the importance of Hiawatha's work among the Iroquois nations.

REVIEW AND APPLY

- Native Americans first came to America from Asia between 20,000 and 50,000 years ago.

- Native Americans developed many different cultures based on the geography and the climate of where they lived.

- The Pueblo used irrigation to grow food in the dry Southwest.

- Native Americans on the Great Plains depended on the buffalo to survive.

- To keep peace, five Iroquois nations formed the Iroquois Confederation. Some ideas for the government of the United States are based on the ideas of the Iroquois Confederation.

- The Maya, Aztec, and Inca developed great civilizations in Mexico, Central America, and South America.

VOCABULARY

Finish the Sentence ■ **Choose one of the words or phrases from the box to complete each sentence. In your social studies notebook, write the numbers 1 through 8. Next to each number, write the correct word or phrase. You will not use all the words in the box.**

1. An _____ studies old bones to learn how people lived long ago.

2. An _____ is a tool or object that was made by a person.

3. How people live, what they eat, and how they dress are all parts

   of the _____ of a group.

4. An _____ is a ditch that carries water to dry land so people can grow crops.

5. An _____ is land or people that are ruled by one nation.

6. A _____ is a tent that is made from animal skins and bones.

7. Native Americans of the Northwest used carved and painted _____ as symbols of their families.

8. The Iroquois joined together as a _____ to keep peace.

empire
culture
archaeologist
totem poles
tepee
irrigation canal
confederation
pyramids
artifact

11

USING INFORMATION

Journal Writing ■ Write a paragraph in your journal that explains with which Native Americans you would want to live and why.

COMPREHENSION CHECK

Finish the Paragraph ■ Use the words in the box to finish the paragraph. In your social studies notebook, write the numbers 1 through 6. Next to each number, write the correct word. There is an extra word that you will not use.

buffalo	Maya	gatherers	Bering Sea
	burning	cotton	villages

Between 20,000 and 50,000 years ago, people first came to America by crossing the __1__ on a land bridge. These people were __2__ because they moved from place to place, searching for food. After people learned to farm, they started to live in __3__. The Native Americans of the Great Plains hunted __4__. In the eastern forests, Native Americans farmed by first chopping down trees and then __5__ the stumps. The __6__ built a civilization in Mexico and Central America.

CRITICAL THINKING

Categories ■ Read the words in each group. In your social studies notebook, write the numbers 1 through 4. Next to each number, write the correct title for each group. You may use the words in the box for all or part of each title. There is one title in the box that you will not need.

Pueblo	Iroquois	Inca
Aztec	Mound Builders	

1. lived in longhouses
   planted corn, beans, and squash
   joined a confederation

2. lived in the Southwest of the United States
   built apartment houses
   built irrigation canals

3. their capital city was Tenochtitlan
   ruled an empire in Mexico
   believed in many gods

4. grew food on mountain terraces
   ruled a huge empire in South America
   built roads to connect cities

SOCIAL STUDIES SKILLS

Locating Oceans and Continents

Most of Earth is covered with water from four large bodies of water called oceans:

Pacific Ocean   Atlantic Ocean
Indian Ocean   Arctic Ocean

Earth also has very large bodies of land called continents:

Asia   Africa
North America   South America
Antarctica
Australia

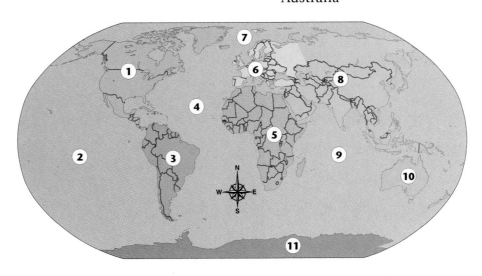

A. Number your paper from 1 to 11. Next to each number, write the name of the ocean or continent represented by the numbers on the map above. Use the world map on page 460.

B. Write the answer to each question in the assignment section of your social studies notebook.

1. Which ocean is located between Africa and South America?

2. Which ocean is located between Africa and Australia?

3. Which continent is connected to South America?

4. Which continent is connected to Europe?

5. Which ocean is located between Asia and North America?

Chapter 2
EUROPEANS EXPLORE THE AMERICAS

◀ *Astrolabe from Portugal from about 1555*

People

Christopher Columbus •
Marco Polo • Queen
Isabella • Tainos • Amerigo
Vespucci • Ferdinand
Magellan • La Salle •
Estevanico • Zuni

St. Lawrence River •
Quebec • Gulf of Mexico •
Louisiana • Florida •
Mexico City

Places

England • Spain • France •
Portugal • Strait of Magellan •
Philippines • Canada •

New Vocabulary

technology • compass •
astrolabe • monarchs •
mainland • colonies •
circumnavigate •
tributaries • log

Focus on Main Ideas

1. Why were Europeans ready for exploration in the 1400s?
2. How did Prince Henry help sailors from Portugal reach Asia 20 years after his death?
3. How did America get its name?
4. Why did explorers continue to look for new routes to Asia after Christopher Columbus came to America?

About the year 1000, Vikings sailed across the Atlantic Ocean and reached North America. The Vikings may have been the first people from Europe to reach America. But it was not until about five hundred years later that Christopher Columbus and others began to explore America.

Why Did Europeans Become Explorers in the 1400s?

For hundreds of years, people in Europe knew little about other parts of the world. European mapmakers believed there were only three continents—Europe, Asia, and Africa. Europeans wanted more trade with Asia after they learned about the travels of Marco Polo. Marco Polo had left Italy in 1271 and had spent 24 years traveling in central Asia and China. He had returned to Europe with beautiful silks and jewels. He had written a book about his travels that made other people want to trade with Asia.

People in Europe also wanted to trade with Asian countries to get spices for their food. Spices were valuable because there were no refrigerators at that time, and spices helped food stay fresher and taste better. In order to trade with Asia,

Europeans had to make a long journey through dangerous lands. Because the journey over land was so long and dangerous, Europeans wanted to find an easier water route to Asia.

There were three reasons why Europeans were ready to start exploring for new ways to reach Asia. First, by the 1400s **technology** had improved ocean travel. Europeans had learned to build ships with better sails that could sail against the wind. They had learned to use the **compass**, which showed sailors which direction was north. Another instrument, the **astrolabe**, helped sailors know how far they were from the equator. Improved technology made it possible to travel and explore more than ever before.

Second, there was also great interest in learning new ideas at this time. Johannes Gutenberg invented a printing press in 1455, and many new books were printed. Through books people could spread ideas and information about travel and exploration.

A third reason was that England, Spain, France, and Portugal had become very strong nations that were ruled by powerful **monarchs**. Monarchs are kings and queens. These nations had the money and the power to send explorers on far-off journeys. Each of these nations wanted to become more powerful than the others. By controlling trade with Asia, a nation could become rich and powerful.

Prince Henry of Portugal brought together mapmakers and sailors from all over Europe to help sailors from Portugal explore the coast of Africa.

Vasco da Gama reached Asia by sailing around Africa. His father had been asked by the king of Portugal to lead the voyage. Da Gama took over after his father died.

Christopher Columbus presents his plans to Queen Isabella and King Ferdinand of Spain. Columbus had first gone to other rulers in Europe, but they had refused to help him.

The Portuguese Become Explorers First

Prince Henry of Portugal believed it was possible to reach Asia by sailing around Africa. So Henry started a school where men could learn to be sailors and learn how to build better ships. Europeans knew very little about Africa, so Prince Henry encouraged sailors to explore the west coast of Africa.

Finally in 1487, almost twenty years after Prince Henry "the Navigator" had died, a Portuguese explorer named Bartolomeu Dias sailed past the southern tip of Africa. Ten years later another Portuguese explorer, Vasco da Gama, sailed around Africa and through the Indian Ocean to India. At last Europeans had found a water route to Asia. Portugal became the leader in trade with Asia.

Christopher Columbus Sails West

Christopher Columbus was born in Italy and became a sailor. He believed that sailing west across the Atlantic Ocean would be a shorter, faster way to reach Asia than sailing around Africa. Like other people at that time, Columbus did not know there were two American continents between Europe and Asia. He also did not know about the huge Pacific Ocean.

Columbus needed sailors and ships in order to sail west across the Atlantic Ocean. He asked the king of Portugal for ships, but the king refused because he thought Columbus's ideas were wrong. Then Columbus went to Spain where he presented his plans to Queen Isabella. After six years Isabella agreed to help Columbus. Isabella hoped Columbus might find gold in Asia so Spain would become a richer nation. She gave Columbus three ships and ninety sailors. Columbus's ships—the *Niña*, the *Pinta*, and the *Santa Maria*—began the long trip across the Atlantic Ocean in August 1492.

Columbus thought the Atlantic Ocean was much smaller than it really is, so the trip across the ocean took much longer than he expected. The sailors thought they were lost at sea because for weeks all they saw was the ocean all around them.

By October 9, 1492, the sailors were so frightened they told Columbus he must turn back to Spain. Columbus promised that he would turn back if they did not see land in three days. But three days later, on October 12, 1492, they reached land.

Columbus believed he had reached an island near India. He put a large cross and a Spanish flag on the island and said the land belonged to Spain. Columbus had reached the island of San Salvador in the Caribbean Sea. He did not know that he was on an island in the Americas. The Native Americans who lived on San Salvador were friendly people called Tainos. Columbus called the people he met Indians because he thought he was in India. To welcome Columbus the Tainos gave him presents that included small pieces of gold. Then Columbus explored other nearby islands as he and his crew searched for gold.

Christopher Columbus was a hero when he returned to Spain. He had forced six Tainos to go back to Spain with him, and they became slaves in Spain. Queen Isabella believed Columbus had reached Asia. She wanted him to return there and find more gold.

Columbus made three more trips to America. As he explored more islands in the Caribbean, he forced Indians to work as slaves to search for gold. Many Indians died from the cruel treatment they received. Columbus never found much gold.

Columbus always believed that the islands he was exploring were close to Asia's **mainland**, the land on the continent. Until the end of his life, Columbus always believed he had found a new way to reach Asia.

Since Spain and Portugal were both sending explorers to find new routes to Asia, the two nations began to argue about which one would rule new lands that were found. Both nations wanted to rule **colonies** in other parts of the world. By ruling colonies they would become more powerful. If gold and spices were found in the colonies, the ruling nation would be richer. The leader of the Roman Catholic Church, Pope Alexander VI, drew a line on a map from north to south that divided the Atlantic Ocean into two parts. The Pope said Spain would rule all new land that was found to the west of the line. Portugal would rule the land that was found to the east of the line. The Pope's decision was called the Treaty of Tordesillas. Portugal and Spain signed the treaty in 1494. When Portuguese explorer Pedro Cabral landed in the country we now call Brazil, the Portuguese said Brazil belonged to them because it was to the east of the Pope's line. Brazil became the only country in South America that was ruled by Portugal.

Other Europeans Explore America to Reach Asia

Soon after 1492 other explorers tried to find water routes to Asia. Amerigo Vespucci came from Italy and sailed for Portugal. He explored the coast of South America. Vespucci realized that South America was not part of Asia as Columbus believed. Vespucci said the land was a new continent and he called it a "New World." The continent was a new world only to the people in Europe who never knew about South America. It was not a new world to the

Native Americans who had been there for thousands of years.

Vespucci wrote about his discovery, and a mapmaker read his work. When the mapmaker made a map that included the New World, the mapmaker decided to name the new continents America after Amerigo Vespucci.

Ferdinand Magellan was another explorer who tried to reach Asia by sailing west. He thought he could find a water route through America that went to Asia. Magellan sailed from Spain in 1519 with five ships and a crew of about 250 men. He reached South America and sailed south to a waterway that we now call the Strait of Magellan. The sea was so stormy it took more than a month to sail through the Strait of Magellan. After sailing through the dangerous waters, Magellan reached a huge calm ocean. Magellan named this ocean the Pacific, which means peaceful.

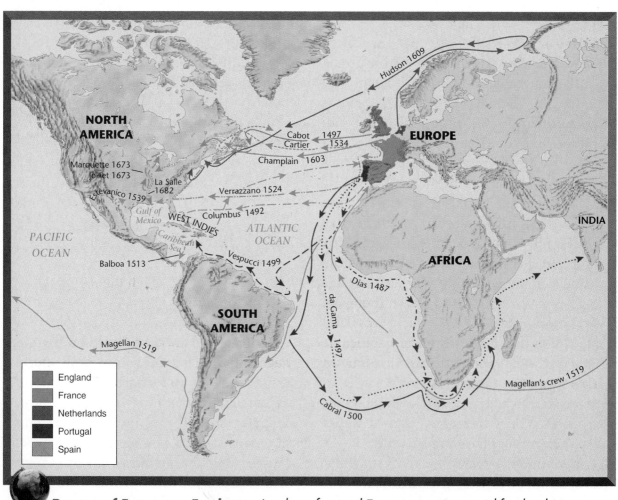

Routes of European Explorers *Leaders of several European nations paid for the ships and crews of explorers. The colors on the map show for which country each explorer was working. Which explorers shown on the map were exploring for Spain?*

18

Magellan did not know that the Pacific was much larger than the Atlantic Ocean. Magellan's trip across the Pacific was long and dangerous. For months the sailors did not see land. After they finished all the food on their ships, they ate all the rats they could find so they would not starve to death. Four ships were destroyed, and most of the sailors died along the way. Magellan was killed in a battle in the Philippines. After three years at sea, one ship with only eighteen men returned to Spain. These men who survived the voyage were the first to **circumnavigate**, or sail around, the world.

Some Europeans believed there was a Northwest Passage, or a northern water route, through North America to Asia. Many explorers tried to find the northern water route. The first was John Cabot who sailed for England. Cabot did not find the Northwest Passage, but he explored parts of Canada. Because of Cabot's work, England claimed the right to rule land in North America.

France also wanted to find a water route to Asia. Jacques Cartier searched for the Northwest Passage. He explored the St. Lawrence River and claimed all the land around that river for France. Samuel de Champlain made eleven trips to America for France. He started the French city of Quebec in Canada.

René-Robert Cavalier was another French explorer. He is also known by the name La Salle. He was born in France, and at age 23 he moved to Canada. In 1682 La Salle explored the entire Mississippi River, the longest river in the United States. He sailed from the north of the river in the

For 20 years La Salle explored parts of North America claiming land for France. In 1685 he set up a French colony on the Gulf of Mexico. The colony failed, and La Salle was killed by angry colonists.

area of the Great Lakes all the way south to the Gulf of Mexico. He claimed all the land around the river and its **tributaries**, or branches, for France. La Salle named this huge area Louisiana in honor of his king, King Louis XIV of France. France now claimed a large part of North America.

Before long, Europeans wanted to settle on and control the land in America. As Europeans tried to rule America, they fought with the Indians who were already there. In the next chapter you will learn how Europeans settled in America and what happened to the Indians who lived there.

Voices from the Past

The Log of Christopher Columbus

Christopher Columbus wrote about his first journey across the Atlantic Ocean in a log, or a journal. He wrote something about his travels every day. From his journal we learn that Columbus was a very religious man. The log also tells us that his goals were to find gold and to teach the Indians to be Christians. Here is part of his log for three days in October 1492.

Thursday, 11 October 1492

I saw several things that were indications [signs] of land. At one time a large flock of sea birds flew overhead, and a green reed was found floating near the ship. The crew of the Pinta spotted some of the same reeds…they also saw what looked like a small board or plank. A stick was recovered that looks manmade.…But even these few made the crew breathe easier; in fact, the men have even become cheerful.…A special thanksgiving was offered to God for giving us renewed hope through the many signs of land He has provided.

… Then at two hours after midnight, the Pinta fired a cannon, my prearranged signal for the sighting of land.

Friday, 12 October 1492

At dawn we saw naked people, and I went ashore.… I unfurled the royal banner and the captains brought the flags which displayed a large green cross with the letters F and Y at the left and right side of the cross. After a prayer of thanksgiving, I ordered the captains of the Pinta and Niña to witness that I was taking possession of this island for the King and Queen. To this island I gave the name San Salvador, in honor of our Blessed Lord.

People began to come to the beach.… They are very well-built people, with handsome bodies and very fine faces. Many of the natives paint their faces; others paint their whole bodies; some, only the eyes or nose. Some are painted black, some white, some red; others are of different colors.

They are friendly… people who bear no arms except for small spears, and they have no iron. I showed one my sword, and through ignorance he grabbed it by the blade and cut himself. Their spears are made of wood, to which they attach a fish tooth at one end, or some other sharp thing. I want the

> *Then at two hours after midnight, the Pinta fired a cannon, my…signal for the sighting of land.*

natives to develop a friendly attitude toward us because I know that they are a people who can be made free and converted to our Holy Faith more by love than by force. I therefore gave red caps to some and glass beads to others. They hung the beads around their necks, along with some other things of slight value that I gave them…. They traded and gave everything they had with good will, but it seems to me that they have very little and are poor in everything…. This afternoon the people of San Salvador came swimming to our ships and in boats made from one log. They brought us parrots, balls of cotton thread, spears, and many other things….

They ought to make good and skilled servants, for they repeat very quickly whatever we say to them. I think they can easily be made Christians, for they seem to have no religion. If it please Our Lord, I will take six of them to Your Highnesses when I depart, in order that they may learn our language.

Saturday, 13 October 1492

I have been very attentive and have tried very hard to find out if there is any gold here. I have seen a few natives who wear a little piece of gold hanging from a hole made in the nose…. I have learned that by going to the south, I can find a king who possesses a lot of gold…. I have tried to find some natives who will take me to this great king, but none seems inclined to make the journey. Tomorrow afternoon I intend to… look for gold and precious stones.

Write Your Answers

Answer these questions in the assignment section of your notebook.

1. How did Columbus know he was near land?

2. How did Columbus describe the native people that he met?

3. Why did Columbus believe these people were peaceful?

4. What did Columbus want to do with the Indians?

5. How did Columbus expect to find gold?

Estevanico 1500(?)–1539

Estevanico was an African slave who explored for gold in Florida and in what is now the Southwest of the United States.

In 1528 the Spanish explorer Panfilo de Narváez led 400 men on a search for gold in Florida. They did not find gold, and they were attacked by Indians. So the Spanish tried to escape by building rafts and sailing to Mexico. Most of the men were killed in a hurricane off the coast of present-day Texas. Eight years later, four survivors of the doomed expedition reached Mexico City. Estevanico was one of those survivors.

Estevanico and the other three men had spent eight years trying to reach Mexico. They traveled through what is now Texas, New Mexico, and Arizona. Along the way Estevanico learned to speak several Indian languages. He was the first African the Indians had ever seen. They thought Estevanico might be a god, so they gave him gifts. They told Estevanico stories about a place called Cibola. In these stories Cibola had seven cities made of gold.

When Estevanico and the other three men reached Mexico City, they told the stories about Cibola. The Spanish wanted to find gold, so the governor of Mexico asked a priest, Father Marcos de Niza, to search for Cibola. Father Niza told Estevanico to help him since Estevanico had already traveled through the Southwest.

During the journey Estevanico was sent ahead of the group so that he could send information about Cibola back to Father Niza. Estevanico sent information to the priest about villages with tall houses that were covered with beautiful stones. Estevanico was killed by Zuni Indians in one of the villages he visited. After he died, the Zunis told legends about the tall African explorer. The Spanish later used what they learned from Estevanico to continue exploring the Southwest, but they never found cities of gold.

In Your Own Words

Write a paragraph in the journal section of your notebook that describes Estevanico's travels and explorations.

REVIEW AND APPLY

- New technology led Europeans to explore at the end of the 1400s.

- The Portuguese were the first Europeans to search for a water route around Africa to Asia.

- Christopher Columbus made four trips to America. He thought he had reached Asia.

- Columbus called the Taino, who lived on the island that he explored, Indians.

- America was named for the explorer Amerigo Vespucci.

- Ferdinand Magellan's crew was the first to circumnavigate the world.

- John Cabot explored parts of Canada for England.

- Jacques Cartier explored the St. Lawrence River for France.

- René-Robert Cavalier, also known as La Salle, explored the Mississippi River and claimed it for France. He named the region Louisiana for King Louis XIV of France.

VOCABULARY

Analogies ■ **Use a word in the box to finish each sentence. In your social studies notebook, write the numbers 1 through 5. Next to each number, write the correct word. You will not use all of the words in the box.**

tributary	log	technology
compass	mainland	circumnavigating

1. Journal is to _____ as king is to monarch.

2. Branch is to tree as _____ is to river.

3. North America is to _____ as San Salvador is to island.

4. Scale is to weight as _____ is to direction.

5. Cartier's expedition is to exploring the St. Laurence as Magellan's expedition is to _____ Earth.

USING INFORMATION

Essay Writing ■ **There were three main reasons why Europeans began exploring in the 1400s. Write an essay that explains two of the reasons. Give one or two examples for each reason. Start your essay with a topic sentence.**

COMPREHENSION CHECK

Create an Information Chart ■ In your social studies notebook, copy and then complete the chart about important explorers. Part of the chart has already been done for you.

Explorer	For which Country Did He Explore?	What Did He Do?
Christopher Columbus		
Pedro Cabral		
Amerigo Vespucci		*Explored coast of South America; said it was a new continent*
Ferdinand Magellan		
John Cabot	*England*	
Robert de La Salle		

CRITICAL THINKING

Drawing Conclusions ■ Read the paragraph below and the five sentences that follow it. In your social studies notebook, write the conclusions that can be drawn from the paragraph. You should write three conclusions.

Christopher Columbus explored the Caribbean islands of the Americas for Spain. Soon after Columbus's voyages, the Spanish began to settle in the Americas. Ferdinand Magellan tried to find a water route to Asia by sailing west. Three years later, only one of Magellan's five ships returned to Spain after it sailed all the way around the world. Other explorers of North America included John Cabot of England and Jacques Cartier of France.

1. Because of Columbus, Spain would claim colonies in the Americas.

2. Brazil would become Portugal's colony.

3. Magellan's trip was very dangerous.

4. Magellan's trip proved it was possible to sail around the world.

5. America was named for Amerigo Vespucci.

Chapter 3 — EUROPEANS SETTLE AMERICA

◀ *Gold coin from Spain*

People

Hernan Cortés •
Moctezuma • Francisco
Pizarro • Ponce de León •
Hernando de Soto •
Francisco de Coronado •
Father Junípero Serra •
Popé • Henry Hudson •
Bartolomé de Las Casas

Santa Fe • West Africa •
New France • Great Lakes •
Hudson River • Manhattan

Places

New Spain • St. Augustine •

New Vocabulary

conquistadors •
smallpox • settlement •
plantations • Creoles •
mestizos • mulattoes •
viceroys • missions •
revolt • civil wars •
peasants • Huguenots

Focus on Main Ideas

1. What were the goals of the Spanish, French, and Dutch as they settled in the Americas?
2. What happened to Indians as more settlers came from Europe?
3. What did Europeans and Indians learn from each other?

Why would people in Europe make the dangerous trip across the Atlantic Ocean to settle in the Americas? There would be hardships during the voyage and more hardships once they reached America. But there was also the chance to earn riches and build empires. As people from Europe settled in the Americas, life changed in many ways for them and for the Indians who lived there.

The Conquistadors Build an Empire for Spain

Spain was the first nation to build an empire in America. The Spanish came to America to find gold, to teach the Catholic religion to the Indians, and to make Spain a more powerful nation. Brave but often cruel men called **conquistadors**, or conquerors, explored and conquered land in America for Spain.

Hernan Cortés was the conquistador who conquered Mexico for Spain. He landed in Mexico with about 500 soldiers in 1519. Then he led his army through thick jungles in order to reach the Aztec capital called Tenochtitlan. Cortés wanted to conquer the Aztec Empire and find gold for Spain.

Moctezuma, the Aztec emperor, thought Cortés might be one of the Aztec's gods. So Moctezuma did not try to capture Cortés.

Hernan Cortés meets Moctezuma in this Aztec drawing. At first the Aztec gave Cortés presents, but later Cortés conquered them.

Instead Moctezuma gave him gifts of gold. By 1521 Cortés and his army had conquered Mexico and destroyed the entire city of Tenochtitlan. Mexico City was built where the Aztec capital had been. The Spanish called their colony New Spain.

Why was Cortés and his small army able to defeat the huge Aztec Empire? The Spanish had horses, guns, and iron weapons to use against the Aztec. The Aztec did not have these powerful weapons. The most important reason was that Cortés and his army brought from Europe diseases, such as **smallpox** and measles, which were new to the Indians. The diseases spread rapidly among the Indians and thousands died.

Francisco Pizarro, another conquistador, climbed the tall Andes Mountains with 180 soldiers. Then they attacked and conquered the Inca in 1530. The Spanish forced the Inca to work as slaves in gold and silver mines throughout the Andes. Ships carried the gold and silver back to Spain. Spain quickly became a very wealthy nation.

Ponce de León explored Florida in 1513 in order to find gold. He also searched for the Fountain of Youth. Stories were told that people who drank from this fountain would never grow old. Ponce de León did not find gold or the Fountain of Youth, but Florida became another Spanish colony. The Spanish built a **settlement** in Florida called St. Augustine. It is the oldest European settlement in the United States.

The Spanish heard stories about an amazing place called Cibola, the Seven Cities of Gold. They learned about Cibola from the African explorer, Estevanico. Conquistadors explored North America in order to find Cibola.

Hernando de Soto, another conquistador, started his search for Cibola in 1539. Hundreds of soldiers joined de Soto as they explored what is now the Southeast of

Famous Spanish Conquistadors

Conquistador Dates of Exploration and Conquest	What Did the Conquistador Do?
Ponce de León 1513	Explored Florida
Hernan Cortés 1519–1521	Explored Mexico, conquered Aztec Empire
Francisco Pizarro 1530–1532	Explored Peru, conquered Inca Empire
Hernando de Soto 1539–1542	First European to see Mississippi River, explored Southeast of the United States
Francisco de Coronado 1540–1542	Explored Southwest of the United States

the United States. He began his search in Florida and then traveled to the Mississippi River. He became the first European to see the river that La Salle would later claim for France. De Soto never found gold, but the Southeast became a Spanish colony.

Francisco de Coronado, another conquistador, searched for Cibola from 1540 to 1542. With 300 soldiers he explored what is now the Southwest of the United States. He finally reached the place that was supposed to be Cibola. Instead of finding gold, Coronado found Indian villages that were made of mud and clay. Spain claimed a large colony in the Southwest and started a settlement called Santa Fe in 1610.

Spanish Missions and Settlements

By 1542 Spain ruled a huge empire in America. Most of the Spanish settled in Mexico, Central America, and South America where gold and silver were found. Settlers also started huge sugar cane and tobacco **plantations**. Fewer settlers came to North America because gold had not been found there.

The Spanish needed workers for their mines and plantations. At first Indians who were forced into slavery did most of the work. But millions of Indians died from diseases and poor treatment. When the Spanish needed more workers, they

Hernando de Soto's search for Cibola began near Tampa Bay in Florida. After exploring the Southeast, he reached the Mississippi River. After exploring farther west, De Soto became sick and died. His men buried him in the Mississippi River.

27

Father Junípero Serra started the first Spanish missions in California. The first mission was located near San Diego, California.

brought slaves from West Africa to work in the colonies. In Chapter 4, you will read more about Africans in America.

As time passed there were different classes of people in the Spanish colonies. The highest class was the rich nobles who were born in Spain. They held the highest government jobs in the colonies. The next class was the **Creoles**, Spanish people who were born in America. Then came **mestizos**, people who had both Native American and Spanish parents. Indians, Africans, and **mulattoes** were considered the lowest class of people. Mulattoes had African and Spanish or African and Native American parents.

The king of Spain chose governors called **viceroys** to rule different parts of the empire. The viceroys carried out laws that Spain wrote for the colonies. These laws told settlers what crops to grow, where they could build towns, and how they should treat Indians. The viceroys were very strict rulers who gave the people very little freedom.

One of Spain's goals was to teach the Indians to be Catholics. The Spanish built **missions** where priests taught their religion. These missions were located throughout what is now the southeastern and southwestern parts of the United States. Forts were built near the missions to protect priests from attacks by Indians. Although Indians had followed their own religions for hundreds of years, the Spanish did not respect their beliefs. Instead they forced Indians to live at the missions, work for the priests, and become Catholics.

In 1769 Father Junípero Serra, a Spanish priest, started a chain of missions in California. Father Serra traveled on foot from one mission to another. He always made sure Indians were treated fairly. At the missions, priests taught Indians how to raise sheep, goats, and cattle in addition to teaching them the Catholic religion.

Many Indians were angry about being forced to live at the missions. Popé, a Pueblo Indian, led a **revolt** against the Spanish in 1680. During that revolt 8,000 Indians attacked the Spanish in New Mexico. They destroyed the missions and forced the Spanish to leave Santa Fe. These Indians began to practice their own religions again. The Spanish did not control Santa Fe again until 1696.

As Indians and Spanish settlers lived together, there was an important exchange of cultures. The Spanish learned about many types of foods that Europeans did not have. The Indians taught them how to grow these crops. The Spanish brought horses and other animals that were not known by the Indians. The use of horses spread throughout the Great Plains. This changed the way the Indians there hunted buffalo. Riding horses made it easier to hunt buffalo and to follow the herds as they moved across the plains.

The Spanish also gave new technology to the Indians, such as guns and metal tools. The chart on this page shows what these two groups of people learned from each other.

The French Settle in America

The Spanish had settlements in America for about one hundred years before other European settlers came. The French had not been ready to start colonies in America because they were fighting in wars against other nations in Europe. There were also **civil wars** in France between Catholics and Protestants. But the king of France became jealous that Spain had built a huge empire in America. So he sent people to explore and settle North America. Like Spain, France's goals in America were to find wealth and to teach the Catholic religion to the Indians.

French explorers searched for gold but did not find any in North America. Instead they found a different way to become rich. At that time people in Europe enjoyed wearing hats made of beaver fur. By selling beaver furs in Europe, the French could become very rich. So the French learned to trap beavers in the North American forests. They also traded with Indians for beaver furs.

The French Empire in North America was called New France. New France was a huge colony. It included all the land around the Mississippi River, the Ohio River, the Great Lakes, and the St. Lawrence River. The colony's rivers and lakes made it possible to travel by canoe from place to place. French settlements began when Samuel de Champlain started Quebec in 1608. As the French explored the St. Lawrence River and the Great Lakes, they built forts and trading posts.

The French king wanted settlers in New France, but few people came. Only French nobles were allowed to own land in America, so French **peasants**, or poor people, did not want to be settlers. French law did not allow the **Huguenots**, or French Protestants, to settle in America. Only

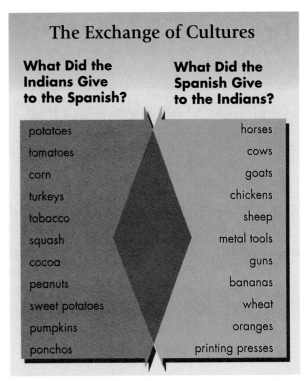

The Exchange of Cultures

What Did the Indians Give to the Spanish?	What Did the Spanish Give to the Indians?
potatoes	horses
tomatoes	cows
corn	goats
turkeys	chickens
tobacco	sheep
squash	metal tools
cocoa	guns
peanuts	bananas
sweet potatoes	wheat
pumpkins	oranges
ponchos	printing presses

French Catholics were allowed to be settlers. So the population of New France remained small, and the settlements were often far from each other.

The king of France chose governors to rule New France. Like the Spanish viceroys, the French governors were very strict. People had little freedom in New France.

Indians had better relationships with the French than with the Spanish. The French started missions to teach the Catholic religion to the Indians. But French priests did not force them to live and work at the missions. They did not force Indians to be their slaves. Instead the French often lived in the woods with Indians as they trapped beavers. The French learned to speak Indian languages and often married Indian women. From Indians the French learned to build canoes, trap beavers, and make snowshoes.

Although the French got along well with most Indians, they became enemies of the Iroquois nations. This problem began when Samuel de Champlain joined with other tribes against the Iroquois. In Chapter 7 you will learn how these problems with the Iroquois helped France lose its empire in America.

The Dutch Settlement in America

Henry Hudson was an explorer who tried to find the Northwest Passage for a small country in Europe called the Netherlands. He explored the river in New York that is now called the Hudson River. The Dutch, the people of the Netherlands, claimed the right to rule the land around the Hudson River. The Dutch wanted to

Henry Hudson explored for both the Dutch and the English. As a result of his trips, both countries claimed land in North America.

become rich from the fur trade. They built trading posts along the Hudson River, and they traded with Indians for beaver furs.

The Dutch colony was called New Netherlands. The Dutch started a town on the island of Manhattan called New Amsterdam. In 1626 the Dutch bought Manhattan from the Indians for only $24 worth of knives, beads, and other goods. People from many countries settled in New Amsterdam. Before long 18 languages were spoken in the colony. But the population of New Netherlands grew slowly. In 1664 England won control of the colony and its name became New York.

As the Spanish, the French, and the Dutch settled in America, Indians lost their lands. Millions of Indians died from European diseases. While the Indian population grew smaller and smaller, the European population grew larger. Europeans would continue to win more control of America.

Bartolomé de Las Casas 1474–1566

Bartolomé de Las Casas became famous for speaking out against using Indians as slaves.

Las Casas was born in Spain. As a teenager he sailed with Columbus on his third voyage to America. He became a landowner in America, and the Indians who lived on his land were his slaves. Las Casas decided to become a priest. In 1510 he was the first person to become a Catholic priest in America.

As Las Casas read the Bible, he became convinced that slavery was wrong and evil. In 1514, at the age of 40, Las Casas decided that he would no longer own slaves. All of his Indian slaves were given their freedom.

Las Casas began to speak out against slavery and the terrible treatment of Indians by the Spanish. His speeches made other Spanish landowners angry. They believed they needed slaves to earn wealth in America.

Church leaders were also angry with Las Casas. They felt he was destroying their efforts to turn Indians into Christians. He believed Indians were the children of God and should be protected by the Catholic Church and by the Spanish government. Las Casas said the Indians, not the Spanish, were the true Christians in America.

Las Casas traveled to Spain and advised the Spanish king, Charles I, to end Indian slavery. King Charles did write laws to end slavery, but it was difficult to carry out those laws in the colonies. When Las Casas returned to America, he wrote books calling for better treatment of Indians. When he was almost 80, he wrote his most famous book, *In Defense of the Indians*.

Las Casas lived to be 92 years old, and he continued working to help Indians until the end of his life. King Charles gave Las Casas the title "Protector of the Indians."

In Your Own Words

Write a paragraph that explains how Las Casas's work and treatment of Indians differed from the treatment they received from other Spanish colonists.

REVIEW AND APPLY

- Hernan Cortés conquered Mexico, and Francisco Pizarro conquered the Inca Empire in Peru.

- Francisco de Coronado explored the Southwest, and Hernando de Soto explored the Southeast, of what would become the United States.

- The Spanish forced Indians to live at the missions, learn the Catholic religion, and work as slaves.

- The French built a large empire in North America called New France.

- The Dutch ruled a colony called New Netherlands.

- Indians gave Europeans foods such as potatoes, tomatoes, corn, and turkey. From the Spanish, Indians got horses, cows, sheep, wheat, and metal tools.

- European diseases caused a decline in Indian population.

VOCABULARY

Matching ■ **Match each vocabulary word in Group B with its definition in Group A. In your social studies notebook, write the numbers 1 through 8. Next to each number, write the letter of the correct answer. You will not use all the words in Group B.**

Group A	Group B
1. This is the Spanish word for a person who conquered and explored an area.	A. revolt
	B. mestizos
2. This disease killed many Indians.	C. peasant
3. This is a large farm where crops such as tobacco and sugar are grown.	D. conquistador
4. This is a place where priests taught the Catholic religion to Indians.	E. mulattoes
	F. viceroy
5. This is a fight against the government.	G. plantation
6. This was a person who was poor.	H. smallpox
7. These people had Indian and Spanish parents.	I. mission
8. These people had African and Spanish or African and Indian parents.	

COMPREHENSION CHECK

Who Said It? ■ Read each statement in Group A. Then match the name of the person in Group B who might have said it. Write the correct answers in your social studies notebook. There is one name you will not use.

Group A

1. "I conquered the Aztec Empire in Mexico and destroyed the city of Tenochtitlan."

2. "I started missions in California where Indians were treated fairly."

3. "In 1608 I started the city of Quebec for France."

4. "I explored a river in New York for the Netherlands."

Group B

A. Francisco Pizarro

B. Henry Hudson

C. Samuel de Champlain

D. Father Junípero Serra

E. Hernan Cortés

CRITICAL THINKING

Fact or Opinion ■ A fact is a true statement. An opinion is a statement that tells what a person thinks about something. In your social studies notebook, write the numbers 1 through 6. Next to each number, write F if the statement is a fact. Write O if the statement is an opinion. If the statement gives both a fact and an opinion, write FO and the part of the sentence that is an opinion.

1. Moctezuma gave Cortés gifts, but he should have tried to capture Cortés.

2. The Spanish found gold and silver in the Inca Empire.

3. De Soto was a better explorer than Ponce de León was.

4. The Spanish king chose viceroys to rule regions of the Americas, but the viceroys were too strict.

5. The French should have allowed peasants to own land in America.

6. The population of New Netherlands grew slowly because the climate was very uncomfortable.

USING INFORMATION

Writing an Opinion ■ Many people believe the Spanish were cruel to the Indians. Write a paragraph that tells your opinion about the Spanish treatment of Indians. Give two or three reasons for your opinion.

Using a Compass Rose and a Map Key

A **compass rose** is used to show directions on a map. The four main, or **cardinal,** directions are north, south, east, and west. There are also four in-between directions. These **intermediate** directions are northeast, southeast, northwest, and southwest. Often cardinal directions are shortened to N, S, E, W, and intermediate directions to NE, SE, NW, SW.

Maps often use **symbols,** or little pictures, to show information on a map. A **map key** tells what the symbols mean. Sometimes the map key will show what different colors on a map mean.

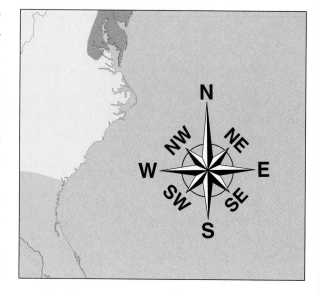

Look at the map key and the compass rose for the map below. In your social studies notebook, write the correct word or phrase that completes each sentence.

1. New France is in the _____ .

   north   south   west

2. Florida is in the _____ .

   northeast   southeast   northwest

3. The Dutch settlements were in the
   _____ .

   northwest   southwest   northeast

4. There are _____ missions on the map.

   20   10   7

5. The French settlements included _____ .

   Florida   New France   Mexico

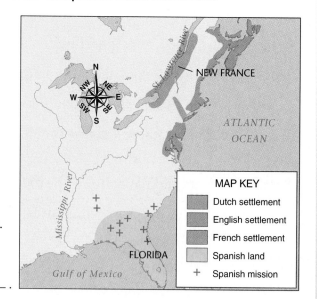

34

Chapter 4

AFRICANS IN AMERICA

◀ *Mansa Musa*

People

Muslims • Mansa Musa •
Africans • English •
Olaudah Equiano

Places

Ghana • North Africa •
Mali • Timbuktu •
Songhai • West Indies •
Barbados • Philadelphia

New Vocabulary

Muslims • converted •
Islam • rum •
Middle Passage •
indentured servants •
fare • contracts •
prejudice

Focus on Main Ideas

1. Which empires did Africans build in western Africa?
2. Why did Europeans start the slave trade?
3. What were the five steps in the slave trade?
4. Why was the Middle Passage so difficult for Africans?
5. What was slavery like in the Spanish and English colonies?

Millions of people came to America with chains on their legs and with fear in their hearts. These people were not like the Spanish and the French who wanted to become rich in America. Instead they were forced to come to America as slaves from their homes in Africa. The slave trade lasted almost 400 years. During that time more than 10 million Africans were forced to come to the Americas as slaves.

Empires of West Africa

Hundreds of years before Europeans were ready to explore Asia and America,

Africans had built empires in West Africa. They developed cultures that were rich with music, dancing, and storytelling. People in these empires created beautiful artwork made from wood and metals. They also used iron to make strong tools and weapons.

The first empire in West Africa was the Empire of Ghana. It lasted from about A.D. 300 to 1200. The empire was rich in gold. So people in Ghana traded their gold for salt, cloth, and horses from North Africa.

Muslims conquered Ghana and built the Empire of Mali that lasted from 1200 to 1400. Mali had a powerful leader named Mansa Musa. He used his army to make

Mali larger, and he captured valuable salt mines that made Mali richer. Mansa Musa had **converted** to the religion of **Islam**, and he had become a Muslim. After that Islam became an important religion in West Africa. The large city of Timbuktu became Mali's center of trade and learning. In this city Africans built a large university where they studied history, law, and Islam. After Mansa Musa died, Mali began to lose its power.

The Empire of Mali was replaced by the Songhai Empire. This empire remained powerful until about 1600. Trade, farming, and Islam were important in Songhai. Timbuktu continued to be an important city. After 1600 the Songhai Empire became weaker and ended.

The Beginning of the European Slave Trade

Slavery had existed in the West African empires and in other parts of Africa for hundreds of years. Slavery in Africa was different in many ways from the kind of slavery that would develop in America. A person captured in war could be made a slave. Africans who could not pay their debts also became slaves. African slaves were often treated as part of the slave owner's family. A slave could marry the master's son or daughter. Children of slaves were not considered slaves. Slaves could earn their freedom through hard work. After winning their freedom, slaves could get important jobs and even become

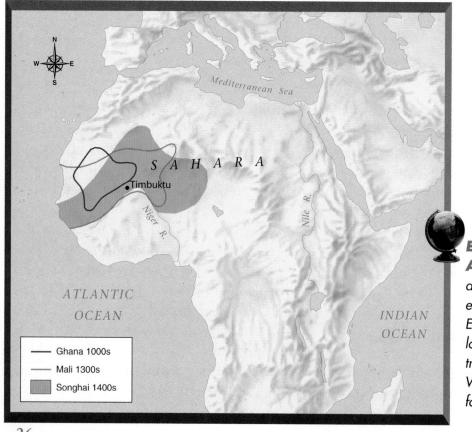

Empires of West Africa Mali, Ghana, and Songhai were three empires of West Africa. Each empire used its location as a center of trade for West Africa. Which river was a border for two of the empires?

leaders of their tribes. Much of this changed after the European slave trade began in Africa.

The European slave trade first began in 1442 when two Portuguese ships went to Africa and returned to Portugal with ten African slaves. These slaves became workers in Portugal. After the Portuguese began settling in Brazil, they began to bring African slaves to this colony. They were the first African slaves in the Americas.

The Spanish brought Africans to America, too. An African sailed with Christopher Columbus in 1492. Cortés, Pizarro, and other conquistadors brought African slaves with them. In 1501 the Spanish king passed a law that said Africans could be used as slaves in the Americas. Before long the Spanish were bringing 10,000 African slaves a year to their colonies. By the year 1600, there were almost 1 million African slaves in Spain's colonies.

Steps in the Slave Trade

The slave trade was carried out by traders from Spain, Portugal, the Netherlands, France, and England. The two goals of the slave traders were to earn large profits by selling African slaves and to provide the colonies with the workers they needed.

There were five steps in the slave trade. First, Africans captured people from different tribes to be sold as slaves. Slave traders depended on these Africans to capture people for them. Slave traders paid for the slaves with European guns, bullets, **rum**, and other products. Second, the captured Africans were forced to march long

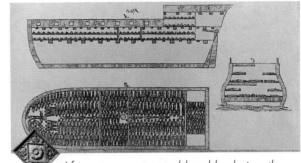

Africans were treated harshly during the Middle Passage. This diagram was drawn to show ship owners how to fit in the most slaves.

distances to the African coast. They marched with iron collars around their necks and with chains around their arms or legs. Many Africans died while they were forced to march.

Third, when they reached the coast of Africa, the captured Africans were held in prisons. They stayed there until they were forced to board ships that would take them on the long trip to America. The fourth step was the long trip from Africa to America, which was called the **Middle Passage**. Slaves were forced to remain in chains in the dark, hot, crowded space below deck.

The Middle Passage often took more than three months. Many slaves died on board the ships during the Middle Passage. They became sick and weak because they were given only small amounts of food and water. On the ships slaves were packed very close together. Diseases spread quickly and many slaves died. Only the strongest people were able to survive the Middle Passage.

The last step in the slave trade took place in the Americas. After slave ships landed at the West Indies, the Africans were sold as slaves. Other Africans were sold in Spanish and English colonies in North and South America.

Slavery in Spanish America

The Spanish needed large numbers of workers for their plantations. At first the Spanish forced Indians to be slaves. But as millions of Indians died from disease, other workers were needed. So the Spanish began using African slaves as plantation workers. These slaves worked on tobacco and sugar cane plantations in Mexico, on islands in the Caribbean Sea, and in Central and South America.

Many slaves in the Spanish colonies tried to run away from their masters, so the Spanish hired Indians to hunt for them. These Indians often helped the Africans to escape. About one tenth of all Africans in Spain's colonies were able to escape because they were helped by Indians.

The Catholic Church tried to protect African slaves in several ways. African men and women were allowed to get married in churches. Families remained together after children were born. Spanish slave owners were not allowed to take children away from their mother and sell them to different owners.

Africans in the English Colonies

Why did the English bring slaves to America? In Chapter 5 you will read about

European slave traders bought African slaves from other Africans. Often these slaves were captured and brought to the coast in chains connected to iron collars around their neck. The Europeans then kept the slaves in prisons until a ship arrived to take them on the Middle Passage to the Americas.

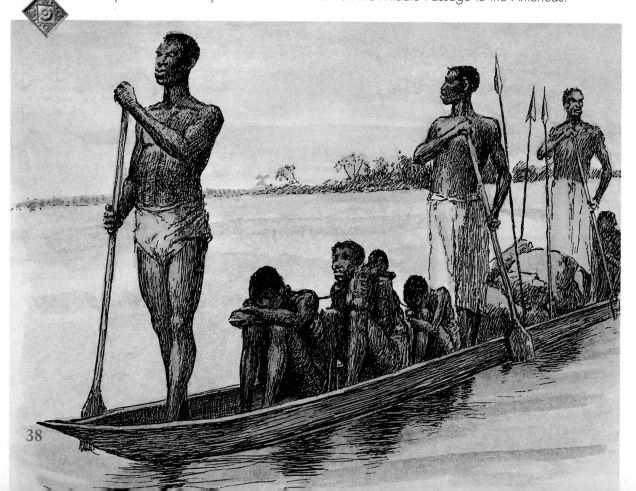

38

the growth of plantations in some of the English colonies. At first the English tried using **indentured servants** as their plantation workers. Indentured servants were people who wanted to come to America but did not have enough money to pay the **fare**. So they signed **contracts** agreeing to work three to seven years for the people who paid their fares. However, not enough people came to America as indentured servants to supply the plantations with all the workers that they needed.

The first Africans were brought to the English colonies in 1619 as indentured servants. After their working period ended, these Africans were free to leave their masters and live where they pleased. But plantation owners needed many workers, and they began to use African slaves. As more plantations were started more slaves were needed.

By the 1700s the English had taken control of most of the slave trade. Each year the English brought more slaves to America on the Middle Passage. Because of the slave trade, the population in the English colonies of the West Indies became about 90 percent African. In some southern colonies of what is now the United States, more than half the people were Africans.

By the 1700s most Africans in the English colonies were slaves. As slaves they could never be free and their children would also be slaves. Slave owners could take children away from their mother and sell them to other plantation owners. Slaves were thought of as property; they did not have the same rights as other people. Free African Americans faced **prejudice** in the English colonies. In most colonies

Slaves brought to the colonies were sold in markets. Merchants and buyers only saw these Africans as property.

they could not get good jobs, vote, or hold government jobs.

The slave trade continued until the 1800s, and it affected Africa and America. The slave trade provided the colonies with the workers they needed, but it brought suffering to millions of Africans. In Africa it caused families to be torn apart as family members were captured and sent to America. But the slave trade also brought some of West Africa's culture to America. African slaves tried to hold on to their traditions, music, dances, and folk tales. That African culture slowly became part of America's culture.

BIOGRAPHY

Olaudah Equiano 1745–1801(?)

Olaudah Equiano was a slave who became a free man and wrote about his life as a slave. Equiano was born in western Africa. He was kidnapped when he was 11 years old, and he was forced to go on a long march to the coast of Africa.

When Equiano finally arrived at Africa's coast, he saw both the ocean and white people for the first time. He was frightened of both the ocean and the white slave traders who were in charge of his group. Since Equiano only knew his own African language, he was unable to speak to the slave traders. He was forced to board a Dutch slave ship to make the long journey to America. He was so frightened and unhappy that he refused to eat. But food was forced down his throat.

The slave ship went to Barbados in the West Indies. There Equiano was bought by his first master. During his time as a slave, Equiano was bought and sold three times. While he was a slave, his name was changed to Gustavus Vessa. One of his owners allowed him to learn to read and write English. Very few slaves were ever taught to read and write.

Equiano was sold for the last time to a merchant in Philadelphia. While working for the merchant, Equiano earned enough money to buy his own freedom. Equiano settled in England where there was no slavery. Equiano's autobiography was published in 1789. It showed the evils of slavery. It convinced many readers that slavery should end. In his book Equiano described his experiences:

"I had a very unhappy.... journey, being in continual fear that the people I was with would murder me. I was now more than a thousand miles from home.... A Dutch ship came into the harbor and they carried me on board. I was exceedingly sea-sick at first.... My master's ship was bound for Barbadoes.... When we came there, I was sold for fifty dollars...."

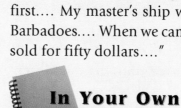

In Your Own Words

Write a paragraph describing Olaudah Equiano's experiences as a slave and his work to end slavery.

REVIEW AND APPLY

- Between A.D. 300 and 1600, Africans built great empires in West Africa.

- The slave trade involved capturing people in Africa, bringing them to the Americas in slave ships, and selling them as slaves for a large profit.

- The slave trade lasted almost 400 years, during which time about 10 million Africans were brought to America.

- The trip to America on slave ships was called the Middle Passage. Many Africans died during this long journey.

- England, Spain, Portugal, France, and the Netherlands took part in the slave trade.

- The English and the Spanish used African slaves for plantation work in their colonies.

VOCABULARY

Find the Meaning ■ In your social studies notebook, write the correct word or phrase that completes each sentence.

1. People who believe in the religion of Islam are _____ .

   Muslims   **Christians**   **Jews**

2. The money paid to ride in a ship, bus, or plane is the _____ .

   colony   **fare**   **mound**

3. The trip to bring slaves from Africa to America was the _____ .

   First Passage   **Northwest Passage** **Middle Passage**

4. Unfair beliefs about another group of people are called _____ .

   culture   **contracts**   **prejudice**

5. A person who agreed to work for someone else for a number of years in order to come to America was a(n) _____ .

   slave   **indentured servant**   **viceroy**

COMPREHENSION CHECK

Write the Answer ■ Write in your social studies notebook one or more sentences to answer each question.

1. About how many Africans were brought to America as slaves?

2. How did Mansa Musa help the Empire of Mali?

41

3. What were two other important West African empires?

4. How was African slavery different from European slavery?

5. Why did many Africans die during the Middle Passage?

6. What European nation was the first to bring African slaves to the Americas?

7. How did the Catholic church help to protect African slaves?

8. Why did the English settlers want slaves instead of indentured servants?

CRITICAL THINKING

Cause and Effect ■ A cause is something that makes something else happen. What happens is called the effect.

Example   **Cause:**
            The tornado stuck the town.

Effect:
Many homes were destroyed.

Choose a cause or an effect in Group B to complete each sentence in Group A. In your social studies notebook, write the letter of the cause or effect that best completes each sentence. Group B has one more answer than you need.

Group A	Group B
1. Mali's ruler, Mansa Musa, became a Muslim, so _____ .	A. The population of the West Indies became 90 percent African
2. _____ , so they put iron collars and chains on the slaves.	B. Islam became an important religion in West Africa
3. _____ , so they brought African slaves to America.	C. The first African Americans in the English colonies were indentured servants
4. _____ , so they were free people when their working period ended.	D. African chiefs did not want their captured slaves to escape as they marched to the coast
	E. Europeans needed many workers for their colonies in the Americas

USING INFORMATION

Journal Writing ■ Africans built three strong empires in West Africa before 1600. Write a paragraph in your journal that tells about one of these early African empires.

THE ENGLISH SETTLE IN NORTH AMERICA

◀ *The Mayflower*

People

Queen Elizabeth I • Francis Drake • King Henry VIII • John Smith • Pilgrims • Puritans • Roger Williams • Anne Hutchinson • William Penn • James Oglethorpe

Places

Roanoke • Jamestown • Virginia • James River • Massachusetts • Providence • Pennsylvania

New Vocabulary

religious freedom • established church • joint stock company • charter • representatives • representative government • royal colony •proprietary colony • proprietor • self-governing colony • debtors

Focus on Main Ideas

1. Why did the English settle in North America?
2. What problems did the settlers have?
3. How did the New England Colonies, the Middle Colonies, and the Southern Colonies get started?

In 1607 England started its first permanent settlement in North America. Slowly more and more English people settled in North America. By the mid-1700s there were 13 English colonies along the Atlantic Ocean.

England Defeats the Spanish Armada

Spain controlled the seas near North and South America. The English had to weaken Spain's power in the Atlantic Ocean before they could start colonies in North America. Queen Elizabeth I was the ruler who weakened Spain's power.

She encouraged English sea captains to capture Spanish ships near America and steal their cargo of gold, silver, and other products. These English captains were called sea dogs.

The most famous sea dog was Francis Drake. In 1578 Drake captured Spanish ships near South America and stole their gold and silver. Then he sailed through the Strait of Magellan into the Pacific Ocean and back to England. His crew was the second to sail around the world. Drake brought a huge amount of gold to England. Francis Drake became England's hero.

King Philip II of Spain was furious that sea dogs were attacking his ships.

Queen Elizabeth ruled England from 1558 to 1603. During this time England defeated the Spanish and built a stronger nation with colonies in America.

He decided to attack England with a huge fleet called the Spanish Armada. In 1588, 130 Spanish ships sailed into the waters close to England. England's smaller navy defeated the Spanish Armada. After the defeat more than half of the Spanish ships were destroyed in a storm. As a result Spain no longer controlled the Atlantic Ocean. England could send ships safely to America to start colonies.

Why Did the English Settle in America?

English settlers came to America for four reasons. First, many came for **religious freedom**. Religious freedom was not allowed in England because all people had to belong to the Church of England. That church began when Queen Elizabeth's father, King Henry VIII, broke away from the Catholic Church and started the Church of England, a Protestant church. Queen Elizabeth made the Church of England the **established church**. At that time this meant that all people in England had to belong to the Church of England and pay taxes to support it. Some people did not want to belong to the Church of England. They decided to follow their own religions in America.

Second, English settlers wanted to become rich. They had heard how the Spanish had become rich from gold and how the French had become rich from the fur trade. The English also hoped to find wealth in America.

Third, people came to America to own land. In England much of the land was used to raise sheep, so it was difficult for people to buy land. Fathers left all their land to their oldest son when they died. It was almost impossible for other family members to own land. Finally, people came to the English colonies to get away from wars in Europe.

The First English Settlements

England's goal was to control all the land along the Atlantic Ocean from French Canada to Spanish Florida. It would take more than one hundred years to meet this goal.

Roanoke was the first English settlement in North America. The settlement was started in 1587 on an island near present-day North Carolina. John White, the leader at

Roanoke, went back to England for supplies and returned to Roanoke after three years. When he returned, all of the settlers were gone. The letters *CRO* had been carved on a tree. To this day no one knows what really happened to the Roanoke settlers.

A lot of money was needed to start a settlement in America. Few people had enough money to pay for the ships and the supplies that were needed. So people were encouraged to buy shares of stock in a **joint stock company**. If the company earned profits from a settlement, the money was shared by all the people who owned stock.

In 1607 Jamestown, Virginia, became the first permanent English settlement in North America. The money for Jamestown came from a joint stock company called the London Company. King James I gave the London Company a **charter**, or a permission paper, to start a colony.

The settlement began in Virginia on the James River with 144 men. They came to America to find gold, but they never found it. The settlers almost starved because they did not want to work or to grow crops. They stayed alive because of food they received from nearby Indians. Their leader, Captain John Smith, forced the men to grow crops. Life at Jamestown was very hard and most of the settlers died. When the settlers learned to grow tobacco in 1612, life began to improve. They sold tobacco to England for a large profit. Each year they grew larger crops of tobacco.

The year 1619 was important in Jamestown for three reasons. In that year the first women from England came to live in the settlement. Also, in 1619 Africans were brought to the English colony to work

The first Africans were brought to the English settlement in Jamestown in 1619. They were considered indentured servants, not slaves, so they were freed after several years.

as indentured servants. Finally, the Virginia House of Burgesses was started. This was the group of **representatives** who wrote laws for the colony. These representatives were chosen by the group of men who were allowed to vote. This was the beginning of **representative government** in the English colonies.

In 1620 a group of people called Pilgrims started a colony in Massachusetts. The Pilgrims came to America for religious freedom. The 102 Pilgrims traveled aboard a small ship called the *Mayflower*. They landed at Cape Cod, Massachusetts. Before leaving their ship, the men signed an agreement called the Mayflower Compact. In this agreement the Pilgrims promised to work together to make laws that would be fair to all. This was the first plan in America for a government in which people would govern themselves.

The Pilgrims spent a month searching for a good place to settle. They chose Plymouth Harbor and started a town there. During the first winter, many Pilgrims died from hunger and disease. Others survived because Indians helped them. Indians taught them how to fish and hunt and grow crops such as corn and squash. The following year the Pilgrims had enough food for the winter. They invited the Indians to join them at a thanksgiving celebration. They thanked God for their good harvest. The American holiday of Thanksgiving began with the first Pilgrim celebration of thanksgiving in 1621.

The Growth of the English Colonies

Before long more colonies were started. As more settlers came to America, they forced Indians to leave their lands. The settlers and the Indians fought wars against each other over control of land. The Indian population grew smaller as Indians died from wars and European diseases. Some Indian nations disappeared completely.

There were three types of colonies. In a **royal colony**, the king controlled the colony and chose the governor who ruled the colony. Each **proprietary colony** had one person or several people who owned the colony. The king gave a **proprietor** a charter to start a colony. The proprietor

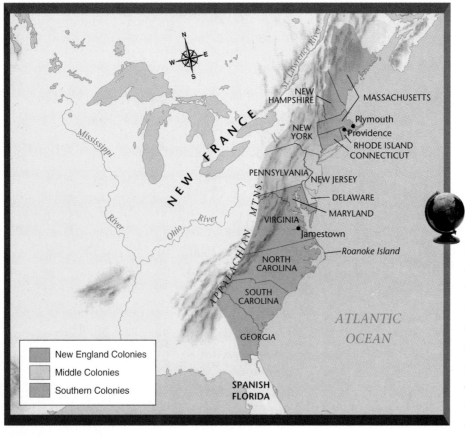

Thirteen English Colonies The 13 English colonies developed differently in 3 regions— New England, the Middle Colonies, and the Southern Colonies. In which region is Jamestown located? In which region is Plymouth located?

The Thanksgiving holiday celebrated in November is a reminder of the Pilgrims' first Thanksgiving. The Pilgrims gave thanks to God and celebrated with the Indians who helped them through their difficult first year.

chose the governor and controlled the colony. The third type was a **self-governing colony**. In these colonies people voted for their own governor and for representatives to make laws for the colony. There were three groups of colonies: The New England Colonies, the Middle Colonies, and the Southern Colonies. Find the names and locations of the 13 colonies on the map on page 46 and the chart on page 48.

The New England Colonies

In 1630 about 1,000 people called Puritans started the Massachusetts Bay Colony. They came to America because they were unhappy with the Church of England.

They believed churches should look plainer, and church leaders should encourage more Bible study. The Puritans did not allow people to follow other religions in their colony. Only church members were allowed to vote. Puritan leaders controlled the colony's government.

Roger Williams lived in the Massachusetts Bay Colony, but he disagreed with many Puritan ideas. Williams believed all people should have freedom of religion. He said that religion and government should be completely separate from each other. Williams's ideas angered the Puritans, and they forced him to leave Massachusetts.

Williams fled to what is now Rhode Island. He met Indians who helped him.

The Thirteen English Colonies

	Name of Colony	Date Started	First Leaders	Reason Started
New England Colonies	Massachusetts	1620 (Plymouth), 1630 (Massachusetts Bay Colony)	William Bradford, John Winthrop	for religious freedom
	New Hampshire	1623	Ferdinando Gorges, John Mason	to earn money from trade and fishing
	Rhode Island	1636	Roger Williams	for religious freedom
	Connecticut	1636	Thomas Hooker	for religious freedom and trade
Middle Colonies	New York	1624 (Dutch colony), 1664 (English colony)	Peter Minuit (of the Netherlands)	to earn money from trade
	New Jersey	1664	John Berkeley, George Carteret	to earn money by selling land
	Delaware	1638	settlers from Sweden	to earn money from trade
	Pennsylvania	1682	William Penn	for religious freedom for Quakers
Southern Colonies	Virginia	1607	John Smith, John Rolfe	to find gold
	Maryland	1632	George Calvert (Lord Baltimore)	for religious freedom for Catholics
	North Carolina	1663	Anthony Cooper, John Colleton, William Berkeley	to earn money from trade and selling land
	South Carolina	1663	Anthony Cooper, John Colleton, William Berkeley	to earn money from trade and selling land
	Georgia	1732	James Oglethorpe	new life for debtors

He bought land from them, and he started the town of Providence. All men were allowed to vote, and Providence became the first American city where all people had religious freedom. In 1644 Rhode Island became a self-governing colony.

Anne Hutchinson was another person who angered the Puritans by talking about different religious ideas. She was forced to leave Massachusetts. She went to Rhode Island and started a new settlement there. Other people moved away from Massachusetts and settled what would become the colonies of New Hampshire and Connecticut.

The Middle Colonies

The Dutch colony of New Netherlands was south of the New England Colonies.

The English wanted control of the Dutch colony. In 1664 England sent warships to fight for New Netherlands. The Dutch surrendered to the English without fighting. New Netherlands was renamed New York. This area included land that would later become parts of New Jersey, Connecticut, Delaware, and Pennsylvania.

The Pennsylvania colony was started in 1682 as a place where Quakers could have freedom of religion. The Quakers, another group of Protestants, refused to pray in the Church of England. The king gave William Penn, a wealthy Quaker leader, land in America where he could start a colony. Penn paid the Indians for all the land that he took from them. Penn allowed all people to have religious freedom in the colony, so people from many parts of Europe came to Pennsylvania.

The Southern Colonies

The Virginia colony grew from the original settlement at Jamestown. It was the largest of the Southern Colonies. Maryland was the second colony started in the South. It was started in 1632 by George Calvert, who was also called Lord Baltimore. He started the colony as a place where Catholics would have religious freedom. In 1649 a law called the Toleration Act was passed in Maryland. This law allowed all Christians to have religious freedom in Maryland. Jews were not allowed in the colony.

North Carolina and South Carolina started as a single proprietary colony called Carolana. Later the colony became two royal colonies. In 1732 James Oglethorpe started Georgia, the last of the 13 colonies. Georgia began as a colony for **debtors**. People in England who did not have enough money to pay their debts were sent to jail. Georgia was a place to go to for debtors who had been released from prison. The Georgia colony was north of Spanish Florida. English soldiers stayed in Georgia to stop attacks on the colonies from Spanish Florida.

By 1732 England controlled 13 colonies along the Atlantic Ocean. Each year more and more people from Europe settled in the English colonies.

This village near Jamestown, Virginia, shows people today what life was like for the Powhatan Indians who lived in the area when the English settlers arrived. There were about 8,500 Indians living in more than 150 villages in the area.

BIOGRAPHY

William Penn 1644–1718

William Penn started the colony of Pennsylvania in America. As a young man, William Penn began to study at Oxford University. Penn's life at Oxford changed when he became a Quaker. The Quakers believed that all people, both men and women, were equal. They believed that slavery was wrong and that all wars were wrong. They would not bow to another person because they bowed only to God. Quakers said it was important to respect all religions. They refused to pay taxes to the Church of England. Most people in England hated the Quakers because of their ideas. After Penn became a Quaker, he was forced to leave Oxford. The English government passed a law called the Quaker Act. Under this law not more than five Quakers could pray together at one time. William Penn was arrested for praying with a large group of Quakers. He spent many months in jail.

King Charles II had once borrowed a lot of money from William Penn's father. The king had not repaid the money while Penn's father was alive. So after his father died, Penn asked the king to repay the loan. Instead of money Penn asked for land in America. King Charles agreed and gave Penn a charter for Pennsylvania. It was a proprietary colony because William Penn owned it.

In 1682 William Penn went to start the new colony. Penn bought land from Indians and made peace treaties with them. The laws in the new colony gave religious freedom to all people who believed in God. Thousands of people from England, Germany, and the Netherlands moved to Pennsylvania.

William Penn planned the colony's capital, Philadelphia. By the time William Penn died, thousands of people of different religions were living together in peace in Pennsylvania.

In Your Own Words

Write a paragraph in the journal section of your social studies notebook that tells if you think William Penn should be admired and why.

REVIEW AND APPLY

CHAPTER 5 MAIN IDEAS

- English settlers came to America to have religious freedom, to gain wealth, to own land, and to get away from wars in Europe.

- The first permanent English settlement in North America was Jamestown. In 1620 the Pilgrims started a colony in Massachusetts.

- There were three types of English colonies—royal colonies, proprietary colonies, and self-governing colonies.

- The Puritans started the Massachusetts Bay Colony in 1630. Rhode Island, New Hampshire, and Connecticut were started by settlers who left Massachusetts.

- The English captured New Netherlands in 1664 and renamed it New York. Pennsylvania was started as a place where Quakers could have religious freedom.

VOCABULARY

Writing with Vocabulary Words ■ Use seven or more vocabulary terms below to write a paragraph that tells how the English settled in North America. Write your paragraph in the vocabulary section of your social studies notebook.

religious freedom	royal colony	charter
joint stock company	established church	representative government
debtors	representatives	proprietary colony

CRITICAL THINKING

Sequencing ■ In your social studies notebook, write the following sentences in their correct order.

The Puritans start the Massachusetts Bay Colony.

William Penn starts the colony of Pennsylvania so that Quakers can have religious freedom.

The first Africans are brought to Jamestown, Virginia, in 1619 as indentured servants.

The English Navy defeats the Spanish Armada.

James Oglethorpe starts the Georgia colony.

In 1607 Jamestown, Virginia, becomes the first permanent English settlement in America.

COMPREHENSION CHECK

Reviewing Important Facts ■ Match each sentence in Group A with the word or phrase from Group B that the sentence explains. Write the letter of the correct answer in your social studies notebook. You will not use all the words in Group B.

<table>
<tr><td>Group A</td><td>Group B</td></tr>
</table>

Group A

1. Since few people had enough money to start a colony, many colonies were started by this type of business.

2. This crop brought profit to the English settlement in Jamestown, Virginia.

3. This was the first representative government in the colonies.

4. Puritans, Pilgrims, and Roger Williams started colonies in this region.

5. This was the first plan for self-government in the colonies.

6. These people lost their land and died from European diseases as the English settled in America.

7. This colony was once part of New Netherlands.

8. Lord Baltimore started this colony to give religious freedom to Catholics.

Group B

A. New York

B. Indians

C. Mayflower Compact

D. joint stock company

E. Virginia House of Burgesses

F. Maryland

G. Georgia

H. New England

I. tobacco

USING INFORMATION

Writing an Essay ■ The English started colonies in America for many different reasons. Choose 2 of the 13 colonies. Explain how and why they were started. Write your essay in the assignment section of your social studies notebook. Begin the essay with a topic sentence. End your essay with a sentence that summarizes the main idea.

AMERICAN GEOGRAPHY

Movement: People, Products, and Ideas

Movement shows us how people, ideas, and products move from place to place. In Unit 1 you learned how people from Africa, Asia, and Europe moved to the Americas. These people brought ideas, animals, resources, goods, and religions from one part of the world to another. Look at the map below. Each numbered arrow shows a large movement of people from one continent or place to another.

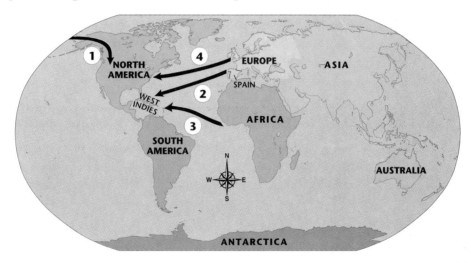

A. In the assignment section of your notebook, write a sentence that explains the movement of people that is represented by each of the four numbered arrows on the map.

B. In your notebook write sentences that tell where arrows for each of the following movements should be placed.

1. Movement of Indians from Alaska across North America and South America.

2. Movement of gold from America to Spain.

3. Movement of different religions from Europe to America.

4. The exchange of goods between the Spanish and the Indians.

C. Select one of the eight movements described above. Write a paragraph in the journal section of your notebook that describes what it was like to be one of the people involved in this movement.

Unit 1 Review

Study the time line on this page. You may want to read parts of Unit 1 again. In the assignment section of your notebook, write the numbers 1 through 14. Then use the words and dates in the box to finish the paragraphs. The box has one possible answer that you will not use.

1492
Christopher Columbus sails west from Spain in search of Asia.

1539
Hernando de Soto explores the Southeast.

1610
Santa Fe is started as a Spanish mission.

1682
La Salle claims Louisiana for France.

1400 — 1500 — 1600

1487
Dias sails around the southern tip of Africa.

1513
Ponce de Léon searches for the Fountain of Youth in Florida.

1608
Champlain Starts Quebec in Canada.

1632
George Calvert starts Maryland.

Iroquois	1539	Mexico
Aztec	North America	plantations
artifacts	Columbus	Middle Passage
Asia	astrolabe	religious
1682	debtors	1492

Thousands of years ago, during the Ice Age, a land bridge connected Asia and Alaska. More than 20,000 years ago, people in Asia crossed the land bridge and walked to __1__ . Archaeologists have learned about these early Americans by studying __2__ . In the eastern forest, the __3__ formed the Confederation of Five Nations that kept peace for a long time. In Mexico the __4__ built their capital,

Tenochtitlan, on an island in a lake. Native Americans did not use the wheel before Europeans came to America. Native Americans and Europeans first met after explorers began to look for a shorter route to ___5___ . The compass and the ___6___ made it possible for ships to sail far out in the ocean. The famous explorer Christopher ___7___ tried to reach Asia by sailing west, but instead he reached America. After the explorations of La Salle in ___8___ , France claimed all the land around the Mississippi River and called it Louisiana.

The Spanish settled in America to find gold and to teach the Catholic religion to Native Americans. Hernan Cortés conquered the Aztec Empire in ___9___ . Hernando de Soto explored for gold in the Southeast in ___10___ and reached the Mississippi River. Europeans needed workers for their ___11___ , so they brought Africans to work as slaves. Many Africans did not survive the ___12___ to America. English settlers came to America for ___13___ freedom and to get land. In 1732 James Oglethorpe started Georgia as a colony for ___14___ .

Looking Ahead to Unit 2

For more than two centuries, Europeans had claimed, explored, conquered, and colonized the Americas. During the 1700s the 13 English colonies grew. For many years American colonists had been proud to be ruled by England. Each year more and more people came to live in the 13 colonies. Most people enjoyed more freedom in the colonies than they had in Europe. Life would change in the colonies after George III became the new king of England. The colonists grew angry about the changes brought by the new king. As you read Unit 2, you will learn how the 13 English colonies were able to become the new United States of America.

Unit 2

FROM COLONIES TO A NATION

Americans in the 13 English colonies were so angry with their king in 1775 that they decided to fight for more freedom. As they prepared to battle, they called themselves Minutemen because they needed only a minute to be ready to fight. They did not have uniforms or enough weapons, but they had a cause that they were willing to die for. By 1781 Americans would defeat the powerful British Army.

As you read Unit 2, you will learn how some Americans created a new, independent nation with a new type of government.

THINK ABOUT IT

- The first public-school laws in the colonies were passed by the Puritans. Why did the Puritans need public schools?

- Americans began to fight in the American Revolution in 1775. Why did they wait until July 4, 1776, to say they were free?

- George Washington led the American Army during the American Revolution. He lost more battles than he won. Why did Americans call Washington a great hero?

1200	1650	1700	1750

1215
King John signs the Magna Carta.

1651
England passes first Navigation Act.

1689
William and Mary sign the English Bill of Rights.

1707
England, Scotland, Wales, and Northern Ireland form Great Britain.

1754
French and Indian War begins.

1763
French and Indian War ends.

▲ *Modern patriots play the role of Minutemen.*

1773
Sons of Liberty have
the Boston Tea Party.

The American Revolution
begins at Lexington
and Concord.
1775

1776
The Declaration
of Independence
is signed.

1783
United States
and Great
Britain sign
Treaty of Paris.

1788
The Constitution
is ratified.

1775

1800

1770
Five colonists
are killed in
the Boston
Massacre.

1774
First
Continental
Congress
meets in
Philadelphia.

1775
Second Continental
Congress meets in
Philadelphia.

1781
The British Army
surrenders
at Yorktown.

1787
The
Constitution
is written.

1791
The Bill
of Rights
is ratified.

Chapter 6

LIFE IN THE THIRTEEN COLONIES

◀ *Hornbooks were used to teach reading.*

People

Congregationalists •
Eliza Lucas Pinckney •
Jonathan Edwards •
Benjamin Franklin

Places

New York City • Sweden •
Scotland • Harvard
College • Boston

New Vocabulary

democracy • cash crops •
manufacturing • planter •
Episcopal Church • indigo •
Great Awakening •
grammar schools • dame
schools • apprentice •
journeyman •
mercantilism • favorable
balance of trade •
Navigation Acts • triangular
trade routes

Focus on Main Ideas

1. What were some of the differences between the Colonies New England, the Middle Colonies, and the Southern Colonies?
2. What were the responsibilities of women in the colonies?
3. How did public schools and colleges develop in the colonies?

There were three groups of colonies: the New England Colonies, the Middle Colonies, and the Southern Colonies. The climate, the geography, and the way of life differed in each of these regions.

Life in the Three Groups of Colonies

The New England Colonies had long, cold winters. The rocky soil made it difficult to grow food. Settlers used the trees from the region's forests for shipbuilding. People in New England used the Atlantic Ocean for fishing, for hunting whales, and for trading.

In New England, religion was the center of life. Most of the people were Puritans whose families came from England. Puritans were also called Congregationalists in America. The Puritans believed that God rewarded people who worked hard. In most towns they built meeting houses where they held Sunday services and town meetings. Some of the problems that were discussed at town meetings included how much the new schoolmaster should be paid and which roads needed to be repaired. All men who were church members and property owners could speak and vote at these meetings. Town meetings helped build **democracy** in America because they gave a large group of people a voice in their government.

The region to the south of New England, the Middle Colonies, had a milder climate and better soil. The Middle Colonies had settlers who came from many nations in Europe, including Germany, Sweden, France, and Scotland. Most people in the Middle Colonies earned their living through farming. These colonies were called the "breadbasket colonies" because they grew large amounts of wheat and other grains as **cash crops**. Farmers used the area's three main rivers to ship their products to Philadelphia and New York City. These busy port cities became the largest cities of the Middle Colonies. Besides trade, **manufacturing** was important, too.

In the Southern Colonies, the climate was warmer than in the other two regions. The warm climate made it possible to grow crops throughout the year. Also, there was a larger area of flat land with good soil for farming. In these colonies people grew tobacco and rice on large plantations. These cash crops were sold to other colonies and to England.

Almost everything a **planter**, or plantation owner, and his family needed was made on the plantation. The planter lived in a large house with his family. The owner's wife ran the house and often managed the

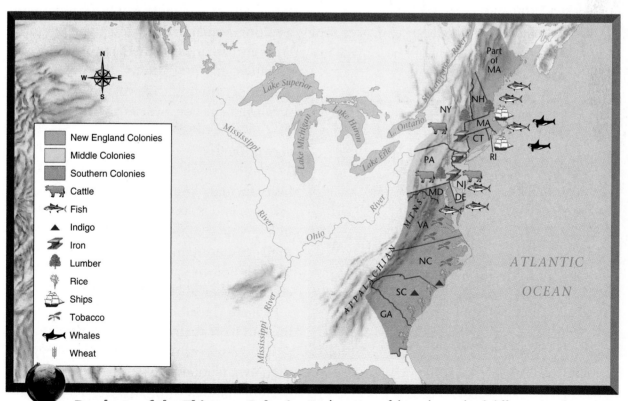

Products of the Thirteen Colonies *Each region of the colonies had different products. Use the map key to identify the products. Which region produced cattle?*

slaves that worked in the house. Planters depended on African slaves to do most of the field work. Laws called "slave codes" were passed to control the slaves. According to these laws, slaves were the property of their owner and had no rights. Teaching slaves to read and write was against the law. Although there were some African slaves in the Middle Colonies and in New England, most slaves were in the Southern Colonies. By 1775 slaves were one fifth of the population in the 13 colonies.

Unlike the Middle Colonies, most people in the Southern Colonies came from England. And unlike New England, most people belonged to the Church of England, which was called the **Episcopal Church** in America. The Episcopal Church was also called the Anglican Church. Laws in Virginia required all people to pay taxes to the Episcopal Church.

Throughout the colonies skilled workers made products that people needed. This worker makes leather goods the same way they were made back in the time of the colonies.

Most southerners owned small farms. But the wealthy planters controlled businesses, slaves, and governments in the Southern Colonies.

Family Life, Role of Women, and Social Classes

The family was the most important social group in the colonies. The father was the head of the house, and he expected his family to obey him. Women had few rights in the 13 colonies. A woman could not vote or work in a colonial government. In order to own land, start a business, or sign a contract, a woman had to have permission from her husband or from her father.

All women were expected to do many kinds of work for their family, but wealthy women had servants to help them. Women had to feed their family, so they grew vegetable gardens that provided some of their food. Women cooked meals in large pots over a fire in a fireplace. Pies filled with meat and vegetables were very popular.

Women took care of all children who lived in their home. Women made soap, candles, and clothing by hand. By working quickly, a woman might make two hundred candles in one day. To make clothing, women had to spin thread, weave it into cloth, and sew the cloth into clothing.

Finally, most women worked with their husband on their farm or in their shops and businesses. A few women managed their own plantations. Eliza Lucas Pinckney became famous for managing her father's plantation. She turned **indigo** into an important cash crop in South Carolina.

Social classes were important in the colonies. Yet colonists had more opportunities to move to a higher social class than did people in England. The highest social class was the upper class. The upper class included the wealthy and the well educated. Ministers, lawyers, southern planters, and rich merchants were part of the upper class. Only upper-class women could afford to wear silk dresses. Upper-class men often wore fancy white wigs. The largest class of people in the colonies was the middle class. Small farmers, shopkeepers, and skilled workers were part of the middle class. Farm workers and servants were in the lower class. Slaves were the lowest level of society and had the fewest rights.

Jonathan Edwards was an important leader of the Great Awakening. He was from Connecticut, and he became a minister in his grandfather's church in Massachusetts.

Religion and Education

Religion was important throughout the 13 colonies. A religious movement called the **Great Awakening** began during the early 1700s. Jonathan Edwards, a Protestant minister in Massachusetts, was an important leader of this movement. All people were equal before God, Edwards told his followers. Edwards taught that people should not depend on ministers to teach them about God. Instead they could learn about God by reading the Bible by themselves. The Great Awakening helped democracy because it spread the idea that all people are equal.

New England became the leader in the development of public schools because the Puritans believed everyone should be able to read the Bible. In 1647 Massachusetts passed America's first public school law. The law required towns with more than 50 families to hire a teacher for the town's children. Towns with more than 100 families had to start **grammar schools** for boys. These grammar schools, the first public schools in America, were small, one-room schools. They were for both rich and poor boys, and tax money supported the schools. Girls often went to **dame schools**, which women ran in their home.

There was little public education in the Middle Colonies and in the Southern Colonies. Most schools in the Middle Colonies were private schools that charged fees. In the Southern Colonies, wealthy children were taught at home.

At the age of 12, many middle- and lower-class children received an education by becoming an **apprentice**. An apprentice lived and worked with a master craftsman. A boy could be an apprentice to a printer,

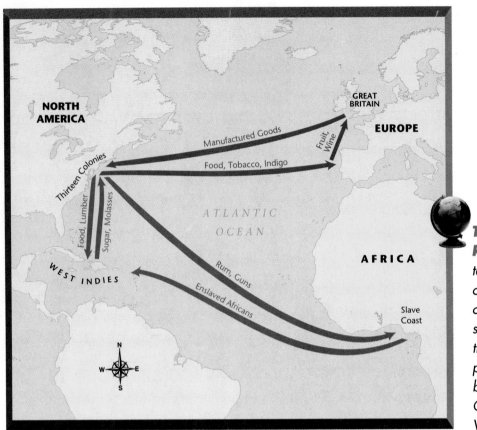

Triangular Trade Routes *Much trade took place between the colonies, Europe, and other places. This map shows some of these trade routes. What products were traded between the Thirteen Colonies and the West Indies?*

shoemaker, glassmaker, silversmith, or other craftsman. The craftsman taught reading, writing, and his trade, or business, to the apprentice. After about seven years, the apprentice could work on his own as a **journeyman**. Later, when he was experienced, he was considered a master craftsman who could have his own apprentices.

The first colleges in the colonies were started as schools to train ministers. In 1636 the Puritans started Harvard College, the first college in the colonies.

Colonial Trade and Cities

Most colonial trade was with other colonies and with England. During the 1600s and the 1700s, Europeans believed in an idea called **mercantilism**. Under mercantilism a nation could be rich only by gaining wealth from rival nations. To get this wealth, a nation needed a **favorable balance of trade**. This means a nation had to sell more products to other countries than it bought from other countries. These products would be sold in exchange for gold and silver. Europeans believed that colonies were needed in order to have a favorable balance of trade. Colonies were a good place to sell products, and they were a good place to get raw materials to make more products.

Beginning in 1651, England passed laws called the **Navigation Acts** to control trade with its colonies. These laws tried to make England richer by forcing the colonies to trade mainly with England. The colonies were not allowed to make products that they could buy from England. All trade had to be done on English ships or on ships that were built in the colonies.

New England, a leader in shipbuilding, sent trading ships to England and to English colonies in all parts of the world. Colonial products, such as lumber and fish, were traded in England for manufactured goods, such as furniture and fine clothing. But much trading took place among the 13 colonies. New England merchants shipped fish and lumber to the other colonies. The Southern Colonies sent rice and tobacco to New England. Grain and flour from the Middle Colonies went to the Southern Colonies and to New England.

In order to trade with countries other than England, the colonies developed **triangular trade routes**. To trade with European merchants, the colonial merchants shipped their products to European ports. There they were traded for goods that were not available in England, such as fruits and wine. Next, the fruits and wine were traded in England for manufactured goods. Finally, the manufactured goods from England were sold in the colonies.

Another triangular trade route brought African slaves to America. First, colonists traded their products for sugar and molasses in the West Indies. Ships carried sugar and molasses back to the colonies, where they were made into rum. In the next step, ships carried rum and guns to Africa.

In Africa these were exchanged for slaves. Then African slaves were shipped to the West Indies or to the colonies.

Trade helped port cities in the colonies grow larger. By 1770 Boston was the busiest port, and Philadelphia was the largest city in the colonies. Cities grew larger each year, but most colonists continued to live on farms and in towns.

By 1760 there were almost 2 million people living in the 13 colonies. About half of the colonists came from European nations other than England. They spoke many languages, belonged to many religions, and earned their living in many different ways. They thought of themselves as Virginians, New Yorkers, or members of other colonies. Read on to learn how problems with England would help the colonists join together to become Americans.

Cities such as Philadelphia and Boston became centers of trade. But in the Southern Colonies, ships sailed directly to the plantations.

63

Benjamin Franklin 1706–1790

Benjamin Franklin was famous for his work as a printer, a writer, a scientist, an inventor, and a leader in the 13 colonies. People around the world admired him because he could do so many things very well.

Franklin was born in Boston and was the fifteenth child in a family with seventeen children. Because his family had little money, Franklin spent only two years in school. But he educated himself by reading every book he could find.

Franklin became an apprentice in his older brother's printing shop. He enjoyed being a printer, but he did not get along with his brother. So at age 17, he ran away to Philadelphia.

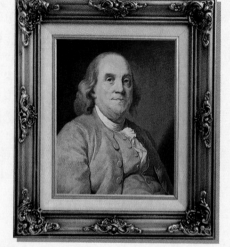

After a few years, Franklin published his own newspaper in Philadelphia. He was the first American to use maps and cartoons in a newspaper. He also published a book each year called *Poor Richard's Almanac*. It was filled with wise sayings like "Early to bed and early to rise, makes a man healthy, wealthy, and wise."

Franklin became famous for his work as an inventor and a scientist. He invented the Franklin stove, which did a good job of warming a cold room because it used less fuel and gave more heat. Scientists around the world admired his experiment that proved that lightning was one form of electricity.

Franklin also contributed to the city of Philadelphia. Franklin started the first hospital, library, and fire department. He also started a school that would later become the University of Pennsylvania.

Later in life Franklin worked hard to help the colonies win their freedom from England. At age 81 he helped write the Constitution, a new set of laws for the United States. He continued to work for Philadelphia and his country until the end of his life at age 84.

In Your Own Words

Write a paragraph in the journal section of your social studies notebook that explains the many ways Ben Franklin helped his city and his country. Although Franklin did many jobs well, what do you think was his most important work?

REVIEW AND APPLY

■ Puritans in New England held town meetings so the people could solve problems together.

■ The Middle Colonies had the most diverse population because there were immigrants from many different European nations.

■ Public-school education began in New England.

■ Most people in the Southern Colonies owned small farms, but rich plantation owners controlled government and businesses.

■ Colonial women could not vote or work in the government.

■ The triangular trade routes helped the colonies trade with the West Indies, Europe, and Africa.

VOCABULARY

Finish the Sentence ■ Choose one of the words or phrases from the box to complete each sentence. Write the correct word or phrase in your social studies notebook. You will not use all the words in the box.

1. In a _____ the government is ruled by the people.

2. Crops, that are grown for profit such as tobacco and indigo, are called _____ .

3. An _____ was a boy who lived and worked with a master craftsman in order to learn his trade.

4. A _____ owned a large plantation.

5. _____ means producing goods by machine.

6. The system that helped a nation get rich by gaining wealth from rival nations was called _____ .

7. _____ were laws that forced the colonies to trade mainly with England.

> Navigation Acts
> planter
> debtor
> democracy
> mercantilism
> cash crops
> dame school
> apprentice
> manufacturing

USING INFORMATION

Journal Writing ■ Write a paragraph in the journal section of your notebook that explains the responsibilities of colonial women.

Choose the Answer ■ In your social studies notebook, write the letter of the word or phrase that best answers each question.

1. What right did colonial women **not** have?

   a. to teach
   b. to vote
   c. to cook

2. Who was a leader of the Great Awakening?

   a. Jonathan Edwards
   b. John Smith
   c. Roger Williams

3. Which people belonged to the upper class?

   a. farm workers and servants
   b. farmers and shopkeepers
   c. ministers, planters, lawyers, and rich merchants

4. Which city was the busiest port in the colonies?

   a. Boston
   b. Providence
   c. Jamestown

5. Where did most people live in the Southern Colonies?

   a. big cities
   b. large plantations
   c. small farms

6. About how many people lived in the 13 colonies in 1760?

   a. almost 2 thousand
   b. almost 2 million
   c. almost 20 million

CRITICAL THINKING

Comparing and Contrasting ■ In this chapter, you read about the differences between the New England, Middle, and Southern colonies. Compare and contrast the three regions by copying and completing the chart below. One box is already done for you.

Region	New England	Middle	Southern
Climate			
Education			
The ways people earned a living	shipbuilding, fishing, whale hunting, trade		

AMERICAN GEOGRAPHY

Location: The Thirteen Colonies

Location tells us where a place is. We can use map directions and latitude and longitude to identify the location of a place. We can also identify the location of a place by comparing it to the location of another place. For example, North Carolina can be described as being a Southern Colony located on the Atlantic Ocean between South Carolina and Virginia. Philadelphia can be described as a city in Pennsylvania on the border of New Jersey.

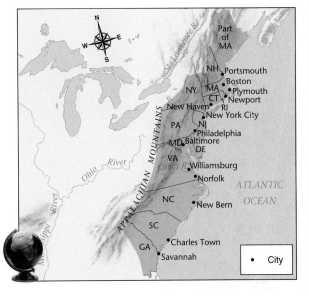

A. Location of Cities ■ Study the map and then write in your social studies notebook about the location of each city.

1. Williamsburg, Virginia

2. Boston

3. New York City

4. Charles Town

5. Baltimore

6. New Haven

B. Location of the Colonies ■ Describe the location of each colony.

1. Connecticut

2. New York

3. Georgia

4. Pennsylvania

5. Virginia

6. New Jersey

Chapter 7

THE ROAD TO REVOLUTION

◄ *Stamp used to show that tax was paid*

People

King John • British •
King George III •
George Washington •
Pontiac • Sons of Liberty •
Daughters of Liberty •
Crispus Attucks • Sam
Adams • John Adams •
Patrick Henry • Minutemen

Places

Wales • Great Britain •
Ohio Valley • Appalachian
Mountains • Montreal •
Lexington • Concord

New Vocabulary

Magna Carta • Parliament •
frontier • surrendered •
treaty • ally •
proclamation •
representation • taxation •
boycott • Committee of
Correspondence •
Intolerable Acts • militia

Focus on Main Ideas

1. What events in England led to the development of representative government?
2. What kinds of representative governments did the colonies have?
3. How did the French and Indian War change the relationship between Great Britain and the 13 colonies?
4. Which events between 1763 and 1775 led Americans to fight against Great Britain?

In 1760 Americans in the 13 colonies were proud to be ruled by Great Britain. After all, Great Britain was the world's most powerful nation. As you read this chapter, think about why the colonies were at war with Great Britain only 15 years later.

Government in England and in the Thirteen Colonies

In order to understand why Americans fought against England, it is necessary to know how representative government developed in England. In the year 1215, a group of nobles forced King John to sign a paper called the **Magna Carta**. The Magna Carta was important because it was the first set of laws in England to limit the king's power. It did this by allowing nobles to help write the nation's laws. This was the beginning of the lawmaking group called **Parliament**. Members of Parliament worked together to make laws for England. Men who had the right to vote voted for leaders to represent them in Parliament. England had a representative government because of its Parliament.

In 1688 Parliament forced its king, James II, to leave England during the Glorious Revolution. No one was killed

68

during this revolution, and Parliament asked William and Mary to become the new monarchs. In 1689 William and Mary signed a group of laws called the English Bill of Rights. The Bill of Rights said that only Parliament had the power to raise an army or to collect taxes. The Glorious Revolution and the English Bill of Rights were important because they made Parliament more powerful than the king.

England had been an independent country for hundreds of years. In 1536 Henry VIII united the kingdoms of England and Wales. In 1707 the Kingdom of England and Wales was united with the Kingdom of Scotland to form one nation. The new nation was called Great Britain. The people who lived in Great Britain were called the British.

In 1760 King George III became the ruler of Great Britain. Before 1760 Parliament made few laws for its American colonies. Each colonial government made its own laws. Each colony had an assembly with two houses, a lower house and an upper house. Colonists voted for representatives to make laws for them in the lower house. The lower house passed tax laws and controlled the colony's money. The upper house had men who were chosen by the governor of the colony. By 1750 most white men who owned property could vote in the colonies. When he became king, George III decided to take stronger control of the colonies. One reason for this change was the cost of fighting wars against France.

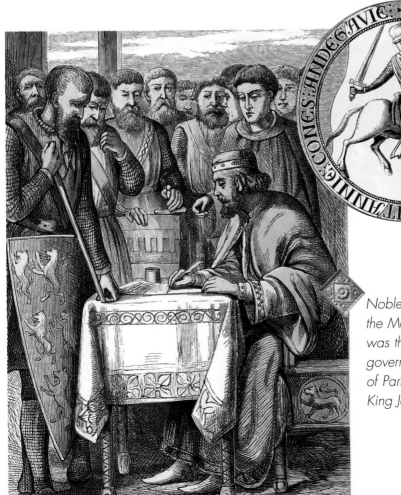

Nobles in England made King John sign the Magna Carta in 1215. This event was the beginning of representative government in England. Now members of Parliament helped the king write laws. King John's seal is shown above.

69

The French and Indian War

In Unit 1 you learned how the English and the French first settled in America. The French built a large empire called New France. Canada and Louisiana were parts of New France. Both England and France wanted to rule the land around the Ohio River called the Ohio Valley. French fur traders were the first people from Europe to reach the Ohio Valley. They built forts in the Valley, but few French people settled there.

British settlers began to move west across the Appalachian Mountains into the Ohio Valley. They called the area the **frontier** because it had no cities or towns. Settlers in the frontier cleared the land of trees to start farms. The trees were used to build log cabins and fences. Life on the frontier was difficult. Many settlers died from hunger, disease, and wars with Indians.

The French and the Indians united to attack British settlers in the Ohio Valley. In 1754 the French and Indian War began between the French and the British. Many Indian nations fought alongside the French. They hoped that if the French won, British settlers would no longer be allowed in the Ohio Valley. Only the powerful Iroquois nations fought alongside the British. The Iroquois and the French had been enemies since 1609.

At the start of the war, the British asked George Washington, a 21-year-old soldier from Virginia, to help them fight the French. They told Washington to force the French to leave a fort they had built in western Pennsylvania. Washington and his soldiers were defeated in their early battles with the French. Although Washington lost these battles, he learned how to fight on the frontier. Because Washington showed great courage, he became a war hero in the colonies.

The British captured the French city of Quebec in 1759. The next year the British captured Montreal and the French **surrendered**. While the French and the British fought in America, they also fought each other in Europe during the Seven Years War. The French lost that war, too.

In 1763 the French and the British signed a peace **treaty** called the Treaty of Paris. The treaty said that France lost all its land in North America except for four small islands. Spain, France's **ally** in the war, gave Florida to Great Britain. Louisiana was split at the Mississippi River. The land east of the river was given to Great Britain. The land west of the river was given to Spain. Great Britain gained more than just the Ohio Valley. It also ruled Canada and all the land along the Atlantic Ocean.

Problems After the French and Indian War

After the French and Indian War, King George III and the leaders of Parliament angered the people in the American colonies. King George first angered the colonists by writing a **proclamation**, a type of law, that said colonists could not settle in the Ohio Valley. The colonists thought the new law was very unfair. After all, they had fought and died to win the Ohio Valley during the French and Indian War.

The Proclamation of 1763 was written after Pontiac's Rebellion, which occurred earlier that same year. Pontiac, an Ottawa leader, led attacks by a number of Indian nations against British settlements and forts in the Ohio Valley. They destroyed most of the British forts in the area and killed about 2,000 settlers. The fighting stopped at the end of the French and Indian War. The king wrote the proclamation because the British thought it would be expensive and difficult to protect colonists from more Indian attacks.

The colonists were also angry when Parliament began to pass tax laws for the colonies. Money from the colonies would be sent to Great Britain to help pay the debts from the French and Indian War. The chart on this page shows the laws passed by Parliament to tax and control the colonies.

The tax laws angered the colonists. They said Parliament could not tax the colonists because they did not have **representation** in Parliament. "No **taxation** without representation" were the words said throughout the colonies. Representatives from the colonies were not allowed in Parliament. The lawmakers in Parliament believed they had every right to tax the colonies and make laws for them because the colonies belonged to Great Britain.

The American Colonists Begin to Unite

Rage toward the British began to unite the colonists. They began to work together against Great Britain. Many colonists stopped seeing themselves as British citizens. Instead they began to think of themselves as Americans. Colonists started protest groups called the Sons of Liberty and the Daughters of Liberty. To end unfair tax

Events Leading to War

Proclamation of 1763	British said colonists could not settle in the Ohio Valley.
Sugar Act (1764)	Taxes on sugar and molasses.
Stamp Act (1765)	Colonists must buy stamps for all printed material.
Quartering Act (1765)	British soldiers must be given food and housing in colonies.
Declaratory Act (1767)	Parliament ended the Stamp and Sugar Acts but said it had the right to tax the colonies.
Townshend Acts (1767)	Taxes on paint, glass, lead, paper, and tea.
Boston Massacre (1770)	A snowball fight leads to British soldiers shooting five Americans.
Tea Act (1773)	Tax on tea.
Boston Tea Party (1773)	Colonists dump tea into Boston Harbor.
Intolerable Acts (1774)	The British passed laws to punish Boston for the Boston Tea Party. They closed Boston Harbor.
First Continental Congress (1774)	Delegates from 12 colonies meet and send a letter to King George.
Lexington and Concord (April 1775)	The American Revolution begins.

Colonists showed their anger at the new tax laws in many ways. Here colonists burn stamps that were used to show that a tax had been paid.

laws, the colonists started a **boycott** against products from Great Britain. When the boycott hurt Britain's trade, Parliament ended some of the tax laws.

Some colonists in Boston used violence to protest. So the British sent soldiers to Boston. On March 5, 1770, a group of American men and boys began throwing rocks and snowballs at a small group of British soldiers. To stop Americans from throwing rocks, British soldiers fired their guns. Five colonists were killed. Crispus Attucks, an African American, was among those killed. The colonists called this the Boston Massacre.

Sam Adams became one of the famous protest leaders in Boston. He started a group called the **Committee of Correspondence.**

Five colonists, including Crispus Attucks, were killed in the Boston Massacre. The Committee of Correspondence was started to tell other colonists about the Boston Massacre.

More committees were started in the other colonies. These committees sent information to each other about the Boston Massacre. As people in every colony learned about the Boston Massacre, bitter feelings towards King George grew stronger.

After the British passed the Tea Act in 1773, the Sons of Liberty took action. In New York City and in Philadelphia, they quietly sent tea ships back to Great Britain. But in Boston, Sam Adams planned the Boston Tea Party. One dark night members of the Sons of Liberty put on Indian clothes and boarded the tea ships. They broke open tea chests and threw thousands of pounds of tea into the water.

Back in Great Britain, King George was furious. Parliament passed new laws to punish the people of Boston. The new laws took away self-government from Massachusetts. Boston Harbor was closed until the colonists paid for the tea. More British soldiers were sent to Boston to carry out the laws. The colonists hated these laws so much that they called these laws the **Intolerable Acts**.

The Colonies Prepare for War

To solve their problems with King George, protest leaders from 12 colonies met in Philadelphia. Georgia did not send its leaders to the meeting of the First Continental Congress in 1774, but that colony agreed to follow the decisions made by the Congress. The best leaders of the colonies were in the Congress. Sam Adams and John Adams came from Massachusetts. Patrick Henry and George Washington were there from Virginia.

The members of the Continental Congress wrote a letter to King George. It said that the colonies were loyal to the king, but laws for the colonies must be made by their own elected representatives. The letter included a list of problems the colonists wanted corrected. The leaders decided that the colonies would boycott British goods until the problems were solved. Each colony would start its own **militia** so the colonies would be prepared if they had to fight the British. Finally they agreed to meet again in May 1775.

The Shot Heard Round the World

In the months that followed, colonists formed militias. Each colony had militia soldiers who called themselves Minutemen because they needed only one minute to be ready to fight the British. The colonists in Massachusetts began to store weapons in the town of Concord near Boston.

In April 1775 more British soldiers were sent to Massachusetts. The Sons of Liberty learned that the soldiers planned to attack Concord and capture the colonists' weapons. On April 18, 1775, Paul Revere and two other members of the Sons of Liberty rode through the night and warned the people of Concord and Lexington that British soldiers were coming. The next day the Minutemen were ready to fight.

The first battle between the colonists and the British began in Lexington. Eight Minutemen died in that battle. Then the British marched on to Concord where they

Minutemen would quickly leave their homes, farms, and families to fight the British. The Minutemen are remembered with the statue above in Massachusetts.

fought the Minutemen again. The British were forced back to Boston.

The fighting at Lexington and Concord has been called "the shot heard round the world." People around the world learned about these famous battles for freedom and representative government. It gave people in other lands the hope that someday they could fight for better governments, too.

Lexington and Concord were the first battles in the American Revolution. When the war began in 1775, Americans were fighting to have the same rights as all British citizens. They wanted self-government in the colonies and representation in Parliament. Read on in Chapter 8 to learn how the American Revolution became a fight for freedom.

$\mathcal{B}$IOGRAPHY

Paul Revere 1735–1818

Paul Revere was a famous leader in the American Revolution who helped the United States become a free nation.

Paul Revere was born in Boston. His father was a silversmith, and Revere became a silversmith, too. Revere became a member of the Sons of Liberty. After the Boston Massacre in 1770, Revere made an engraving of the event that became famous.

Revere worked with Sam Adams to plan the Boston Tea Party in 1773. He was one of the men who dumped tea into Boston Harbor. But he is best known for his ride on April 18, 1775, which was made famous by the poem "Paul Revere's Ride," by Henry Wadsworth Longfellow.

Some Americans had learned that the British were planning to attack Concord to capture American weapons. Revere and William Dawes were sent to warn the colonists in Concord and to warn Sam Adams in Lexington. They arrived at Lexington around midnight and warned the colonists that the British would arrive in the morning.

One hour later Revere, Dawes, and Dr. Samuel Prescott began riding to Concord. On the way British soldiers stopped them. Dawes and Prescott escaped, and Prescott reached Concord. The British allowed Revere to return to Lexington the next day without his horse. After walking to Lexington, Revere and Adams escaped to safety. When the British troops from Boston reached Lexington, the Minutemen were ready for them, thanks to Paul Revere.

Revere served in the army in New England during the American Revolution. He also produced gunpowder and cannons for the army. Revere printed the first paper money for the nation.

After the war Paul Revere continued his work as a silversmith. His silver objects were so popular that Revere became as famous for his work with silver as he was for his famous ride on April 18, 1775.

In Your Own Words

Write a paragraph in the journal section of your notebook that describes Paul Revere's achievements before, during, and after the American Revolution.

REVIEW AND APPLY

- In 1215 England's King John signed the Magna Carta, which limited the king's power and allowed nobles to start Parliament.

- After the French and Indian War, France lost most of its empire in North America. Great Britain gained Canada and the Ohio Valley.

- After the French and Indian War, the British Parliament passed tax laws for the colonies to help pay for the British war debts. The colonists protested these taxes because the colonists were not represented in the British Parliament.

- The American Revolution started in 1775 with the battles of Lexington and Concord.

VOCABULARY

Choose the Meaning ■ In your social studies notebook, write the letter of the word or phrase that best completes each sentence.

1. The Magna Carta was a paper that limited the power of the _____ .

   a. British king
   b. French king
   c. colonial government

2. Parliament is a _____ .

   a. British colony
   b. British trading group
   c. British lawmaking body

3. During a boycott people _____ .

   a. vote to pay taxes
   b. get elected to Parliament
   c. refuse to use or buy something

4. A nation that surrenders during a war _____ .

   a. wins the war
   b. gives up fighting the war
   c. decides to continue fighting the war

5. Taxation is a way for a government to _____ .

   a. raise money
   b. fight a war
   c. start new colonies

6. An ally during a war _____ .

   a. helps your enemy
   b. fights with you against your enemy
   c. is your enemy

7. A militia is a group of citizens that are trained to be _____ .

   a. craftsman
   b. soldiers
   c. farmers

8. The frontier is a region with few _____ .

   a. Indians
   b. trees
   c. settlers

COMPREHENSION CHECK

Write the Answer ■ In your social studies notebook, write one or more sentences to answer each question.

1. How did the Magna Carta and the English Bill of Rights help the growth of representative government in England?

2. What groups made up the two sides that fought the French and Indian War?

3. What were the results of the French and Indian War?

4. What changes did King George make in the way the colonies were ruled after the French and Indian War?

5. Why did Pontiac lead a rebellion in the Ohio Valley?

6. What does the phrase "No taxation without representation!" mean?

7. What was one way the colonists protested against British taxes?

8. What happened at the Boston Tea Party?

9. What happened at Lexington and Concord in Massachusetts on April 19, 1775?

10. Why did the Americans decide to fight the British, starting in 1775?

CRITICAL THINKING

Distinguishing Relevant Information ■ Imagine you are telling a friend why many colonists decided to protest and fight against Great Britain. Read each sentence below. Decide which sentences are relevant to what you will say. Write the relevant sentences in your social studies notebook. There are three relevant sentences.

1. The British passed the Tea Act in 1773.

2. George III became the king of England in 1760.

3. The British would not allow the colonies to have representation in Parliament.

4. Settlers cleared trees and started farms in the Ohio Valley.

5. The British closed Boston Harbor after the Boston Tea Party.

USING INFORMATION

Writing an Opinion ■ Do you think that the colonists were right or wrong for protesting the tax laws made by Parliament? In your notebook write a paragraph that explains your opinion.

76

SOCIAL STUDIES SKILLS

Comparing Historical Maps

A historical map shows how a region looked during a certain period of history. You can learn how events have changed a region by comparing two maps of the same place that represent different time periods.

The historical map on the left shows North America when the French and Indian War began in 1754. The map on the right shows how European control of North America changed in 1763 as a result of the war.

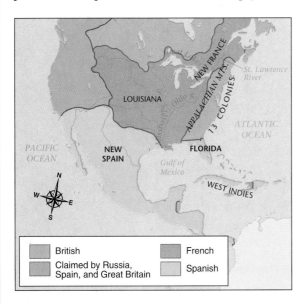

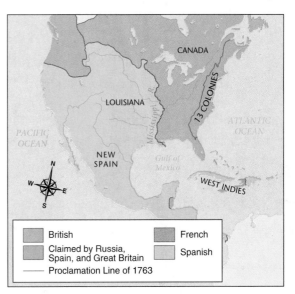

Compare the two maps of North America and write the answer to each question.

1. Which nation ruled Louisiana in 1754? In 1763?

2. Which nation ruled east of the Mississippi River in 1763?

3. Which nation ruled Florida in 1754? In 1763?

4. What land did France lose in 1763?

5. What land did England control in 1763?

6. How did the French and Indian War change Great Britain's control in North America?

7. How did control of New Spain change between 1754 and 1763?

8. How did the land claimed by Russia, Spain, and Great Britain change between 1754 and 1763?

Chapter 8

THE AMERICAN REVOLUTION

◀ *The Liberty Bell*

People

Thomas Paine • Thomas Jefferson • John Locke • Phillis Wheatley • Marquis de Lafayette • Friedrich von Steuben • Bernardo de Gálvez • Benedict Arnold • General Cornwallis • Joseph Brant • Peter Salem

Places

Fort Ticonderoga • Bunker Hill • Trenton • Princeton • Saratoga • Valley Forge • Yorktown

New Vocabulary

delegates • commander in chief • blockade • pamphlet • Loyalists • neutral • Patriots • Enlightenment • unalienable rights • pursuit of happiness • traitors • retreat • turning point • morale

Focus on Main Ideas

1. What important ideas were in the Declaration of Independence?
2. What were the strengths and the weaknesses of the British and American armies?
3. Who were some important people during the American Revolution? How did they help Americans win the war?

At the start of the American Revolution, the British Army was the strongest in the world. As you read this chapter, think about how Americans were able to defeat the powerful British Army.

The Second Continental Congress

Soon after the battles of Lexington and Concord, **delegates** from all 13 colonies held the Second Continental Congress. The Congress began in May 1775 in Philadelphia. The Continental Congress decided to form an army with soldiers from all of the colonies. All the delegates agreed that George Washington should be the **commander in chief** of the new Continental Army. Washington had come to the Congress as a delegate. Dressed in his army uniform, Washington looked ready for the difficult job. The Continental Congress also decided to send Benjamin Franklin to France to ask for French help.

While American delegates were working in the Continental Congress, American soldiers had captured British cannons and supplies at Fort Ticonderoga in New York. In June 1775 American troops moved to Breeds Hill and Bunker Hill, two hills near Boston. On these hills American and

British troops fought the Battle of Bunker Hill. The Americans lost the battle, but more than a thousand British soldiers died at Bunker Hill.

Back at the Continental Congress in Philadelphia, the delegates sent a letter to King George called the Olive Branch Petition. It said the colonists wanted peace, and they wanted to be ruled by Great Britain. But the colonists also wanted to have the same rights as British citizens.

A few delegates, one being Patrick Henry, were ready for the colonies to break away from Great Britain and become an independent nation. In one of his famous speeches, Patrick Henry said, "I know not what course others may take, but as for me, give me liberty or give me death!" However most delegates still wanted the colonies to be ruled by Great Britain.

Those feelings changed at the end of 1775. King George refused to read the Olive Branch Petition. Instead British ships were sent to **blockade** American ports.

In January 1776 Thomas Paine convinced many Americans that they should be a free nation. Paine had come to live in America from England. He wrote a **pamphlet** called "Common Sense," which said the colonies should break all ties with Great Britain. Many people in the colonies agreed with "Common Sense."

In the Battle of Bunker Hill, the Americans had very little gunpowder. They waited until the British came very close before they began to shoot. When they ran out of gunpowder, they used their rifles as clubs. The Americans fought bravely, but they lost the battle.

79

Benjamin Franklin, John Adams, and Thomas Jefferson (shown left to right above) were in the committee of five delegates that wrote the Declaration of Independence.

Not all colonists agreed with Thomas Paine. About one third of the colonists wanted to remain part of the British Empire. These colonists were called **Loyalists** because they were loyal to King George. Many Loyalists moved to England and Canada during the American Revolution, but thousands stayed and fought for the British. About one third of the colonists wanted to be **neutral** and not fight for either side. One third of the colonists wanted independence; they were called **Patriots**.

The Declaration of Independence

In June 1776 the delegates at the Congress decided to tell the world that the colonies were an independent nation.

They decided to explain their reasons in a paper called the Declaration of Independence. A committee was given the job of writing the Declaration. They asked Thomas Jefferson, a young delegate from Virginia, to do most of the writing.

Thomas Jefferson used ideas from the **Enlightenment** when he wrote the Declaration. The Enlightenment was a period during the 1600s and 1700s when great thinkers wrote new ideas about government. John Locke was one of the great thinkers of the Enlightenment. He believed that God gave rights that belong to all people and can not be taken away. Locke also believed that people have the right to have a revolution against their government if the government does not protect the rights of the people.

The Declaration of Independence explained that "all men are created equal" and that God gave all people **unalienable rights**. These rights, which can not be taken away, are "life, liberty, and the **pursuit of happiness**." Jefferson used Locke's ideas when he wrote in the Declaration that people can change their government if it tries to take away these rights. The Declaration listed the many ways King George had taken away the rights of the colonists. The Declaration ended by saying the 13 colonies were "free and independent states." Soon Americans began to call their free nation the United States of America.

Jefferson wrote "all men are created equal" at a time when one fifth of the people in the colonies were slaves. Women did not have the right to vote in any of the colonies. Jefferson wanted the Declaration to include sentences that spoke out against slavery.

But when delegates from the Southern Colonies refused to sign the Declaration, those sentences about slavery were removed. All people were not treated equally in America in 1776, but the Declaration set high goals for equal treatment in the future.

On July 4, 1776, the delegates signed and adopted the Declaration of Independence. It took great courage to say the colonies were a free nation. To King George all of the signers were **traitors**. If Americans lost their fight to be free, all of the signers would be punished with death.

George Washington Becomes Commander in Chief

In July 1776 George Washington went to Boston to take charge of the Continental Army. Washington faced many problems. The Continental Congress could not collect taxes, so there was little money to pay for an army. The soldiers had no uniforms, and they had to buy their own guns. Often the army did not have enough food.

Washington became a hero as commander in chief. He taught the soldiers to work together as an army. Although Washington lost more battles than he won, he refused to give up. He knew when to **retreat** and when to move to another place. Then the army could fight again.

Comparing the American and British Armies

In 1776 the British were sure they would win the war. They had the strongest army in the world, and they had a large,

Phillis Wheatley, a poet, admired Washington. She published a poem about Washington's greatness. He read the poem, liked it, and later met Phillis Wheatley to thank her.

powerful navy. The Americans lacked supplies, but they knew how to fight in forests and on the frontier. The British soldiers and their leaders did not.

Since Great Britain ruled many colonies around the world, the British Army had soldiers in many far-off places. The British did not have enough soldiers to fight in America. So they hired Hessian soldiers from Germany. The Hessians were paid to fight, and they really did not care which side won. The American soldiers believed in the cause for which they were fighting.

The Early Years of the War

Soon after the Declaration of Independence was signed, Americans

On the snowy Christmas Eve of 1776, Washington crossed the icy Delaware River with 2,400 soldiers. The next day they made a surprise attack on a group of Hessian soldiers in Trenton, New Jersey. The Americans captured 900 Hessian soldiers and not one American was killed.

fought the British in New York. When Washington lost the Battle of Long Island, he retreated to Manhattan. Washington then escaped with his army to New Jersey. Great Britain had won control of New York City and Long Island.

Nathan Hale was a brave American spy at the Battle of Long Island. He was caught by the British and hanged. Just before he died, Hale said, "My only regret is that I have but one life to give for my country."

Washington had two victories at the end of 1776. The first victory was the surprise attack in Trenton after crossing the icy Delaware River. Then the Americans went to nearby Princeton, where they won another small battle. These two victories

encouraged the American soldiers to continue fighting.

In September 1777 the British captured Philadelphia. But a few weeks later, in October, Americans won a very important victory in Saratoga, New York. The Americans captured almost 6,000 British prisoners. The Battle of Saratoga became the **turning point** in the war. It proved that the Americans were strong enough to defeat the British. So France decided to send soldiers, ships, and supplies to help the new nation. France's goal was to defeat its old enemy, Great Britain.

Marquis de Lafayette became a French hero during the American Revolution. In 1777 he used his own money to buy a ship, and then he sailed to America with French soldiers. Lafayette fought alongside the Americans until the last battle ended.

The War After the Battle of Saratoga

After the Battle of Saratoga, Washington led his army to Valley Forge in Pennsylvania. There they spent a long, cold winter. **Morale** was so low that many soldiers left the army to return home. There was not enough food or clothing. Thousands of soldiers wrapped rags around their feet because they did not have shoes to wear. But the men who stayed at Valley Forge that winter became better soldiers, thanks to

the work of German General Friedrich von Steuben. Von Steuben drilled the soldiers on how to use weapons, and he taught them the best ways to fight.

After the winter at Valley Forge, more fighting took place in the South and in the West. The British won many battles in the South, but it cost them many lives. In the West, Americans had a victory at Vincennes in the Ohio Valley.

In 1779 Spain started to help the American Army. Bernardo de Gálvez, the Spanish governor of Louisiana, sent gun powder, food, medicine, and money to the American Army. He led a Spanish army that captured British forts and cities along the Gulf of Mexico from Louisiana to Florida.

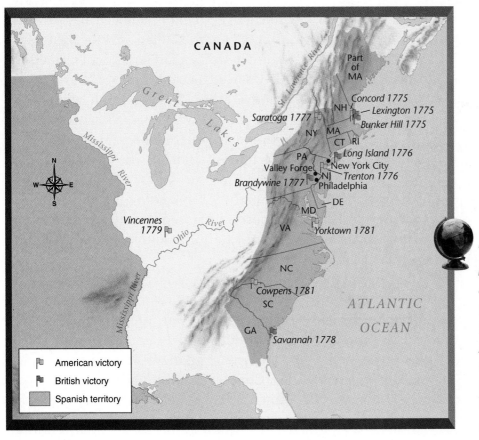

The American Revolution Many of the earlier battles of the war took place in New England and the Middle Colonies. Later the British tried to capture the Southern Colonies. Where was the last battle of the war?

83

One of the best American generals, Benedict Arnold, became a traitor. He wanted to surrender the American fort at West Point, New York, to the British. When Americans learned that Arnold was a traitor, they tried to capture him. But Arnold escaped and became a general in the British Army.

By 1781 General Cornwallis, the leader of the British Army, was losing the war in the South. From August until October, Americans fought Cornwallis at Yorktown, Virginia. With the help of the French Army and the French Navy, the British army was trapped. On October 19 Cornwallis surrendered to Washington. Americans had won their independence!

In 1783 the Americans and the British signed the Treaty of Paris. In this peace treaty, Great Britain recognized the United States as an independent nation. Although Great Britain still ruled Canada, the United States ruled all the land to the east of the Mississippi River.

Who Fought in the American Revolution?

Many kinds of people fought in the war. Most Indians fought for the British. They hoped that the British would stop Americans from settling on Indian lands. Joseph Brant, a Mohawk leader, helped the British win the Battle of Long Island.

About five thousand African Americans fought for American freedom during the war. Free African Americans and slaves were in the American Army. They fought in every important battle. Peter Salem, a Minuteman, fought the British at Lexington. Later Salem shot a British commander in the Battle of Bunker Hill. James Armistead, an African American slave, served as a spy for Lafayette. He became a free man after the war.

Large numbers of Irish Americans fought for freedom. Many of these soldiers became generals in the Continental Army.

Jewish Americans fought for American freedom. David Emmanuel became a hero in Georgia. Haym Salomon, a spy for the American Army, was arrested twice by the British. Both times he escaped. He also raised money for the Continental Army.

Thaddeus Kosciusko, a Polish engineer, became good friends with George Washington. Kosciusko's work during the Battle of Saratoga helped Americans win this important battle.

Women were important during the American Revolution, although they were not allowed to be soldiers. While men were fighting, women ran farms and businesses. They served as cooks, nurses, and doctors for the army. Some women worked as spies. George Washington's wife, Martha, spent each winter of the war with the army. She nursed soldiers who were hurt and sewed up the holes in their clothes. Deborah Sampson fought as a soldier. Sampson disguised herself as a man, wore an army uniform, and fought in the Battle of Yorktown.

Americans were proud that they had worked together to win their independence. Early in the war, the Declaration of Independence had said Americans wanted a government that would serve the people. In Chapter 9 you will find out how Americans planned a new government that would protect their rights and freedoms.

BIOGRAPHY

Thomas Jefferson 1743–1826

Farmer, lawyer, architect, inventor, governor, President, and writer were all jobs that Thomas Jefferson did well during his long life.

Jefferson was born on his family's farm in Virginia. Jefferson was well educated. He learned several languages and played the violin. He attended college and became a lawyer. Jefferson was elected to the Virginia House of Burgesses in 1769.

Jefferson became a Patriot who spoke out against unfair British laws. He had studied John Locke's ideas about government, and he believed the British were taking away the rights of Americans. So he was glad to be one of Virginia's delegates at the First Continental Congress.

Delegates at the Second Continental Congress asked Jefferson to write the Declaration of Independence. It took two weeks of hard work to write the Declaration. A few men like Benjamin Franklin and John Adams shortened the Declaration after it was finished. The Declaration told why the colonies wanted independence, and it explained that governments should get their power from the people.

Jefferson strongly believed that all people should have religious freedom. So during the American Revolution he wrote the "Virginia Statute for Religious Freedom." This law gave religious freedom to all people. During the war Jefferson also served as governor of Virginia.

After the British surrendered, Jefferson helped write the Treaty of Paris. He wrote treaties with other European nations for the United States.

Jefferson was elected the third President of the United States in 1800. He served two terms. In 1817 he started the University of Virginia. Thomas Jefferson and his good friend John Adams both died on July 4, 1826. This was exactly fifty years after the Declaration of Independence had been adopted.

In Your Own Words

Write a paragraph in the journal section of your social studies notebook that describes Thomas Jefferson's important work. How do you think his work helped American freedom?

Voices from the Past

John Adams was a cousin of Sam Adams and another leader in America's fight for independence. Adams was a delegate from Massachusetts at both the First and Second Continental Congresses. He was away from home for long periods of time during the American Revolution. Abigail Adams, his wife and the mother of their five children, agreed that the colonies should be independent. John and Abigail wrote to each other while he was away from home. Their letters show their love for each other and their support for American independence.

Letter from Abigail Adams to John
19 August, 1774

"The great distance between us makes the time appear very long to me. It seems already a month since you left me. The great anxiety I feel for my country, for you, and for our family renders the day tedious and the night unpleasant.... I want much to hear from you.... The little flock remember Papa, and kindly wish to see him; so does your most affectionate. Abigail Adams"

Letter from John Adams to Abigail
7 October 1774

"I wish I could write to you a dozen letters every day. But the business before me...takes up my time so entirely....

There is a great spirit in the Congress. But our people must be peaceable.... Let them furnish themselves with artillery, arms, and ammunition.... But let them avoid war if possible...."

Letter from John Adams to Abigail
17 June, 1775

"I can now inform you that the Congress have made choice of the modest and virtuous, the amiable, generous, and brave George Washington, Esquire, to be General of the American Army.... I hope the people...will treat the General with all...that politeness and respect, which is due to one of the most important characters in the world...."

Letter from John Adams to Abigail
7 July, 1775

"Your description of the distresses of the worthy inhabitants of Boston and other seaport towns is enough to melt a heart of stone....

It gives me more pleasure than I can express, to learn that you sustain the shocks and terrors of the times. You are really brave, my dear. You are a heroine.... I am forever yours."

Letter from Abigail Adams to John
9 March, 1776

"You ask what is thought of 'Common Sense.' There is a great deal of good sense delivered in clear, simple, concise, and nervous style."

Letter from John Adams to Abigail
29 March, 1776

"...I am waiting with great impatience for letters from you.... We are taking precautions to defend every place that is in danger, the Carolinas, Virginia, New York, Canada. I can think of nothing but fortifying Boston harbor. I want more cannon than are to be had...."

Letter from Abigail Adams to John
31 March, 1776

"I wish you would ever write me a letter half as long as I write you... I long to hear that you have declared an independency. And, by the way, in the new code of laws which I suppose it will be necessary for you to make, I desire you would remember the ladies and be more generous and favorable to them than your ancestors. Do not put such unlimited power into the hands of the husbands. Remember, all men would be tyrants if they could. If particular care and attention is not paid to the ladies, we are determined to foment a rebellion, and will not hold ourselves bound by any laws in which we have no voice or representation."

Letter from John Adams to Abigail
3 July, 1776

July, 1776, will be the most memorable...in the history of America. I...believe that it will be celebrated by succeeding generations as the great anniversary festival."

Write Your Answers

Write the answer to each question in the assignment section of your notebook.

1. In 1774 what did John say the people must do?

2. What did John Adams think of George Washington?

3. What did Abigail think of Thomas Paine's "Common Sense"?

4. What did Abigail tell John to put into the new code of laws?

5. How did John think that July 1776 would be remembered?

REVIEW AND APPLY

- The Second Continental Congress first met in May 1775. It created a Continental Army and made George Washington commander in chief of the Continental Army.

- When the Declaration of Independence was approved on July 4, 1776, Americans announced their independence from Great Britain.

- The Battle of Saratoga was considered the turning point of the American Revolution because after this American victory, France began to help the Continental Army.

- The Americans won the American Revolution after the British were defeated at the Battle of Yorktown on October 19, 1783.

VOCABULARY

Defining and Using Vocabulary ■ Use the glossary to find the meaning of each word or phrase listed below. Write each word's definition in your social studies notebook. Then use each word in a sentence.

blockade	neutral	traitor
commander in chief	pamphlet	turning point
delegate	retreat	

COMPREHENSION CHECK

Biography Cards ■ In your social studies notebook, copy and complete the index cards by explaining how each person helped the United States win independence.

Name _Thomas Jefferson_

How he helped:

Name _Haym Salomon_

How he helped:

Name _Thomas Paine_

How he helped:

Name _George Washington_

How he helped:

Name _Marquis de Lafayette_	Name _James Armistead_
How he helped:	How he helped:

CRITICAL THINKING

Making Predictions ■ Making predictions means using information that we know in order to think about what probably will happen next.

Example   **Fact:**   **Prediction:**
It rained hard for ten days.   There will be a flood.

Read the paragraph below about the end of the American revolution. Next, read the four sentences below the paragraph. In your social studies notebook write the two sentences that predict what will happen after the war.

The American Army was defeated in many battles during the American Revolution, but George Washington continued to lead the fight for independence. After 7 long years of war, the American army defeated the British at Yorktown. The 13 colonies became one free and independent nation.

1. The United States will develop a plan for a new government.

2. Most Americans will want to stay part of Great Britain.

3. The new nation will give some land back to Great Britain.

4. Americans will choose a leader for their nation.

USING INFORMATION

Writing an Essay ■ There were many battles fought during the American Revolution. Select the battle that you think was the most important to the American victory. Explain why you feel the battle was so important. Start your essay with a topic sentence. End your essay with a sentence that summarizes the main idea. Write your essay in your social studies notebook.

SOCIAL STUDIES SKILLS

Interpreting a Line Graph

A line graph uses lines to show how something has changed over a period of time. The line graph below shows how the population in the American colonies changed from 1680 to 1780. A line graph can also show a trend during a period of time. The graph below shows that the trend was for the American population to increase.

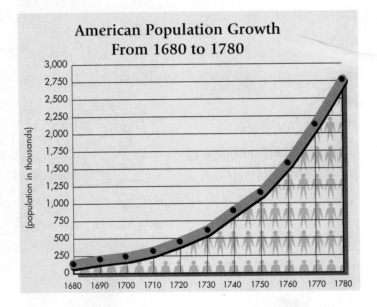

Study the graph. Then write the answers to the following questions in the assignment section of your social studies notebook.

1. In what year did the colonies have the smallest population?

2. Which 40-year period showed the slowest growth?

3. Which 30-year period showed the greatest growth?

4. When was the population less than 250,000?

5. When was the population between 500,000 and 1 million?

6. When did the population become more than 1 million?

7. When did the population become more than 2 million?

8. What effect did the American Revolution have on population in the colonies?

9. Do you think the population continued to grow after 1780? Why?

DECLARATION of INDEPENDENCE

When in the course of human events, it becomes necessary for one people to dissolve the political bands which have connected them with another, and to assume among the powers of the earth the separate and equal station to which the laws of nature and of nature's God entitle them, a decent respect to the opinions of mankind requires that they should declare the causes which impel them to the separation.

Sometimes in history, one group of people must become independent from the nation that rules it. The people who are breaking ties must then explain their reasons to the world. That is the purpose of this Declaration of Independence.

We hold these truths to be self-evident: that all men are created equal, that they are endowed by their Creator with certain unalienable rights, that among these are life, liberty, and the pursuit of happiness.

We believe the following things are always true. All people are equal. God gave all people the natural rights of life, liberty, and working for happiness.

That to secure these rights, governments are instituted among men, deriving their just powers from the consent of the governed; that whenever any form of government becomes destructive of these ends, it is the right of the people to alter or to abolish it, and to institute new government, laying its foundation on such principles and organizing its powers in such form as to them shall seem most likely to effect their safety and happiness. Prudence, indeed, will dictate that governments long established should not be changed for light and transient causes; and accordingly all experience hath shown, that mankind are more disposed to suffer while evils are sufferable, than to right themselves by abolishing the forms to which they are accustomed. But when a long train of abuses and usurpations, pursuing invariably the same object, evinces a design to reduce them under absolute despotism, it is their right, it is their duty, to throw off such government, and to provide new guards for their future security.

Governments are created by people to protect the people's rights. Governments get their power by the consent of the people they rule. People have the right to change or end a government that takes away their natural rights. The people must then start a new government that will protect natural rights. People should never revolt for only a few, unimportant reasons. However, when there is a long history of repeated abuses, then it is the right and the duty of the people to overthrow the ruling government and start a new government that will safeguard the rights of all people.

Such has been the patient sufferance of these colonies; and such is now the necessity which constrains them to alter their former systems of government. The history of the present king of Great Britain is a history of repeated injuries and usurpations, all having in direct object the establishment of an absolute tyranny over these states. To prove this, let facts be submitted to a candid world.

For a long time, the colonies have suffered abuses from the king's government, and so we must

change our government. King George, through
many unfair actions, has shown that his goals are
to take away our rights and to have complete
control over the colonies. We want the world to
know the following facts about the king's abuses:

He has refused his assent to laws, the most
wholesome and necessary for the public good.

The king has refused to approve laws necessary
for the good of the colonies.

He has forbidden his governors to pass laws
of immediate and pressing importance, unless
suspended in their operation till his assent
should be obtained, and when so suspended,
he has utterly neglected to attend to them.

He has not allowed laws to be passed without
his approval. And he has taken a long time to
approve those he allows.

He has refused to pass other laws for the
accommodation of large districts of people,
unless those people would relinquish the
right of representation in the legislature, a
right inestimable to them and formidable to
tyrants only.

He has not allowed all people to have equal
representation in the legislatures.

He has called together legislative bodies
at places unusual, uncomfortable, and distant
from the depository of their public records,
for the sole purpose of fatiguing them into
compliance with his measures.

He has forced representatives to meet in
strange, uncomfortable, and far-off places
in order to make them so tired that they
would obey his orders.

He has dissolved Representative Houses
repeatedly, for opposing with manly firmness
his invasions on the rights of the people.

He has shut down colonial legislatures many
times when they criticized the king's abuses of
the people.

He has refused for a long time, after such
dissolutions, to cause others to be elected;
whereby the legislative powers, incapable of
annihilation, have returned to the people at
large for their exercise; the state remaining, in
the mean time, exposed to all the dangers of
invasion from without, and convulsions within.

After shutting down legislatures, he has taken a
long time before holding new elections. The people
were in danger because their colonial governments
could not make laws to protect them.

He has endeavored to prevent the population
of these states; for that purpose obstructing the
laws of naturalization of foreigners, refusing to
pass others to encourage their migration hither,
and raising the conditions of new appropriations
of lands.

King George has tried to stop the colonial
population from growing by making it difficult for
Europeans to come to the colonies. He has made
it difficult to buy land in America.

He has obstructed the administration of
justice, by refusing his assent to laws for
establishing judiciary powers.

He stopped us from carrying out justice by
refusing to let us set up courts.

He has made judges dependent on his will
alone, for the tenure of their offices, and the
amount and payment of their salaries.

Judges depend on the king for their salaries and their jobs, so they make unfair decisions to keep their jobs.

He has erected a multitude of new offices, and sent hither swarms of officers to harass our people, and eat out their substance.

The king sent large numbers of government people to bother us and use up our resources.

He has kept among us, in times of peace, standing armies without the consent of our legislatures.

Even in peaceful times, the king has kept his armies in the colonies without the consent of our legislatures.

He has affected to render the military independent of and superior to the civil power.

He has tried to make the military free from, and more powerful than, our government.

He has combined with others to subject us to a jurisdiction foreign to our constitution, and unacknowledged by our laws; giving his assent to their acts of pretended legislation:

King George has worked with Parliament to give us these unfair laws that we did not help write:

For quartering large bodies of armed troops among us;

They forced us to allow British soldiers to stay in our homes.

For protecting them, by a mock trial, from punishment for any murders which they should commit on the inhabitants of these states;

They protected soldiers who murdered our people by giving them fake trials.

For cutting off our trade with all parts of the world;

They stopped us from trading with other nations.

For imposing taxes on us without our consent;

They made unfair tax laws for us.

For depriving us, in many cases, of the benefits of trial by jury;

They often took away our right to have fair jury trials.

For transporting us beyond seas to be tried for pretended offenses;

They forced some of our people to go to Great Britain for trials for crimes they never committed.

For abolishing the free system of English laws in a neighboring province, establishing therein an arbitrary government, and enlarging its boundaries so as to render it at once an example and fit instrument for introducing the same absolute rule into these colonies;

They took away Quebec's fair government and gave Quebec an unfair government. They can use Quebec as an example of how to bring absolute government to the colonies.

For taking away our charters, abolishing our most valuable laws, and altering fundamentally the forms of our governments;

They took away our charters, they changed our most important laws, and they changed the kind of government we have.

For suspending our own legislatures, and declaring themselves invested with power to legislate for us in all cases whatsoever.

They have stopped us from meeting in our legislatures. They say they have the power to make all laws for us.

He has abdicated government here, by declaring us out of his protection and waging war against us.

King George has given up his power to rule us since he says he cannot protect us and is now fighting a war against us.

He has plundered our seas, ravaged our coasts, burnt our towns, and destroyed the lives of our people.

The king has attacked our ships, destroyed our ports, burned our towns, and destroyed our lives.

He is at this time transporting large armies of foreign mercenaries to complete the works of death, desolation, and tyranny, already begun with circumstances of cruelty and perfidy scarcely paralleled in the most barbarous ages, and totally unworthy the head of a civilized nation.

He is bringing foreign armies to kill us and destroy the colonies. These soldiers show cruelty that should not be allowed by a modern king.

He has constrained our fellow citizens taken captive on the high seas to bear arms against their country, to become the executioners of their friends and brethren, or to fall themselves by their hands.

He has taken Americans off our ships at sea and has forced them to fight against their own people.

He has excited domestic insurrections amongst us, and has endeavored to bring on the inhabitants of our frontiers, the merciless Indian savages, whose known rule of warfare, is an undistinguished destruction of all ages, sexes and conditions.

He has told our slaves and servants to fight against us, and he has encouraged the Indians to attack us.

In every stage of these oppressions we have petitioned for redress in the most humble terms; our repeated petitions have been answered only by repeated injury. A prince whose character is thus marked by every act which may define a tyrant is unfit to be the ruler of a free people.

We have asked the king to end the unfair treatment of the colonies many times, but each time new abuses were added. A king who acts so unfairly is unfit to rule a free people.

Nor have we been wanting in attentions to our British brethren. We have warned them from time to time of attempts by their legislature to extend an unwarrantable jurisdiction over us. We have reminded them of the circumstances of our emigration and settlement here. We have appealed to their native justice and magnanimity, and we have conjured them by the ties of our common kindred to disavow these usurpations, which would inevitably interrupt our connections and correspondence. They too have been deaf to the voice of justice and of consanguinity. We must, therefore, acquiesce in the necessity which denounces our separation, and hold them, as we hold the rest of mankind, enemies in war, in peace friends.

We have hoped the British people would help us end the abuses, so we sent many messages to them. We have told them how Parliament has mistreated us. The British people have not listened to our messages. Therefore, we must declare that we are a separate nation. We will treat Great Britain as we treat all other nations.

We, therefore, the representatives of the United States of America, in General Congress assembled, appealing to the Supreme Judge of the world for the rectitude of our intentions, do, in the name, and by authority of the good people of these colonies, solemnly publish and declare, that these united colonies are, and of right ought to be, free and independent states; that they are absolved from all allegiance to the British crown, and that all political connection between them and the state of Great Britain is, and ought to be, totally dissolved; and that as free and independent states, they have full power to levy war, conclude peace, contract alliances, establish commerce, and to do all other acts and things which independent states may of right do.

As representatives of the people of the United States, we declare that these united colonies are one independent nation. We have completely cut ties to Great Britain. As an independent nation, we have the right to wage war, make peace treaties, have trade with all nations, and do all the things a nation does.

And for the support of this declaration, with a firm reliance on the protection of Divine Providence, we mutually pledge to each other our lives, our fortunes and our sacred honor.

We now trust that God will protect us. We promise to support this Declaration with our lives, our money, and our honor.

John Hancock
(President,
Massachusetts)

Georgia
Button Gwinnett
Lyman Hall
George Walton

North Carolina
William Hooper
Joseph Hewes
John Penn

South Carolina
Edward Rutledge
Thomas Heyward, Jr.
Thomas Lynch, Jr.
Arthur Middleton

Maryland
Samuel Chase
William Paca
Thomas Stone
Charles Carroll of
Carrollton

Virginia
George Wythe
Richard Henry Lee
Thomas Jefferson
Benjamin Harrison
Thomas Nelson, Jr.
Francis Lightfoot Lee
Carter Braxton

Pennsylvania
Robert Morris
Benjamin Rush
Benjamin Franklin
John Morton
George Clymer
James Smith
George Taylor
James Wilson
George Ross

Delaware
Caesar Rodney
George Read
Thomas McKean

New York
William Floyd
Philip Livingston
Francis Lewis
Lewis Morris

New Jersey
Richard Stockton
John Witherspoon
Francis Hopkinson
John Hart
Abraham Clark

New Hampshire
Josiah Bartlett
William Whipple
Matthew Thornton

Massachusetts
John Adams
Samuel Adams
Robert Treat Paine
Elbridge Gerry

Rhode Island
Stephen Hopkins
William Ellery

Connecticut
Roger Sherman
Samuel Huntington
William Williams
Oliver Wolcott

Chapter 9

THE NATION'S NEW CONSTITUTION

◀ Miss Liberty, symbol of the new nation

People

Daniel Shays • James Madison • Montesquieu • Federalists • Antifederalists • John Jay • Alexander Hamilton

New Vocabulary

central government • ratified • compromises • senators • principles • federalism • federal • separation of powers • legislative • executive • judicial • checks and balances • flexibility • amendments

Places

Northwest Territory • Athens

Focus on Main Ideas

1. What were some of the problems with the Articles of Confederation?
2. What compromises were used to write the Constitution?
3. What six principles were included in the Constitution?

In 1787 American leaders planned a new kind of government for their new nation. As you read this chapter, think about how our leaders created a government that protects the rights of its people.

Problems Under the Articles of Confederation

During the American Revolution, the delegates at the Second Continental Congress planned a **central government** for the United States. The laws for this government were called the Articles of Confederation. All 13 states **ratified,** or

voted for, the Articles of Confederation in 1781. Under the new laws, the nation was ruled by Congress. Each state had one vote in Congress. To pass a new law, at least nine states had to vote for it.

The Articles of Confederation helped the nation in a few ways. Under the Articles of Confederation, the United States and Great Britain signed the Treaty of Paris. The new government also passed an important law called the Northwest Ordinance of 1787. This law helped the new nation govern the Northwest Territory, the land between the Ohio and Mississippi rivers and the Great Lakes.

Under the Northwest Ordinance, the Northwest Territory was divided into smaller territories. When each territory had 60,000 people, it could write a constitution. Then it could ask Congress to allow it to become a state.

The Articles of Confederation created a very weak government. The delegates who created it feared that a strong government would take away the rights of the people. The government did not have a president to lead the nation. It also did not have courts to settle problems between states.

The central government was so weak under the Articles of Confederation that the new nation had many problems. Congress could not collect taxes, so the central government had little money. Each state was allowed to print its own money, and money from one state could not be used in another state. Congress could not raise an army, so there was no way to protect the nation.

Shays's Rebellion in 1786 proved that the nation needed a much stronger central government. Many farms and businesses were not able to earn much money after the war. Poor farmers like Daniel Shays of Massachusetts could not pay their state taxes. The courts began taking away their farms. Daniel Shays gathered about one thousand angry farmers and attacked several courthouses. Then he tried to take over buildings where weapons were stored. There was no army to stop Daniel Shays. Finally a group of businesspeople hired their own soldiers to end the fighting. This event showed that the nation needed a strong central government with the power to have an army.

The Constitutional Convention

In May 1787, 55 delegates met in Philadelphia to correct the problems in the Articles of Confederation. They quickly realized that there were too many problems to correct. They decided to write a new plan of government. They wrote the United States Constitution, the laws that govern our nation today.

The meetings that were held to write the Constitution were called the Constitutional Convention. All delegates agreed that

Shays's Rebellion proved that the nation needed a stronger government. Daniel Shays had been a captain in the army during the American Revolution.

97

George Washington should be president of the Convention. At the age of 81, Benjamin Franklin was the oldest delegate. James Madison of Virginia came to the Convention with more ideas for planning the new government than any other person.

The delegates wanted secrecy during their meetings so they could speak and argue freely. Since they did not want anyone outside the Convention to learn what was said, they kept all doors and windows closed each day. Delegates were not allowed to speak to newspaper reporters.

All of the delegates agreed that the United States should have a representative government. To plan the Constitution, the delegates used ideas that they had learned about earlier governments. The delegates wanted the United States government to be a democracy. They had learned about democracy by studying the government of ancient Athens. All citizens in ancient

Athens could vote and help write new laws. The delegates knew that representative government had first started in England with the Magna Carta and had grown stronger as Parliament gained more power. Finally, the delegates had learned Jewish and Christian values about kindness, fairness, and responsibility by studying the Bible.

Compromises of the Constitution

The delegates to the convention agreed that the new government should have a Congress to make laws. Each state would send representatives to the Congress. But the delegates could not agree on how many representatives each state should have. States with large populations, like Virginia, wanted more representatives than the smaller states. The smaller states wanted every state to have the same number of representatives.

The problem was solved because the delegates agreed to the first of several **compromises**. The Great Compromise created a Congress with two parts. One part, the Senate, would have two **senators** from each state. All states would have equal representation in the Senate. The other part, the House of Representatives, would have more representatives from states with larger populations. States with smaller populations would have fewer representatives.

The delegates also made two compromises about slavery. One compromise allowed the slave trade to continue until 1808. After that year Congress could pass laws to end the slave trade. The other compromise, known as the Three-fifths Compromise, solved the problem about how to count slaves for taxes and for representation in Congress.

During the meeting of the Constitutional Convention, George Washington used this chair and this pen and ink set.

Delegates from northern states, which did not have a lot of slaves, said that slaves should not be counted for representation since they could not vote. Southern delegates wanted to count slaves because there were many slaves in the South. If slaves were counted, the southern states would have more representatives in Congress. The delegates compromised by allowing three fifths of the number of slaves to be counted as part of each state's population.

Principles of the Constitution

The Constitution begins with a paragraph called the Preamble. This paragraph states the goals of the Constitution. These goals focus on the weaknesses of the Articles of Confederation. Justice, peace, safety, and freedom are the goals of the nation's government. Then the Constitution explains how the government works. The full text of the Constitution, with explanations, follows this chapter on pages 108–135 in your textbook.

The delegates included six important principles, or ideas, in the Constitution. They used these six principles to create a government that would be a democracy and a representative government. These principles would protect the rights of the people.

The first principle is that the government gets its power from the people. The first words of the Constitution, "We the people of the United States…," show that it is the American people who decide what the government will do.

The second principle is **federalism**. This means power is shared between the state governments and the **federal**, or central, government. This is shown in the diagram below. For example, both can collect taxes. While power is shared, each government also has certain powers that the other does not. The federal government can print money, but only the state governments can pass education laws.

If power is shared, what happens when federal and state laws disagree? The delegates decided that the Constitution is the nation's highest law. So all federal and state laws must obey the Constitution. Likewise, all federal laws must be obeyed over state laws.

Third, the delegates believed in limited government. This means that the federal government only has the powers that are written in the Constitution.

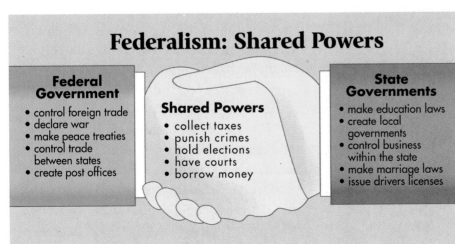

Federalism: Shared Powers

Federal Government
- control foreign trade
- declare war
- make peace treaties
- control trade between states
- create post offices

Shared Powers
- collect taxes
- punish crimes
- hold elections
- have courts
- borrow money

State Governments
- make education laws
- create local governments
- control business within the state
- make marriage laws
- issue drivers licenses

The fourth principle is the **separation of powers**. This means the powers of the government are divided among three branches of government. Dividing power prevents one part of the government from becoming too powerful. Montesquieu, a well-known French thinker during the Enlightenment, developed the idea of the three branches of government. The **legislative** branch is led by Congress, which makes laws. The **executive** branch carries out the laws passed by Congress. The executive branch is led by the President and the Vice President. The **judicial** branch of the government includes the federal court system. The Supreme Court is the nation's highest court.

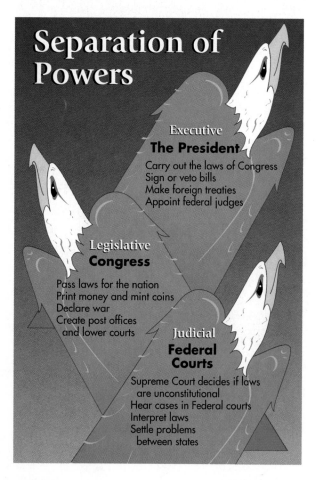

Separation of Powers

Executive
The President
Carry out the laws of Congress
Sign or veto bills
Make foreign treaties
Appoint federal judges

Legislative
Congress
Pass laws for the nation
Print money and mint coins
Declare war
Create post offices
   and lower courts

Judicial
Federal Courts
Supreme Court decides if laws
   are unconstitutional
Hear cases in Federal courts
Interpret laws
Settle problems
   between states

The fifth principle uses **checks and balances** to stop one branch of the government from gaining too much power over the other branches. For example, the President has the power to choose judges for federal courts, but the Senate must vote to approve each of these judges.

The sixth principle is **flexibility**. The Constitution must meet the needs of a changing nation. The Elastic Clause of the Constitution allows Congress to pass new laws to carry out its powers. The Constitution also allows new laws called **amendments** to be added to the original Constitution. An amendment can be added if two thirds of the members in both houses of Congress vote for it. Then three fourths of the state governments must vote for it. Twenty-seven amendments have been added to the Constitution.

Ratifying the Constitution

The delegates at the Constitutional Convention worked hard throughout the long, hot summer of 1787. By September they had finished this difficult job. On September 17, 1787, most delegates voted to accept the Constitution. Nine of the thirteen states had to ratify the Constitution in order for it to become the law of the land.

Not all of the delegates were happy with the Constitution. Many delegates feared the federal government would become too strong and would take away the rights of the people. These delegates believed that the new Constitution needed a Bill of Rights similar to the English Bill of Rights. The delegates decided that a Bill of Rights would soon be added to the Constitution.

Before long there were arguments about the Constitution between two groups of people, the Federalists and the Antifederalists. The Federalists supported the Constitution. James Madison, John Jay, and Alexander Hamilton became the most famous Federalists. George Washington and Benjamin Franklin also supported the Constitution. Many Federalists were traders, business owners, or planters. These wealthy people believed a strong central government would protect the nation and its businesses.

The Antifederalists were led by Patrick Henry and Sam Adams. They believed that a strong central government would destroy the rights of the people. They felt state governments needed more power. They were afraid that the President of the United States would act like the king they hated, George III.

By June 1788 nine states had ratified the Constitution. But the Federalists wanted the largest states, New York and Virginia, to ratify it, too. So James Madison and George Washington convinced Virginians to vote for it. In New York, Alexander Hamilton, John Jay, and James Madison wrote many

Some of the new nation's best leaders, including Benjamin Franklin, were at the Constitutional Convention. George Washington was president of the convention. Among the 55 delegates were 8 who had signed the Declaration of Independence and 7 who had been state governors.

The First Amendment in the Bill of Rights protects the rights to free speech and to gather in groups. It is the First Amendment that allows people to tell each other and the government their opinion about issues that are important to them. Without this freedom there would be no democracy.

newspaper articles called the "Federalist Papers." These articles explained how the new Constitution would help the nation. Finally New York became the eleventh state to ratify the Constitution.

The Bill of Rights

The Bill of Rights is laws that protect important rights for every American. These laws, the first ten amendments to the Constitution, were ratified in 1791.

The First Amendment of the Bill of Rights says that the government cannot take away your rights to religious freedom, freedom of speech, or freedom of the press. It says people have the right to gather in groups. The First Amendment says there must be a separation of church and state. This means the government cannot pass laws about religion. Tax money cannot be used to help churches or religious schools. You do not have to belong to a church in order to have the right to vote.

Another amendment says that accused people have the right to a fair, speedy trial. Still another amendment says your property cannot be searched without permission from a judge.

Since 1791 the Constitution and the Bill of Rights have been the laws of the United States. For more than 200 years, those laws have allowed our nation to be a democracy where the rights of all people are respected.

BIOGRAPHY

James Madison 1751–1836

James Madison was called the "Great Little Madison" by his friends. Perhaps it was because he weighed less than one hundred pounds and was very short. But it was probably because this man did more to create the Constitution than any other American.

Madison came from Virginia and had written a constitution for that state. When Madison saw the problems that the United States had under the Articles of Confederation, he began to study other types of governments. He believed a strong central government was needed to prevent problems like Shays's Rebellion.

In 1787 Madison became a delegate to the Constitutional Convention. Before going to the Convention, he had written his own plan for a constitution. His plan was known as the Virginia Plan. It included checks and balances, separation of powers, and sharing power between state and federal governments. Most of Madison's ideas became part of the Constitution. To convince delegates to sign the Constitution, Madison made more than one hundred speeches. To get states to ratify the constitution, he wrote the "Federalist Papers" with Alexander Hamilton and John Jay. The "Federalist Papers" were put into a book. It is one of the most important books ever written about government.

After the nation's Constitution was ratified in 1788, Madison wrote the Bill of Rights. His work became the first ten amendments to the Constitution.

Madison kept a journal in which he wrote down everything that was said each day at the Constitutional Convention. Since all meetings were held in secrecy, it is from Madison's journal that we know what happened there.

Madison went on to become the fourth President of the United States. But he is best known as the "Father of the Constitution" because of all he did to create good laws for the United States.

In Your Own Words

Write a paragraph in the journal section of your social studies notebook that explains why James Madison deserves to be called the "Father of the Constitution."

REVIEW AND APPLY

- The Articles of Confederation were the first set of laws for the United States.

- The Northwest Ordinance of 1787 divided the Northwest Territory into five territories. These territories became five new states in the United States.

- In May 1787, 55 delegates met in Philadelphia and wrote a new Constitution.

- Antifederalists and federalists argued over the Constitution, which was ratified in 1788.

- Six principles of the Constitution are popular sovereignty, federalism, limited government, separation of powers, checks and balances, and flexibility.

- The first ten amendments of the Constitution are called the Bill of Rights. They protect the individual rights and freedoms of Americans.

VOCABULARY

Finish the Sentence ■ In your social studies notebook, write the correct word or phrase from the box that best completes each sentence. You will not use all the words in the box.

1. New laws that are added to the Constitution are called _____ .

2. A _____ is an important basic belief.

3. Sharing power between the state governments and the national government is called _____ .

4. Being able to change in order to meet new conditions is called _____ .

5. The _____ branch of government is based in Washington, D.C.

6. To _____ is to approve.

7. The principle that allows the branches of government to limit each other's powers is called _____ .

> principle
> judicial
> federal
> senator
> checks and balances
> amendments
> flexibility
> federalism
> ratify
> compromise

USING INFORMATION

Journal Writing ■ Write a paragraph in your journal that explains why you would have voted for or against the Constitution.

COMPREHENSION CHECK

Reviewing Important Facts ■ Match the sentence in Group A with the word or phrase from Group B that the sentence explains. In your social studies notebook, write the letter of the correct word or phrase. You will not use all the words in Group B.

Group A

1. The Second Continental Congress created this plan for governing the country.

2. This law helped the United States govern the land between the Ohio and Mississippi rivers and the Great Lakes.

3. This plan gave each state two members in the Senate and representation in the House of Representatives based on each state's population.

4. This is the highest law in the United States.

5. The President leads this branch of government.

6. This branch of government passes bills.

Group B

A. Constitution

B. Great Compromise

C. Articles of Confederation

D. executive branch

E. Northwest Ordinance

F. Three-fifths Compromise

G. legislative branch

CRITICAL THINKING

Categories ■ Read the words in each group. Choose one of the phrases from the box as a title for the group. Write the title in your social studies notebook.

| Weaknesses of the Articles of Confederation | Goals of the Constitution |
| Parts of the Constitution | Principles of the Constitution |

1. no President to lead the nation
   Congress could not raise an army
   Congress could not collect taxes

2. peace
   freedom
   justice and safety

3. Preamble
   articles
   amendments

4. federalism
   flexibility
   checks and balances

Unit 2 Review

Study the time line on this page. You may want to read parts of Unit 2 again. In the assignment section of your notebook, write the numbers 1 through 14. Then use the words and dates in the box to finish the paragraphs. The box has one possible answer that you will not use.

1765
The British pass the Stamp Act.

1775
The American Revolution begins.

1777
Americans win the Battle of Saratoga.

1787
The Constitution is written.

1791
The Bill of Rights is ratified.

1750

1651
The British pass first Navigation Act.

1754
The French and Indian War begins.

1776
The Declaration of Independence is signed.

1781
The British surrender at Yorktown.

1788
The Constitution is ratified.

1754	Navigation Acts	Saratoga
Harvard College	branches	Great Compromise
triangular	American Revolution	July 4, 1776
Great Britain	Treaty of Paris	Stamp Act
Yorktown	Philadelphia	Bill of Rights

Starting in 1651, the British passed ___1___ to control trade with the American colonies. The colonies developed ___2___ trade routes in order to trade with many nations. Starting in ___3___ , Great Britain and France fought to win control of the Ohio Valley. After France lost the French and Indian War, ___4___ ruled all of Canada, the Ohio Valley, and the colonies along the Atlantic Ocean. To raise money to help

pay for the war, Parliament passed new tax laws. One of the new laws passed was the
____5____ , a tax law that required colonists to buy stamps for newspapers, letters, and printed
papers. American colonists were angry about the new tax laws.

The ____6____ began in April 1775 with battles at Lexington and Concord. On ____7____ ,
Americans used the Declaration of Independence to tell the world the colonies were an
independent nation. The turning point of the war was the American victory at the Battle
of ____8____ . Finally, in 1781 the British surrendered to George Washington at ____9____ ,
Virginia. The British and the Americans agreed to peace when they signed the ____10____
in 1783.

Delegates met in ____11____ to write the Constitution. To prevent the federal government
from becoming too powerful, they divided power between three ____12____ of government.
The ____13____ solved the problem of representation in Congress. A ____14____ was added to
the Constitution in 1791. The Constitution has governed the United States for more
than 200 years.

Looking Ahead to Unit 3

After the year 1800, the United States grew larger and stronger. The young nation doubled in size with the Louisiana Purchase in 1803. Then in 1812 the United States fought a second war against Great Britain.

During the 1800s slavery became a bigger problem between the North and the South.

The Missouri Compromise of 1820 prevented a war between North and South. During the 1800s many people wanted to improve American education, end slavery, and win more rights for women. As you read Unit 3, learn how the 1800s brought growth, change, and problems to the United States.

THE CONSTITUTION
of the United States of America

PREAMBLE

We, the People of the United States, in order to form a more perfect Union, establish justice, insure domestic tranquility, provide for the common defense, promote the general welfare, and secure the blessings of liberty to ourselves and our posterity, do ordain and establish this Constitution for the United States of America.

The preamble is an introduction that states the goals of the Constitution.

We, the people of the United States, want to create a better nation, create a justice system, encourage peace within the nation, defend the nation from enemies, promote the well-being of the people, and protect the freedom of the people now and in future times.

ARTICLE I. THE LEGISLATIVE BRANCH

Section 1. The Congress

All legislative powers herein granted shall be vested in a Congress of the United States, which shall consist of a Senate and House of Representatives.

The power to make laws shall be given to Congress. Congress will have a Senate and a House of Representatives.

Section 2. The House of Representatives

The House of Representatives shall be composed of members chosen every second year by the people of the several states, and the electors in each state shall have the qualifications requisite for electors of the most numerous branch of the state legislature.

Members of the House of Representatives shall be elected by voters every two years. Each state decides its own voting requirements, but states must allow all people who vote for members of their state legislatures to vote for members of the House of Representatives.

According to the Fifteenth and Nineteenth Amendments, states cannot take away the right to vote because of race or sex.

No person shall be a Representative who shall not have attained the age of 25 years, and been seven years a citizen of the United States, and who shall not, when elected, be an inhabitant of that state in which he shall be chosen.

To be a member of the House of Representatives, a person must be at least 25 years old, have been an American citizen for at least seven years, and live in the state he or she represents.

Representatives and direct taxes shall be apportioned among the several states which may be included within this Union, according to their respective numbers, which shall be determined by adding to the whole number of free persons, including those bound to service for a term of years, and excluding Indians not taxed, three fifths of all other persons. The actual enumeration shall be made within three years after the first meeting of the Congress of the United States, and within every subsequent term of ten years, in such manner as they shall by law direct. The number of Representatives shall not exceed one for every 30,000, but each state shall have at least one Representative; and until such enumeration shall be made, the state of New Hampshire shall be entitled to choose three, Massachusetts eight, Rhode Island and Providence Plantations one, Connecticut five, New York six, New Jersey four, Pennsylvania eight, Delaware one, Maryland six, Virginia ten, North Carolina five, South Carolina five, and Georgia three.

Representation for each state is based on its population. Every state must have at least one representative. The population of each state must be counted in a census every ten years. The number of representatives from a state can change as the population changes.

The lines in the original Constitution are crossed out because they no longer apply. These lines explain how slaves were to be counted as a result of the Three-Fifths Compromise. The law was overturned by section 2 of the Fourteenth Amendment.

When vacancies happen in the representation from any state, the executive authority thereof shall issue writs of election to fill such vacancies.

When a seat becomes vacant in the House, it must be filled. The state governor must call a special election to fill the seat.

The House of Representatives shall choose their Speaker and other officers; and shall have the sole power of impeachment.

The members of the House must elect a Speaker and other officers. Only the House of Representatives has the power to impeach a member of the federal government.

Section 3. The Senate

The Senate of the United States shall be composed of two Senators from each state, chosen by the legislature thereof, for six years; and each Senator shall have one vote.

Each state shall send two senators. Senators serve a six-year term. These senators shall be chosen by the state legislatures.

As part of the Great Compromise, the Framers agreed that all states would have equal representation in the Senate, but representation in the House would be based on population. Since the Seventeenth Amendment was added to the Constitution in 1913, all senators are elected by the voters in every state.

Immediately after they shall be assembled in consequence of the first election, they shall be divided as equally as may be into three classes. The seats of the Senators of the first class shall be vacated at the expiration of the second year, of the second class at the expiration of the fourth year, and of the third class at the expiration of the sixth year, so that one third may be chosen every second year; and if vacancies happen by resignation, or otherwise, during the recess of the legislature of any state, the executive thereof may make temporary appointments until the next meeting of the legislature, which shall then fill such vacancies.

The senators were divided into three groups when they met for the first time in 1789. This was done so that one third of the senator seats would come up for election every two years, while the remaining two thirds of the senators would continue to serve.

The Senate, unlike the House, is a continuing body because only one third of its members are elected at a time.

No person shall be a Senator who shall not have attained the age of thirty years, and been nine years a citizen of the United States, and who shall not, when elected, be an inhabitant of that state for which he shall be chosen.

To be a United States senator, a person must be at least thirty years old, be a citizen for at least nine years, and live in the state he or she represents.

The Vice President of the United States shall be President of the Senate, but shall have no vote, unless they be equally divided.

The Vice President acts as president of the Senate. He or she can vote only to break a tie.

The Senate shall choose their other officers, and also a President *pro tempore*, in the absence of the Vice President, or when he shall exercise the office of President of the United States.

The senators shall elect officers to lead Senate meetings. One of these officers will be a President *pro tempore*, who will lead the Senate when the Vice President cannot attend meetings.

The Senate shall have the sole power to try all impeachments. When sitting for that purpose, they shall be on oath or affirmation. When the President of the United States is tried, the Chief Justice shall preside: and no person shall be convicted without the concurrence of two thirds of the members present.

After the members of the House have voted to impeach a government leader, the impeachment trial can be held only by the Senate. The Chief Justice of the Supreme Court must preside at a trial of the President. A two-thirds vote is needed to convict a leader.

Judgment in cases of impeachment shall not extend further than to removal from office, and disqualification to hold and enjoy any office of honor, trust, or profit, under the United States: but the party convicted shall nevertheless be liable and subject to indictment, trial, judgment, and punishment, according to law.

When a government leader is found guilty by the Senate, that leader is removed from office and is never allowed to hold another government office. This is the only way a person can be punished by the Senate. However, the guilty leader can be given a regular jury trial and receive punishment from a judge.

Since 1789, only seven people have been found guilty during Senate trials. They were removed from office but never put on trial before a regular court.

Section 4. Elections

The times, places, and manner of holding elections for Senators and Representatives, shall be prescribed in each state by the legislature thereof; but the Congress may at any time by law make or alter such regulations, except as to the places of choosing Senators.

State legislatures shall decide the places, times, and ways to hold elections for senators and representatives. Congress can make laws to change state decisions on the times and ways to hold elections. It cannot change state decisions on the places for holding elections.

All states hold elections for members of Congress on the first Tuesday after the first Monday in November of even-numbered years.

The Congress shall assemble at least once in every year, and such meeting shall be on the first Monday in December, unless they shall by law appoint a different day.

Congress must meet at least once a year.

Section 5. Meetings of Congress

Each House shall be the judge of the elections, returns, and qualifications of its own members, and a majority of each shall constitute a quorum to do business; but a smaller number may adjourn from day to day, and may be authorized to compel the attendance of absent members, in such manner, and under such penalties as each House may provide.

Each house decides whether its members meet the qualifications that were stated in Sections 2 and 3 and whether they were legally elected. A quorum, or majority, of members must be present for each house to do business. Each house can decide on punishment for members who miss meetings.

Meetings are often held without a quorum, but a quorum is always needed when voting on a bill.

Each House may determine the rules of its proceedings, punish its members for disorderly behavior, and, with the concurrence of two thirds, expel a member.

Each house makes its own rules for running meetings and deciding how members who disobey rules should be punished. A house can expel one of its members with a two-thirds vote.

Each house has different rules for debates. These rules allow the Senate to have long debates and filibusters, while the House limits debating time.

Each House shall keep a journal of its proceedings, and from time to time publish the same, excepting such parts as may in their judgment require secrecy; and the yeas and nays of the members of either House on any question, shall, at the desire of one fifth of those present, be entered on the journal.

Each house shall publish a journal that tells what happened at each session. Secret information that affects the nation's security may not be published. Voting records on bills are published when one fifth of the members present vote for publication.

Congress's journal, *The Congressional Record*, can be found in public libraries.

Neither House, during the session of Congress, shall, without the consent of the other, adjourn for more than three days, nor to any other place than that in which the two Houses shall be sitting.

Both houses must agree on when to end a session for more than three days. Each house must always meet in the same place.

Section 6. Salaries and Rules

The Senators and Representatives shall receive a compensation for their services, to be ascertained by law, and paid out of the Treasury of the United States. They shall in all cases, except treason, felony, and breach of the peace, be privileged from arrest during their attendance at the session of their respective Houses, and in going to and returning from the same; and for any speech or debate in either House, they shall not be questioned in any other place.

Members of Congress shall be paid salaries that are decided in laws passed by Congress. Salaries are paid from the nation's treasury. Members cannot be arrested while going to and from their work in Congress unless they commit serious crimes. They cannot be arrested for anything they say or write as part of their work during a session.

No Senator or Representative shall, during the time for which he was elected, be appointed to any civil office under the authority of the United States, which shall have been created, or the emoluments whereof shall have been increased during such time; and no person holding any office under the United States, shall be a member of either House during his continuance in office.

Members of Congress cannot be appointed to government jobs that were created or given a higher salary while they were in office. People cannot serve in Congress while they hold a government job. This clause helps to keep a separation of powers.

Section 7. Bills

All bills for raising revenue shall originate in the House of Representatives; but the Senate may propose or concur with amendments as on other bills.

All tax bills must start in the House of Representatives. After the bills are passed by the House, they are sent to the Senate. The Senate can approve or amend them.

Every bill which shall have passed the House of Representatives and the Senate, shall, before it become a law, be presented to the President of the United States; if he approve he shall sign it, but if not he shall return it, with his objections, to that House in which it shall have originated, who shall enter the objections at large on their journal, and proceed to reconsider it. If after such reconsideration two thirds of that House shall agree to pass the bill, it shall be sent, together with the objections, to the other House, by which it shall likewise be reconsidered, and if approved by two thirds of that House, it shall become a law. But in all such cases the votes of both Houses shall be determined by yeas and nays, and the names of the persons voting for and against the bill shall be entered on the journal of each House respectively. If any bill shall not be returned by the President within ten days (Sundays excepted) after it shall have been presented to him, the same shall be a law, in like manner as if he had signed it, unless the Congress by their adjournment prevent its return, in which case it shall not be a law.

Every bill that is passed by the House and Senate must then be read by the President. A bill becomes a law if the President signs it within ten days, not counting Sundays. If the President does not approve of the bill, he can veto it by returning the bill unsigned to the house that introduced it. Congress can override the President's veto if two thirds of the members of both houses vote for the bill. Congress's journal must show how the members voted. A bill also becomes a law if the President holds it for ten days, without counting Sundays, and does not sign it. If Congress adjourns and the President holds a bill without signing it for ten days, not counting Sundays, the bill cannot become a law. This last method of defeating a bill is called a pocket veto.

Every order, resolution, or vote, to which the concurrence of the Senate and House of Representatives may be necessary (except on a question of adjournment), shall be presented to the President of the United States; and before the same shall take effect, shall be approved by him, or being disapproved by him, shall be repassed by two thirds of the Senate and House of Representatives, according to the rules and limitations prescribed in the case of a bill.

Every order and joint resolution that is passed by both the Senate and the House needs the President's approval. The President must approve or veto resolutions just as he does bills.

Section 8. Powers of Congress
The Congress shall have power:

Congress shall have these powers:

To lay and collect taxes, duties, imposts, and excises, to pay the debts and provide for the common defense and general welfare of the United States; but all duties, imposts, and excises shall be uniform throughout the United States;

To collect different kinds of taxes in order to pay for the nation's government and defense; Federal taxes must be the same for every part of the nation.

To borrow money on the credit of the United States;

To borrow money;

112

The government borrows money by selling bonds. It must repay borrowed money.

To regulate commerce with foreign nations, and among the several states, and with the Indian tribes;

To control commerce with foreign nations, between the states of the nation, and with the Indian tribes;

Commerce means trade and business. This commerce clause allows Congress to pass all laws necessary for helping business between states. It also allows Congress to pass laws that control transportation between states.

To establish a uniform rule of naturalization, and uniform laws on the subject of bankruptcies throughout the United States;

To make laws on how people can become citizens; to pass laws about bankruptcy, or losing all of one's money, for the entire nation;

To coin money, regulate the value thereof, and of foreign coin, and fix the standard of weights and measures;

To print and coin money and decide how much that money is worth; to decide how much foreign money is worth in the United States; to set standards for weights and measures;

To provide for the punishment of counterfeiting the securities and current coin of the United States;

To make laws about punishing people who produce counterfeit money, stamps, and government bonds;

To establish post offices and post roads;

To set up post offices and create routes for delivering mail;

To promote the progress of science and useful arts, by securing for limited times to authors and inventors the exclusive right to their respective writings and discoveries;

To promote art and science in the nation by issuing copyrights and patents;

To constitute tribunals inferior to the Supreme Court;

To create a system of lower federal courts;
The Framers planned the highest court, the Supreme Court, but gave to Congress the job planning all lower courts.

To define and punish piracies and felonies committed on the high seas, and offenses against the law of nations;

To punish crimes committed on the seas and against other nations;

To declare war, grant letters of marque and reprisal, and make rules concerning captures on land and water;

To declare war and issue letters of marque and reprisal;
The President can send troops to fight in any part of the world, but only Congress can declare war. Letters of marque and reprisal were documents issued to allow private ships to attack enemy ships. Since the Civil War, the United States has obeyed an international law that does not allow the use of letters of marque and reprisal.

To raise and support armies; but no appropriation of money to that use shall be for a longer term than two years;

To create and pay for an army; Congress can provide enough money to support the army for two years at a time;

This clause keeps the army under civilian control and limits its power. Since the army depends on Congress for money, it cannot become so powerful that it will take control of the government.

To provide and maintain a navy;

To provide and take care of a navy;

To make rules for the government and regulation of the land and naval forces;

To make rules for controlling the army and navy; In 1950, Congress used this power to pass military laws called the Uniform Code of Military Justice. Since then, amendments have been added to that law.

To provide for calling forth the militia to execute the laws of the Union, suppress insurrections and repel invasions;

To call the militia, or National Guard, into action in order to carry out the nation's laws, put down riots and revolts, and fight against invading enemies;

To provide for organizing, arming, and disciplining the militia, and for governing such part of them as may be employed in the service of the United States, reserving to the states respectively, the appointment of the officers, and the authority of training the militia according to the discipline prescribed by Congress;

To make rules for organizing, controlling, and arming the state militia; states can appoint officers for the Guard, but all soldiers must be trained according to the laws of Congress; Since the National Defense Act was passed in 1916, federal money has been used to help pay for the National Guard. The President can call on the National Guard to help during an emergency or to fight during a war.

To exercise exclusive legislation, in all cases whatsoever, over such district (not exceeding ten miles square) as may, by cession of particular states, and the acceptance of Congress, become the seat of the government of the United States, and to exercise like authority over all places purchased by the consent of the legislature of the state in which the same shall be, for the erection of forts, magazines, arsenals, dockyards, and other needful buildings. And,

To make all laws for the District of Columbia, where the nation's capital is located; to make laws for land owned by the federal government; This land includes national parks, forests, and post offices.

To make all laws which shall be necessary and proper for carrying into execution the foregoing powers, and all other powers vested by this Constitution in the government of the United States, or in any department or officer thereof.

To make all necessary laws so Congress can carry out the powers listed in the Constitution. This clause is called the elastic clause because it allows Congress to write laws that are needed for a changing nation.

Section 9. Powers Not Given to Congress

The migration or importation of such persons as any of the states now existing shall think proper to admit, shall not be prohibited by the Congress prior to the year 1808; but a tax or duty may be imposed on such importation, not exceeding ten dollars for each person.

Congress could not make laws to stop the slave trade until the year 1808. This clause was one of the compromises made by the Framers. In 1808, Congress passed a law that stopped the nation from importing slaves from Africa.

The privilege of the writ of *habeas corpus* shall not be suspended, unless when in cases of rebellion or invasion the public safety may require it.

Congress cannot take away the right of *habeas corpus* except if there is a revolution or war.

The writ of habeas corpus is a legal order that says a police officer or sheriff must appear before a judge with a person who is being held in jail. The judge decides whether the accused person is being held legally, and if not, the person must be released. The writ of habeas corpus protects people from being kept in jail without a fair trial.

No bill of attainder or *ex post facto* law shall be passed.

Congress cannot pass a bill of attainder or an *ex post facto* law.

This clause protects a person from being punished without a trial and from being punished for something that was made illegal after he or she did it.

No capitation, or other direct tax, shall be laid, unless in proportion to the census or enumeration herein before directed to be taken.

Congress cannot collect a tax on each person unless the tax is based on state populations in the last census.

This clause was changed by the Sixteenth Amendment in 1913. That amendment allows Congress to collect a direct tax on people's income.

No tax or duty shall be laid on articles exported from any state.

Congress cannot tax goods that are exported from one state to another.

No preference shall be given by any regulation of commerce or revenue to the ports of one state over those of another: nor shall vessels bound to, or from, one state be obliged to enter, clear, or pay duties in another.

Congress cannot favor any state when making laws to control trade between states. Ships shall not be taxed when they go from one state to another.

No money shall be drawn from the treasury, but in consequence of appropriations made by law; and a regular statement and account of the receipts and expenditures of all public money shall be published from time to time.

Federal money can only be spent to pay for legislation passed by Congress. It must publish records that show how money is spent.

The power of Congress to spend money is very important. The President can plan programs and policies, but only Congress can provide the money to pay for them.

No title of nobility shall be granted by the United States; and no person holding any office of profit or trust under them, shall, without the consent of the Congress, accept of any present, emolument, office, or title, of any kind whatever, from any king, prince, or foreign state.

Congress is not allowed to give titles of nobility, such as prince, king, or duke, to any person. Members of the government cannot accept gifts or titles from foreign nations without permission from Congress.

This clause is based on the idea from the Declaration of Independence that all people are equal. The Framers did not want the nation to have a noble class of titled people who were more powerful and important than the rest of the population.

Section 10. Powers Not Given to the States

No state shall enter into any treaty, alliance, or confederation; grant letters of marque and reprisal; coin money; emit bills of credit; make any thing but gold and silver coin a tender in payment of debts; pass any bill of attainder, *ex post facto* law, or law impairing the obligation of contracts, or grant any title of nobility.

States shall not have the power to make treaties and alliances with foreign nations or to coin money. These powers belong to the federal government. Neither state nor federal governments have the power to pass bills of attainder and *ex post facto* laws or to grant titles of nobility.

No state shall, without the consent of the Congress, lay any imposts or duties on imports or exports, except what may be absolutely necessary for executing its inspection laws: and the net produce of all duties and imposts, laid by any state on imports or exports, shall be for the use of the Treasury of the United States; and all such laws shall be subject to the revision and control of the Congress.

States are not allowed to tax imported or exported goods without permission from Congress. They may charge a small fee for the inspection of goods that enter the state. If Congress does permit states to tax goods, the tax money must belong to the United States Treasury. These laws can be changed by Congress.

No state shall, without the consent of Congress, lay any duty of tonnage, keep troops, or ships of war in time of peace, enter into any agreement or compact with another state, or with a foreign power, or engage in war, unless actually invaded, or in such imminent danger as will not admit of delay.

States cannot tax goods on ships. They cannot have their own army and navy, but they can have soldiers in the National Guard. States cannot make treaties or declare war against other nations unless the state is invaded.

Our system of federalism gives all powers of foreign policy and national defense to the federal government.

ARTICLE II. THE EXECUTIVE BRANCH

Section 1. President and Vice President

The executive power shall be vested in a President of the United States of America. He shall hold his office during the term of four years, and, together with the Vice President, chosen for the same term, be elected, as follows:

The executive power is given to a President of the United States. The President and the Vice President shall serve four-year terms and be elected as follows:

Each state shall appoint, in such manner as the legislature thereof may direct, a number of electors equal to the whole number of Senators and Representatives to which the state may be entitled in the Congress: but no Senator or Representative, or person holding an office of trust or profit under the United States, shall be appointed an elector.

Each state shall choose a group of people called electors to elect the President. The number of electors from a state must equal the number of senators and representatives from that state. Members of Congress and other government officials cannot be electors.

~~The electors shall meet in their respective states, and vote by ballot for two persons, of whom one at least shall not be an inhabitant of the same state with themselves. And they shall make a list of all the persons voted for, and of the number of votes for each; which list they shall sign and certify, and transmit sealed to the seat of the government of the~~

United States, directed to the President of the Senate. The President of the Senate shall, in the presence of the Senate and House of Representatives, open all the certificates, and the votes shall then be counted. The person having the greatest number of votes shall be the President, if such number be a majority of the whole number of electors appointed; and if there be more than one who have such majority, and have an equal number of votes, then the House of Representatives shall immediately choose by ballot one of them for President; and if no person have a majority, then from the five highest on the list the said House shall in like manner choose the President. But in choosing the President, the votes shall be taken by states, the representation from each state having one vote; a quorum for this purpose shall consist of a member or members from two thirds of the states, and a majority of all the states shall be necessary to a choice. In every case, after the choice of the President, the person having the greatest number of votes of the electors shall be the Vice President. But if there should remain two or more who have equal votes, the Senate shall choose from them by ballot the Vice President.

This clause, or paragraph, explains how to elect the President and Vice President. It was changed by the Twelfth Amendment, in 1804.

The Congress may determine the time of choosing the electors, and the day on which they shall give their votes; which day shall be the same throughout the United States.

Congress sets one date for choosing electors and sets another date for electors to vote for President. The dates must be the same for the entire nation.

Electors are chosen every fourth year on Election Day, which is the first Tuesday after the first Monday in November.

No person except a natural-born citizen, or a citizen of the United States, at the time of the adoption of this Constitution, shall be eligible to the office of President; neither shall any person be eligible to that office who shall not have attained the age of 35 years, and been 14 years a resident within the United States.

To be President, a person must be a citizen who was born in the United States, be at least 35 years old, and live in the nation for at least 14 years.

In case of the removal of the President from office, or of his death, resignation, or inability to discharge the powers and duties of the said office, the same shall devolve on the Vice President, and the Congress may by law provide for the case of removal, death, resignation, or inability, both of the President and Vice President, declaring what officer shall then act as President, and such officer shall act accordingly until the disability be removed, or a President shall be elected.

The Vice President shall become the President if the nation's President dies, resigns, or is unable to work. Congress must decide who becomes President if the nation does not have a Vice President.

The Twenty-fifth Amendment tells when the Vice President becomes the President and how another person must then be chosen to be the new Vice President.

The President shall, at stated times, receive for his services a compensation, which shall neither be increased nor diminished during the period for which he shall have been elected, and he shall not receive within that period any other emolument from the United States, or any of them.

The President shall receive a salary. The amount will be decided by Congress, and it cannot be changed while the President is in office. A President cannot receive money from any state or from any other part of the federal government while in office.

Before he enter on the execution of his office, he shall take the following oath or affirmation:

"I do solemnly swear (or affirm) that I will faithfully execute the office of President of the United States, and will to the best of my ability, preserve, protect, and defend the Constitution of the United States."

On the day a President takes office, he must take the Presidential Oath. With this oath, the new President swears to carry out the duties of the presidency and to protect and defend the United States Constitution.

Section 2. President's Powers

The President shall be Commander in Chief of the Army and Navy of the United States, and of the militia of the several states, when called into the actual service of the United States; he may require the opinion, in writing, of the principal officer in each of the executive departments, upon any subject relating to the duties of their respective offices, and he shall have power to grant reprieves and pardons for offenses against the United States, except in cases of impeachment.

The President shall be the commander in chief of the Army, Navy, and National Guard. He may order the leaders of executive departments to report on their work. The President has the power to grant pardons for federal crimes. Pardons cannot be granted to a person who has been impeached.

This clause puts the military under civilian control. The clause also allows the President to create a cabinet with executive department leaders.

He shall have power, by and with the advice and consent of the Senate, to make treaties,

provided two thirds of the Senators present concur; and he shall nominate, and by and with the advice and consent of the Senate, shall appoint ambassadors, other public ministers and consuls, judges of the Supreme Court, and all other officers of the United States, whose appointments are not herein otherwise provided for, and which shall be established by law: but the Congress may by law vest the appointment of such inferior officers, as they think proper, in the President alone, in the courts of law, or in the heads of departments.

The President can make treaties with foreign nations, but the treaties cannot be used unless two thirds of the senators vote for them. The President appoints ambassadors to foreign nations and judges to the Supreme Court. These appointments must receive a majority of votes in the Senate. The President can appoint people to less-important government offices. Senate approval is not needed for less-important positions.

This clause gives the President the power to make foreign policy. The Senate checks the President's power of making appointments.

The President shall have power to fill up all vacancies that may happen during the recess of the Senate, by granting commissions which shall expire at the end of their next session.

The President can appoint people to government jobs when the Senate is not in session. These jobs will be temporary, since the appointments were not approved by the Senate.

Section 3. Other Powers

He shall from time to time give to the Congress information of the state of the Union, and recommend to their consideration such measures as he shall judge necessary and expedient; he may, on extraordinary occasions, convene both Houses, or either of them, and in case of disagreement between them, with respect to the time of adjournment, he may adjourn them to such time as he shall think proper; he shall receive ambassadors and other public ministers; he shall take care that the laws be faithfully executed, and shall commission all the officers of the United States.

The President shall deliver a State of the Union address to both houses of Congress. When necessary, he shall recommend to Congress new laws that the nation needs. To deal with emergencies and serious problems, the President may call on Congress to meet in special sessions after it has adjourned. If the two houses cannot agree on when to adjourn, then the President shall decide when Congress shall adjourn. The President shall meet with ambassadors and leaders from other nations. The President must make sure the laws of Congress are carried out properly. The President gives federal officers the power to have their jobs and to do their responsibilities.

Planning the nation's budget is one of the President's major responsibilities. After the President prepares the budget, it must be passed by Congress. Congress checks the President's power because it can vote against the budget or not provide the money the President wants for new programs. Very few special sessions of Congress are called since Congress now meets for most of the year.

Section 4. Impeachment
The President, Vice President, and all civil officers of the United States, shall be removed from office on impeachment for, and conviction of, treason, bribery, or other high crimes and misdemeanors.

The President, Vice President, and all officers not in the military can be removed from office through impeachment. A President and other officials can be impeached for treason, or giving help to enemy nations, for bribery, and for committing crimes.

Andrew Johnson was the only President to be impeached. The Senate lacked one vote for the required two-thirds vote that was needed to find him guilty.

ARTICLE III. THE JUDICIAL BRANCH

Section 1. Judges
The judicial power of the United States, shall be vested in one Supreme Court, and in such inferior courts as the Congress may from time to time ordain and establish. The judges, both of the Supreme and inferior courts, shall hold their offices during good behavior, and shall, at stated times, receive for their services, a compensation, which shall not be diminished during their continuance in office.

Judicial power is given to the Supreme Court and to lower courts that are set up by Congress. Judges of the Supreme Court and the lower federal courts are appointed for lifetime terms, unless they are impeached for wrongdoing. Judges shall be paid salaries that cannot be lowered while they are in office.

The Framers wanted the courts to be separate from the other branches so that judges would not be pressured by Congress or the President to make unfair decisions.

Section 2. Federal Courts
The judicial power shall extend to all cases, in law and equity, arising under this Constitution, the laws of the United States, and treaties made, or which shall be made, under their authority; to all cases affecting ambassadors, other public ministers and consuls; to all cases of admiralty and maritime jurisdiction; to controversies to which the United States shall be a party; to controversies between two or more states, between a state and citizens of another state; between citizens of different states; between citizens of the same state claiming lands under grants of different states, and between a state, or

the citizens thereof, and foreign states, citizens
or subjects.

Federal courts have the power to hear many
different kinds of cases. They can hear all cases
that deal with the Constitution, the laws of
Congress, ambassadors, ships at sea, the
actions of government leaders, problems between
two states, and problems between citizens and
their state.

The Eleventh Amendment, in 1795, changed
this clause slightly. Only state governments can
deal with problems between a state and citizens
of another state or nation.

This clause gives the Supreme Court the power
of judicial review, which is the right to overturn
any law that is found unconstitutional. Judicial
review is one of the most important powers of
the Supreme Court. For example, the Supreme
Court used this power to overturn state segregation laws.

In all cases affecting ambassadors, other public ministers and consuls, and those in which a
state shall be party, the Supreme Court shall
have original jurisdiction. In all the other cases
before mentioned, the Supreme Court shall have
appellate jurisdiction, both as to law and fact,
with such exceptions, and under such regulations, as the Congress shall make.

The Supreme Court has two kinds of jurisdiction,
or power, to hear cases. It has original jurisdiction,
which is the power to hear cases the first time
they go to court; it has appellate jurisdiction,
which is the power to hear cases that were decided
in a lower court and appealed to the Supreme
Court. The Supreme Court has original jurisdiction
in cases that involve states or ambassadors.
These cases are presented directly to the
Supreme Court. Most cases that are heard by
the Supreme Court have appellate jurisdiction.
Congress can make rules about appealing cases
to the Supreme Court.

The trial of all crimes, except in cases of
impeachment, shall be by jury; and such trial
shall be held in the state where the said crimes
shall have been committed; but when not
committed within any state, the trial shall be at
such place or places as the Congress may by law
have directed.

All cases dealing with federal crimes shall be
decided by a jury trial in a federal court in the
state where the crime was committed.

The right to a jury trial is one of the most
important constitutional rights. It began with
the Magna Carta in 1215. The Fifth and
Sixth Amendments guarantee the rights of
accused people.

Section 3. Treason

Treason against the United States, shall
consist only in levying war against them, or in
adhering to their enemies, giving them aid and
comfort. No person shall be convicted of treason
unless on the testimony of two witnesses to the
same overt act, or on confession in open court.

A person commits treason against the United
States by making war against the nation or by
helping the enemies of the nation. A person can
be convicted of treason only if two people state
before a judge that they witnessed the same act
of treason, or if the person confesses to the crime
in an open court.

The Congress shall have power to declare the
punishment of treason, but no attainder of treason shall work corruption of blood, or forfeiture
except during the life of the person attainted.

Congress has the power to make laws for the
punishment of treason. Only the person who
committed treason, and not the person's family,
can be punished.

ARTICLE IV. RELATIONS BETWEEN STATES

Section 1. Laws

Full faith and credit shall be given in each state to the public acts, records, and judicial proceedings of every other state. And the Congress may by general laws prescribe the manner in which such acts, records, and proceedings shall be proved, and the effect thereof.

Every state must respect the laws, records, and court decisions of every other state.

For example, every state has its own marriage laws. A marriage that takes place in one state is accepted in every other state.

Section 2. Citizens

The citizens of each state shall be entitled to all privileges and immunities of citizens in the several states.

When citizens visit another state, they must be given the same rights as the people of that state. States cannot treat citizens of other states unfairly.

A person charged in any state with treason, felony, or other crimes, who shall flee from justice, and be found in another state, shall, on demand of the executive authority of the state from which he fled, be delivered up, to be removed to the state having jurisdiction of the crime.

If a person charged with a crime escapes to another state, that person must be found and returned to the state he or she ran away from.

Returning an accused person to the state or nation where the crime took place is called extradition.

No person held to service or labor in one state, under the laws thereof, escaping into another, shall, in consequence of any laws or regulation therein, be discharged from such ser-vice or labor, but shall be delivered up on claim of the party to whom such service or labor may be due.

This clause is about returning runaway slaves. This clause was overturned in 1865 by the Thirteenth Amendment, which ended slavery.

Section 3. States and Territories

New states may be admitted by the Congress into this Union; but no new state shall be formed or erected within the jurisdiction of any other state; nor any state be formed by the junction of two or more states, or parts of states, without the consent of the legislatures of the states concerned, as well as of the Congress.

Congress has the power to admit new states to the Union. New states cannot be created by dividing one state or by joining two or more states, or parts of states, unless the states and Congress agree.

Since 1787, 37 states have become part of the United States. They were all admitted to the Union by Congress. Five of them—Vermont, Kentucky, Tennessee, Maine, and West Virginia—were formed from older states, with their consent.

The Congress shall have power to dispose of and make all needful rules and regulations respecting the territory or other property belonging to the United States; and nothing in this Constitution shall be so construed as to prejudice any claims of the United States, or of any particular state.

Congress shall make rules for selling and controlling federal property and territory.

Section 4. Protecting the States

The United States shall guarantee to every state in this Union a republican form of government, and shall protect each of them against invasion; and on application of the legislature, or of the executive (when the legislature cannot be convened) against domestic violence.

The United States guarantees that every state shall have a representative government. The federal government shall protect states from enemy invasions. If fighting and violence start in a state, the state legislature or governor can request help from the federal government.

ARTICLE V. ADDING AMENDMENTS

The Congress, whenever two thirds of both Houses shall deem it necessary, shall propose amendments to this Constitution, or, on the application of the legislatures of two thirds of the several states, shall call a convention for proposing amendments, which, in either case, shall be valid to all intents and purposes, as part of this Constitution, when ratified by the legislatures of three fourths of the several states, or by conventions in three fourths thereof, as the one or the other mode of ratification may be proposed by the Congress; provided that no amendment which may be made prior to the year 1808 shall in any manner affect the first and fourth clauses in the ninth section of the first article; and that no state, without its consent, shall be deprived of its equal suffrage in the Senate.

Amendments can be added to change the Constitution. The process to add amendments begins by proposing the new amendment. A proposal is made by a two-thirds vote for an amendment in both the Senate and House. One can also be made by two thirds of the state legislatures voting to have a national convention to propose an amendment. There are two ratification methods. Three fourths of the state legislatures must vote for the amendment, or three fourths of the state conventions must ratify it. Congress has the power to decide which method should be used for ratification.

Because the Framers made it difficult to add amendments, only 27 have been added to the Constitution. The Twenty-first Amendment was the only one ratified by state conventions. Amendments have allowed the Constitution to be a flexible document.

ARTICLE VI. THE SUPREME LAW OF THE LAND

All debts contracted and engagements entered into, before the adoption of this Constitution, shall be as valid against the United States, under this Constitution, as under the Confederation.

The United States government must repay debts on money that was borrowed before the Constitution was adopted.

The United States borrowed large amounts of money for the American Revolution and during the years after the war. The Framers wanted the money repaid so that people and other nations would trust the government of the new nation.

This Constitution, and the laws of the United States which shall be made in pursuance thereof; and all treaties made, or which shall be made, under the authority of the United States, shall be the supreme law of the land; and the judges, in every state, shall be bound thereby, anything in the constitution or laws of any state to the contrary notwithstanding.

The Constitution, the laws of Congress, and all treaties are the highest laws of the nation. State judges must understand that the United States Constitution is supreme over state laws.

This clause is called the Supremacy Clause. All state and local laws must agree with the Constitution. The Supreme Court can overturn laws that do not agree with the Constitution.

The Senators and Representatives before mentioned, and the members of the several state legislatures, and all executive and judicial officers, both of the United States and of the several states, shall be bound, by oath or affirmation, to support this Constitution; but no religious test shall ever be required as a qualification to any office or public trust under the United States.

All members of Congress, members of state legislatures, and all executive and judicial branch workers must take an oath and promise to obey the United States Constitution. There can be no religious requirements for people who apply for government jobs.

This clause shows the supremacy of the Constitution. Leaders of state and local governments must promise to obey the United States Constitution and to accept it as the highest law of the nation.

ARTICLE VII. RATIFICATION

The ratification of the conventions of nine states, shall be sufficient for the establishment of this Constitution between the states so ratifying the same.

The Constitution will become the nation's law when nine states ratify it. Each state will hold a convention to vote on ratification.

Done in convention by the unanimous consent of the states present the 17th day of September in the year of our Lord 1787 and of the independence of the United States of America the 12th. IN WITNESS whereof we have hereunto subscribed our names,

The Constitution was signed by delegates from all 12 states at the Convention. It was signed on September 17, 1787. The nation became independent 12 years before the Constitution was written. Here are the names of the states and their delegates who signed:

George Washington
President and deputy from Virginia
attest: William Jackson, Secretary

New Hampshire
John Langdon
Nicholas Gilman

Massachusetts
Nathaniel Gorham
Rufus King

Connecticut
William Samuel Johnson
Roger Sherman

New York
Alexander Hamilton

New Jersey
William Livingston
David Brearley
William Paterson
Jonathan Dayton

Pennsylvania
Benjamin Franklin
Thomas Mifflin
Robert Morris
George Clymer
Thomas FitzSimons
Jared Ingersoll
James Wilson
Gouverneur Morris

Delaware
George Read
Gunning Bedford, Jr.
John Dickinson
Richard Bassett
Jacob Broom

Maryland
James McHenry
Daniel of St. Thomas Jenifer
Daniel Carroll

Virginia
John Blair
James Madison, Jr.

North Carolina
William Blount
Richard Dobbs Spaight
Hugh Williamson

South Carolina
John Rutledge
Charles Cotesworth Pinckney
Charles Pinckney
Pierce Butler

Georgia
William Few
Abraham Baldwin

The Constitution was ratified in 1788. Under the laws of this Constitution, Congress met for the first time in 1789. George Washington became the nation's first President in that same year.

AMENDMENTS

The first ten amendments are called the Bill of Rights. They were ratified on December 15, 1791. The other amendments were ratified in the years shown in parentheses.

AMENDMENT I. Freedom of Religion, Speech, Press, Assembly, and Petition
Congress shall make no law respecting an establishment of religion, or prohibiting the free exercise thereof; or abridging the freedom of speech, or of the press; or the right of the people peaceably to assemble, and to petition the government for a redress of grievances.

Congress cannot make laws to establish a religion for the nation. It cannot stop people from having freedom of religion. Congress cannot pass laws that take away freedom of speech, freedom of the press, or the right to assemble peacefully in groups. It cannot stop people from asking government leaders to correct something that the people think is wrong.

At the time the Bill of Rights was written, the United States was one of the first nations to allow freedom of religion. The separation of church and state clause in the First Amendment requires that religion be completely separate from the government. This differed from British law, which allowed an official religion that was supported with government money.

Americans use their First Amendment rights when they form groups that work for causes and when they write letters to government leaders. People are not allowed to use their rights to hurt others.

AMENDMENT II. The Right to Bear Arms
A well regulated militia, being necessary to the security of a free state, the right of the people to keep and bear arms shall not be infringed.

Every state needs a well-armed militia to protect the people. The federal government cannot take away the right of the people to have guns.
State governments can pass laws to control the ownership of guns. The Second Amendment has been used to prevent Congress from passing gun-control laws.

AMENDMENT III. The Housing of Soldiers
No soldier shall, in time of peace, be quartered in any house, without the consent of the owner, nor in time of war, but in a manner to be prescribed by law.

People cannot be forced to have soldiers eat and sleep in their homes in peaceful times. In order for soldiers to stay in civilian homes during a war, Congress must pass a special law.

AMENDMENT IV. Search and Arrest
The right of the people to be secure in their persons, houses, papers, and effects, against unreasonable searches and seizures, shall not be violated, and no warrants shall issue, but upon

probable cause, supported by oath or affirmation, and particularly describing the place to be searched, and the persons or things to be seized.

People have the right to be safe from police searches and arrests in their homes. Police are not allowed to search people or their homes, arrest people, or seize evidence without a court order or warrant from a judge. A judge can only issue a warrant for very good reasons. Evidence that is taken without a warrant cannot be used to convict a person.

AMENDMENT V. The Rights of Accused Persons

No person shall be held to answer for a capital, or otherwise infamous crime, unless on a presentment or indictment of a grand jury, except in cases arising in the land or naval forces, or in the militia, when in actual service, in time of war or public danger; nor shall any person be subject for the same offenses to be twice put in jeopardy of life or limb; nor shall be compelled in any criminal case to be a witness against himself, nor be deprived of life, liberty, or property, without due process of law; nor shall private property be taken for public use without just compensation.

A person can stand trial for a capital crime or other serious crime only after being accused of the crime by a grand jury. A capital crime is a crime that can be punished with the death penalty. Once a jury decides that a person is not guilty, that person cannot be tried again for the same crime in the same court. This is known as double jeopardy. Accused people cannot be forced to speak or provide evidence against themselves. Every accused person has the right to due process. This means they must receive fair treatment according to the law. The government must pay a fair price to people when it takes private property for government use.

AMENDMENT VI. The Right to a Fair Trial

In all criminal prosecutions, the accused shall enjoy the right to a speedy and public trial, by an impartial jury of the state and district wherein the crime shall have been committed, which district shall have been previously ascertained by law, and to be informed of the nature and cause of the accusation; to be confronted with the witnesses against him; to have compulsory process for obtaining witnesses in his favor; and to have the assistance of counsel for his defense.

Every accused person has the right to a speedy trial. The accused must be given a public trial by a fair jury. Accused people must be told what crimes they have been charged with. At the trial, they have the right to question witnesses who present evidence against them. Accused people can have their own witnesses with evidence to support their case. An accused person has the right to be defended in court by a lawyer.

The Framers believed in the importance of a speedy trial. They had seen how accused people in Great Britain were sometimes held in jail for a long time without a trial. Accused people have the right to a jury trial only when they say that they are innocent of the crime. A person who pleads guilty to a crime is sentenced by a judge and does not stand trial. The Sixth Amendment also gives accused people the right to a defense lawyer. In the 1963 case *Gideon* v. *Wainwright,* the Supreme Court decided that a person cannot receive a fair trial without a defense lawyer. Because of that decision, states must provide lawyers to all people who cannot pay for their own defense.

AMENDMENT VII. Civil Cases

In suits at common law, where the value in controversy shall exceed twenty dollars, the right of trial by jury shall be preserved, and no fact tried by a jury, shall be otherwise re-examined in any court of the United States, than according to the rules of the common law.

This amendment guarantees the right to a jury trial in civil cases that involve at least twenty dollars.

Civil cases are about problems between people, such as money, property, and divorce. Although the Seventh Amendment applies to federal courts, most states also allow jury trials for civil cases.

AMENDMENT VIII. Bail and Punishment

Excessive bail shall not be required, nor excessive fines imposed, nor cruel and unusual punishments inflicted.

Courts cannot ask accused people to pay unfair amounts of bail money. People cannot be punished with fines that are too high. A person who is found guilty should not be given a cruel or unfair punishment for the kind of crime committed. Bail is money that a judge orders an accused person to give to the court. Bail money is held by the court until the trial, and then returned when the accused person goes on trial. Since bail money is used to guarantee that the accused person will not run away, the money is not returned if the accused does not come to the trial. If an accused person cannot pay bail, that person must wait in jail until the trial begins. The Framers did not want the amount of bail to be so high that accused people would be forced to wait in jail for their trials.

AMENDMENT IX. Other Rights

The enumeration in the Constitution, of certain rights, shall not be construed to deny or disparage others retained by the people.

The Constitution explains certain rights that the government must protect. The people have many other important rights that are not listed in the Constitution, and those rights must be protected by the government.

AMENDMENT X. Powers Belonging to States

The powers not delegated to the United States by the Constitution, nor prohibited by it to the states, are reserved to the states respectively, or to the people.

All of the powers that the Constitution did not give to the federal government and did not keep from the states belong to state governments and to their people.

When the Constitution was written, many people feared that the federal government would have too much power over the states. The Tenth Amendment showed that federalism allows both a strong federal government and separate state governments with many powers of their own.

AMENDMENT XI. Cases Against States (1795)

The judicial power of the United States shall not be construed to extend to any suit in law or equity, commenced or prosecuted against one of the United States by citizens of any state, or by citizens or subjects of any foreign state.

A state cannot be sued in a federal court by a citizen from another state or from a foreign nation.

AMENDMENT XII. Election of the President and Vice President (1804)

The electors shall meet in their respective states and vote by ballot for President and Vice President, one of whom, at least, shall not be an inhabitant of the same state with themselves; they shall name in their ballots the person voted for as President, and in distinct ballots the person voted for as Vice President, and they shall make distinct lists of all persons voted for as President, and of all persons voted for as Vice President, and of the number of votes for each, which lists they shall sign and certify, and transmit sealed to the seat of the government of the United States, directed to the President of the Senate; the President of the Senate shall, in the presence of the Senate and House of Representatives, open all the certificates and the votes shall then be counted. The person having the greatest number of votes for President shall be the President, if such number be a majority of the whole number of electors appointed; and if no person have such majority, then from the persons having the highest numbers, not exceeding three on the list of those voted for as President, the House of Representatives shall choose immediately, by ballot, the President. But in choosing the President, the votes shall be taken by states, the representation from each state having one vote; a quorum for this purpose shall consist of a member or members from two-thirds of the states, and a majority of all the states shall be necessary to a choice. ~~And if the House of Representatives shall not choose a President whenever the right of choice shall devolve upon them, before the fourth day of March next following, then the Vice President shall act as President, as in the case of the death or other constitutional disability of the President.~~ The person having the greatest number of votes as Vice President, shall be the Vice President, if such number be a majority of the whole number of electors appointed, and if no person have a majority, then from the two highest numbers on the list, the Senate shall choose the Vice President; a quorum for the purpose shall consist of two-thirds of the whole number of Senators, and a majority of the whole number shall be necessary to a choice. But no person constitutionally ineligible to the office of President shall be eligible to that of Vice President of the United States.

To elect a President, electors shall meet in their own states and cast one ballot for a presidential candidate and another ballot for a vice-presidential candidate. When all electors have voted, the ballots are sent to the president of the United States Senate. The president of the Senate shall count the votes for each candidate in front of both houses of Congress. The presidential candidate with the greatest number of votes shall be

President. The winning candidate must receive more than half of the electoral votes. If none of the candidates receive a majority of votes, then the House of Representatives must choose one of the candidates to be President. Each state is allowed only one vote when electing the President. At least two thirds of the states must cast votes. To be elected, a candidate must receive a majority of votes in the House. If the House does not choose a President by March 4, the Vice President shall act as President. (The date of March 4 was later changed to January 20 in the Twentieth Amendment.) The vice-presidential candidate with the greatest number of electoral votes shall be the Vice President. If none of the candidates receive a majority of votes, then the Senate shall choose the Vice President. Two thirds of the senators must vote. The candidate who receives a majority of votes shall be Vice President. The Vice President must meet the same constitutional requirements of age, residency, and citizenship as the President.

The Twelfth Amendment overturned the procedures for electing a President that were listed in Article 2, Section 1, Clause 3. Much of the presidential election process is not included in the Constitution. Thomas Jefferson and John Quincy Adams were the only presidents that were chosen by the House of Representatives.

AMENDMENT XIII. Slavery (1865)

Section 1. Neither slavery nor involuntary servitude, except as a punishment for a crime whereof the party shall have been duly convicted, shall exist within the United States, or any place subject to their jurisdiction.

Section 2. Congress shall have power to enforce this article by appropriate legislation.

This amendment ended slavery. It said that slavery shall not exist in the United States or in territories ruled by this nation. Forced labor can be used only as a punishment for crime.

Congress shall have the power to make laws to carry out this amendment.

AMENDMENT XIV. Rights of Citizens (1868)

Section 1. All persons born or naturalized in the United States, and subject to the jurisdiction thereof, are citizens of the United States and of the state wherein they reside. No state shall make or enforce any law which shall abridge the privileges or immunities of citizens of the United States; nor shall any state deprive any person of life, liberty, or property, without due process of law; nor deny to any person within its jurisdiction the equal protection of the laws.

All people who are born or naturalized in the United States are citizens of both the nation and the state where they live. A naturalized citizen is a person who was born in a different nation, moved to the United States, and went through a legal process to become a citizen. States cannot make laws that take away the rights of citizens. States must give all people the right to due process. They cannot punish people by taking away their life, freedom, or property without due process. Every person in a state must be given equal protection by the laws.

The first sentence in this amendment gave citizenship to African Americans. The Fifth Amendment guaranteed due process to people accused of crimes by the federal government. The Fourteenth Amendment guarantees that state governments will also allow due process to all people. Many civil rights laws that have been passed by Congress are based on the Fourteenth Amendment. The equal protection clause was used by the Supreme Court when it ruled on the *Brown v. Topeka Board of Education* case. The Supreme Court decided that separate schools for African American children and white children did not allow equal protection. That decision and the Fourteenth Amendment were used to overturn state segregation laws across the nation.

Section 2. Representatives shall be apportioned among the several states according to their respective numbers, counting the whole number of persons in each state, excluding Indians not taxed. But when the right to vote at any election for the choice of electors for President and Vice President of the United States, representatives in Congress, the executive and judicial officers of a state, or the members of the legislature thereof, is denied to any of the male inhabitants of such state, being 21 years of age, and citizens of the United States, or in anyway abridged, except for participation in rebellion or other crime, the basis of representation therein shall be reduced in the proportion which the number of such male citizens shall bear to the whole number of male citizens 21 years of age in such state.

The number of members from each state in the House of Representatives depends on the state's population. This clause overturned the Three-Fifths Compromise that was used in Article 1. This clause says that everyone is counted in the census except Indians, who are not taxed. States cannot take away the right to vote in state or federal elections unless a person has committed a serious crime. States that unfairly take away the right to vote will have fewer representatives in Congress. States must allow all men who are over the age of 21 to vote.

This amendment says states that take away voting rights can be punished by losing some of their representatives in Congress, but this punishment has never been used. Voting rights were given to women in the Nineteenth Amendment and to people as young as eighteen in the Twenty-sixth Amendment.

Section 3. No person shall be a Senator or Representative in Congress, or elector of President and Vice President, or hold any office, civil or military, under the United States, or under any state, who, having previously taken an oath, as a member of Congress, or as an officer of the United States, or as a member of any state legislature, or as an executive or judicial officer of any state, to support the Constitution of the United States, shall have engaged in insurrection or rebellion against the same, or given aid or comfort to the enemies thereof. But Congress may, by a vote of two-thirds of each house, remove such disability.

This section was added to punish people who had been Confederate leaders during the Civil War. It says that they cannot hold office in the federal government. Congress can vote to remove this penalty.

In 1898, Congress removed this punishment for Confederate leaders.

Section 4. The validity of the public debt of the United States, authorized by law, including debts incurred for payment of pensions and bounties for services in suppressing insurrection or rebellion, shall not be questioned. But neither the United States nor any state shall assume or pay any debt or obligation incurred in aid of insurrection or rebellion against the United States, or any claim for the loss or emancipation of any slave; but all such debts, obligations and claims shall be held illegal and void.

The United States is required by law to pay its debts on money borrowed for the Civil War. Neither the United States government nor the state governments are allowed to pay the war debts of the Confederate States. People who once owned slaves will not be paid for the loss of their slaves.

Section 5. The Congress shall have power to enforce, by appropriate legislation. the provisions of this article.

Congress shall have the power to make the laws that are needed to carry out this amendment.

AMENDMENT XV. Right to Vote (1870)
Section 1. The right of citizens of the United States to vote shall not be denied or abridged by the United States or by any state on account of race, color, or previous condition of servitude.

Citizens cannot be prevented from voting because of race, color, or because they have been slaves.

Section 2. The Congress shall have power to enforce this article by appropriate legislation.

Congress shall have the power to make laws to enforce this amendment.
The Fifteenth Amendment could only be carried out by laws of Congress. Many states passed laws that made it difficult for African Americans to vote. Martin Luther King, Jr., worked hard to win fair voting laws. His work influenced Congress, and in 1965 the Voting Rights Act was passed.

AMENDMENT XVI. Income Tax (1913)
The Congress shall have power to lay and collect taxes on incomes, from whatever source derived, without apportionment among the several states, and without regard to any census or enumeration.

Congress shall have the power to collect taxes on income. The amount of tax money collected does not depend on state populations.
Almost half of the money in the federal budget now comes from personal income taxes.

AMENDMENT XVII. Election of Senators (1913)
The Senate of the United States shall be composed of two Senators from each state, elected by the people thereof, for six years; and each Senator shall have one vote. The electors in each state shall have the qualifications requisite for electors of the most numerous branch of the state legislatures.

When vacancies happen in the representation of any state in the Senate, the executive authority of such state shall issue writs of election to fill such vacancies: *Provided*, That the legislature of any state may empower the executive thereof to make temporary appointments until the people fill the vacancies by election as the legislature may direct.

This amendment shall not be so construed as to effect the election or term of any Senator chosen before it becomes valid as part of the Constitution.

The United States Senate shall have two senators from each state. They shall be elected by the people of their states to serve six-year terms. Each senator shall have one vote. When there is a vacant seat in the Senate because a senator can no longer represent the state, the governor of that state shall call an election for a new senator. The state legislature can allow the governor to appoint a temporary senator, who will serve until the election takes place.

This amendment overturned the method of choosing senators that was discussed in Article 1, Section 3, Clauses 1 and 2, of the Constitution. Article 1 required that senators be elected by state legislatures. This amendment allows senators to be elected directly by the people in the same way that members of the House of Representatives are chosen. The amendment gives people a greater voice in government since they can choose their own representatives for both houses of Congress.

AMENDMENT XVIII. Prohibition of Liquor (1919)

Section 1. After one year from the ratification of this article the manufacture, sale, or transportation of intoxicating liquors within, the importation thereof into, or the exportation thereof from the United States and all territory subject to the jurisdiction thereof for beverage purposes is hereby prohibited.

One year after this amendment is ratified, liquor cannot be manufactured, sold, imported, or exported in the United States.

Section 2. The Congress and the several states shall have concurrent power to enforce this article by appropriate legislation.

Congress and the states have the power to make laws to enforce this amendment.

Section 3. This article shall be inoperative unless it shall have been ratified as an amendment to the Constitution by the legislatures of the several states, as provided in the Constitution, within seven years from the date of the submission hereof to the states by the Congress.

This amendment must be ratified within seven years or it cannot be part of the Constitution.

This amendment was repealed in 1933 by the Twenty-first Amendment. The laws against liquor were called Prohibition Laws. During the time known as Prohibition, a great deal of liquor was manufactured and sold illegally.

AMENDMENT XIX. Woman Suffrage (1920)

The right of citizens of the United States to vote shall not be denied or abridged by the United States or by any state on account of sex.

Citizens of the United States shall not be prevented from voting because of their sex.

Congress shall have power to enforce this article by appropriate legislation.

Congress shall have the power to pass laws to carry out this amendment.

Wyoming was the first state to give women the right to vote in state elections. Later, other states gave this right to women. But women in all states wanted to vote in national elections, so they worked for the woman suffrage amendment. From 1878 to 1918, an amendment on woman suffrage was proposed and defeated each year in Congress. Finally, the House approved the amendment in 1918, and the Senate did so in 1919. When it was ratified in 1920, woman had the right to vote in local, state, and national elections.

AMENDMENT XX. Lame Duck Amendment (1933)

Section 1. The terms of the President and Vice President shall end at noon on the 20th day of January, and the terms of Senators and Representatives at noon on the third day of January, of the years in which such terms would have ended if this article had not been ratified; and the terms of their successors shall then begin.

The term of office of the President and Vice President shall end on January 20 at noon. The term of office for senators and representatives of Congress shall end on January 3 at noon. The new President and Vice President will take office on January 20. New members of Congress will take office on January 3.

Members of Congress who were defeated in the November elections are considered to have less power from that time until the new members are sworn in. These defeated members are called lame ducks. This amendment shortened the length of time a Lame Duck could remain in office.

Until this amendment, newly elected members did not begin work until March 4. This was so because when the Constitution was written, it took a long time for mail to reach the members and inform them of their new job. Then it took a while for them to travel to the capital to begin their work.

Section 2. The Congress shall assemble at least once in every year, and such meeting shall begin at noon on the third day of January, unless they shall by law appoint a different day.

Congress shall meet at least once each year.

The meetings shall begin on January 3 at noon.

Section 3. If, at the time fixed for the beginning of the term of the President, the President elect shall have died, the Vice President elect shall become President. If a President shall not have been chosen before the time fixed for the beginning of his term, or if the President elect shall have failed to qualify, then the Vice President elect shall act as President until a President shall have qualified; and the Congress may by law provide for the case wherein neither a President elect nor a Vice President elect shall have qualified, declaring who shall then act as President, or the manner in which one who is to act shall be selected, and such person shall act accordingly until a President or Vice President shall have qualified.

If the President elect dies, the Vice President elect shall become the new President. If a new President has not been chosen before the time the new term is to begin, the Vice President elect will act as President. Congress can pass laws to decide who will be a temporary President if the nation does not have a President elect or a Vice President elect.

This section discusses problems that have never happened in the history of the United States.

Section 4. The Congress may by law provide for the case of the death of any of the persons from whom the House of Representatives may choose a President whenever the right of choice shall have devolved upon them, and for the case of the death of any of the persons from whom the Senate may choose a Vice President whenever the right of choice shall have devolved upon them.

The Twelfth Amendment required the House of Representatives to choose a President if none of the presidential candidates received a majority of electoral votes. If one of the three presidential candidates dies, Congress can pass a law on how to choose a President. This also applied to the Vice President.

This situation has never occurred, and Congress has never had to pass this type of law.

Section 5. Sections 1 and 2 shall take effect on the 15th day of October following the ratification of this article.

After this amendment is ratified, Sections 1 and 2 will take effect on October 15.

Section 6. This article shall be inoperative unless it shall have been ratified as an amendment to the Constitution by the legislatures of three-fourths of the several states within seven years from the date of its submission.

This amendment must be ratified within seven years by three fourths of the state legislatures.

AMENDMENT XXI. Repeal of the Eighteenth Amendment (1933)

Section 1. The Eighteenth article of amendment to the Constitution of the United States is hereby repealed.

The Eighteenth Amendment on prohibition is no longer a law of the United States.

Section 2. The transportation or importation into any state, territory, or possession of the United States for delivery or use therein of intoxicating liquors, in violation of the laws thereof, is hereby prohibited.

States can make their own laws about selling, transporting, or prohibiting liquor. It is a federal crime to disobey a state's liquor laws.

Section 3. This article shall be inoperative unless it shall have been ratified as an

amendment to the Constitution by conventions in the several states, as provided in the Constitution, within seven years from the date of the submission hereof to the states by the Congress.

To become an amendment, this law must be ratified by state conventions within seven years.

The Twenty-first Amendment was the only amendment ratified by state conventions. Although Americans drank less liquor during the years the Prohibition Amendment was in effect, the amendment encouraged people to break the law in order to buy, sell, and manufacture liquor.

AMENDMENT XXII. Terms of the Presidency (1951)

Section 1. No person shall be elected to the office of the President more than twice, and no person who has held the office of President, or acted as President, for more than two years of a term to which some other person was elected President shall be elected to the office of the President more than once. But this article shall not apply to any person holding the office of President when this article was proposed by the Congress, and shall not prevent any person who may be holding the office of President, or acting as President, during the term within which this article becomes operative from holding the office of President or acting as President during the remainder of such term.

No person shall be elected to more than two terms of presidential office. A President who serves two years of another President's elected term can be elected to two more terms. A President shall not serve for more than ten years.

Section 2. This article shall be inoperative unless it shall have been ratified as an amendment to the Constitution by the legislatures of three fourths of the several States within seven years from the date of its submission to the States by Congress.

This amendment cannot be part of the Constitution unless it is ratified by three fourths of the state legislatures within seven years.

George Washington served only two terms of office. This tradition was followed by every President until Franklin D. Roosevelt was elected to four terms. Many Americans felt a President could become too powerful if he remained in office for more than ten years. So this amendment was added to the Constitution.

AMENDMENT XXIII. Voting in the District of Columbia (1961)

Section 1. The district constituting the seat of government of the United States shall appoint in such manner as the Congress may direct: A number of electors of President and Vice President equal to the whole number of Senators and Representatives in Congress to which the district would be entitled if it were a state, but in no event more than the least populous state; they shall be in addition to those appointed by the states, but they shall be considered, for the purposes of the election of the President and Vice President, to be electors appointed by a state; and they shall meet in the district and perform such duties as provided by the Twelfth article of amendment.

The people of the District of Columbia, as residents of the nation's capital and seat of government, shall vote for electors in presidential elections. The number of electors is to be the same as if the District of Columbia were a state. It cannot have more electors than the state with the smallest population. The electors shall help elect a President by following the rules of the Twelfth Amendment.

Section 2. The Congress shall have power to enforce this article by appropriate legislation.

Congress has the power to make laws to enforce this amendment.

Until 1961, citizens of Washington, D.C., could not vote in presidential elections. The District of Columbia is an area that is located between Maryland and Virginia. Since it is not a state, its citizens were not allowed to vote for President.

AMENDMENT XXIV. Poll Taxes (1964)

Section 1. The right of citizens of the United States to vote in any primary or other election for President or Vice President, for electors for President or Vice President, or for Senator or Representative in Congress, shall not be denied or abridged by the United States or any state by reason of failure to pay any poll tax or other tax.

It is the right of every citizen to vote in primary elections and presidential elections. Every citizen has the right to vote for senators and representatives in Congress. The federal and state governments cannot take away these rights because a person does not pay a poll tax or other kind of tax.

Section 2. The Congress shall have the power to enforce this article by appropriate legislation.

Congress has the power to make laws to enforce this amendment.

After 1889, eleven southern states had poll taxes. The poll-tax laws were used to prevent African Americans from voting. The Twenty-fourth Amendment said poll taxes could not be used to take away voting rights in federal elections. The amendment did not prevent states from having poll taxes for state and local elections. In 1966, the Supreme Court ruled that poll taxes were against the Equal Protection Clause of the Fourteenth Amendment. All poll taxes were declared unconstitutional, and they could no longer be used to stop people from voting.

AMENDMENT XXV. Presidential Succession (1967)

Section 1. In case of the removal of the President from office or his death or resignation, the Vice President shall become President.

The Vice President shall become President if the President dies, resigns, or is removed from office.

Section 2. Whenever there is a vacancy in the office of the Vice President, the President shall nominate a Vice President who shall take office upon confirmation by a majority vote of both houses of Congress.

Since the nation must have a Vice President, this office must be filled if it becomes vacant. The President shall nominate a person for Vice President. If a majority of senators and representatives vote for the nominated person, that person becomes the new Vice President.

Checks and balances are used since the House and Senate can check the President's choice for Vice President.

Section 3. Whenever the President transmits to the president *pro tempore* of the Senate and the Speaker of the House of Representatives his written declaration that he is unable to discharge the powers and duties of his office, and until he transmits to them a written declaration to the contrary, such powers and duties shall be discharged by the Vice President as Acting President.

If a President is unable to carry out his duties, he must write and tell the president pro tempore *of the Senate and the Speaker of the House. Then the Vice President must be acting President until the President is able to work again.*

In 1985, Vice President George Bush acted as President while Ronald Reagan had surgery.

Section 4. Whenever the Vice President and a majority of either the principal officers of the executive departments or of such other body as Congress may by law provide, transmit to the President pro tempore of the Senate and the Speaker of the House of Representatives their written declaration that the President is unable to discharge the powers and duties of his office, the Vice President shall immediately assume the powers and duties of the office as Acting President.

Thereafter, when the President transmits to the President pro tempore of the Senate and the Speaker of the House of Representatives his written declaration that no inability exists, he shall resume the powers and duties of his office unless the Vice President and a majority of either the principal officers of the executive department or of such other body as Congress may by law provide, transmit within four days to the President pro tempore of the Senate and the Speaker of the House of Representatives their written declaration that the President is unable to discharge the powers and duties of his office. Thereupon Congress shall decide the issue, assembling within 48 hours for that purpose if not in session. If the Congress, within 21 days after receipt of the latter written declaration, or, if Congress is not in session, within 21 days after Congress is required to assemble, determines by two-thirds vote of both houses that the President is unable to discharge the powers and duties of his office, the Vice President shall continue to discharge the same as Acting President; otherwise, the President shall resume the powers and duties of his office.

If the Vice President and a majority of cabinet leaders or Congress feels that the President is unable to carry out his duties, then they must tell this in writing to the president pro tempore *of the Senate and the Speaker of the House. Then the Vice President shall be acting President. Then, if the President writes that he is again able to carry out his duties, he will do so. However, the Vice*

President and a majority of cabinet leaders can write declaring the President still unfit. Both houses must vote on the President's condition within 21 days. The Vice President will remain acting President if two thirds of the members of both houses vote for the Vice President. If there are not enough votes for the Vice President, the President can start to work again.

This amendment was added to make clear just what steps would be followed to decide whether the President is unable to carry out his duties. This was not made clear in Article 2, Section 1, Clause 6.

AMENDMENT XXVI. Voting Age of 18 (1971)

Section 1. The right of citizens of the United States, who are 18 years of age or older, to vote shall not be denied or abridged by the United States or by any state on account of age.

All citizens who are at least 18 years of age shall be allowed to vote in state and federal elections.

Section 2. The Congress shall have power to enforce this article by appropriate legislation.

Congress shall have the power to pass laws to enforce this amendment.

The Constitution in 1787 gave the right to vote to white men. After the Civil War, the right to vote was given to African Americans. Then woman suffrage became law with the Nineteenth Amendment. Voting rights were given to the people of Washington, D.C., in 1961. Finally in 1971, the right to vote was given to 18-year-olds.

AMENDMENT XXVII. Congressional Pay (1992)

No law varying the compensation for the services of the Senators and Representatives shall take effect, until an election of Representatives shall have intervened.

Salary increases given to members of Congress will not take effect until after the next congressional election. This amendment prevents the members of Congress in session from giving themselves higher pay.

This amendment was originally introduced in 1789, but was not ratified for the Constitution by the necessary three fourths of the states until 1992.

Unit 3

THE NATION GROWS AND CHANGES

A brave young Shoshone woman named Sacagawea and her French-Canadian husband helped a group of explorers cross the Rocky Mountains. The group, led by Meriwether Lewis and William Clark, traveled to the Pacific Ocean. They brought exciting information about the West back to President Thomas Jefferson.

As you read Unit 3, you will learn how the nation grew larger and stronger. Find out why Americans fought wars in 1812 and 1848. Learn how Americans moved west when gold was found in California.

THINK ABOUT IT

- George Washington was the only President who did not join a political party. Why?
- Andrew Jackson became a war hero after the Battle of New Orleans, but this battle should not have been fought. Why?
- The invention of the cotton gin made slaves more valuable than ever. Why?
- One state was once an independent republic with its own president. Which state?

1750   **1800**

1789
George Washington becomes first President.

1791
Bank of the United States begins.

1793
Eli Whitney invents the cotton gin.

1803
United States buys Louisiana.

1807
The Embargo Act stops trade with France and Great Britain.

▲ *Lewis and Clark expedition, 1804-1806*

1814
Treaty of Ghent
ends War of
1812.

1823
President Monroe
delivers the
Monroe Doctrine.

1832
South Carolina
passes the
Nullification Act.

1846
United States and
Great Britain
compromise over
Oregon.

1853
Mexico agrees
to the Gadsden
purchase.

1850

1812
War of 1812
begins.

1820
The Missouri
Compromise
is written.

1828
Andrew
Jackson
is elected
President.

1836
Texas wins
independence
from Mexico.

1849
Gold Rush
begins in
California.

THE START OF THE NEW NATION

◀ *George Washington coins from 1790*

People

Benjamin Banneker •
Anthony Wayne • Pierre
L'Enfant • Maurice de
Talleyrand • Napoleon
Bonaparte • Charles
Pinckney • Aaron Burr •
Richard Henry Lee

Places

Mount Vernon • District of
Columbia • Potomac River •
Washington, D.C.

New Vocabulary

precedents • appointed •
Cabinet • rebel •
foreign affairs •
political parties •
foreign minister •
unconstitutional •
electoral college •
electors • candidates

Focus on Main Ideas

1. How did Alexander Hamilton's plans help the United States pay its debts?
2. What difficult decisions did George Washington and John Adams make as Presidents?
3. Why did the House of Representatives elect the President in 1800?

In April 1789 George Washington left the home he loved in Virginia and traveled with his wife, Martha, to New York City. That city, the largest in the country, was the nation's first capital. Crowds cheered for Washington as he traveled through towns on his way to New York. On April 30, 1789, Washington was inaugurated as the nation's first President.

The New Government Begins

In 1788 the Constitution had been ratified, and the new Congress started meeting in March 1789. The first job for Congress was to write the Bill of Rights. Congress also created executive departments to help the President carry out his duties. George Washington knew that his actions would create **precedents**, or examples, that future Presidents would follow. So he was careful about every decision he made. Washington **appointed**, or selected, people to advise him and to lead the new executive departments. These people were called the **Cabinet**. Every President has followed Washington's precedent and has had a Cabinet of leaders.

The Constitution gave Congress the power to create a federal court system.

To do this, Congress passed a law called the Judiciary Act. It gave the nation's highest court, the Supreme Court, six judges called justices. The leader of the Court is called the Chief Justice. Today the Supreme Court has nine justices. The Judiciary Act also created federal courts that heard cases in different parts of the nation.

Paying the Nation's Debts

In 1789 the new government had huge war debts. To pay for the American Revolution, the Continental Congress had borrowed millions of dollars from other nations and from the American people by selling bonds. After a certain period of time, the government had to repay the money it borrowed, with interest. If the new country could not pay its debts, no nation and no person would ever lend money to the American government again.

Alexander Hamilton, secretary of the treasury, made plans for the United States to pay all its debts. He asked Congress to pass new tax laws. Hamilton also wanted to create a Bank of the United States where the federal government would keep the tax money it collected. This bank would lend money to businesses in order to help them grow. The taxes these businesses paid would help the nation grow.

The men pictured here with George Washington were members of the first Cabinet. From the right they are Attorney General Edmund Randolph, Secretary of State Thomas Jefferson, Secretary of the Treasury Alexander Hamilton, and Secretary of War Henry Knox.

Washington chose Benjamin Banneker, a free African American, to survey the land for the nation's new capital city.

Thomas Jefferson and James Madison believed that the Constitution did not give Congress power to create the Bank of the United States. But Hamilton said the Elastic Clause in the Constitution allowed Congress to pass laws to carry out its powers. The Bank would help Congress carry out its power to collect taxes. In 1791 Congress passed a law creating the Bank of the United States.

Alexander Hamilton's plans worked well. Slowly the government collected enough tax money to repay its debts, and the American economy grew stronger.

Problems and Decisions for the New Government

The Northwest Ordinance of 1787 said settlers could not take land away from the Indians of the region. But American settlers moved into the Northwest Territory and settled on Indian land. There were many fights between the settlers and the Indians of the region. In 1793 George Washington sent General Anthony Wayne to the Northwest Territory to protect the settlers. After two years of fighting, the Indians surrendered and signed the Treaty of Greenville.

After Congress put a tax on whiskey in 1791, frontier farmers started the Whiskey Rebellion. The farmers grew corn that they made into whiskey. Many farmers earned most of their money from the sale of whiskey. In 1794 the farmers prepared to fight to end the whiskey tax. President Washington led about 13,000 soldiers against the frontier farmers. When they reached the frontier, none of the **rebel** farmers could be found. Unlike Shays's Rebellion in 1786, the Whiskey Rebellion ended quickly. The new government was strong enough to stop rebellions and keep order in the nation.

Washington had to make difficult decisions about the nation's **foreign affairs**. In 1793 Great Britain went to war against France. The British seized American ships that were trading with France. Many Americans wanted the United States to help France and go to war against Great Britain. But Washington felt the United States was not strong enough to fight another war against Britain. Instead he sent John Jay to Great Britain to discuss a peace treaty. Although many people thought Jay's Treaty was unfair to the United States, Washington accepted the treaty in order to avoid war. By avoiding war the United States had time to grow stronger.

By the end of his first term as President, Washington wanted to retire. But members of the Cabinet asked him to serve another term. In 1796 Washington decided not to serve a third term as President. This decision set the precedent that Presidents should serve only two terms. For the next 145 years, no President served more than two terms.

At the end of his term, Washington wrote his famous Farewell Address. He told the American people to remain united at home and to develop more trade with other nations. He warned his country to remain neutral and to not favor any foreign nation: "Tis our true policy to steer clear of permanent alliances with any portion of the foreign world."

President Washington retired to his home at Mount Vernon. On the way home, he stopped to visit the site where the nation's new capital was being built.

Congress had passed a bill that allowed the nation to build a new capital city. Washington had helped plan the District of Columbia along the Potomac River between Virginia and Maryland. He had asked Pierre L'Enfant of France to plan the capital. That city became Washington, D.C.

The United States Under President John Adams

Disagreements between two Cabinet members, Thomas Jefferson and Alexander Hamilton, led to the development of the first **political parties**. Jefferson's party became the Democratic Republican party. Its members were often called Republicans. This is not the same as the modern Republican party, which began in the 1850s. Alexander Hamilton's party became the Federalist party. John Adams, a Federalist, was elected President in 1796.

Soon after Adams became President, he faced serious problems with France. The French had seized American ships that were trading in the West Indies. Adams sent three Americans to France to end this problem. The **foreign minister** of France, Maurice de Talleyrand, sent three men to meet secretly with the

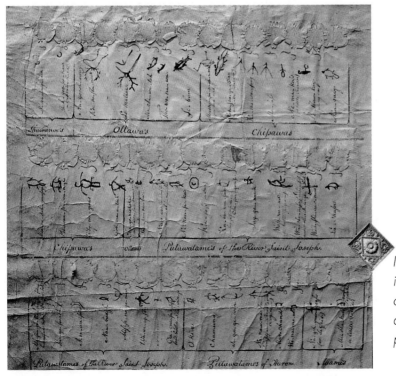

In 1795 the chiefs of 12 Indian nations in the Northwest Territory signed the Treaty of Greenville. In this treaty the Indians agreed to give the United States a large part of what is now the state of Ohio.

141

Americans. The French men said France would stop seizing ships if the United States paid ten million dollars to France. The three French men were called Mr. X, Mr. Y, and Mr. Z, so the problem with the French became known as the XYZ Affair.

The American people were furious about the XYZ Affair. The words "Millions for defense, but not one cent for tribute" were heard everywhere. In other words, Americans would spend money to defend their nation, but they would not spend money to pay for favors. Adams made an agreement with the new French leader, Napoleon Bonaparte, without paying the money. France agreed to stop seizing American ships.

In 1798 the Federalists in Congress passed several unfair laws called the Alien and Sedition acts. The Alien act forced people from foreign countries to wait 14 years instead of 5 years to become American citizens. The Sedition Act said it was a crime to write or print anything against the government. This law took away rights that were protected by the First Amendment of the Constitution.

Thomas Jefferson and James Madison believed the new laws were **unconstitutional**. So in 1798 Jefferson wrote the Kentucky Resolution. It said Kentucky did not have to obey a federal law that was unconstitutional. Madison wrote almost the same thing in the Virginia Resolution. Because of these resolutions, many people wondered if state governments should have more power or less power than the federal government. This question would continue to be a problem for the next 65 years of American history.

The Election of 1800

The Constitution states that the President must be elected by the **electoral college**. Each state chooses delegates called **electors** for the electoral college. The number of electors chosen by a state is the same as the number of representatives and senators the state sends to Congress. Electors meet to vote for the President and the Vice President. During the nation's early years, the person who received the most electoral votes became President. The person who received the second largest number of votes became Vice President.

In the election of 1800, John Adams and Charles Pinckney were the Federalist **candidates**. Thomas Jefferson and Aaron Burr were the Republican candidates. Adams lost the election when Jefferson and Burr received more votes. But Jefferson and Burr received the same number of votes.

The Constitution said the House of Representatives must elect the President when there is a tie vote. For six days members of the House voted, and each time there was a tie vote. Then Alexander Hamilton advised other Federalists to vote for Jefferson because he would be a better leader than Burr. Jefferson was elected President, and Burr became Vice President. Because of this election, the Twelfth Amendment was added to the Constitution in 1804. It required separate voting for President and Vice President.

The election of 1800 gave power to the Republican party. Thomas Jefferson, the man who wrote the Declaration of Independence, became the nation's third President.

BIOGRAPHY

George Washington 1732-1799

George Washington has been called the "father of our country." He earned that honor by leading the United States during the country's difficult early years.

Washington was born in Virginia. He led soldiers from Virginia against the French during the French and Indian War. He spent 16 years as a farmer after the war. He also became a judge in a Virginia court. He was elected to the Virginia House of Burgesses where he helped write laws for the colony.

Washington married Martha Custis. Martha had been married before, and Washington adopted Martha's children, John and Patsy.

Washington was a delegate to the First and Second Continental Congresses. He was chosen as commander in chief of the American Army. Washington led Americans to victory in 1781.

After the war Washington was glad to return to his plantation at Mount Vernon. He studied ways to grow better crops and raise healthier farm animals. But when the United States needed a Constitution, Washington agreed to lead the Constitutional Convention. When the new nation chose its first President, Americans wanted Washington. He became President, and Congress passed a law that gave him a salary of $25,000 each year. That was a large salary in 1789.

Washington disliked political parties, and he was the only President who never belonged to one. Some people complained that he behaved like a king. He rode white horses, wore expensive clothes, and had many servants. But he never wanted more power. In 1797 he retired and became a farmer again. Washington died in 1799. The new capital city was named Washington, D.C., to honor the nation's first President.

After his death, Washington's close friend Richard Henry Lee said that Washington was "first in war, first in peace, and first in the hearts of his countrymen."

In Your Own Words

Write a paragraph in your notebook that tells how George Washington served his country in war and in peace.

REVIEW AND APPLY

- After the Constitution was ratified in 1788, the new government was started.

- George Washington, the country's first President, selected people to advise him. These people became known as the President's Cabinet.

- The challenges that faced the new government included paying the debt from the American Revolution, stopping the rebellion against taxes by frontier farmers, and settling the Northwest Territory.

- George Washington served two terms as President. He was followed by President John Adams and President Thomas Jefferson.

- The election of 1796 saw the creation of the country's first political parties, the Democratic Republicans and the Federalists.

VOCABULARY

Finish the Sentence ■ In your social studies notebook, write the correct word or phrase from the box that best completes each sentence. You will not use all the words in the box.

1. George Washington set a _____ , or example, for future Presidents by not serving a third term as President.

2. President Washington's _____ advised him on issues such as the national debt and foreign affairs.

3. The Democratic Republicans and the Federalists were the country's first _____ .

4. Thomas Jefferson and James Madison believed that Americans should not obey laws that were _____ , or against the Constitution.

5. The Constitution states that the President must be elected by the _____ .

6. The French _____ tried to get the United States to pay a bribe of ten million dollars to France.

> unconstitutional
> precedent
> candidates
> Cabinet
> political parties
> foreign minister
> electoral college

USING INFORMATION

Writing an Opinion ■ The election of 1800 was decided by a vote in the House of Representatives. Whom would you have voted for if you had been a member of the House of Representatives in 1800?

COMPREHENSION CHECK

Who Said It? ■ Read each statement in Group A. Then look in Group B for the person who might have said it. You will not use all the words in Group B.

Group A	Group B
1. "I was the first President of the United States."	A. Pierre L'Enfant
2. "My plan for paying off the country's debts included creating the Bank of the United States."	B. John Jay
	C. George Washington
3. "I was sent to the Northwest Territory to protect settlers."	D. Thomas Jefferson
4. "I planned the city of Washington, D.C."	E. Benjamin Banneker
5. "As President, I refused to pay the French any bribe money."	F. Alexander Hamilton
	G. John Adams
6. "I wrote the Declaration of Independence."	H. Anthony Wayne
7. "I surveyed the land for the nation's capital."	I. Napoleon Bonaparte

CRITICAL THINKING

Categories ■ Read the words in each group. In your social studies notebook, write the correct title for each group. You may use the words in the box for all or part of each title. There is one title in the box that you will not need to use.

> Political Parties   The Bank of the United States   The XYZ Affair
> The President's Cabinet   The Electoral College

1. included Secretary of Treasury
   Alexander Hamilton
   advised President Washington
   every President has had one to
   give advice

2. created to pay off country's debts
   first proposed by Alexander Hamilton
   lent money to American businesses

3. occurred with the country of France
   made the American people very angry
   America was asked to pay ten million
   dollars

4. has representatives from each state
   created in the Constitution
   meets to elect the President and
   the Vice President

145

Chapter 11

A TIME OF GROWTH AND WAR

◀ *Scales of Justice*

People

James Monroe • William Marbury • John Marshall • Meriwether Lewis • William Clark • York • Shoshone • Sacagawea • William Henry Harrison • Tecumseh • Henry Clay • Dolley Madison • Francis Scott Key • Andrew Jackson • Seminoles • Simón Bolívar • José de San Martín

Places

New Orleans • St. Louis • Tippecanoe Creek • Fort McHenry • Latin America

New Vocabulary

repealed • judicial review • impressed • Embargo Act • War Hawks • anthem

Focus on Main Ideas

1. Why was *Marbury v. Madison* an important Supreme Court case?
2. How did the Louisiana Purchase help the United States?
3. Why did the United States fight in the War of 1812?
4. What important ideas were in the Monroe Doctrine?

The years between 1800 and 1825 were a time of growth, war, and change for the United States. During these twenty-five years, the nation was led by three Virginians—Thomas Jefferson, James Madison, and James Monroe.

The Age of Jefferson Begins

The election of Jefferson in 1800 was a victory for his Democratic Republican party. But Jefferson did not want the differences between Republicans and Federalists to tear the nation apart. In his first speech as President, Jefferson said, "We are all Republicans, we are all Federalists." He kept many of the laws and ideas of the Federalists. Jefferson continued Hamilton's program of paying off the nation's debts. He also kept the Bank of the United States. But Jefferson also made changes. During his first term, the Alien and Sedition acts ended, and the Whiskey Tax was **repealed**.

The Louisiana Purchase

Louisiana was a huge region to the west of the Mississippi River. Louisiana and New Orleans belonged to France until France gave them to Spain in 1762. Spain allowed American farmers to use the port of New Orleans. Farmers west of the Appalachian Mountains would send their products down the river to the port. In New Orleans, products were moved from river boats to oceangoing ships.

In 1800 Napoleon Bonaparte, the ruler of France, won control of Louisiana. Jefferson wanted the United States to control New Orleans. So he sent James Monroe to France to buy the important port. Napoleon needed money for his wars in Europe, so he offered to sell Louisiana and New Orleans for $15 million. In 1803 Jefferson signed a treaty agreeing to purchase, or buy, Louisiana.

The Louisiana Purchase doubled the size of the United States. The nation now owned all the land between the Atlantic Ocean and the Rocky Mountains. Jefferson wanted to learn about the land of the Louisiana Purchase. He hired Meriwether Lewis and William Clark to explore Louisiana. In May 1804 the Lewis and Clark expedition left from St. Louis, Missouri, with about 40 men. One of these men, York, was Clark's African American slave. York was a great help to the expedition because he had the ability to make friends with the Indians they met. The expedition traveled northwest until cold weather forced them to spend the winter in North

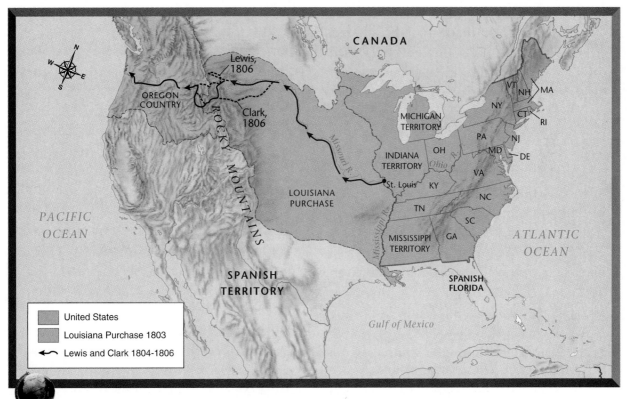

The Louisiana Purchase *The Louisiana Purchase in 1803 doubled the size of the United States. President Jefferson sent Meriwether Lewis and William Clark on an expedition to explore this area. After leaving St. Louis, on what river did the expedition travel into Louisiana?*

Dakota. There they met a young Shoshone woman named Sacagawea. She and her French-Canadian husband agreed to join the expedition and help them cross the Rocky Mountains. In November 1805 they finally reached the Pacific Ocean. Then the group began the long trip home. They reached St. Louis in September 1806. York became free at the end of the expedition. Lewis and Clark gave Jefferson new maps and information about Louisiana.

Marbury v. Madison

The *Marbury* v. *Madison* case of 1803 became one of the most important cases the Supreme Court has ever heard. Just before leaving office, President Adams had appointed William Marbury to be a judge. The Judiciary Act that Congress had passed in 1789 allowed President Adams to do this. But the new secretary of state, James Madison, refused to give Marbury this job. Marbury took his case to the United States Supreme Court.

At the time John Marshall was Chief Justice of the United States. Marshall and the other justices decided that the Judiciary Act of 1789 was unconstitutional. Because that law was used to appoint Marbury as a judge, Marbury could not have the job given to him. Marshall's decision was important because it gave the Supreme Court the power of **judicial review**. This means that the United States Supreme Court has the power to decide if any federal or state law is unconstitutional. This decision made the federal government more powerful because the Supreme Court could decide if state laws had to be changed.

Problems That Led to the War of 1812

When Napoleon went to war against Britain, it became difficult for the United States to be neutral. Both Britain and France seized hundreds of American trading ships, but the large British Navy captured most of them. The British often **impressed**, or forced, American sailors from these captured ships into the British Navy. The United States insisted that both nations respect America's right to have freedom of the seas.

In 1807 President Jefferson asked Congress to pass the **Embargo Act**. This law stopped all American trade with other countries. New England lost money because it depended on trade. The Embargo Act hurt Americans far more than it hurt Britain or France. The Embargo Act made so many Americans unhappy that Congress repealed it.

By the end of 1808, Thomas Jefferson had served two terms as President. He followed Washington's precedent and retired. James Madison was elected President.

While Americans tried to solve their problems with the British, they also faced problems with Indians in the Northwest Territory. As Americans moved onto Indian lands in Indiana, they faced new Indian attacks. In 1809 the governor of the Indiana Territory, General William Henry Harrison, pressured the Indians into signing an unfair treaty. In this treaty the Indians sold a large amount of Indiana land to the United States for very little money.

A Shawnee chief, Tecumseh, became furious when he learned about the treaty.

Tecumseh had fought the Americans during the American Revolution. Since then he had fought to slow the spread of settlers onto Indian lands. In 1811 General Harrison prepared to attack Tecumseh's village on Tippecanoe Creek in Indiana. Tecumseh was away, but his brother was defeated when he led an attack against Harrison. After defeating the Shawnees in the Battle of Tippecanoe, Harrison destroyed their village. Tecumseh would fight against the United States again later.

The War of 1812

The British continued to seize American ships and impress American sailors. The question of going to war against Britain divided the nation. People in New England did not want war because war would prevent trade with other nations. People in the South and in the West favored going to war. These people, called **War Hawks**, were led by Senator Henry Clay of Kentucky. They wanted to end British attacks on American ships. In June 1812 President Madison asked Congress to declare war against Great Britain. The War of 1812 had begun.

The United States was not prepared for war in 1812. Its army and navy were small. But the war was difficult for Britain, too. Until 1814 most British soldiers and sailors were fighting a war against Napoleon.

In 1813 American troops captured the Canadian city of York, which is now called Toronto. Americans burned the government buildings in York. But Canada remained part of Great Britain. Later that year, Tecumseh was killed while fighting Americans in Canada.

Tecumseh fought to slow the spread of settlers onto Indian lands. He tried to unite several Indian nations into a confederation that would not sell land to settlers.

In 1814 Napoleon was defeated in Europe, and British soldiers stopped fighting the French. The British sent many more ships, sailors, and soldiers to fight against the United States. In August 1814 the British prepared to attack Washington, D.C.

President Madison was with the army in Maryland when the British attacked Washington. Madison sent a message to his wife, Dolley, telling her to escape from the capital as quickly as possible. Dolley packed important government papers in trunks. She packed a famous painting of George Washington that had been hanging in the White House dining room. Then she left the capital. The British entered the city and burned many buildings.

Next the British planned to capture Baltimore, but the city's harbor was protected by Fort McHenry. Francis Scott Key, an American who watched the battle at Fort McHenry, was filled with joy when he saw the American flag flying over the fort after the long battle. He wrote a poem called "The Star Spangled Banner" about the flag. That poem became our country's national **anthem**.

Peace talks to end the war began in August 1814. On December 24, 1814, the United States and Great Britain signed a peace treaty called the Treaty of Ghent.

The last battle of the War of 1812 was actually fought in January 1815, not long after the peace treaty was signed. News about the treaty did not reach the United States until February. General Andrew Jackson had learned that the British wanted to capture New Orleans. So he gathered more than 5,000 soldiers to defend the city. Many free African Americans joined Jackson's army. During the Battle of New Orleans, 2,200 British soldiers were wounded or killed, and only 8 Americans died. Jackson became a war hero.

The United States did not win new land in the War of 1812. But the United States did win respect from Great Britain and other European nations.

Many of the battles during the War of 1812 were fought along the border of Canada. In the Battle of Lake Erie, Oliver Hazard Perry defeated a British fleet and took control of Lake Erie. His ship was damaged during the battle, and he had to take a rowboat to get to another American ship.

The Era of Good Feelings

The Republican party was so popular after the War of 1812 that the Federalist party lost most of its members. In the election of 1816, the Republican candidate, James Monroe, won 183 out of 217 electoral votes.

The years when Monroe was President have been called the Era of Good Feelings. During this time the nation grew larger. By 1821 the nation had 24 states. Businesses were growing, and many Americans were earning more money.

While Monroe was President, many slaves in the South ran away to Spanish Florida to hide among the Seminole Indians. Monroe sent General Jackson to Florida to attack the Seminoles and capture runaway slaves. Jackson fought battles against the Seminoles and destroyed their villages. But he also captured two Spanish forts. The Spanish were too weak to fight back. In 1819 Spain signed the Adams-Onís Treaty, which gave Florida to the United States for about $5 million.

The Monroe Doctrine

For a few hundred years, Spain had ruled a large empire in America. But in the early 1800s, Spain's colonies began to fight for independence. The fight for freedom in Latin America began in Mexico in 1810. In South America Simón Bolívar and José de San Martín helped Spanish colonies win freedom. By 1822 most nations in Central and South America were independent.

President Monroe feared that other European nations might try to start colonies in Latin America. To prevent this

Simón Bolívar led five South American nations to independence from Spain. He is known as the George Washington of South America.

from happening, Monroe gave a speech to Congress that is now called the Monroe Doctrine. Monroe stated that the United States would not allow European countries to start new colonies in Latin America. The United States might even go to war to prevent new European colonies. European nations must stay out of the Americas. In return the United States would stay out of Europe's affairs. The Monroe Doctrine helped many future Presidents decide how to handle problems with Latin America.

The United States had grown stronger, larger, and more powerful when Jefferson, Madison, and Monroe served as Presidents. In the next chapter, you will learn about other changes that took place in the nation during this time.

BIOGRAPHY

Sacagawea

Sacagawea helped Lewis and Clark reach the Pacific Ocean. Most of what is known about this woman comes from the journals that Lewis and Clark wrote during their expedition.

Sacagawea was born a Shoshone, but she was kidnapped at about age 12 by the Minnetaree Indians. She lived with them in what is now North or South Dakota. Toussaint Charbonneau, a French Canadian fur trapper, was also living with the Minnetarees. He bought Sacagawea from them when she was about 14 years old and married her in an Indian ceremony.

Sacagawea met Lewis and Clark during the winter that they spent in North Dakota. They hired her husband to be an interpreter for them because he knew Indian sign language. Sacagawea was also hired because she knew the Shoshone language.

During the winter in North Dakota, Sacagawea gave birth to a baby boy. Although she had to care for a baby, Sacagawea kept up with the expedition.

As the expedition traveled through Shoshone country, Lewis and Clark met the Shoshone chief Cumeahwait. To Sacagawea's surprise, the chief was her brother. She had not seen him since the day she had been kidnapped.

Sacagawea's knowledge of the plants of the region helped her to show the men which plants were safe to eat. Because Sacagawea and her baby were traveling with Lewis and Clark, the Indian groups that they met were friendly towards the expedition. Sacagawea helped Lewis and Clark cross the Rocky Mountains and reach the Pacific. When the expedition ended, Sacagawea, her husband, and her son returned to live with the Shoshone. No one is certain what happened to Sacagawea later in life. Some believe she died of illness when she was only 25. Others believe Sacagawea lived with the Shoshone in Wyoming until she died in 1884. She would have been almost 100 years old.

In Your Own Words

Write a paragraph in the journal section of your notebook explaining how Sacagawea helped Lewis and Clark.

REVIEW AND APPLY

■ The early 1800s was a time of growth, war, and change for the United States.

■ The United States nearly doubled its size when it purchased the Louisiana Territory from France for $15 million.

■ The War of 1812 was fought because the British had seized American ships and impressed American sailors.

■ James Monroe was elected President in 1816 and brought in the Era of Good Feelings. American businesses and the nation were growing.

■ The Monroe Doctrine offered Latin American countries help from the United States if European nations tried to make colonies in Latin America.

VOCABULARY

Choose the Meaning ■ In the assignment section of your notebook, write the letter of the word or phrase that best completes each sentence.

1. A **republic** is a _____ .

   a. form of government
   b. political party
   c. branch of government

2. **Repeal** means to _____ .

   a. fight against
   b. do away with
   c. declare something unconstitutional

3. The **Embargo Act** _____ .

   a. stopped other countries from trading with the United States
   b. stopped the United States from trading with other countries
   c. stopped all trade to and from the United States

4. To **impress** means to _____ .

   a. sign
   b. fight
   c. draft

5. **War Hawks** were people who _____ .

   a. wanted war
   b. opposed war
   c. wanted to remain neutral

6. Our country's national **anthem** is a _____ .

   a. book
   b. song
   c. flag

USING INFORMATION

Writing an Essay ■ During the early 1800s, the United States went through a period of growth, war, and change. Select one of these three areas and write an essay relating it to the United States during this time.

COMPREHENSION CHECK

Understanding Events in History ■ Copy and complete the graphic organizer below with information about the Louisiana Purchase.

What two leaders were involved?

Why did France sell this land?

The United States Bought the Louisiana Territory

In what year did it happen?

What are two results of this event?

CRITICAL THINKING

Cause and Effect ■ Choose a cause or an effect from Group B to complete each sentence in Group A. Group B has one more answer than you need.

Group A

1. The Supreme Court decided that the Judiciary Act of 1789 was unconstitutional, so _____ .

2. _____ , so France sold Louisiana to the United States for $15 million.

3. News of the peace treaty ending the War of 1812 did not reach the United States until two months later, _____ .

4. _____ , so his time as President became known as the Era of Good Feelings.

5. President Monroe was afraid that European nations would try to set up colonies in Latin America, _____ .

6. Lewis and Clark needed help crossing the Rocky Mountains, _____ .

7. _____ , so Americans could not trade with other countries.

Group B

A. so Jay's Treaty was signed

B. France needed to pay off its war debts

C. While James Monroe was President the country grew

D. so they asked Sacagawea to help them

E. the *Marbury* v. *Madison* court case gave the Supreme Court the power of judicial review

F. Congress passed the Embargo Act

G. so the Battle of New Orleans was fought after the war was over

H. so he gave a speech that is now called the Monroe Doctrine

Chapter 12
GROWTH AND SECTIONALISM

◀ *Eli Whitney's cotton gin*

People

Samuel Slater • Robert
Fulton • John Quincy
Adams • John C. Calhoun •
Creek • Cherokee •
Choctaw • Chickasaw •
Sequoya • Osceola • Black
Hawk • Sauk • Fox

Places

Erie Canal • Rock River

New Vocabulary

Industrial Revolution •
textile mills • fibers •
cotton gin • sectionalism •
tariffs • Union •
majority • spoils system •
states' rights • nullify

Focus on Main Ideas

1. How did the Industrial Revolution affect the North and the South?
2. How did North, South, and West differ in their ideas about slavery, building roads, and tariffs?
3. What important decisions did Andrew Jackson make as President?

During the Era of Good Feelings, feelings of unity among Americans grew stronger. While events like the War of 1812 united most Americans, other forces were dividing the nation.

The Industrial Revolution

The **Industrial Revolution** was a change from making products by hand at home to making products by machine in factories. It began in the 1700s in Great Britain with the invention of machines that could spin cotton thread. Then weaving machines were invented. Factories called **textile mills** were built where workers used these new machines to spin thread and weave cloth. In 1789 Samuel Slater came to America from England. In Rhode Island Slater built factories that had spinning machines. Before long there were many textile mills in the North.

The textile mills in the North needed the cotton **fibers** taken from cotton plants that were grown in the South. It took many hours of work to remove the cotton seeds from the cotton fibers. Eli Whitney helped solve this problem when he invented the **cotton gin** in 1793. This machine quickly separated the cotton seeds from the fibers.

One cotton gin could do the work of many people. Because of the cotton gin, southern planters could grow and harvest large amounts of cotton. As more factories were built in the North, more cotton was needed. Soon cotton became the most important southern crop, and people began saying "Cotton is king."

Southern planters wanted to start new plantations in the West to grow more cotton. They insisted on bringing their slaves to work on these new cotton plantations. The spread of slavery was one of several issues that would divide the nation.

The Growth of Sectionalism

In each section of the nation—the North, the South, and the West—people cared more about the needs and interests of their part of the country than about what was good for the entire nation. This division of the nation into regions with different interests has been called **sectionalism**.

By 1820 three important issues were dividing the nation. The first issue was the use of **tariffs**, or taxes on goods brought into the country from other countries. Tariffs helped industries in the North and West because they encouraged people to buy less expensive American-made products. Southerners did not want tariffs that would make European products more expensive.

A second issue was that states in the North and West wanted to use federal money to build roads across the country. The South had less need for roads. It had many rivers that it used for transportation and shipping. A National Road was built from Maryland to Illinois.

During this time other improvements in transportation were made. Steamboats and canals improved water transportation. Robert Fulton's invention of the steamboat in 1807 made it possible for ships to sail upstream quickly. The Erie Canal was built to create a water route from the Great Lakes to the Hudson River. Trade between New York City and the West increased greatly.

The most serious issue that divided the nation was slavery. The slave trade from Africa had ended in 1808, but buying and selling slaves continued within the United States. Americans argued about allowing slavery in the new territories in the West. The people in these territories wanted to join the **Union** as new states. The South wanted slavery in these new states. The North and the West wanted these new states to be free from slavery.

The Missouri Compromise

The issue of slavery almost tore the nation apart in 1820. Missouri wanted to join the Union as a slave state. At that time there were 11 slave states and 11 free states. If Missouri joined the Union, the slave states would have more representation in the Senate than the free states. The slave states would have more power to pass laws that favored slavery. In 1820 Henry Clay suggested a compromise.

In this compromise Missouri joined the Union as a slave state and Maine joined as a free state. Then a line was drawn from Missouri's southern border across the Louisiana Purchase. All land north of that line would be free territory. All land south of that line would be slave territory.

The invention of the cotton gin and the new textile mills in the North increased the demand for cotton grown on plantations in the South. Greater demand for cotton led southern planters to use more slaves to work in the fields.

The compromise provided a way to allow Missouri to join the Union and still keep the balance between slave and free states.

The Elections of 1824 and 1828

James Monroe had served two terms as a very popular President. In the election of 1824, the candidates were all Republicans. They represented different sections of the nation. John Quincy Adams was the candidate from the North. His father, John Adams, had been the second President. William H. Crawford came from the South. Both Henry Clay and Andrew Jackson were candidates from the West. Although Clay was respected in Congress, he was far less popular than Jackson. In the election of 1824, more people voted for Jackson than for the other candidates, but none of the candidates won a **majority** of electoral votes. So the House of Representatives had to elect the President. The House elected John Quincy Adams.

As President, John Quincy Adams tried to improve roads, canals, and industry. But Adams was not popular, and Congress would not pass laws to put his plans into action.

In the election of 1828, Jackson and Adams were the main candidates. Jackson and his followers from the Republican party formed a new political party, the Democratic party. Jackson won the election.

Jackson's opponents became known as the Whigs. The Federalist party and the Republican party had lost all their power.

The Age of Jackson

The inauguration of Andrew Jackson was an exciting event. People traveled hundreds of miles to watch the man they loved become President. Jackson, who was from Tennessee, became the first President from west of the Appalachian Mountains. After the inauguration people crowded into the White House to meet the new President. They broke furniture and dishes as they pushed to get close to Jackson. He spent the night in a hotel to get away from the crowds.

Because Jackson favored the common people, he was called the "people's President." He believed that the common people should have power in government. While he was President, more white men in the western states won the right to vote because voting rules about owning property were removed.

Jackson created a **spoils system** that gave government jobs to the people who supported him. Although other Presidents had also given jobs to their supporters, Jackson was the first to brag about his actions.

Before Jackson became President, Congress had passed high tariffs. The southern states were angry because these tariffs made products from Europe more

The Missouri Compromise In this compromise, Maine and Missouri became states, and a line was drawn to separate free territory from slave territory. According to the Missouri Compromise is the Unorganized Territory supposed to be free or slave territory?

expensive. John C. Calhoun, Jackson's Vice President, led the fight against the tariffs. He believed in **states' rights,** which meant that the state governments should have more power than the federal government. He said states had the right to **nullify** laws they believed were unconstitutional.

Many people thought President Jackson, a man who owned slaves, would agree with Calhoun. But Jackson strongly disagreed. At a dinner party, Jackson stood up and said, "Our Union—it must be preserved." In other words the United States could be a nation only if all states obeyed its laws.

In 1832 South Carolina passed a law that said the tariff laws were unconstitutional. The new law said South Carolina would leave the Union if it was forced to pay the tariffs. Jackson said he would send soldiers to South Carolina to force that state to obey the tariff law. He said that no state had the right to nullify the laws of Congress or leave the Union. Henry Clay wrote a compromise law that lowered the tariffs. South Carolina agreed to pay the tariffs. "Do states have the right to disobey federal laws that they believe are unconstitutional?" would continue to be a question that would trouble the nation.

The Bank of the United States had been started by Alexander Hamilton. Jackson disliked the Bank because he felt it favored the wealthy. In 1832 Congress wrote a bill to give the Bank a new charter, but Jackson

Andrew Jackson had fought in the American Revolution at age 13. He had become a lawyer and a senator. Jackson became a hero by winning the Battle of New Orleans at the end of the War of 1812. In this painting, Jackson is giving a speech while running for President.

vetoed that bill. After he was reelected, Jackson had the government take its money out of the Bank. The Bank could not do its work without government money. In 1836 the Bank no longer existed.

The Trail of Tears

In 1830 Congress passed the Indian Removal Act, which forced Indians to move west across the Mississippi River. From 1830 to the early 1840s, the United States Army forced about 100,000 Indians—such as Creek, Cherokee, Choctaw, Chickasaw, and Seminole—to leave their homes. Because thousands of Indians died along the way from hunger, disease, and cold weather, the trip west has been called the "Trail of Tears."

The Cherokee had become farmers, built schools and churches, and had a representative government. One Cherokee, Sequoya, had developed an alphabet for the language of his people. The Cherokee took their case to the Supreme Court. The Supreme Court decided that the Cherokee should keep their land. But Jackson refused to obey the Supreme Court's decision.

In Florida the Seminole, led by Osceola, fought against the American Army. After winning several battles, Osceola was captured. Other Seminole continued the fight, but by 1840 there were few Indians east of the Mississippi River.

About 100,000 Indians were forced to leave their homes and travel hundreds of miles to settle in Oklahoma. Because thousands of Indians died from hunger, disease, and cold weather, the trip west has been called the "Trail of Tears."

BIOGRAPHY

Black Hawk 1767-1838

Black Hawk, a leader of the Sauk and Fox nations, decided to fight for the land that belonged to his people. Black Hawk was born near the Rock River in Illinois. Black Hawk began fighting for his people soon after the Sauk were tricked into signing an unfair treaty in 1804. Five Sauk leaders were tricked by William Henry Harrison. He gave them whiskey. While the Sauk were drunk, they signed a treaty that gave all of their land east of the Mississippi River to the United States. In return the United States would pay the Sauk about $3,000.

Black Hawk was furious when he learned about the treaty. Black Hawk decided to fight the United States. During the War of 1812, he fought with Tecumseh on the side of the British.

The United States government wanted the Sauk and Fox nations to move west to Iowa. The chief of the Sauk agreed to move. By 1830 most of the Sauk and the Fox had settled in Iowa.

Black Hawk refused to leave Illinois. Instead, in 1832 Black Hawk and his sons led a group of Sauk and Fox against the United States Army. The war became known as the Black Hawk War. Black Hawk and his men fought bravely, but the American Army had more soldiers and better weapons. The war ended in August 1832 when Black Hawk and his sons were captured. They were taken to Washington, D.C., as prisoners.

While Black Hawk was a prisoner, he told the story of his life to a soldier, and it was published as Black Hawk's autobiography. From this autobiography we know how Black Hawk fought to keep Sauk lands. Black Hawk returned to his people and settled with them in Iowa. He remained there until he died in 1838. Although Black Hawk failed to keep his land, he is now admired for his brave fight to protect the rights of his people.

In Your Own Words

How did Black Hawk work to protect the rights of the Sauk and Fox nations? Write your answer in a paragraph of five or more sentences in your notebook.

REVIEW AND APPLY

- Issues such as slavery, sectionalism, and states' rights were starting to divide the nation in the early part of the 1800s.

- The Industrial Revolution resulted in the invention of more machines and the growth of American factories in the North.

- The Missouri Compromise tried to keep a balance between slave states and free states.

- Andrew Jackson, "the people's President," served two terms in office.

- President Jackson would not let South Carolina nullify laws. He also stopped the Bank of the United States.

- Jackson had Indians removed from the Southeast. The move west became known as the Trail of Tears.

VOCABULARY

Matching ■ **Match the vocabulary word or phrase in Group B with its definition in Group A. You will not use all the words in Group B.**

Group A	Group B
1. This was a change from making products by hand to making products by machine.	A. tariffs
2. These were factories where machines would spin cotton thread.	B. spoils system
3. This invention made it easier to remove cotton seeds from the cotton fibers.	C. textile mills
4. These are taxes on goods brought into the country.	D. sectionalism
5. This means having one more than half.	E. Industrial Revolution
6. This was a way that politicians gave jobs to people who supported them.	F. cotton gin
7. This was a belief that the state governments should have more power than the federal government.	G. majority
8. This is a division of a nation into regions based on different interests.	H. states' rights
	I. Union

162

USING INFORMATION

Journal Writing ■ Write a paragraph in your journal that answers the following questions. **What three important decisions did Andrew Jackson make as President? Would you have made the same decisions if you were President?**

COMPREHENSION CHECK

Write the Answer ■ Write one or more sentences to answer each question.

1. How did the Industrial Revolution change the North and the South?

2. Who was Samuel Slater, and what effect did he have on American industry?

3. What issue did the Missouri Compromise help to resolve?

4. Who was elected President in 1824?

5. What was Andrew Jackson's nickname as President, and how did he get that name?

6. What was the Trail of Tears?

7. How did Andrew Jackson feel about states' rights?

8. What happened to the Bank of the United States while Jackson was in office?

9. Who developed an alphabet for the Cherokee language?

10. Who was Osceola?

CRITICAL THINKING

Comparing and Contrasting ■ In this chapter you read about the differences that were dividing the sections of the United States in the 1800s. Compare and contrast North, South, and West by copying and completing the chart below.

TOPIC	NORTH	SOUTH	WEST
Taxes			
Building Roads			
Slavery			

SOCIAL STUDIES SKILLS

Reading a Bar Graph

A **bar graph** uses bars of different lengths and colors to show facts. The bar graph below compares the population of three sections of the nation for the years 1800, 1820, and 1850.

To read the graph, compare the height of the bar to the numbers on the left side of the graph. Notice that each color bar represents a different part of the country—North, South, and West.

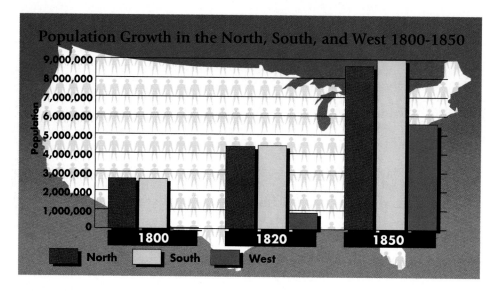

Population Growth in the North, South, and West 1800-1850

Study the graph. Then write the answer to each question below in the assignment section of your notebook.

1. Which section had the smallest population in 1800?

2. Which section had the largest population in 1850?

3. Which section showed the largest growth from 1800 to 1850?

4. Which section had less than 1 million people in 1820?

5. Which two sections had almost the same population for each date?

6. According to this graph, was the total population of the United States greater or less than 4 million people in 1800?

Chapter 13

WORKING FOR REFORM AND CULTURE

◀ *Working to reform women's rights*

People

Horace Mann • Noah Webster • Emma Willard • Mary Lyon • Thomas Gallaudet • William Lloyd Garrison • Paul Cuffee • Frederick Douglass • Angelina Grimké • Sarah Grimké • Sojourner Truth • Lucretia Mott • Elizabeth Cady Stanton • Dorothea Dix • Joseph Smith

Places

Liberia • Great Salt Lake

New Vocabulary

reform • disabilities • abolition • abolitionists • political rights • public office • mental illnesses • criminals • asylums • labor • labor unions • transcendentalists • persecution

Focus on Main Ideas

1. What were some accomplishments of the reform movements?
2. In what ways were the reform movements unsuccessful?
3. What important religious movements began in the 1800s?

In the early 1800s most children did not go to school, thousands of people were slaves, and women did not vote. During the 1800s, **reform** movements took on the job of correcting the nation's problems. Some goals of these reform movements were to improve education, end slavery, and win more rights for women.

Working for Better Education

Before 1820 most American children did not go to school. Wealthy people paid to send their children to private schools, but there were few free public schools. Children who lived on the frontier went to church schools or were taught by their parents at home. In towns and cities, many children went to dame schools that women ran in their home.

A better education system was needed as more men were allowed to vote. A democracy needs educated people who can read about the nation's problems and make wise voting decisions. In the 1820s a law was passed in New York that required elementary schools for all children.

Horace Mann worked to reform education in Massachusetts. He worked with the state's lawmakers to pass laws requiring children to attend school. He believed that schools needed well-trained teachers, so three colleges were opened to train teachers. Other states copied Horace Mann's ideas. By the 1860s most white boys in the North went to free public elementary schools. There were few public high schools in the country, and there were few schools for girls or for African American children.

Noah Webster improved American education by writing the first American dictionary. His *Spelling Book* and *Reader* became best sellers that helped children throughout the nation learn how to read and to spell. Women had fewer educational opportunities than men. In 1821 Emma Willard opened the nation's first high school for girls. In 1837 Mary Lyon opened the first college for women, Mount Holyoke Seminary, in Massachusetts. By 1900 some colleges for men began accepting female students.

Schools for children with **disabilities** were started. In Connecticut, Reverend Thomas Gallaudet opened the nation's first school for deaf children. Dr. Samuel Gridley Howe started a school for blind children.

The reform movement to change education led to more free public elementary schools. Leaders like Horace Mann convinced lawmakers to build more elementary schools and to pay teachers better salaries. These children are in the schoolyard of a public school in New York City.

The Abolition Movement

In 1776 the writers of the Declaration of Independence had written that "all men are created equal," but slavery had always been allowed in the United States. The Constitution allowed slavery. Slavery ended in the North by the early 1800s because slaves were not needed for northern businesses, factories, and small farms. The Industrial Revolution caused slavery to become more important in the South. Laws in the South protected the rights of slave owners.

In the early 1800s, many Americans worked to end slavery. Some wanted to prevent slavery in the West. Others wanted all slaves to be freed. Some thought slavery should end slowly. Others believed all slaves should be freed at once. The movement to end slavery was called the **abolition** movement. People who worked to win freedom for all slaves were called **abolitionists**.

The abolitionists faced a very difficult fight in the South and in the North. No southern state would agree to pass laws to end slavery. Nor would the South agree to change the Constitution by passing an amendment to end slavery. Many factory owners in the North opposed the abolitionists. They wanted southern slaves to continue growing cotton for their textile mills.

The abolition movement first began with religious groups. In 1776 the Quakers were the first group to stop owning slaves. They believed it was wrong for one person to own another. Other religious groups later joined the fight against slavery.

One of the most famous abolitionists was William Lloyd Garrison. Garrison wanted all slaves to be given their freedom immediately. To spread his beliefs, he began to publish a newspaper called *The Liberator*. In the first issue he wrote powerful

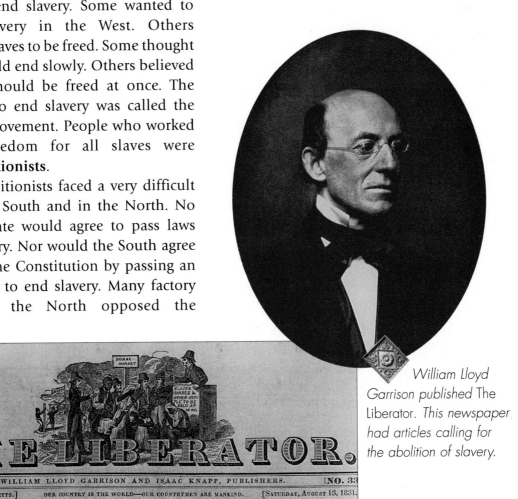

William Lloyd Garrison published The Liberator. *This newspaper had articles calling for the abolition of slavery.*

167

All of these women were abolitionists and leaders in the women's rights movement. Pictured from left to right are Elizabeth Cady Stanton, Lucretia Mott, Susan B. Anthony, and Sojourner Truth. Stanton and Mott organized the convention in Seneca Falls, New York, where Stanton lived.

sentences about what he planned to do: "I will be as harsh as truth…. I will not excuse. I will not retreat a single inch—and I will be heard."

Some abolitionists started a colony in West Africa called Liberia. Liberia became an independent African nation. Paul Cuffee, a wealthy, free African American, used his own money to send a group of freed slaves to settle in West Africa. But it was too expensive to send large groups to live in Africa. Few African Americans wanted to leave their family and move thousands of miles to live in Africa. Only a few thousand freed slaves moved to Liberia.

Frederick Douglass had been a slave, but he escaped to the North in 1838. As a free African American, he did not enjoy the same rights that white people enjoyed. So he spent several years in England where he could enjoy full freedom. Then he returned

to the United States where he published his own newspaper, *The North Star*. In *The North Star*, Douglass encouraged people to work to end slavery. Douglass also gave speeches about his experiences as a slave. Many people who heard him joined the abolition movement.

Angelina and Sarah Grimké were sisters who became abolitionists. Their parents owned slaves on their large southern plantation. The sisters had seen the evils of slavery. They gave many speeches to convince people to work to end slavery.

The abolition movement grew during the 1840s and 1850s. It made feelings of sectionalism stronger in the North and in the South. However, the abolitionists did not succeed in passing laws to end slavery. They helped only some slaves escape to freedom. But they did make many Americans think more about the problem of slavery.

The Women's Rights Movement

Many abolitionists were women. These women soon realized that they needed more **political rights** for themselves before they could help slaves win their freedom. In the 1800s women were controlled by their husbands and fathers. They could not vote, serve on juries, own property, or be elected to **public office**.

Some abolitionists began working to win more rights for women. Frederick Douglass and the Grimké sisters worked for women's rights. Angelina Grimké said that working for the rights of slaves helped her understand the rights that she needed as a woman.

Sojourner Truth had been a slave and had escaped to freedom. She became famous for her powerful speeches for the abolition of slavery and for the women's rights movement.

In 1848 Lucretia Mott and Elizabeth Cady Stanton organized the first conference to work for women's rights. At a conference in Seneca Falls, New York, they presented "The Declaration of Sentiments." This Declaration was written to sound like the Declaration of Independence. It included a sentence that said "all men and women are created equal." Then it went on to explain how women were treated unfairly by men. The Declaration of Sentiments ended by saying that women wanted the same rights as men, including the right to vote.

Frederick Douglass spoke at the conference and urged the delegates to accept the Declaration. Because of Douglass's powerful speech, delegates voted to accept it. But many delegates did not agree that women should have the right to vote.

Very slowly more schools and jobs opened for women. Some states passed laws that allowed women to own property. But it would take more than seventy years of hard work before women would win the right to vote.

Other Reform Movements

When Dorothea Dix visited a prison in 1841, she was upset to find people with **mental illnesses** held there. Dix believed that people with mental illnesses should be treated as sick people, not as **criminals**. She visited many states and succeeded in getting special hospitals, or **asylums**, built for people with mental illnesses.

Dix visited hundreds of prisons, and she was unhappy with the terrible conditions she found. People who could not pay their debts were in jail for long periods of time. Children who were in jail for crimes were held in prison cells with adults.

Dix worked hard to reform prisons throughout the nation. She succeeded in getting lighter sentences for those who did less serious crimes. Fewer people were placed in each prison cell. Children were punished differently for crimes than adults were punished. People who could not pay their debts were not treated as criminals.

The Industrial Revolution created a need for **labor** reform. More and more people were factory workers who worked from morning to night for low salaries. Factory workers formed groups called **labor unions** so they could fight for better salaries and shorter workdays. But factory owners did not have to listen to the demands of labor unions because thousands of poor immigrants had come to America from 1820 to 1840. These immigrants were willing to work at any job to earn some money for their family. Labor unions really did not succeed in helping factory workers until the late 1800s.

Creating an American Culture

During the early 1800s Americans began creating their own writing styles. The chart below provides information on some of the writers from this time period.

Washington Irving was the first American writer to become famous in Europe. Some New England writers, such as Ralph Waldo Emerson and Henry David Thoreau, were called **transcendentalists**. They stressed the importance of each person, and they believed in living close to nature.

American religion was also changing. A Protestant movement called the Second Great Awakening began in the 1820s. Religious leaders taught that everyone could get forgiveness from God for their sins. People became much more excited about religion. Thousands of people attended large religious gatherings called revivals, or camp meetings.

Joseph Smith started a new church called the Mormon church in New York in 1830. Smith's followers were called Mormons because Smith claimed he was given a holy book, *The Book of Mormon*, by an angel. Smith used that book to teach his new religion. One of Smith's many teachings was that a man could have more than one wife. Smith was killed by a mob of people who disliked his religious ideas. Brigham Young took over as leader of the Mormon church. To escape **persecution**, Young led his followers west to the Great Salt Lake in Utah. At that time Utah was part of Mexico. In Utah the Mormon church grew larger each year.

Because Americans worked for reform, better schools were built, and women won more rights. Prisoners and people with mental illnesses received better treatment. But the reform movements did not win for women the right to vote. They did not end slavery in the United States. Because Americans were not able to solve the problem of slavery, that problem would continue to divide the North and the South.

American Writers of the Early 1800s

Writer	Title of Important Work	What Was the Work About?
Washington Irving	"Rip Van Winkle," "The Legend of Sleepy Hollow"	Early American life in New York
James Fenimore Cooper	The Last of the Mohicans	American frontier life
Ralph Waldo Emerson	Nature	The ideas of the transcendentalists
Edgar Alan Poe	"The Raven"	Despair over death
Emily Dickinson	"Because I Could Not Stop for Death"	Living and death
Nathaniel Hawthorne	The Scarlet Letter	Life in Puritan New England
Herman Melville	Moby Dick	The struggle between good and evil during a whale hunt
Henry David Thoreau	Walden	Living close to nature
Walt Whitman	Leaves of Grass	Poems that praise America

Elizabeth Blackwell 1821–1910

There was a time in this country when women could not be doctors. Elizabeth Blackwell faced this problem, and she became the first woman doctor in the United States.

Blackwell was born in England but moved to New York at age eleven. Although education for girls at that time stressed music, sewing, and cooking, Elizabeth's education included math, science, and history.

Blackwell worked as a teacher for a while. But her real goal was to become a doctor. So she began to study medical books. Later she was taught by a doctor. Then she began applying to medical schools.

Blackwell soon learned that no medical school wanted a female student. She applied to 29 schools but was not accepted. Finally, she was accepted to the medical school at Geneva College in New York. She graduated in 1849.

Blackwell thought she would have greater opportunities to work as a doctor in Europe. She sailed to Europe and worked in England and France.

In 1851 Blackwell returned to New York to practice medicine. Because she was a woman, male doctors refused to accept her as a doctor. She was not allowed to treat patients in any hospitals. Blackwell solved these problems by opening her own hospital in 1857. Her sister Emily, who had also become a doctor, worked with her. Together they started the New York Infirmary for Women and Children. It included a medical school to train women to be doctors. Women worked in the hospital, and most of the patients were poor.

Since 1949 an award called the Elizabeth Blackwell Medal has been given to women doctors who have done outstanding work in medicine. This award helps Americans remember that Elizabeth Blackwell made it possible for many other women to become doctors.

In Your Own Words

In the journal section of your notebook, write what steps Elizabeth Blackwell took to become a doctor and to help other women become doctors.

Voices from the Past

Frederick Douglass: The Life of an American Slave

Frederick Douglass was born a slave. When he was eight, his owner's wife began to teach Douglass how to read. He became a good reader and an excellent writer. In 1838 he escaped to Massachusetts, where he began a new life as a free man. Although he was free, as an African American, Douglass was treated unfairly. He spent his life working to end slavery and to help African Americans and women win equal rights. Douglass told the story of his life in his autobiography, *Narrative Life of an American Slave*.

"I received my first impressions of slavery on this plantation.... Colonel Lloyd kept from three to four hundred slaves on his home plantation and owned a large number more on the neighboring farms belonging to him....

The men and women slaves received, as their monthly allowance of food, eight pounds of pork, or its equivalent in fish, and one bushel of corn meal. Their yearly clothing consisted of two coarse linen shirts, one pair of linen trousers, like the shirts, one jacket, one pair of trousers for winter, made of coarse negro cloth, one pair of stockings, and one pair of shoes; the whole of which could not have cost more than seven dollars....

I was seldom whipped by my old master, and suffered little from anything else than hunger and cold. I suffered much from hunger, but much more from cold. In hottest summer and coldest winter, I was kept almost naked.... I had no bed.... The coldest nights, I used to steal a bag which was used for carrying corn to the mill. I would crawl into this bag, and there sleep on the cold, damp, clay floor....

I was probably between seven and eight years old when I left Colonel Lloyd's plantation. My old master [Anthony] had determined to let me go to Baltimore, to live with Mr. Hugh Auld, brother to my old master's son-in-law....

Very soon after I went to live with Mr. and Mrs. Auld, she kindly commenced to teach me the A, B, C. After I had learned this, she assisted [helped] me in learning to spell words of three or four letters. Just at this point of my progress, Mr. Auld found out what was going on, and at once forbade [would not allow] Mrs. Auld to instruct me further, telling her, among other things, that it was unlawful, as well as unsafe, to teach a

> **"You will be free as soon as you are twenty-one, but I am a slave for life!"**

slave to read.... I was saddened by the thought of losing the aid of my kind mistress. I set out with high hope to learn how to read.

I lived in Master Hugh's family about seven years. During this time, I succeeded in learning to read and write.... The plan which I adopted...was that of making friends of all the little white boys whom I met in the street.... I would say to them, I wished I could be as free as they would be when they got to 21.... "You will be free as soon as you are twenty-one, but I am a slave for life! Have not I as good a right to be free as you have?" These words used to trouble them....

I was not about twelve years old, and the thought of being a slave for life began to bear heavily upon my heart.... Every little while, I could hear something about the abolitionists.... If a slave ran away and succeeded in getting clear, or if a slave killed his master, set fire to a barn, or did any thing very wrong in the mind of a slaveholder, it was spoken of as the fruit of abolition....

My old master, Captain Anthony, died.... Now all the property of my old master was in the hands of strangers.... Not a slave was left free. All remained slaves, from the youngest to the old-ers.... [My old grandmother] had served my old master faithfully from youth to old age.... She was nevertheless left a slave—a slave for life.... She saw her children, her grandchildren, and her great grandchildren, divided like so many sheep.... My determination to run away was again revived.... When that time came, I was determined to be off."

Write Your Answers

Write the answer to each question in your notebook.

1. What was the monthly allowance of food for slaves on Colonel Lloyd's plantation?

2. What did Douglass do to fight the cold?

3. Who began to teach Douglass how to read?

4. Why did Douglass's words trouble the other children?

5. What made Douglass determined to run away?

REVIEW AND APPLY

■ During the 1800s many reform movements tried to correct the nation's problems.

■ Horace Mann, Noah Webster, Emma Willard, and Thomas Gallaudet worked for better education in the United States.

■ Abolitionists, such as William Lloyd Garrison and Fredrick Douglass, worked to end slavery.

■ Reformers, such as Lucretia Mott and Elizabeth Cady Stanton, fought for women's rights such as the rights to vote, to own property, and to be elected to public office.

■ Other reform movements worked toward improving prisons, hospitals, and workplaces.

■ During the 1800s an American culture continued to develop.

VOCABULARY

Writing with Vocabulary Words ■ **Use six or more vocabulary words to write a paragraph in your social studies notebook about some of the reform movements of the 1800s.**

committed	disabilities	asylums
reform	public office	labor
abolition	mental illness	labor union
political rights	criminals	literature

COMPREHENSION CHECK

Choose the Answer ■ **Write the letter of the word or phrase that best answers each question.**

1. Which statement describes American education before 1820?

   a. Most children went to public schools.
   b. Most children did not go to school.
   c. Most children went to private schools.

2. Who started the first school for deaf children?

   a. Reverend Thomas Gallaudet
   b. Emma Willard
   c. Mary Lyon

3. Where was the first conference on women's rights held?

   a. Boston, Massachusetts
   b. Seneca Falls, New York
   c. Washington, D.C.

4. In what reform movement was Dorothea Dix a leader?

   a. prison reform
   b. labor reform
   c. education reform

5. What did labor unions work for?

   a. prison reform
   b. a shorter workday
   c. to close factories

6. What religion did Joseph Smith start?

   a. Quaker
   b. Protestant
   c. Mormon

7. Which of the following people was a transcendentalist?

   a. Fredrick Douglass
   b. Henry David Thoreau
   c. Sojourner Truth

8. What was the Second Great Awakening?

   a. a religious movement
   b. a book by Ralph Waldo Emerson
   c. a prison reform group

CRITICAL THINKING

Distinguishing Relevant Information ■ Imagine you are telling a friend about the reform movements of the 1800s. Read each sentence below. Decide which sentences are relevant to what you will say. Write those sentences in your social studies notebook. There are four relevant sentences.

1. In the 1800s, women had very few political and social rights.

2. Many children in the 1800s had disabilities.

3. Some abolitionists started a colony called Liberia in West Africa.

4. Many women in the 1800s wore dresses.

5. In the 1800s many people with mental illnesses were treated like criminals.

6. Ralph Waldo Emerson was a good writer.

USING INFORMATION

Writing an Opinion ■ During the 1800s there were many reform movements. If you could have chosen only one of those movements to support, which one would it have been? Explain your answer.

Chapter 14

AMERICANS MOVE WESTWARD

◀ *Gold from California*

People

Moses Austin • Stephen Austin • Antonio López de Santa Anna • Sam Houston • Suzanna Dickenson • James Marshall • John Sutter

Places

Santa Fe • Oregon Country • Alamo • Goliad • San Jacinto River • Rio Grande • American River • Houston

New Vocabulary

execution • Manifest Destiny • missionaries • fertile • parallel • slogan • latitude • pass • blended • vaqueros • diverse

Focus on Main Ideas

1. How did Americans travel to Oregon and the Southwest in the 1800s?
2. How did Texas become an independent republic in 1836?
3. How did the ideas about Manifest Destiny affect the United States?
4. How did the United States win control of Texas, Oregon, and the Southwest?

As thousands of settlers moved west in the 1800s, they often traveled in long wagon trains. At times more than 100 covered wagons formed one wagon train. As they traveled, their wheels made deep cuts in the ground that formed trails. Those cuts can still be seen in the West today.

Americans Travel West

Thousands of Americans wanted to travel west to places like Santa Fe and the Oregon Country, but there were no roads or rivers to these areas. People had to travel in covered wagons. In 1821 a group of settlers met in St. Louis, Missouri. They formed a wagon train with their covered wagons, and together they traveled slowly to Santa Fe. The route they followed was known as the Santa Fe Trail. Thousands of people took this trail to the Southwest.

Other people headed west on the Oregon Trail to reach the Oregon Country. There were hardships and dangers on the Oregon Trail as people traveled across rivers, the Great Plains, and the Rocky Mountains. Wagon wheels could break, wagons could turn over, and there could be attacks from Indians along the way. At times it was difficult to find food.

People often traveled 12 hours each day. The wagon trains could not go faster than a few miles an hour, so it took many months to reach Oregon. Between 1843 and 1860, about 50,000 people traveled west on the Oregon Trail.

Americans dreamed of being able to travel by railroad from the East Coast on the Atlantic Ocean to the West Coast on the Pacific Ocean. By 1840 there were many railroads throughout the Northeast. A railroad was built that went as far west as Illinois. But railroads would not connect the Atlantic and Pacific coasts until 1869.

Many settlers headed west in covered wagons. Usually people did not ride in the slow-moving wagons because the wagons were filled with belongings.

Texas Becomes a Republic

Soon after Columbus reached the Americas in 1492, the Spanish explored Mexico and what is now the southwestern part of the United States. The Spanish called the region New Spain, and they ruled it for almost 300 years. Texas, Nevada, New Mexico, and California were in the northern part of New Spain. People who were born in Spain, instead of in America, held all the power. The Spanish governors who ruled New Spain did not allow representative government.

At that time Texas was part of northern Mexico. Many Indians lived in Texas, but only about 5,000 Mexicans had settled there. In 1820 Moses Austin, an American, asked the government of New Spain if he could start a colony in Texas. The government agreed because they wanted Americans to develop the area. Moses Austin died before he could start the colony.

Mexicans fought a long war to win independence from Spain. In 1821 Mexico won its freedom from Spain. The new Mexican government allowed Stephen Austin to carry out his father's plan for a colony in Texas. The Mexican government made five important rules for the American colonists. Americans had to speak Spanish, become Catholics, and become Mexican citizens. They had to obey Mexican laws, and they could not bring slaves to Texas.

Americans came to Texas because land was very cheap. By 1830 there were 20,000 settlers. There were more Americans than Mexicans in Texas. The Mexicans became angry because the Americans had brought 2,000 slaves to Texas, and the settlers were

177

The battle of San Jacinto ended the Texas Revolution. Santa Anna was captured and brought to Sam Houston, who was injured during the battle.

into the Alamo and killed every soldier. Fifteen women and children survived the battle. Santa Anna sent one woman, Suzanna Dickenson, to warn other Texans to end the revolt.

Meanwhile part of Santa Anna's army captured the town of Goliad. Santa Anna ordered the **execution** of nearly 400 Texans who were captured at Goliad. Texans were furious about what had happened at the Alamo and at Goliad.

On April 21, 1836, Sam Houston and the Texans attacked Santa Anna's army at the San Jacinto River. "Remember the Alamo! Remember Goliad!" they shouted as they fought the Mexican Army. In only 18 minutes the battle was over. Santa Anna and the Mexicans surrendered. The next day Santa Anna signed a treaty that said Texas was free.

Texas became an independent republic. Texans elected Sam Houston as their first president. They wrote a constitution that allowed slavery.

Most Texans wanted Texas to join the Union in 1836. But Andrew Jackson, the President at that time, was worried that there would be war with Mexico if Texas became a state. Also, the North did not want another slave state to join the Union. So Texas remained a republic until 1845. In that year Congress voted for Texas to become a state.

not obeying the five rules. Mexican leaders decided not to allow any more Americans to settle in Texas.

In 1835 the Texans decided they wanted to be free from Mexico. The president of Mexico, General Antonio López de Santa Anna, led soldiers to Texas to end the revolt. The war became known as the Texas Revolution. In March 1836, 59 delegates met in a convention in Texas. They wrote and signed the Texas Declaration of Independence. They also chose Sam Houston as their commander in chief.

While the convention was meeting, Santa Anna and 3,000 Mexican soldiers attacked a mission called the Alamo in the town of San Antonio. Inside the Alamo were only 187 Texan soldiers. Free African Americans as well as several slaves fought with the Texans. After many days of fighting, Santa Anna's soldiers forced their way

Manifest Destiny

During the 1840s many Americans believed that the United States should rule all the land between the Atlantic Ocean and the Pacific Ocean. This idea was called

Manifest Destiny. In 1845 James K. Polk became President. Before he was elected, Polk had promised to carry out the idea of Manifest Destiny. He had said that Oregon, Texas, and California would become part of the United States.

Since 1818 the United States and Great Britain had ruled the Oregon Country together. The Oregon Country was much larger than the state of Oregon today. It included what is now Idaho as well as part of Canada. At first, few Americans or British settled in Oregon. Then, in the 1830s, American **missionaries** became the first American settlers in Oregon. Their goal was to teach the Indians to be Christians.

Slowly more Americans traveled west along the Oregon Trail and settled in Oregon. People liked the **fertile** soil and pleasant climate of the Oregon Country. By 1846 there were more Americans than British in Oregon.

President Polk wanted the United States to rule all of Oregon. As you can see on the map on page 180, Oregon's northern border was at the 54°40′ **parallel**. Before the election Polk said he would fight to have all of Oregon. His **slogan** became "54°40′ or Fight."

In 1846 President Polk agreed to a compromise with Great Britain. The Oregon Country was divided at the 49th parallel, or 49° line of **latitude**. All of the land north of that line was part of Canada and was to be ruled by Great Britain. All of the land to the south of 49° became part of the United States and was called the Oregon Territory. This land would later become parts of three states—Oregon, Washington, and Idaho.

War with Mexico

Texas became a state shortly before Polk became President. Polk also wanted California and all land between California and Texas to belong to the United States. But Mexico ruled this land. When Polk asked Mexico to sell the land to the United States, the Mexican government refused.

The Mexicans were very angry when Texas became a state. Their anger grew when Mexico and the United States did not agree on where the southern border of Texas should be. The United States said the Texas border was a river called the Rio Grande. Mexico insisted that Texas should be smaller. Both nations sent soldiers to the Rio Grande in 1846. The Mexicans crossed the Rio Grande, and a short battle took place. American and Mexican soldiers were killed. Polk asked Congress to declare war against Mexico. After all, Polk said, Mexico had attacked Americans in Texas. But the Mexicans believed that it was the Americans who had been on Mexican land. Congress declared war in 1846, and the Mexican War began.

During the Mexican War, Americans captured California. The American Army went south into Mexico. After many months of fighting, Americans captured the Mexican capital, Mexico City. Although Mexicans had fought bravely throughout the war, they agreed to surrender.

In 1848 the leaders of Mexico and the United States signed a peace treaty called the Treaty of Guadalupe Hidalgo. The treaty said that Texas was part of the United States, and the southern border of Texas was the Rio Grande. California and the land between Texas and California belonged to the United States. The United States agreed to pay Mexico $15 million for its land. Mexico had lost half of its land to the United States. The treaty allowed all Mexicans in the Southwest to become United States citizens.

The land the United States won in 1848 was called the Mexican Cession. As you can see on the map below, the Mexican Cession would become five states—California, Nevada, Utah, Arizona, and New Mexico—as well as parts of three other states.

In 1853 Mexico agreed to sell another piece of land to the United States for $10 million. This land to the south of the Mexican Cession was called the Gadsden Purchase. The United States bought this land because there was a **pass**, or a path, through its mountains. Americans planned to build a railroad through the pass.

The Blending of Cultures in the Southwest

Mexicans in the Southwest became American citizens after the Mexican War. Parts of Mexican culture and American culture have **blended** together in the Southwest. Many years before, the Indian and Spanish cultures had blended to form Mexican culture.

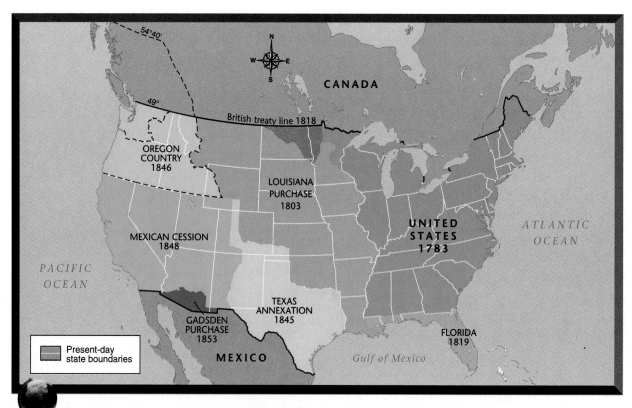

The United States Grows 1783–1853 *The idea of Manifest Destiny came true as the nation grew to include Texas, Oregon, and the Mexican Cession. What part of the United States was added in 1853?*

The blending of cultures and the influence of Spain and Mexico can be seen in these two photographs. The town on the left is in Mexico. The building on the right is in Oregon. Notice how both the style of the homes and the use of tiles is similar.

The first people in the region, the Indians, had developed irrigation systems to water their crops. The Indians were the first to grow corn, wheat, beans, and cotton. They also grew spicy chili peppers.

When the Spanish conquered Mexico, the Spanish built missions where they taught the Catholic religion to the Indians. The Spanish also brought the first horses and cows to America from Europe. They built huge ranches where they forced Indians to work at caring for cattle and sheep. Years later Americans would learn these skills from Mexican cowboys, who were called **vaqueros**.

Mexican culture included great respect for parents. Mexican food included both Spanish and Indian foods. Like the Spanish, Mexicans built houses with white walls and red tiled roofs. That style continues to be popular in the Southwest today.

When the Mexican Cession became part of the United States, Americans and Mexicans learned from each other. Americans taught Mexicans to have jury trials for people who were accused of crimes. They showed Mexicans how to use better seeds and tools to grow crops.

From the Mexicans, Americans learned how to irrigate the dry desert and to mine silver and other metals. Americans also adopted two Mexican laws. One law allowed married women to own property together with their husband. Another law said landowners could not take away a neighbor's water supply. This law helped protect the way water was used in the dry Southwest.

181

Forty-niners looked for gold by separating it from gravel. The gravel was shoveled into water, which was then stirred. The lighter gravel would float, leaving the heavier gold at the bottom.

The blend of Mexican and American cultures created a new southwestern culture. This culture can be seen today in laws, foods, music, and houses of the region.

There's Gold in California

In January 1848 a man named James Marshall was building a mill on the American River for John Sutter. While building Sutter's Mill, Marshall discovered gold. The news that there was gold in California spread quickly. By 1849 California had a gold rush.

The people who went to California in 1849 to find gold were called forty-niners.

Teachers left their schools and farmers left their farms as they rushed to look for gold in California. Some slave owners brought their slaves to California to help them look for gold. Free African Americans also searched for gold in California.

Some people traveled by ship all the way around South America to reach California. Most people traveled in covered wagons and followed trails over the mountains. Often they stopped along the way at the Mormon settlement at the Great Salt Lake. The Mormons grew wealthy as the forty-niners bought food and supplies for their trip to California. People from every part of the world rushed to California to find gold. Many came from Europe. Thousands came from Asia. In 1851 about 20,000 Chinese came to find gold.

Some lucky people found gold in California and became very rich. Most people did not become rich. But California's population grew quickly because of the gold rush. San Francisco grew from a small town into a busy city. By 1850 California had enough people to become a state. In that year California joined the Union as a free state.

Because of the gold rush, California's population became **diverse**. Chinese immigrants, African Americans, and white settlers went to California and stayed. More Indians and Mexicans joined the ones who were already there. Each group helped to create a special culture in California.

Americans had reached their goal of Manifest Destiny. By 1848 the United States ruled all the land between the Atlantic and Pacific oceans.

Sam Houston 1793-1863

Sam Houston was a leader in Texas for almost thirty years. But he did many other things before arriving in Texas. Houston is the only person in American history to serve as the governor of two states.

Sam Houston ran away from his home in Tennessee to live with the Cherokee when he was 15. Later he fought in the War of 1812, opened a new school, became a lawyer, and was elected to Congress. Then he was elected governor of Tennessee. While he was governor, Houston's wife left him and returned to her family. An unhappy Houston gave up his job as governor.

Houston moved to Texas and later became a leader in the Texas Revolution. He was chosen as commander in chief of the Texas Army. He led the Texans to win the Battle of San Jacinto. Santa Anna and his soldiers had taken an afternoon nap when Houston and his soldiers made a surprise attack. The Mexican Army surrendered. Texas became an independent republic.

Houston was elected as the first president of Texas. After Texas joined the Union, Houston was elected to the United States Senate. He represented Texas for 13 years.

Sam Houston ran for governor of Texas in 1857. To win votes Houston made 67 speeches in different parts of Texas. Houston lost the 1857 election, but he ran again and won in 1859.

While Houston was governor, the battle between the North and the South over slavery grew angrier. In 1861 Texans decided to leave the Union because of the slavery issue. When Houston refused to allow Texas to leave the Union, he was forced to resign as governor. People called him a traitor. He died two years later during the Civil War.

The city of Houston, Texas, was named to honor the man who helped Texas become both an independent republic and a state.

In Your Own Words

Use examples from Houston's biography to write a paragraph that tells what kind of person you think Houston was, a hero or a traitor.

AMERICAN GEOGRAPHY

Human/Environmental Interaction: The Oregon Trail

Starting in 1843, thousands of Americans traveled west on the Oregon Trail. Their wagon wheels made deep cuts in the earth that we can still see today. As they climbed into the Rocky Mountains, they had to make their wagons lighter. So they left a trail as they threw away their belongings. Forts were built on the trail to protect settlers from Indian attacks. Forts became places where people could get supplies. During the long trip, people learned how to be on their own by fixing wagon wheels and hunting buffalo.

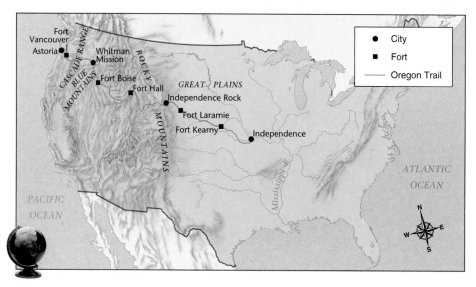

Study the map and read the paragraphs above to learn about changes in the West as people traveled on the Oregon Trail. Then answer the questions.

1. Where did the Oregon Trail begin?

2. List four forts that were built along the trail.

3. Why were forts useful to travelers on the Oregon Trail?

4. Which three mountain ranges did the pioneers cross?

5. Name a city built along the trail.

6. How did people change the landscape along the Oregon Trail?

7. People changed during the trip to Oregon. Give an example of how they changed.

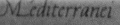

REVIEW AND APPLY

- In the mid-1800s, travelers formed wagon trains and traveled together to places such as Santa Fe and the Oregon Country.

- In 1836 Texas became independent from Mexico and started its own republic. Nine years later it became the forty-fifth state in the United States.

- During the 1840s many Americans believed in Manifest Destiny, the idea that the United States should rule all the land between the Atlantic and Pacific oceans.

- The United States and Great Britain reached an agreement dividing Oregon.

- The United States and Mexico went to war in 1846. After the war the United States gained control of the Southwest.

- Parts of the Mexican and the American cultures have blended together in the Southwest.

- A gold rush in California led to California becoming a state in 1850.

VOCABULARY

Find the Meaning ■ In the assignment section of your social studies notebook, write the word or phrase that best completes each sentence.

1. In an **execution** a person is ———— .
   killed   elected to public office   made a citizen

2. **Manifest Destiny** was a(n) ———— .
   law   idea   new colony

3. As a result of the **Mexican Cession**, the United States ——— territory.
   sold   lost   purchased

4. The **Gadsden Purchase** was made by ———— .
   Mexico   the United States   Spain

5. A **pass** is a ———— .
   wagon   river   path

6. Things that have **blended** have ———— .
   come together   separated   fought against one another

7. A **vaquero** is a Mexican ———— .
   cowboy   politician   soldier

8. A **diverse** population is one that has people from ———— .
   the same place   many different places   the same continent

COMPREHENSION CHECK

Finish the Paragraph ■ Use the words in the box to finish the paragraph. In your social studies notebook, write the numbers 1 through 8. Next to each number, write the correct word or phrase. There is an extra word that you will not use.

> republic   Mexico   colony   Oregon Trail
> Manifest Destiny   Utah   forty-niners   Texas   Cession

In the 1800s Americans were moving west. People using the __1__ crossed rivers and the Rocky Mountains on their way to the Oregon Country. Some Americans followed Stephen Austin into __2__ to start a colony there. Texas became an independent __3__ in 1836 and a state in the United States in 1845. Many Americans of this time believed in the idea of __4__ . The United States did reach from coast to coast as a result of the war in 1848 with __5__ . The purchase of the Mexican __6__ gave the United States land that would become the states of California, Nevada, New Mexico, Arizona, and __7__ . Miners who rushed to California in 1849 became known as __8__ .

CRITICAL THINKING

Sequencing Information ■ In your social studies notebook, write the following sentences in their correct order.

Gold is discovered in California.

In 1845 James Polk becomes President of the United States.

California becomes a state.

In 1830 there are more Americans than Mexicans living in Texas.

The Mexican War begins.

The Battle of the Alamo takes place during the Texas Revolution.

USING INFORMATION

Writing an Essay ■ During the 1840s the boundaries of the United States expanded. Write an essay explaining how the United States gained one of the following: the Oregon Country, Texas, or the Mexican Cession.

186

SOCIAL STUDIES SKILLS

Using Lines of Latitude and Longitude

Lines of **latitude** and **longitude** are imaginary lines that form a grid that helps you find places on maps and globes. Lines of latitude run east and west around the earth. Lines of longitude run north and south. Lines of latitude and longitude are identi-fied with a direction and a number that stands for the degrees, or parts, of a circle. For example, New Orleans has a latitude of 30°N, read as "thirty degrees north." The longitude of New Orleans is 90°W. We say its latitude and longitude are 30°N/90°W.

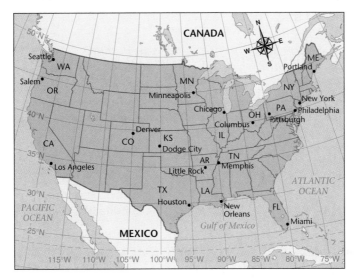

A. Study the map. Then write the latitude for each city.

1. Philadelphia, PA

2. Minneapolis, MN

3. Little Rock, AR

4. Salem, OR

B. Write the longitude for each city.

1. Philadelphia, PA

2. Dodge City, KS

3. Denver, CO

4. Pittsburgh, PA

C. Write the latitude and the longitude for each city. Always write the latitude first.

1. Philadelphia, PA

2. Memphis, TN

3. Houston, TX

Unit 3 Review

Study the time line on this page. You may want to read parts of Unit 3 again. In the assignment section of your notebook, write the numbers 1 through 14. Then use the words and the dates in the box to finish the paragraphs. The box has one possible answer that you will not use.

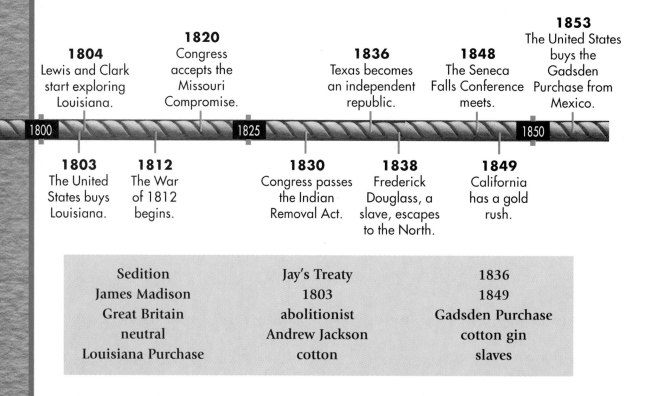

1853
The United States buys the Gadsden Purchase from Mexico.

1804
Lewis and Clark start exploring Louisiana.

1820
Congress accepts the Missouri Compromise.

1836
Texas becomes an independent republic.

1848
The Seneca Falls Conference meets.

1800   1825   1850

1803
The United States buys Louisiana.

1812
The War of 1812 begins.

1830
Congress passes the Indian Removal Act.

1838
Frederick Douglass, a slave, escapes to the North.

1849
California has a gold rush.

Sedition	Jay's Treaty	1836
James Madison	1803	1849
Great Britain	abolitionist	Gadsden Purchase
neutral	Andrew Jackson	cotton gin
Louisiana Purchase	cotton	slaves

    In 1789 George Washington became the first President. Washington believed the United States should be ___1___ when dealing with other nations. To avoid war with Great Britain, George Washington approved ___2___ in 1794. While John Adams was President, the Alien and ___3___ acts were passed. In ___4___ President

Thomas Jefferson agreed to buy Louisiana from France for $15 million. Then in 1804 Jefferson asked Lewis and Clark to explore the __5__. Although __6__ seized many American ships at sea, Jefferson avoided going to war. Later, Henry Clay and the War Hawks urged President __7__ to fight Great Britain in the War of 1812.

After the __8__ was invented in 1793, southern planters grew more cotton. Planters needed more __9__ to work in the cotton fields. During the Industrial Revolution, many textile mills were built in the North. These mills needed __10__ from the South.

President __11__ approved the Indian Removal Act in 1830, and thousands of Indians were forced to move to Oklahoma. Frederick Douglass escaped to freedom and became an important __12__. Texas became an independent republic in __13__. Mexico lost a lot of land after the United States won the Mexican War. The population of California grew rapidly during the gold rush of __14__.

Looking Ahead to Unit 4

The differences between North and South grew stronger as western territories wanted to become states. The question of whether the new states should be free states or slave states continued to tear the nation apart. After 1850 the North and South grew farther apart. From 1861 to 1865 the North and South fought the Civil War.

As you read Unit 4, think about the people who led the North and South during the Civil War. Find out why the North defeated the South. Find out how life changed for African Americans during this time. Read on to learn how events led the North and South to fight the terrible Civil War.

Unit 4

THE CIVIL WAR AND RECONSTRUCTION

As they marched into battle, many Northern soldiers asked themselves "Will I be fighting against my Southern cousin or best friend today?" Southern soldiers shared the same worries. The Civil War divided American families and friends in both the North and the South. In 1865, after 600,000 soldiers died, the North and the South became one nation again.

As you read Unit 4, you will learn how slavery and other problems divided the nation. Find out how the long Civil War changed the United States. Discover how Americans rebuilt their nation.

1850			1860			

1852
Harriet Beecher Stowe writes *Uncle Tom's Cabin*.

1857
The Supreme Court makes the Dred Scott Decision.

1860
Abraham Lincoln is elected President.

1861
The Civil War begins at Fort Sumter.

1862
The battle of Antietam is fought.

1863
Lincoln signs the Emancipation Proclamation.

Americans today act as Union soldiers marching into battle.

1865
The Confederate Army surrenders.

1867
Congress passes its first Reconstruction Act.

1870
The Fifteenth Amendment is ratified.

1881
The first Jim Crow law is passed.

1870

1865
Congress passes the Thirteenth Amendment to end slavery.

1868
The Fourteenth Amendment is ratified.

1877
Reconstruction ends.

1896
The Supreme Court's decision in *Plessy* v. *Ferguson* allows segregation.

Chapter 15 — NORTH AND SOUTH DISAGREE

◀ cotton plant

People

Gabriel Prosser • Nat Turner • Harriet Tubman • Daniel Webster • Harriet Beecher Stowe • Stephen Douglas • James Buchanan • Dred Scott • Roger B. Taney • John Brown • Abraham Lincoln • Jefferson Davis

Places

Richmond • Harpers Ferry

New Vocabulary

rebellions • secede • popular sovereignty • debates • novel • Free Soilers • opposed • arsenal • nominated • Confederate States of America • Confederacy

Focus on Main Ideas

1. How did the Compromise of 1850 keep peace in the United States for ten years?
2. How did Bleeding Kansas, John Brown, and the Dred Scott decision further divide the North and the South?
3. What caused some Southern states to form their own nation?

As the years passed, the differences between the North and the South grew stronger. By 1861 those differences were so serious that some Southern states decided they could no longer be part of the United States.

Differences Between the North and the South

By 1850 the North and the South had grown further apart. The North had changed into a region of factories, railroads, and large cities. Millions of immigrants had settled throughout the North. African Americans in the North were not allowed to vote in most states. People in the North believed that the nation needed a strong federal government.

The South, with its smaller population, small farms, and large plantations, was very different from the North. The South had fewer cities, immigrants, factories, and railroads. The South's economy depended on slaves to work on cotton, sugar, and tobacco plantations. Most Southerners believed in states' rights and wanted the federal government to have less power.

The biggest problem between the North and the South was over the issue of slavery.

Northern abolitionists wanted to end slavery. Most Southerners were against all efforts to end slavery.

Slaves Struggle for Freedom

Slave owners lived in fear that their slaves might rebel against them. Sometimes **rebellions** did happen. One slave rebellion was led by a slave named Gabriel Prosser in 1800. He gathered about 1,000 slaves and planned to attack Richmond, Virginia. The rebellion failed, and Prosser and 36 of his followers were hanged. Nat Turner led a slave rebellion in Virginia in 1831 that frightened slave owners in the South.

Some slaves won their freedom by running away to the North and to Canada. They received help from a secret organization called the Underground Railroad. Members, or "conductors," hid runaway slaves in homes and barns as they escaped to the North.

Most slaves never returned to the South after they escaped, but a few brave people came back to help others. Harriet Tubman returned many times and led about 300 slaves to freedom. Another slave, Arnold Cragston, escaped to the North. He returned to the South many times and rowed hundreds of runaway slaves across the Ohio River to freedom.

Nat Turner led a slave rebellion in Virginia in 1831. Turner and his followers killed 57 slave owners on several plantations. It took about two months for soldiers to capture Turner. He and about 20 of his followers were hanged.

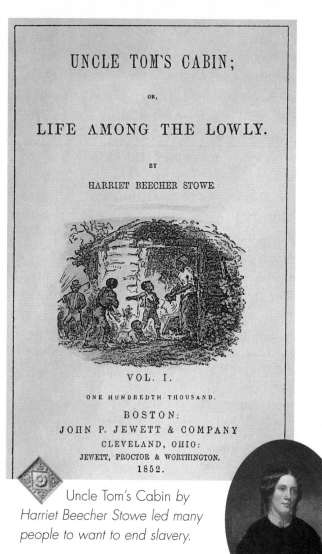

Uncle Tom's Cabin by Harriet Beecher Stowe led many people to want to end slavery.

The Compromise of 1850

As Americans moved west, slavery became an issue in the territories of the Mexican Cession. California wanted to join the Union as a free state. The South did not want this to happen. If California joined the Union as a free state, there would be more free states than slave states. Since the North would then have more power in the Senate, it could pass laws against slavery. Some Southern states threatened to **secede,** or leave the Union, if slavery was not allowed in the Western territories.

Southerners were also angry because Northerners were helping slaves escape to freedom. When Northerners wanted to abolish slavery in the nation's capital, people in the South grew angrier.

Once again the nation turned to Senator Henry Clay. In 1820 he had written the Missouri Compromise. Clay was now old and sick, but he wanted to save his country. So he put together another compromise plan that became known as the Compromise of 1850.

The Compromise of 1850 had four main parts. First, California would join the Union as a free state. Second, the people's vote, or **popular sovereignty**, would be used to decide if there would be slavery in the New Mexico and Utah territories. Third, a stricter Fugitive Slave Act would force people in the North to return runaway slaves to the South. Fourth, slaves would no longer be bought and sold in Washington, D.C., but slavery was still allowed in the capital.

No one was really happy with the Compromise of 1850. But it seemed to be the only way to keep the nation together. Senator Daniel Webster of Massachusetts urged Congress to pass the Compromise in order to save the nation. After seven months of **debates**, Congress passed the laws that formed the Compromise of 1850.

Uncle Tom's Cabin

In 1852 a new **novel** called *Uncle Tom's Cabin* turned thousands of people against slavery. Harriet Beecher Stowe, an abolitionist, wrote the book to show the evils of slavery. The book quickly became a bestseller. It was made into a play and performed in theaters across the country. After reading the book or seeing the play, many Northerners wanted to end slavery. People in the South accused Stowe of telling lies about slave owners. This paragraph from *Uncle Tom's Cabin* shows how cruel slavery could be:

"My master bought my oldest sister. At first I was glad she was bought, for I had one friend near me. I was soon sorry for it.... I have stood at the door and heard her whipped, when it seemed as if every blow cut into my naked heart, and I couldn't do anything to help her...."

Trouble in Kansas

Senator Stephen Douglas wanted to build a railroad across the West through his state of Illinois. But Douglas needed votes from Southern states to pass the bill that would approve the railroad. Douglas knew that the Southern states wanted slavery to be allowed in every state. However, the Missouri Compromise prevented slavery on land north of Missouri's southern border. To get the votes from Southern states, Douglas wrote the Kansas-Nebraska Act of 1854. This law created two new territories, Kansas and Nebraska. The new law allowed popular sovereignty to decide if slavery would be allowed in these territories. The Kansas-Nebraska Act repealed the Missouri Compromise.

Kansas would be the first territory to vote on whether to allow slavery. People who favored slavery and people who were against slavery quickly moved into Kansas.

Each side was determined to have a majority of voters. When the election took place, there were enough votes to allow slavery in Kansas. The people who were against slavery, the **Free Soilers**, refused to accept this decision. The Free Soilers started their own government in Kansas. Kansas then had two governments, one that favored slavery and another that **opposed** it. Terrible fighting broke out between the two sides. By 1856 more than 200 people had been killed and so many others were hurt that the Kansas territory became known as "Bleeding Kansas."

Eventually the Free Soilers won control of the government in Kansas. They passed laws to end slavery. Kansas wanted to join the Union as a free state, but Southerners in Congress voted against it.

"Bleeding Kansas" affected the presidential election in 1856. A new party, the Republican party, was formed. Its goal was to stop the spread of slavery into the West. This party was not the same Republican party of Thomas Jefferson.

The Democratic party, once Andrew Jackson's party, was now a divided party. It was split between Southern Democrats, who favored slavery, and Northern Democrats, who opposed slavery. James Buchanan, a Northern Democrat, was elected President in 1856. Buchanan supported popular sovereignty.

The Dred Scott Decision

The North and the South moved even further apart when the United States Supreme Court ruled on the court case of Dred Scott in 1857. Dred Scott was a slave

Although the Supreme Court ruled in 1857 that Dred Scott was property, his owner freed him shortly after the decision.

The decision in the Dred Scott case told the nation that slavery must be allowed in all territories. The Supreme Court used its power of judicial review in this decision. The Court decided that the Missouri Compromise was unconstitutional because it prevented slaveholders from bringing their property, in the form of slaves, into the Western territories. The Dred Scott decision pleased Southerners, but it made Northerners furious.

After the Dred Scott decision, some Americans felt that only fighting would end slavery. One of these people was an abolitionist named John Brown. In 1859 Brown captured the federal **arsenal** and its weapons in Harpers Ferry, Virginia. He planned to give the weapons to slaves so they could attack their owners. Brown was captured before he could carry out his plans. Brown and his followers were put on trial, found guilty, and hanged.

To many abolitionists in the North, John Brown was a great hero. When Southerners saw how much abolitionists admired Brown, they were convinced that the North wanted to end slavery.

The Republican Party Wins Power

The main goal of the Republican party was to stop the spread of slavery into the West. Republicans also wanted high tariffs to protect Northern industries. Most party members were from the North and the West. One member was a tall, thin lawyer from Illinois named Abraham Lincoln.

In 1858 the Republican party in Illinois **nominated** Lincoln to be its candidate for the United States Senate. When Lincoln

in Missouri. He had worked for his owner in a free territory and in the free state of Illinois. After they moved back to Missouri, Scott's owner died. In 1846 Scott sued for his freedom. Scott said that he should be free because he had lived on free soil. The Dred Scott case went to the Supreme Court.

In 1857 the Supreme Court ruled against Scott and said he was still a slave. Chief Justice Roger B. Taney wrote that Scott was not a citizen because African Americans were not citizens and did not have the right to bring their cases to court. Taney added that since Scott was a slave, he was the property of his owner. The Fifth Amendment to the Constitution protects a person's right to own property. Taney concluded that the Fifth Amendment allowed people to take their property, including their slaves, anywhere in the nation.

agreed to run for the Senate, he made a speech that said the nation could not continue to be divided over slavery:

"A house divided against itself cannot stand. I believe this government cannot endure permanently half slave and half free...."

In the election for the Senate, Lincoln ran against Senator Stephen Douglas. Douglas agreed to be in debates with Lincoln throughout Illinois. Because newspapers throughout the nation had stories about the debates, the two candidates became famous in every part of the country. Douglas won the Senate election in 1858.

In 1860 there were four candidates for President. The Republican party chose Abraham Lincoln as its candidate. The Democratic party split into Northern Democrats and Southern Democrats. Stephen Douglas, promising to allow popular sovereignty, was the candidate of the Northern Democrats. The Southern Democrats chose John C. Breckinridge, who supported slavery. A new political party, the Constitutional-Union party, nominated John Bell of Tennessee. Bell did not favor or oppose slavery.

Lincoln won the election of 1860. He received a majority of electoral votes, but none were from the South.

The South Secedes

Southerners had threatened to secede if Lincoln won the election. Although Lincoln won the election in November 1860, he would not be inaugurated until March 1861.

South Carolina did not wait until March. In December 1860 South Carolina

CHARLESTON
MERCURY
EXTRA:

Passed unanimously at 1.15 o'clock, P. M. December 20th, 1860.

AN ORDINANCE

To dissolve the Union between the State of South Carolina and other States united with her under the compact entitled "The Constitution of the United States of America."

We, the People of the State of South Carolina, in Convention assembled, do declare and ordain, and it is hereby declared and ordained,

That the Ordinance adopted by us in Convention, on the twenty-third day of May, in the year of our Lord one thousand seven hundred and eighty-eight, whereby the Constitution of the United States of America was ratified, and also, all Acts and parts of Acts of the General Assembly of this State, ratifying amendments of the said Constitution, are hereby repealed; and that the union now subsisting between South Carolina and other States, under the name of "The United States of America," is hereby dissolved.

THE
UNION
IS
DISSOLVED!

This headline from a newspaper in Charleston, South Carolina, announced that South Carolina had seceded from the Union.

seceded. Before Lincoln's inauguration, six more Southern states seceded. Their leaders formed a new nation, the **Confederate States of America**. They wrote a constitution that protected slavery and favored states' rights. Jefferson Davis was elected president of the **Confederacy**.

The struggle between the North and the South had finally caused the Union to divide. No one knew how very difficult it would be to unite the North and the South into one nation again.

BIOGRAPHY

Harriet Tubman 1820(?)–1913

Harriet Tubman was an escaped slave who helped groups of slaves escape to the North. She was one of the most famous leaders of the Underground Railroad which, helped slaves escape to freedom.

Tubman grew up as a slave in Maryland. When she was about 13 years old, she received a terrible blow on her head when she tried to save another slave from punishment. After that Tubman suffered from sleeping spells that could cause her to fall asleep at any time of the day or night.

Harriet Tubman grew up to be a short but very strong woman. Her father taught her how to survive in the woods. From him she learned which plants were safe to eat. She had also learned how to use the North Star to travel north at night. In 1849 with help from the Underground Railroad, Harriet Tubman escaped to freedom in Philadelphia.

Congress passed a strict Fugitive Slave Act as part of the Compromise of 1850. It became more dangerous than ever to help runaway slaves. But danger did not stop Tubman. She made 19 trips back to Maryland. She helped more than 300 slaves, including her parents, escape to the North and to Canada.

Slave catchers throughout the South tried to find and capture Tubman. A reward in the amount of $40,000 would go to the person who caught her. But Tubman used many disguises, and she was never caught.

Harriet Tubman knew John Brown, and she admired him. But she did not join him when he attacked the arsenal at Harpers Ferry in 1859.

During the Civil War, Tubman worked as a nurse. She also served as a spy and a scout for the Union Army.

Tubman lived to be more than ninety years old. Many Americans called this brave woman Moses. Like Moses in the Bible, Tubman led her people from slavery to freedom.

In Your Own Words

In the journal section of your notebook, write a paragraph that explains why Harriet Tubman earned the name "Moses."

REVIEW AND APPLY

- By 1850 slavery was the biggest issue separating the North and the South.

- The Compromise of 1850 was an agreement that kept the nation together.

- The Kansas Territory became known as "Bleeding Kansas" because so many people were hurt or killed while trying to settle the issue of slavery in the territory.

- In 1857 the Supreme Court decided in the Dred Scott case that slaves were the property of their owner and could be taken by their owner anywhere in the nation.

- In 1860 Abraham Lincoln won the presidential election. As a result, seven Southern states seceded from the Union and created the Confederate States of America.

VOCABULARY

Finish the Sentence ■ In your social studies notebook, write the word or phrase from the box that best completes each sentence. You will not use all the words in the box.

1. Some slaves like Gabriel Prosser led _____ against their slave owners.

2. Some Southern states threatened to _____, or leave, the Union if slavery was not allowed in the West.

3. Harriet Beecher Stowe wrote the _____ called *Uncle Tom's Cabin.*

4. John Brown captured the federal _____ in Harpers Ferry, Virginia, where weapons were stored.

5. In 1860 the Republican party _____ Abraham Lincoln to be its candidate for President.

6. _____, or the people's vote, was used in many places to decide on the issue of slavery.

7. _____ was the name given to people who opposed the spread of slavery into new states and territories.

> novel
> rebellions
> opposed
> secede
> nominated
> popular sovereignty
> arsenal
> Free Soilers

USING INFORMATION

Writing an Opinion ■ The Dred Scott Decision was a major setback for people who opposed slavery. Considering the period in which it was made, do you think it was the correct decision to make? Explain your answer.

COMPREHENSION CHECK

Who Said It? ■ Read each statement in Group A. Then match the name of the person in Group B who might have said it. You will not use all the names in Group B.

Group A	Group B
1. "I wrote the Compromise of 1850."	A. Stephen Douglas
2. "My book showed the evils of slavery."	B. John Brown
3. "I was elected senator from Illinois in 1858."	C. Henry Clay
4. "I was the Northern Democrat who was elected President in 1856."	D. Abraham Lincoln
	E. Dred Scott
5. "I helped many slaves to freedom through the Underground Railroad."	F. Harriet Beecher Stowe
6. "I was elected president of the Confederate States of America."	G. Jefferson Davis
	H. James Buchanan
7. "My raid on Harpers Ferry made me a hero to many Northern abolitionists."	I. Harriet Tubman
8. "I was a slave who sued for my freedom."	

CRITICAL THINKING

Categories ■ Read the words in each group. Choose one of the phrases from the box as a title for the group. Write the title in your social studies notebook. One of the titles in the box is not used.

> Dred Scott Decision   Underground Railroad   Compromise of 1850
> Confederate States of America   Nat Turner's Rebellion

1. took place in Virginia in 1831
   57 slave owners were killed
   its leader was captured and hanged

2. made up of seven Southern states
   opposed President Lincoln
   their constitution protected slavery and favored states' rights

3. admitted California to the Union as a free state
   forced Northerners to return runaway slaves
   allowed people in New Mexico and Utah territories to vote on the slavery issue

4. a secret organization
   leaders included Arnold Cragston
   helped many slaves escape to freedom

SOCIAL STUDIES SKILLS

Reading an Election Map

An **election map** shows how different areas vote in an election. The map on this page shows for each state the number of electoral votes each candidate won in the election of 1860. The key identifies which color represents each candidate. For example, Breckinridge won Florida's three electoral votes. This map shows us that sectionalism and slavery affected the election of 1860.

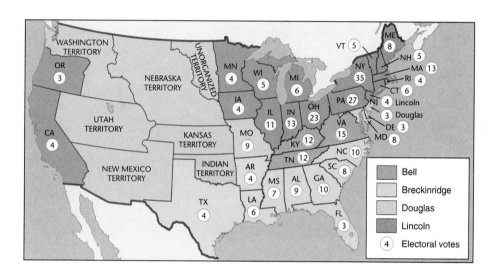

Study the map and its map key. Then answer the questions.

1. Name three states in which John Bell won electoral votes.

2. How many electoral votes did Douglas win?

3. How many states voted for Breckinridge?

4. Which state had the most electoral votes in 1860?

5. In which part of the nation did Breckinridge win electoral votes?

6. For which candidate did the western states vote?

7. In which part of the nation did Lincoln win electoral votes?

8. Did Lincoln win electoral votes in any Southern states?

9. How did the question of slavery affect the election of 1860?

Chapter 16

THE BEGINNING OF THE CIVIL WAR

◀ Civil War cannon

People

Robert E. Lee • Thomas "Stonewall" Jackson • George McClellan • David Farragut • Ulysses S. Grant

Places

Fort Sumter • Manassas • Bull Run • Antietam Creek • Sharpsburg

New Vocabulary

rejoin • ammunition • border states • draft • Anaconda Plan • prey • income tax • defensive war

Focus on Main Ideas

1. How did the Civil War begin?
2. What were the different goals of the Union and the Confederacy during the Civil War?
3. What advantages did each side have during the Civil War?
4. What happened during the early battles of the war?

In 1861 Americans began to fight the worst war the nation had ever known. From the first days of the Civil War, families and friends were divided about which side to support. During this bitter war, brothers, friends, fathers, and sons fought on opposite sides and attacked each other in battles. Even President Lincoln's wife, Mary, had brothers who were Confederate soldiers.

Shots Fired at Fort Sumter

Seven Southern states had formed a new nation called the Confederate States of America shortly before Abraham Lincoln became President. Southerners felt that their differences with the North were too great to allow them to remain part of the United States. The Confederates wanted to leave the Union peacefully. Although Lincoln did not want a war between North and South, he said that he would fight to keep the United States together.

On March 4, 1861, Lincoln became the President of a divided nation. In his inaugural speech, he asked the South to **rejoin** the Union and to avoid war. He told the South, "We are not enemies, but friends. We must not be enemies." But within a few weeks, they were at war.

Fort Sumter in Charleston Harbor, South Carolina, belonged to the United States Army. But the Confederates said that the United States must give Fort Sumter to them because it was on Confederate land. Lincoln refused to surrender the fort. Instead he sent ships with supplies for the Union soldiers at Fort Sumter.

The Confederates said that it was an act of war for the Union to send supplies to a fort on Confederate land. So on April 12, 1861, the Civil War began with the Confederate attack on Fort Sumter. On April 13 the Union soldiers at the fort ran out of **ammunition** and surrendered. The Confederates had won the first battle.

Taking Sides in the Civil War

Each side had different goals during the Civil War. The Confederates were fighting to have their own independent nation. The North was fighting so that the South would remain part of the United States. Ending slavery was not Lincoln's goal in 1861. Lincoln did not talk about the issue of slavery because eight slave states still remained in the Union. These states were called **border states** because they were between the Union and the Confederacy.

Soon after Fort Sumter surrendered, four border states seceded and joined the Confederacy. Virginia, Tennessee,

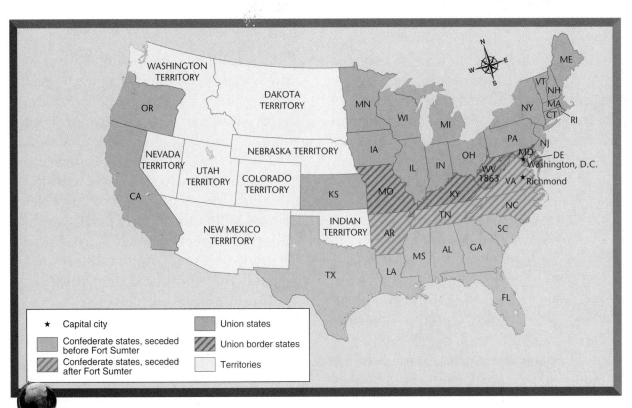

The Nation Divides *Before shots were fired on Fort Sumter, seven states had left the Union. After Fort Sumter four more states left the Union. Part of Virginia would not secede and became West Virginia, a Union state, in 1863. What city was the Confederate capital?*

203

The North was able to produce more war supplies than the South because there were more factories in the North.

Army were often called "Yankees" or "Yanks." People called Confederate soldiers "Rebels" or "Johnny Reb." Confederates wore gray uniforms.

In 1861 the Union and the Confederacy asked for thousands of men to volunteer to be soldiers. At first many men on both sides wanted to fight. They believed that the war would end quickly. As men left home to become soldiers, they often joked that they would be "home in time for dinner." But as the war dragged on and thousands died, many more soldiers were needed. Both the Union and the Confederacy passed **draft** laws that required men to be soldiers.

Each Side Had Advantages

Union soldiers had many reasons to believe that they would win the war and soon be "home for dinner." The Union had almost four times as many soldiers. With almost 23 million people, the Union had a much larger population. The Union also had more money to pay for the war. Union farms grew more food. Most of the nation's factories and railroads were in the North. During the war, the North's factories produced its needed weapons, ammunition, and supplies. The North used its railroads to move its troops and supplies.

The Confederacy seemed to have few advantages in 1861. The Confederate states had less than nine million people. Forty percent of those people were slaves who were not allowed to fight in the war. The Confederacy had less food and fewer factories, soldiers, and railroads. But the people in the Confederacy were fighting to have their

North Carolina, and Arkansas gave the Confederacy 11 states. Richmond, Virginia, became the Confederate capital. People in the western part of Virginia did not want to secede with the rest of Virginia. They formed the new state of West Virginia when they joined the Union in 1863.

Four other border states—Delaware, Maryland, Kentucky, and Missouri—decided to remain in the Union. These states were very important to the Union. Maryland and Delaware were close to Washington, D.C., the Union's capital. Missouri and Kentucky controlled the Mississippi and Ohio rivers. The North used these rivers to move soldiers and supplies. Because of the border states, more than 400,000 slaves were in the Union throughout the war.

As soon as the Civil War began, both sides began to form armies. Union soldiers wore blue uniforms. Soldiers in the Union

own nation. They were willing to fight very hard for their cause. Southerners fought on their own land, which they knew well.

The Confederacy's greatest advantage was its excellent generals. Generals on both sides of the war had been trained at the United States Military Academy at West Point, New York. But many of the Southern generals had more experience. The greatest Confederate general was Robert E. Lee of Virginia. Lee had led American soldiers in the Mexican War. He had captured John Brown after Brown's attack on the arsenal at Harpers Ferry. President Lincoln admired Lee and asked him to lead the Union Army. But Lee would not fight against his own state of Virginia. Instead he led the Confederate Army.

Planning and Paying for War

To defeat the South, the North decided to use the **Anaconda Plan**. It was named for the South American anaconda snake, which crushes its **prey** to death. The North planned to capture the Mississippi River and divide the Confederacy in half. The Union also planned to capture Richmond, the Confederate capital. Northern ships would blockade Southern ports to stop the Confederacy from receiving supplies from Europe. The blockade would also prevent the South from selling its cotton to Great Britain and other nations.

To pay for the war, Congress passed the nation's first **income tax** laws. Americans had to give some of the money they earned to the federal government. The government also sold war bonds to raise money to help pay for the war.

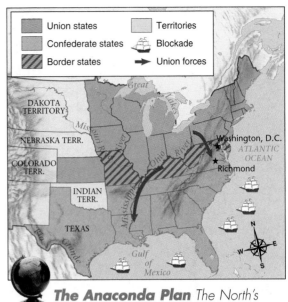

The Anaconda Plan *The North's plan to win the war called for dividing the South and using a blockade on Southern ports.*

The South planned to fight a **defensive war**. Southerners would fight on their own land and defend it. The South thought that the Union would grow tired of fighting and would decide to surrender. The Confederates were also hopeful that Great Britain would provide them with supplies during the war.

To pay for the war, the Confederacy placed taxes on many different products. The Confederate government also sold war bonds. But as the war destroyed farms and businesses, few Southerners had money to buy bonds or to pay taxes. The South did not have enough money to pay for the war, so there was not enough food and ammunition. The lack of supplies weakened the Southern Army.

Confederate Victories in the East

The first major battle of the Civil War took place in Virginia, near a town called Manassas and a stream called Bull Run.

On July 21, 1861, 30,000 Union soldiers fought 22,000 Confederates in this battle. Union troops seemed to be winning early in the day. But Confederate troops led by Thomas J. Jackson held their position and helped turn the battle into a victory. "Stonewall" Jackson became one of the South's best generals. After this battle the Union knew the war would not end quickly.

President Lincoln asked General George McClellan to command the Union Army in the East. McClellan trained 150,000 men to fight against Lee's army. But McClellan was too cautious. He refused to attack Lee's army at times when he could have defeated the Confederates.

General McClellan's goal was to capture Richmond, Virginia. He tried to do this in the Battle of Seven Days in June 1862. But Lee defeated McClellan, and the Confederate

capital would be safe for more than two years. In September 1862 the Union Army fought the Confederates again at the Second Battle of Bull Run. Once again Lee defeated the Union army.

While the Confederates held back the Union forces in the East, the Union was winning battles in the West along the Mississippi. The Union Navy captured the port of New Orleans. After capturing New Orleans, the Union controlled the southern part of the Mississippi River.

Antietam

Confederate leaders hoped that Great Britain would help them fight the Union

The Battle of New Orleans took place in April 1862. David Farragut led a fleet of ships on the Mississippi River in a battle against forts on the shore and ships in the river. Farragut's ships sank most of the Confederate ships, and New Orleans surrendered.

The Second Battle of Bull Run was fought in September 1862. Like the first battle fought at Manassas, this battle was a Confederate victory. In this painting Confederate soldiers from Louisiana defend their position, throwing stones when they ran out of ammunition.

because the British bought cotton from the South. If the South won a major battle in the North, the British might support the South. So President Davis and General Lee decided to invade Maryland. Unfortunately for Lee, his battle plans were found by one of McClellan's soldiers.

On September 17, 1862, Lee led his army against the Union near Antietam Creek outside the small town of Sharpsburg, Maryland. It was the bloodiest day of the Civil War. Thousands of Confederate and Union soldiers died, and thousands more were wounded during that one day of fighting.

The Battle of Antietam became a Union victory. Lee was forced to retreat to Virginia. But General McClellan foolishly waited 19 days before he attacked Lee's army again. President Lincoln was furious with McClellan for waiting. He believed McClellan should have followed Lee's army, destroyed it, and forced Lee to surrender. If McClellan had done that, the war might have ended in 1862. Soon after Antietam, Lincoln chose another general to command the Union Army.

The Union victory at the Battle of Antietam made Great Britain and other European nations decide not to aid the Confederacy. Because the Union had won an important battle, Lincoln felt the time was right to act against slavery. Read on in Chapter 17 to learn how Lincoln took steps to end slavery and how the Civil War ended.

BIOGRAPHY

Robert E. Lee 1807–1870

"Make your sons Americans," Robert E. Lee told Southerners after the Civil War. Although Lee led the Confederate Army for four years, he had a strong love for the United States.

Lee attended the United States Military Academy at West Point. After graduating from West Point second in his class, Lee worked as an army officer. Lee fought bravely in the Mexican War. He fought in the same unit with Ulysses S. Grant, George McClellan, and Thomas "Stonewall" Jackson. All of these men became important generals in the Civil War.

As the disagreements between the North and the South grew stronger, Lee hoped the Southern states would not secede. Lee loved the South, but he hated slavery. He had freed the few slaves he owned long before the Civil War began.

After the Civil War began, Abraham Lincoln asked Lee to lead the Union Army. Lee decided that he could not go to war against his own state. Lee believed the Southern states had the same right to leave the Union that the 13 colonies had when they separated from Great Britain in 1776.

As general of the Army of Northern Virginia, Lee became famous for his brilliant battle plans. Although his army was much smaller than the Union Army, Lee defeated the Union Army again and again. When he won battles, Lee praised the work of his soldiers. When battles were lost, he took full blame upon himself.

By April 1865 Lee knew that it would not be possible for the South to win the war. So General Lee surrendered. Although many Confederates wanted to continue fighting, Lee told them to go home and become good American citizens again. After the war ended, Lee tried to heal the anger between the North and the South.

Robert E. Lee's birthday, January 19, is a legal holiday in most Southern states. Lee continues to be respected as one of the nation's greatest generals.

In Your Own Words

Write a paragraph in your notebook that explains why Robert E. Lee is considered a great general and a hero.

REVIEW AND APPLY

- By the time Abraham Lincoln became President, the nation was divided and preparing for war.

- The first battle of the Civil War took place in April 1861 at Fort Sumter, South Carolina.

- The Confederacy grew from seven states to eleven states when the border states of Virginia, Tennessee, North Carolina, and Arkansas seceded from the Union.

- Each side had its advantages in the war. The North had more people and more industries. The South had better generals and knowledge of the land.

- Early Confederate victories included the Battle of Bull Run and the Second Battle of Bull Run. The Union Army won the Battle of Antietam.

VOCABULARY

Matching ■ **Match the vocabulary word or phrase in Group B with its definition in Group A. You will not use all the words in Group B.**

Group A	Group B
1. This was the name of the war between the North and the South.	A. draft
2. Union soldiers ran out of this and were forced to surrender Fort Sumter.	B. Anaconda Plan
	C. Civil War
3. These were states that were between the Union and the Confederacy.	D. income tax
4. This was the way that the North planned to win the war.	E. defensive war
	F. border states
5. Congress used this to raise money for the war.	G. ammunition
6. This was the way that the Confederacy planned to fight the war.	

USING INFORMATION

Journal Writing ■ **Imagine that you are General Lee or General McClellan. You are writing a report to President Lincoln or President Davis about your victory at Bull Run or Antietam. Explain the importance of your victory to your commander in chief.**

COMPREHENSION CHECK

Write the Answer ■ Write one or more sentences to answer each question.

1. What were President Lincoln's feelings about fighting a war against the Confederacy?

2. Why did the Union and the Confederacy fight over Fort Sumter?

3. Of the eight border states, which ones joined the Confederacy, and which ones stayed in the Union?

4. Why did many Northerners believe the war would be over quickly?

5. Explain the North's plan for winning the war.

6. Explain the South's plan for winning the war.

7. Who was Robert E. Lee, and why did he decide to fight for the Confederacy?

8. Who was Thomas Jackson?

9. Why did the Confederacy hope that European countries would help them fight the war?

CRITICAL THINKING

Comparing and Contrasting ■ In this chapter you read about the early years of the Civil War. Compare and contrast the North and South in the early part of the war by copying and completing the chart below.

TOPIC	NORTH	SOUTH
Reasons for Fighting		
Nicknames and Uniform Colors		
Advantages		
Early Victories		

SOCIAL STUDIES SKILLS

Comparing Circle Graphs

A **circle graph**, also called a **pie graph**, is a circle that has been divided into sections that look like pieces of a pie. All the pie sections add up to 100 percent of the circle. Percent means parts of 100. The two circle graphs below give percents of the populations of the Union and the Confederacy in 1860. The two graphs can be compared.

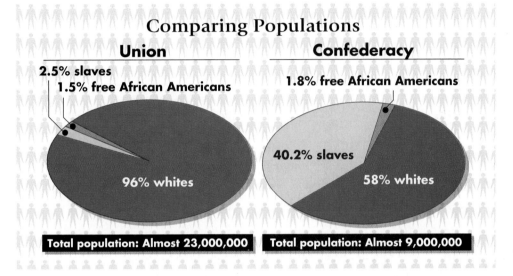

Comparing Populations

Union

2.5% slaves
1.5% free African Americans
96% whites

Total population: Almost 23,000,000

Confederacy

1.8% free African Americans
40.2% slaves
58% whites

Total population: Almost 9,000,000

A. Study the two graphs. Then use your knowledge about multiplying percents to complete each of the following sentences. You will not use one of the possible answers.

1. The Union had more than _____ white people in 1860.

2. The slave population in the Confederacy was about _____.

3. The slave population in the Union was about _____.

4. There were fewer than 1 million African Americans in the _____ in 1860.

5. The white population in the Confederacy was about _____.

a. 5,220,000

b. 575,000

c. 22,000,000

d. Union

e. 3,600,000

f. Confederacy

B. Answer the following question in your notebook.

Compare the populations of the Union and the Confederacy. How were they different?

Chapter 17

THE END OF THE CIVIL WAR

◀ *Young Union soldier*

Focus on Main Ideas

1. How did the Emancipation Proclamation help the Union during the Civil War?
2. How did events at Gettysburg and Vicksburg affect the Civil War?
3. How did Abraham Lincoln want to treat the South after the Civil War?
4. What were the consequences of the Civil War?

People

José Chavez • Edward Solomon • Loretta Valesquez • Judah P. Benjamin • Clara Barton • George C. Meade • William T. Sherman • Ely S. Parker • John Wilkes Booth

Places

Gettysburg • Vicksburg • Atlanta • Savannah • Appomattox Court House

New Vocabulary

Emancipation Proclamation • emancipated • battlefield • Gettysburg Address • unconditional surrender • laid siege • total war • malice • charity • bind up • just • assassinated • dictator

After the Battle of Antietam, both the North and the South knew the war would continue for a long time. New victories gave the Union hope of winning the war.

The Emancipation Proclamation

President Lincoln's goal at the start of the Civil War was to keep the United States together. But Lincoln had always thought slavery was wrong. After the Battle of Antietam, he took action to end it. Lincoln wrote the **Emancipation Proclamation**. This paper said that after the date it was issued, January 1, 1863, all slaves in states that were at war with the Union would be **emancipated**, or freed. Slaves in the Confederacy were filled with joy when they learned that Lincoln said they were free.

However, the Emancipation Proclamation did not free any slaves. It did not free the slaves in the border states or in Southern territory captured by the Union. Only an amendment to the Constitution could end slavery in those areas. The Proclamation could not free slaves in the Confederate states because Lincoln had no power there.

The Emancipation Proclamation did accomplish three important things for the Union. First, it gave Union soldiers two important causes to fight for: freeing the slaves and saving the Union. Second, the Proclamation encouraged African American slaves to escape from their owners and join the Union Army. Third, Great Britain and other European nations decided not to aid the Confederacy when they heard that the Union was trying to end slavery there.

The Contributions of Many Americans

Thousands of African American slaves joined the Union Army soon after the Emancipation Proclamation was written. African American soldiers faced special dangers. If captured by Confederate soldiers, African Americans could be sold into slavery or killed. Twenty-two African Americans won the Congressional Medal of Honor for their courage.

About 440,000 immigrants fought in the Union Army. They came from Ireland, Germany, Italy, Sweden, Poland, and other nations. One of these immigrant soldiers was a Polish man, Wladimir Kryzanowski. He became a general after fighting at Bull Run, Gettysburg, and in other battles.

About 10,000 Hispanic Americans fought for the Union. Lieutenant Colonel José Chavez led a company of Union soldiers that captured Confederate land in the Southwest.

About 6,000 Jewish Americans also fought for the Union Army. One of these soldiers was Colonel Edward Solomon. He led a large group of soldiers from Illinois at the battles of Gettysburg and Atlanta.

Fewer immigrants fought for the Confederacy because fewer immigrants lived in the South. Loretta Valesquez, a Cuban immigrant, dressed as a man and fought in the Confederate Army.

Judah P. Benjamin became the most important Jewish citizen in the Confederacy. He worked in Jefferson Davis's cabinet. Benjamin was attorney general, secretary of state, and secretary of war at different times during the Civil War.

Women played an important role in the Union and in the Confederacy. As men went off to fight, women ran farms, businesses, and plantations. Women worked as nurses and ran hospitals. The nation's first woman doctor, Elizabeth Blackwell, organized a group to train

This soldier is one of the 200,000 African Americans who fought for the Union during the Civil War.

Union nurses. Dorothea Dix, who had helped people with mental illnesses before the war, was in charge of the Union's nurses during the war. Sojourner Truth and Harriet Tubman had once been slaves, but they served as nurses and scouts for the Union Army.

Another brave woman was Clara Barton. Before the war Barton had been a teacher, but she became a Union nurse during the war. At the Battle of Antietam, Barton worked in a small hospital right on the **battlefield**. After Antietam she nursed men at other battles.

Clara Barton was a nurse during the Civil War. After the war ended, Barton started the American Red Cross.

The Battle of Gettysburg

After the Union victory at Antietam, the Union lost two battles in Virginia. Lincoln appointed General George C. Meade to command the Union Army that was fighting in the East.

Robert E. Lee decided to try once again to attack the North. He hoped that a victory would convince the Union to surrender. So Lee planned to invade Pennsylvania. Lee led 75,000 Confederate soldiers and Meade led 90,000 Union soldiers. The two armies met at Gettysburg, Pennsylvania, on July 1, 1863. The Battle of Gettysburg lasted three terrible days.

During the third day, thousands of Confederate soldiers charged across open fields toward the Union forces. Using rifles and cannons, the Union soldiers shot down the Confederate soldiers. The Union won a great victory at Gettysburg. But that victory was expensive. The North lost 23,000 soldiers; the South lost 28,000.

To save his defeated army, Lee retreated to Virginia. Lincoln sent a message to General Meade ordering him to attack Lee's army before it crossed the Potomac River into Virginia. Like General McClellan, Meade waited too many days to attack. Lee's army escaped back into Virginia.

Lee had lost more soldiers than the South's small population could replace. After the Battle of Gettysburg, the South's army would never be as strong as it had once been. The Confederates would never invade the North again.

So many soldiers died at Gettysburg that a military cemetery was built for the Union soldiers who died there. On

November 19, 1863, President Lincoln dedicated the new cemetery. He gave a short speech that is now called the **Gettysburg Address**.

War in the West and the Fall of Vicksburg

To carry out its Anaconda Plan, the Union had to win control of the entire Mississippi River. Then the Confederates would not be able to use the Mississippi to move their soldiers and supplies. The Southern states west of the river would be cut off from the eastern states. The Union controlled part of the Mississippi. Lincoln knew that to control all of the river, Vicksburg, Mississippi, had to be captured. Lincoln ordered General Ulysses S. Grant and his army to capture Vicksburg.

What kind of man was General Grant? Like Robert E. Lee, Grant had studied at West Point and had fought in the Mexican War. When the Civil War began, Grant was working in his father's business in Illinois. He rejoined the army and became a general. When Grant demanded the **unconditional surrender** of a fort early in the war, the newspapers started calling him Unconditional Surrender Grant. President Lincoln liked Grant because he would fight until he won a battle.

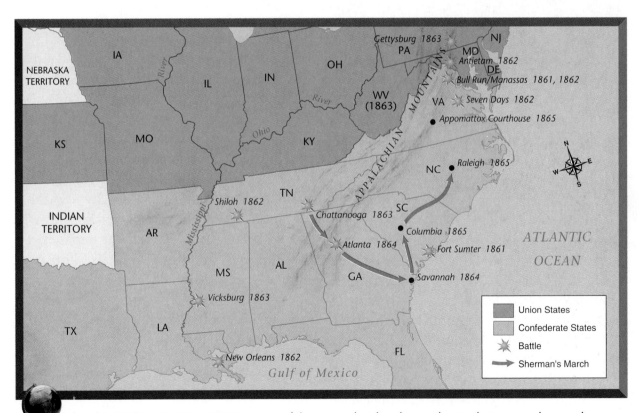

The Civil War 1861–1865 *Some of the major battles during the Civil War are shown above. Many battles occurred in Virginia and along the Mississippi River. Which three major battles were fought in 1863?*

Ulysses S. Grant became the first American general since George Washington to hold the rank of lieutenant general.

From November 1862 to July 1863, Grant fought to capture Vicksburg. By May 1863 Grant's army surrounded the city. But the people of Vicksburg would not surrender. So Grant **laid siege** to the city. No food, supplies, or people could move in or out of the city. By summer the starving people of Vicksburg were eating dogs and rats in order to stay alive. On July 4, 1863, the city surrendered to Grant.

Next the Union captured Port Hudson, Louisiana. Now they controlled the entire Mississippi River. By controlling the river, the Union had split the Confederacy. Without the river the Southern army could not get food from Texas and Arkansas.

The fall of Vicksburg happened one day after the Union won the Battle of Gettysburg. The Union victories at Gettysburg and Vicksburg were turning points in the Civil War. The Confederate army was not ready to surrender, but it had become too weak to win the war.

Sherman's March to the Sea

Early in 1864 President Lincoln appointed Grant commander of all the Union armies. Grant now commanded more than 500,000 soldiers. His goal was to crush the South to make it impossible for the Confederates to continue fighting.

Grant sent General William Tecumseh Sherman to capture the city of Atlanta, Georgia. Sherman led about 100,000 Union soldiers on a march through the South. He started by attacking Atlanta, an important manufacturing and railroad center. Sherman captured the city and set it on fire. Atlanta was completely destroyed. Sherman's actions were called **total war**. His goal was to destroy everything that the South could use to continue the war.

After burning Atlanta, Sherman led his army to Savannah, Georgia, a city near the Atlantic Ocean. Sherman and his soldiers carried out total war as they marched toward the sea. Farm animals, houses, barns, roads, railroads, and bridges were destroyed. Sherman forced the people of Georgia to surrender. But he also caused them to hate people from the North.

Lincoln's Reelection

The news of Sherman's victory in Atlanta swept through the North. People in the Union believed the war would soon be over. The victory made Lincoln popular. In 1864 Lincoln was reelected. He defeated Democrat George McClellan.

In January 1865 Congress passed an amendment to end slavery in the nation. The Thirteenth Amendment was ratified in December 1865.

Lincoln was inaugurated for his second term as President in March 1865. He knew that the North would soon win the war and that the North and the South would be united again. He did not want Northerners to treat the Confederates as traitors. He felt that they had been punished enough by the terrible war. In his inaugural speech, Lincoln asked the Union to forgive the South. He asked the North and the South to work together to rebuild the nation. In his speech he said, "With **malice** toward none, with **charity** for all, with firmness in the right as God gives us to see the right, let us strive on to finish the work we are in, to **bind up** the nation's wounds,…to do all which may achieve and cherish a **just** and lasting peace among ourselves and with all nations."

Final Battles of the Civil War

While Lincoln spoke of peace, the war continued. Sherman's army destroyed everything it could as it marched through South Carolina and North Carolina.

Grant fought hard to capture the Confederate capital at Richmond. To do this, he kept Lee's army under siege in the nearby town of Petersburg for almost a year. During this time, Lee's army had little food and lost many men. Finally, both Petersburg and Richmond were captured. The Union Army completely surrounded Lee's army. Sadly, Lee sent a message to Grant that he was ready to surrender.

On April 9, 1865, the two generals met in a house in a town called Appomattox Court House. Lee signed the surrender papers that Grant had prepared. Grant was kind to the Confederates. All Confederate soldiers were allowed to return to their homes. They could keep their horses and mules. Officers were allowed to keep their pistols and swords. Grant sent food to feed Lee's army.

Lee was introduced to Grant's officers, including General Ely S. Parker, Grant's army secretary. Parker was also a Seneca Indian. Lee said to Parker, "I am glad to

The Civil War ended when General Lee surrendered to General Grant in Appomattox Court House on April 9, 1865.

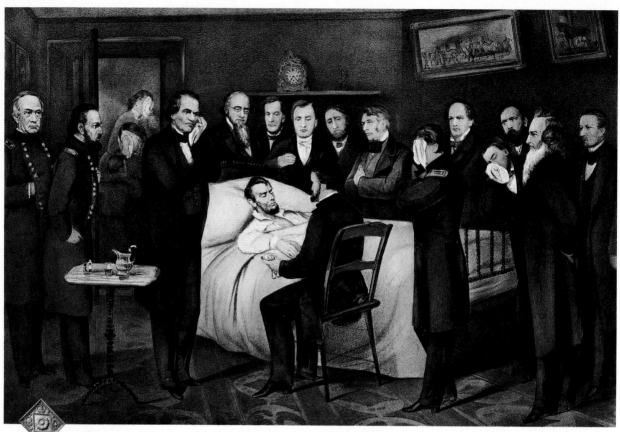

Lincoln was shot in the back of the head as he watched a play with his wife at Ford's Theater in Washington, D.C. He was taken to a room across the street, where he died the next morning. John Wilkes Booth was shot and killed while Union troops tried to capture him in a barn in Virginia.

see one real American here." Parker answered, "We are all Americans." With the war over, the Confederates were Americans once again.

Five days after General Lee surrendered, President Lincoln was **assassinated.** John Wilkes Booth shot him because Booth was angry that the Confederacy had lost the war. People everywhere mourned for Abraham Lincoln.

The Results of the Civil War

The United States had survived four terrible years of war. More than 620,000 men died during the Civil War. No other war in American history has caused so many American deaths. The Civil War ended slavery in the United States. It settled the question about whether or not states could secede. Never again would states leave the Union. As a result of the Civil War, the federal government became stronger than the state governments.

The Civil War destroyed much of the South. It created hatred between people in the North and the South. African Americans were no longer slaves, but they continued to face prejudice from Northerners and Southerners. It would take many years for the nation to recover from the Civil War.

Abraham Lincoln 1809-1865

Abraham Lincoln was born in a small log cabin in Kentucky. His parents were poor and had never learned to read. His mother died when he was nine. After Lincoln's father remarried, Lincoln's stepmother encouraged him to read the Bible and to learn as much as possible. Throughout his life Lincoln read the Bible whenever he had to make difficult decisions. Although he only went to school for about one year, he read as many books as he could.

Lincoln moved to New Salem, Illinois, when he was 22 years old. He studied law on his own and became a lawyer. In 1834 Lincoln was elected to the Illinois state legislature. In 1846 he was elected to the House of Representatives. During his one term in Congress, Lincoln spoke out against President Polk for fighting the Mexican War. In 1858 he ran for the Senate as a Republican, but he lost to Stephen Douglas. However, in 1860 Lincoln was elected President.

No President ever faced the difficult problems that Lincoln faced in 1861. The South had seceded, the Civil War had begun, and slavery had to be ended.

Lincoln was determined to do everything possible to save the Union. He felt that the United States would be a much weaker nation without the South.

During the Civil War, Lincoln took on more power than the Constitution allowed. Some people called Lincoln a **dictator**. But he insisted that everything he did was necessary to save the Union.

Although the war took up most of his time, President Lincoln made other important decisions. He encouraged Congress to pass a law that gave free land to people who settled in the West.

Lincoln was assassinated before he could lead the nation in a time of peace. Millions wept when he died. Today, Lincoln is remembered as the great President who saved the Union.

In Your Own Words

Write a paragraph in the journal section of your notebook that explains why Abraham Lincoln was one of the nation's great leaders.

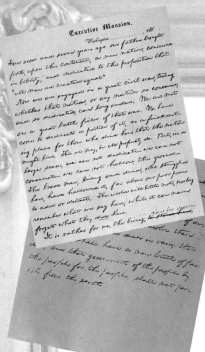

*V*OICES *from the* *P*AST

The Gettysburg Address

A military cemetery was built at Gettysburg for the thousands of Union soldiers who died there. The dedication of the cemetery took place on November 19, 1863. President Lincoln was asked to give a short speech, since he was not the main speaker that day. In his speech Lincoln told Americans that the purpose of the Civil War was to make the United States a democracy with freedom and liberty for all. The Gettysburg Address lasted only two minutes, but today it is considered one of the nation's greatest speeches.

Four score and seven years ago our fathers brought forth on this continent, a new nation, conceived in Liberty, and dedicated to the proposition that all men are created equal.

Now we are engaged in a great civil war, testing whether that nation, or any nation so conceived and so dedicated, can long endure. We are met on a great battlefield of that war. We have come to dedicate a portion of that field, as a final resting place for those who here gave their lives that that nation might live. It is altogether fitting and proper that we should do this.

But, in a large sense, we can not dedicate—we can not consecrate—we can not hallow—this ground. The brave men, living and dead, who struggled here, have consecrated it, far above our poor power to add or detract. The world will little note, nor long remember what we say here, but it can never forget what they did here. It is for us the living, rather, to be dedicated here to the unfinished work which they who fought here have thus far so nobly advanced. It is rather for us to be here dedicated to the great task remaining before us—that from these honored dead we take increased devotion to that cause for which they gave the last full measure of devotion—that we here highly resolve that these dead shall not have died in vain—that this nation, under God, shall have a new birth of freedom—and that government of the people, by the people, for the people, shall not perish from the earth.

Explanation of the Gettysburg Address

Paragraph 1 Eighty-seven years ago, in 1776, our leaders created a new nation based on the idea of liberty.

The United States would exist to prove the statement that "all men are created equal."

Paragraph 2 Now we are fighting a Civil War. This war is a test to see if the United States, or any other nation, can exist for a long time if it is based on the ideas of liberty and equality. We are now meeting at the battlefield of Gettysburg. We have come to dedicate part of the battlefield as a cemetery for soldiers who died here. Those soldiers died fighting so that the United States would continue to be a nation based on ideas of liberty and equality. It is correct and proper that we dedicate this cemetery to honor those dead soldiers.

Paragraph 3 But we really do not have the power to dedicate this cemetery and make this ground holy. We cannot do this because this cemetery has already been made holy by the brave men, living and dead, who fought at Gettysburg. We cannot do anything more to make this cemetery holy than they have already done. The world will not notice or remember what we say here today. But the world can never forget what they did at Gettysburg. It must be our job to dedicate our own lives to the work these soldiers fought for so hard but could not finish. We must dedicate ourselves to the great cause for which these soldiers died. To honor them we must work harder than ever for this cause. We must prove that these soldiers did not die without a reason. We must work hard so that this nation, under God, will have a government that allows equality and liberty for all people. We must make sure that this democratic government will never be destroyed.

Write Your Answers

Answer these questions in the assignment section of your notebook.

1. Why did people gather at Gettysburg on November 19, 1863?

2. Why did Lincoln say "we can not dedicate—we can not consecrate—we can not hallow this ground?"

3. How does Lincoln think Americans should finish the work for which the Union soldiers fought?

AMERICAN GEOGRAPHY

Place: Vicksburg

Place is what makes an area special and what makes it different from other areas. Landscape and culture are two of the features that tell us about a place.

Vicksburg was an important port on the Mississippi River. General Grant wanted to capture Vicksburg because its location would allow the Union to control the Mississippi River. Grant laid siege to Vicksburg. Grant would not allow the city to receive supplies from its port or its railroad. After 47 days the starving city surrendered.

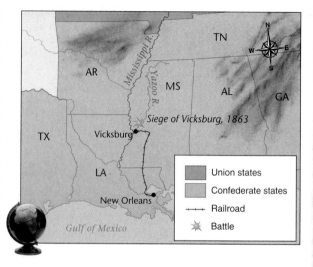

Read the paragraph above. Then study the map of the Mississippi River and Vicksburg. Write the answer for each question below in the assignment section of your social studies notebook.

1. Which two rivers flowed into Vicksburg?

2. Why did the Union want to control these two rivers?

3. Why was control of New Orleans important to the Union's strategy?

4. Which two cities were connected by a railroad?

5. Which Confederate state was west of Vicksburg?

6. Which Confederate state was northwest of Mississippi?

7. How did Grant's control of Vicksburg's railroad help the Union to win control of the city?

8. Why was control of Vicksburg important to the Union?

9. How did Grant capture Vicksburg?

REVIEW AND APPLY

- President Lincoln issued the Emancipation Proclamation. It said that after January 1, 1863, all slaves in the Confederate states would be freed.

- African Americans, European immigrants, Jewish Americans, and women all played important roles for both sides during the Civil War.

- The Battle of Gettysburg was fought from July 1 to July 3, 1863. As a result of this Union victory, the Confederacy would not invade the North again.

- Union victories at Vicksburg and Atlanta greatly weakened the South.

- President Lincoln was reelected in 1864.

- The Civil War came to an end on April 9, 1865, when Lee surrendered to Grant at Appomattox Court House, Virginia.

- Five days after the South's surrender, President Lincoln was assassinated.

VOCABULARY

Writing with Vocabulary Words ■ Use six or more vocabulary words below to write a paragraph about why and how the North won the Civil War. Write your paragraph in your social studies notebook.

emancipated	laid siege	charity
battlefield	total war	just
unconditional surrender	malice	assassinated

COMPREHENSION CHECK

Choose the Answer ■ Write the letter of the word or phrase that best answers each question.

1. What was the name of President Lincoln's speech that honored the soldiers who died at Gettysburg?

   a. Farewell Address
   b. Inaugural Speech
   c. Gettysburg Address

2. What was the name given to General Sherman's actions in Atlanta?

   a. unconditional surrender
   b. total war
   c. defensive war

3. What role did Clara Barton play during the war?

   a. a cook
   b. a photographer
   c. a nurse

4. When did President Lincoln issue the Emancipation Proclamation?

   a. on January 1, 1863
   b. before the Battle of Antietam
   c. after the war was over

5. Who was the Union commander at the Battle of Gettysburg?

   a. George Meade
   b. Robert E. Lee
   c. Ulysses S. Grant

6. Which Constitutional amendment ended slavery in the United States?

   a. Thirteenth Amendment
   b. Fourteenth Amendment
   c. Fifteenth Amendment

7. Where did the Civil War come to an end?

   a. Richmond, Virginia
   b. Atlanta, Georgia
   c. Appomattox Court House, Virginia

8. In what battle was the Union able to split the Confederacy into two parts?

   a. Vicksburg
   b. Antietam
   c. Appomattox

CRITICAL THINKING

Sequencing Information ■ In your social studies notebook, write the following sentences in their correct order.

In January 1865 Congress passes an amendment to end slavery in the United States.

Lincoln is assassinated in Washington, D.C.

The Battle of Gettysburg is fought for three days in July 1863.

On April 9, 1865, the Confederate army surrenders, ending the Civil War.

Lincoln dedicates a new cemetery to the soldiers who died at the Battle of Gettysburg.

USING INFORMATION

Writing an Essay ■ After President Lincoln made Ulysses S. Grant commander of all the Union armies, the tide of the war started to change in favor of the North. Explain the actions taken by General Grant that helped the Union win the war. Start your essay with a topic sentence.

THE RECONSTRUCTION YEARS

◀ Carpetbag

People

Andrew Johnson • Edwin
Stanton • Blanche Bruce •
Samuel Tilden • Rutherford
Hayes • Homer Plessy •
Booker T. Washington

Places

Hampton Institute •
Tuskegee Institute

New Vocabulary

Reconstruction • oath •
Radical Republicans •
freedmen • Civil Rights Act •
campaigned • due process •
public office • impeach •
carpetbaggers • scalawags •
sharecroppers •
Ku Klux Klan • poll tax •
literacy test • grandfather
clauses • segregation

Focus on Main Ideas

1. How did the Republicans help African Americans during Reconstruction?
2. Why were the Fourteenth and Fifteenth Amendments added to the Constitution?
3. What changes took place in the South after Reconstruction?

The United States faced serious problems after the Civil War. Much of the South had been destroyed. During the years known as **Reconstruction**, Southern states would rebuild their economies and become part of the United States again.

Plans for Reconstruction

Lincoln's goals for Reconstruction were to reunite all of the states and to rebuild the country. Lincoln planned to allow Southern states to rejoin the Union if one tenth of their voters would take an **oath** to be loyal to the Union. One group in Congress, which became known as the **Radical Republicans**, disagreed with Lincoln's plan. They believed that the South was to blame for the war and should be punished. Lincoln vetoed the harsh Reconstruction plan passed by Congress. Before Lincoln and the Congress could compromise on a plan, Lincoln was assassinated.

Vice President Andrew Johnson became President. Johnson had a Reconstruction plan that was like the plan Congress had passed, but the Radical Republicans rejected it. The Radical Republicans believed that Johnson's plan did not punish the South enough.

The Radical Republicans became furious when people who had been Confederate leaders were elected to Congress and to state governments. They were also furious when Southern states passed laws called Black Codes. These laws treated African Americans as if they were still slaves. Congress created an agency called the Freedmen's Bureau to help the **freedmen,** slaves who became free after the Civil War. The Black Codes in the South said freedmen could only work as farmers or house servants. Freedmen had to carry special passes when they traveled. They could not serve on juries or vote. Since the Republicans controlled Congress, they decided to use their power to change what was happening in the South.

Congress and Reconstruction

The Radical Republicans created their own Reconstruction plan. Their first action was to pass a **Civil Rights Act** in 1866. This law said that African Americans were American citizens and had equal rights under the law. Next the Republicans wanted to add the Fourteenth Amendment to the Constitution. President Johnson **campaigned** against the amendment and the Radical Republicans. Despite Johnson's efforts, Republicans won control of Congress in

By the end of the Civil War, much of the the South looked like the photograph below of Richmond, Virginia. Many soldiers returned to their homes to find that they had been destroyed. Throughout the South many farms, factories, railroads, bridges, and buildings would have to be rebuilt.

the election of 1866. The Fourteenth Amendment was ratified in 1868.

The Fourteenth Amendment has been called the Equal Rights Amendment. The amendment said that all people born in the United States were citizens of their state and the nation. This included African Americans. The amendment also said that states could not make laws that took away the rights of citizens. States had to give all people **due process** under the law.

In 1867 the Republicans passed the Reconstruction Act. The act had five parts. First, any state governments in the South that had been created under Lincoln's plan or Johnson's plan were not recognized by Congress. Instead federal troops would be sent to rule the South. Second, people who had been Confederate soldiers or leaders could not vote or hold **public office.** Third, all other white men and all African American men could vote and be elected to public office. Fourth, Southern states had to write new state constitutions that guaranteed African American men the right to vote. Fifth, all Southern states had to ratify the Fourteenth Amendment before they could rejoin the Union.

Johnson vetoed Congress's plan for Reconstruction, but Congress passed it again and the Reconstruction Act became law. By 1870 all Southern states had ratified the Fourteenth Amendment and had rejoined the Union.

The Impeachment of Johnson

The Radical Republicans disliked Andrew Johnson because he opposed their Reconstruction plans. They wanted to

After the Civil War, African Americans had the right to vote. Their votes helped to elect African American leaders during the years of Reconstruction.

remove Johnson from the job of President. According to the Constitution, the House of Representatives can **impeach** a President who commits crimes. Then the President is put on trial in the Senate. If two thirds of the senators find the President guilty, the President loses his job.

In 1868 the House of Representatives voted to impeach Johnson. Congress had never before voted to impeach a President. Johnson was accused of not carrying out the Reconstruction plan of Congress and of breaking the Tenure in Office Act. Congress had passed the Tenure of Office Act to have power over the President. This law said that he could not fire anyone without the Senate's approval. When the President fired Edwin Stanton, the secretary of war, Johnson had broken the Tenure of Office Act.

After Johnson was impeached, he had a trial in the Senate that lasted three months.

227

The Senate needed 36 votes to find Johnson guilty. Only 35 senators voted against him. The other senators correctly believed that Johnson was a poor leader and a poor President, but he had not committed crimes. Johnson finished his term as President.

In November 1868 the popular Union war hero, General Ulysses S. Grant, was elected President. For the first time, African Americans were able to vote in an election for President. They helped Grant win. Grant did a poor job as President. Many of the people whom he appointed stole money from the government. Still, in 1872, Grant was reelected to a second term.

Under President Grant, the Fifteenth Amendment became part of the Constitution in 1870. This amendment said citizens cannot be denied the right to vote because of their race. Therefore, African American men had the right to vote. Women were not yet allowed to vote in any state, but they could vote in the Territory of Wyoming.

The South During Reconstruction

During Reconstruction the South was controlled by three groups—**carpetbaggers**, **scalawags**, and African Americans. Carpetbaggers came from the North. They were called carpetbaggers because travelers

Most African Americans who had been slaves remained in the South as farmers. They started small farms on land that they rented from the plantation owners. They paid for the use of the land by giving the owner part of the crops they raised.

carried their clothing in bags made of carpet material. Some carpetbaggers really tried to help the South, but many used their power to get rich. Scalawags were white Republican Southerners. They became the largest group in Reconstruction governments. Before the war, most scalawags had been small farmers. After the war they wanted the power that had belonged to rich plantation owners. Most former Confederates hated the scalawags.

African Americans had a small role in government while the Union Army controlled the South. During Reconstruction many African Americans were elected to public office in state governments. Also, 22 African Americans were elected to Congress. Two of these men became senators. One of these two senators was Blanche Bruce from Mississippi. In the Senate, he worked to help African Americans, Indians, and Chinese immigrants win equal rights. Bruce was respected because he was an honest senator who cared about helping different groups of Americans.

African Americans in the South After the Civil War

After the Civil War, there were four million freedmen who had no money, no land, no jobs, and no education. The Freedmen's Bureau gave African Americans and poor whites food, clothing, and medical care. It started new hospitals and more than 4,000 public schools. The Bureau also started several universities for African Americans.

Freedmen needed jobs after the war, but there were few kinds of work besides farming that they knew how to do. Since they did not have money to buy land, seeds, tools, and farm animals, they were forced to become **sharecroppers**. They rented farmland by giving landowners a share of their crops. They paid for the use of their tools, seeds, and farm animals with another share of their crops. This system forced sharecroppers to give more than half of their crops to the landowners. They had few crops left to sell or to use for themselves, so sharecroppers remained very poor year after year.

In 1866 white Southerners started a secret organization in the South called the **Ku Klux Klan**. Members wore white hoods and white robes. Their goal was to stop freedmen from using the new rights they had won. Many freedmen were beaten and many others were killed by the Klan.

The End of Reconstruction

In 1872, while Grant was President, Congress passed a law that allowed most Confederates to vote and hold public office. Once that happened, Democrats slowly won control of the South just as they had before the Civil War.

During the election of 1876, Democratic Governor Samuel Tilden of New York ran against Republican Governor Rutherford Hayes of Ohio. To win the election, one candidate needed a majority of electoral votes. Each side said it had won a majority of electoral votes. Each side also said there had been cheating during the election. Since it was hard to decide which candidate was the real winner, Congress created a special committee to choose the President. That committee chose Hayes

The decision of the Supreme Court in the 1896 case of Plessy v. Ferguson *kept segregation in the United States until the 1950s.*

as the winner of the election after Democrats and Republicans worked out a compromise.

Under this Compromise of 1877, Hayes promised to remove all federal troops from the South. He also promised that federal money would be used to build Southern railroads. The Democrats accepted this compromise.

In March 1877, Hayes became the new President. He ordered federal troops to leave the South. Reconstruction had ended.

The South After Reconstruction

The Fifteenth Amendment was supposed to protect the right of African Americans to vote. When federal troops left, Southern governments passed laws that took away that right. One law required voters to pay a special **poll tax** in order to vote. Most African Americans were too poor to pay the tax. Another law required people to pass a difficult **literacy test.** In order to allow poor whites to vote, these laws had **grandfather clauses.** These clauses said that people whose grandfather had voted in 1867 did not have to pay poll taxes or pass literacy tests to vote. These laws allowed poor whites to vote but made it impossible for most African Americans to vote.

Governments throughout the South also began to pass **segregation** laws called Jim Crow laws. These laws kept African Americans and whites apart in public places, such as schools, hotels, beaches, churches, and restaurants.

In 1896 the Supreme Court protected segregation in a case called *Plessy* v. *Ferguson.* Homer Plessy, an African American, wanted to ride in the same railroad cars as white people. The Court ruled against Plessy and said that states could pass segregation laws to keep African Americans and white people apart. However, the public places for African Americans had to be equal to those for whites. Whites used this decision to carry out segregation until the 1950s.

In 1776 the United States had started with the goal that this nation would allow all people to have freedom and equality. The years after Reconstruction proved that this goal had not been reached. But the Thirteenth, Fourteenth, and Fifteenth Amendments gave the nation better tools for reaching its goal. Many years later, those amendments would finally allow all Americans to have equal rights.

BIOGRAPHY

Booker T. Washington 1856-1915

Booker T. Washington was born a slave, but he became an important African American leader. He advised governors, Congressmen, and two Presidents on how to help African Americans.

Washington became free when he was nine years old. He wanted an education very badly, so he went to school at the Hampton Institute, a school for African American students. He became a teacher.

In 1881 Washington started the Tuskegee Institute in Alabama. Washington's goal was to teach African Americans different trades at the school so they could get better jobs. Many students at Tuskegee became teachers who later started their own schools for African Americans. Washington was the principal at Tuskegee for 33 years.

While Washington worked at Tuskegee, he often thought about the problems African Americans had in the South. Washington wanted to help African Americans have a better life even though they were not treated fairly. He believed that African Americans needed good jobs so they could earn more money and then buy their own land. By doing this, they would slowly have more power to improve their civil rights.

Washington said these ideas in a famous speech, the Atlanta Compromise. He asked whites to be fair and to give African Americans better jobs. He said that African Americans must accept segregation and not ask for equal rights. As they earned more money, they would receive better treatment. Not all African Americans agreed with Washington's ideas. Some believed African Americans should demand equal rights.

Booker T. Washington succeeded in helping many African Americans get a good education. Today Washington is remembered as one of the most important African American leaders during the years after Reconstruction.

In Your Own Words

Write a paragraph in your notebook that tells how Booker T. Washington tried to help African Americans.

REVIEW AND APPLY

- The years after the Civil War were called Reconstruction.

- After Abraham Lincoln was assassinated, Andrew Johnson became President.

- Radical Republicans, members of Congress who blamed the South for the war and felt the South should be punished, opposed President Johnson's Reconstruction plan.

- Radical Republicans tried, but failed, to impeach President Johnson.

- Reconstruction came to an end in March 1877 when President Hayes ordered federal troops to leave the South.

- After Reconstruction, Southern states passed laws that took many rights away from African Americans. Segregation laws separated African Americans and whites in many public places.

VOCABULARY

Choose the Meaning ■ Write the letter of the word or phrase that best completes each sentence.

1. An **oath** is a _____.

   a. promise to be loyal
   b. a proposed law
   c. a plan

2. **Freedmen** were people who _____.

   a. passed the Black Codes
   b. wanted to stop slaves from gaining their freedom
   c. became free after the Civil War

3. The **Civil Rights Act** said that African Americans _____.

   a. were American citizens
   b. had to pay for their freedom
   c. could not hold any public offices

4. To **impeach** means to _____.

   a. be elected to a public office
   b. be charged with a crime in order to be removed from public office
   c. be chosen to run for political office

5. **Sharecroppers** rented land from landowners in return for _____.

   a. money
   b. labor
   c. crops

6. A **poll tax** had to be paid so that a person could _____.

   a. own land
   b. move to another place
   c. vote

COMPREHENSION CHECK

Understanding Events in History ■ Copy the graphic organizer below to your social studies notebook. Then complete the graphic organizer with information about Reconstruction.

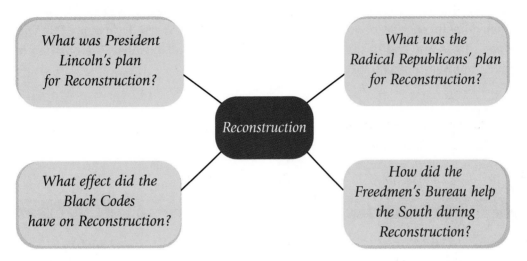

What was President Lincoln's plan for Reconstruction?

What was the Radical Republicans' plan for Reconstruction?

Reconstruction

What effect did the Black Codes have on Reconstruction?

How did the Freedmen's Bureau help the South during Reconstruction?

CRITICAL THINKING

Distinguishing Relevant Information ■ Imagine you are telling a friend about Reconstruction in the South after the Civil War. Read each sentence below. Decide which sentences are relevant to what you will say. Write those sentences in your social studies notebook. There are four relevant sentences.

1. President Lincoln cared about Southerners.

2. President Johnson and the Radical Republicans disagreed over Reconstruction plans.

3. The Fourteenth and Fifteenth amendments were added to the Constitution.

4. Radical Republicans tried to impeach President Johnson.

5. Carpetbaggers, scalawags, and African American Republicans controlled the South during Reconstruction.

6. Samuel Tilden ran for President in 1876.

USING INFORMATION

Writing an Opinion ■ After the Civil War, there were different ideas about rebuilding the South and bringing the Southern states back into the Union. Write a paragraph explaining which plan of Reconstruction you would have supported.

Unit 4 Review

Study the time line on this page. You may want to read parts of Unit 4 again. In the assignment section of your notebook, write the numbers 1 through 18. Then use the words and the dates in the box to finish the paragraphs. The box has one possible answer that you will not use.

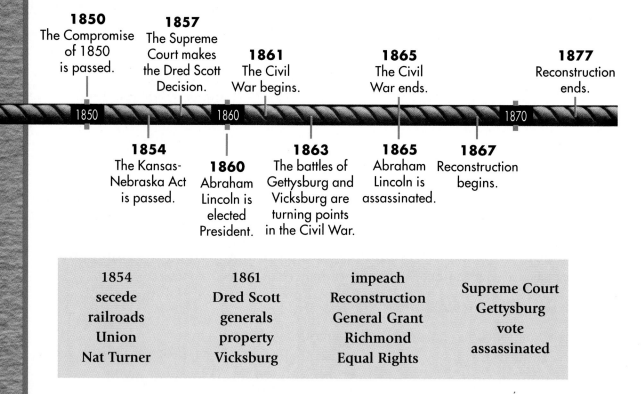

1850
The Compromise of 1850 is passed.

1857
The Supreme Court makes the Dred Scott Decision.

1861
The Civil War begins.

1865
The Civil War ends.

1877
Reconstruction ends.

1854
The Kansas-Nebraska Act is passed.

1860
Abraham Lincoln is elected President.

1863
The battles of Gettysburg and Vicksburg are turning points in the Civil War.

1865
Abraham Lincoln is assassinated.

1867
Reconstruction begins.

1854	1861	impeach	Supreme Court
secede	Dred Scott	Reconstruction	Gettysburg
railroads	generals	General Grant	vote
Union	property	Richmond	assassinated
Nat Turner	Vicksburg	Equal Rights	

Slavery continued to trouble the nation during the 1800s. After ___1___ led a slave rebellion, slave owners were afraid that there would be more rebellions. The Kansas-Nebraska Act of ___2___ allowed the question of slavery to be decided by popular sovereignty. In 1857 the Supreme Court made a decision about a slave named ___3___.

The Court said that Scott was still a slave and all slaves were ___4___, so they could be taken to any part of the country. After Abraham Lincoln was elected President, the Southern states began to ___5___. Lincoln said that his goal was to save the ___6___. The Civil War began in ___7___ when South Carolina attacked Fort Sumter. The Confederates had better ___8___, but the Union had more money, soldiers, supplies, and ___9___.

In 1863 the Union won the three-day battle at ___10___, Pennsylvania. To win control of the Mississippi River, General Grant laid siege to ___11___, Mississippi. In April 1865 the Union captured the Confederate capital of ___12___, Virginia. General Robert E. Lee knew he could not win the war, so he surrendered to ___13___ at Appomattox Court House. On April 14, 1865, Abraham Lincoln was ___14___. In 1867 Congress passed the ___15___ Act so the South could rejoin the Union. In 1868 the House of Representatives voted to ___16___ President Andrew Johnson. The Senate did not have enough votes to find Johnson guilty, so he finished his term as President. The Fourteenth Amendment, often called the ___17___ Amendment, was ratified in 1868. In 1870 the Fifteenth Amendment gave African Americans the right to ___18___. After Reconstruction ended, it became very difficult for African Americans to vote.

Looking Ahead to Unit 5

After the Civil War, Americans began to develop the West, and railroads were built across the nation. While many Americans moved West, others built new factories and businesses in the North and South. The nation changed as millions of people settled in the United States. There were new problems to be solved as cities became crowded and factory workers worked long hours.

As you read Unit 5, think about the Indian leaders who fought to keep their homes in the West. Discover who helped factory workers solve their problems. Read on to learn how the United States became a large industrial nation.

Unit 5

THE UNITED STATES BECOMES AN INDUSTRIAL NATION

In 1876 the nation celebrated its one hundredth birthday at an event called the Centennial Exposition in Philadelphia. Millions of people saw strange new inventions such as the typewriter and the telephone. People agreed that the nation had changed in many ways since 1776.

As you read Unit 5, you will learn how the nation changed after the Civil War. Learn how Americans settled the West and how Indian life changed. Discover how immigrants contributed to the nation and how cities grew and changed. Learn how Americans solved the problems created by the growth of industry.

1862
Congress passes the Homestead Act.

1869
The first transcontinental railroad is finished.

1876
Sioux Indians win the Battle of Little Bighorn.

1879
Thomas Edison invents the electric light bulb.

1860 — 1870 — 1880

1861
Civil War begins.

1865
Civil War ends.

1873
Barbed wire is invented.

1877
Reconstruction ends.

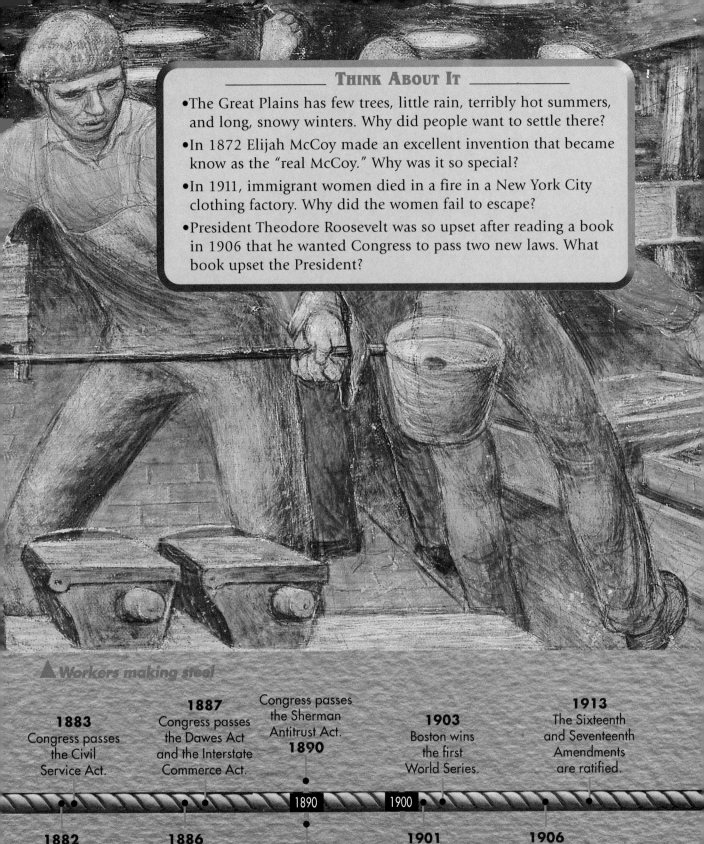

THINK ABOUT IT

- The Great Plains has few trees, little rain, terribly hot summers, and long, snowy winters. Why did people want to settle there?
- In 1872 Elijah McCoy made an excellent invention that became know as the "real McCoy." Why was it so special?
- In 1911, immigrant women died in a fire in a New York City clothing factory. Why did the women fail to escape?
- President Theodore Roosevelt was so upset after reading a book in 1906 that he wanted Congress to pass two new laws. What book upset the President?

▲ Workers making steel

1883
Congress passes the Civil Service Act.

1887
Congress passes the Dawes Act and the Interstate Commerce Act.

Congress passes the Sherman Antitrust Act.
1890

1903
Boston wins the first World Series.

1913
The Sixteenth and Seventeenth Amendments are ratified.

1890

1900

1882
Congress passes the Chinese Exclusion Act.

1886
Samuel Gompers starts the American Federation of Labor.

1890
Indians are massacred at Wounded Knee.

1901
Theodore Roosevelt becomes President after McKinley is assassinated.

1906
Congress passes the Meat Inspection Act and the Pure Food and Drug Act.

Chapter 19
GROWTH IN THE AMERICAN WEST

◀ *Wheat field on the Great Plains*

People

Cyrus McCormick • Leland Stanford • Henry Comstock • Chief Seattle • Cheyenne • Arapaho • Colonel John Chivington • Sioux • Sitting Bull • Crazy Horse • George Custer • Chief Joseph • Nez Percé • Helen Hunt Jackson • Red Cloud • Korczak Ziolkowski

Places

Omaha • Sacramento • Promontory Point • Abilene • Chicago • Black Hills

New Vocabulary

technology • reaper • transcontinental • spike • open range • barbed wire • reservations • poverty

Focus on Main Ideas

1. What problems did people face as they settled on the Great Plains?
2. How did railroads cause the population of the West to grow?
3. How did Indian life change as white settlers moved to the Great Plains?

Would you want to settle on the Great Plains, where there is little rain and very few trees? The summers are blazing hot and the winters are freezing cold. Dust storms, windstorms, snowstorms, and tornadoes are common. Despite these hardships, during the 1860s many Americans began to make the Great Plains their home.

The Homestead Act

Throughout the nation's history, there had been a frontier, land that had few settlers. After the American Revolution, the frontier was the land between the original 13 states and the Mississippi River. As Americans settled that land and moved west, the Great Plains became the frontier.

The Great Plains is the flat region between the Mississippi River and the Rocky Mountains. Because this region received little rain and had few forests, it was called the Great American Desert. Few people wanted to settle there. To encourage people to settle on the Great Plains, Congress passed the Homestead Act in 1862. This law gave settlers 160 acres of free land on the Great Plains. The law required a settler to live on the land, build a house, and farm the land for five years.

238

About two million people moved to the Great Plains because of the Homestead Act.

Life was difficult for the new settlers. People were lonely because they lived far apart and had few neighbors. There were few stores where settlers could shop.

Farming was difficult on the Great Plains, but new **technology** helped the farmers. At first farmers found it difficult to turn over the soil to plant seeds because the thick grass of the Great Plains had very long, strong roots. This problem was solved with the invention of the steel plow, which worked better than iron plows. The lack of rain made it difficult to grow crops. So farmers used windmills to pump water up from deep underground. They also planted special kinds of wheat that needed less water. To harvest large fields of wheat and corn, farmers used a machine called the **reaper**. It had been invented by Cyrus McCormick in 1831.

By the 1890s huge amounts of wheat and corn were being grown on the Great Plains. The region became known as "America's breadbasket."

Railroads Opened the West

In 1860 there were no railroads west of the Missouri River. Building a **transcontinental** railroad would allow

Life was difficult for settlers on the Great Plains. Because there were few trees, homes were built from sod, or squares of grass. The family pictured above might have lived there for some time because they have had time to add glass windows and a new section to the original house.

people to travel from the Atlantic Ocean to the Pacific Ocean. To reach this goal, Congress passed the Pacific Railway Act in 1862. This act allowed the Union Pacific Railroad Company to build a railroad that started in Omaha, Nebraska, and went west. The Central Pacific Railroad Company would build a railroad that would move east from Sacramento, California.

Both companies worked fast to lay as many miles of railroad tracks as possible. It was hard work to build railroads across rivers and mountains. The work was so dangerous that many men died while working on the railroads.

Thousands of immigrants were hired to build the railroads. The Central Pacific hired Chinese immigrants, and the Union Pacific hired Irish immigrants. Immigrants from other European countries, as well as many African Americans, also helped to build these railroads.

On May 10, 1869, the tracks of the Central Pacific and Union Pacific railroads met at a place called Promontory Point in Utah. Leland Stanford, the owner of the Central Pacific, used a silver hammer to drive a golden **spike** into the ground. The spike joined the two railroads together. The nation's first transcontinental railroad was finished. People could travel by train from New York to California in a week. By covered wagon the trip took six months. Soon more transcontinental railroad routes were built.

Mining on the Last Frontier

The 1849 California gold rush was the first of many gold rushes in the West.

Throughout Colorado, Nevada, Idaho, Montana, and the Dakotas, the search for gold, silver, and other metals continued.

In 1859 miners found small amounts of gold and large amounts of silver in Nevada. The place became known as the Comstock Lode, after Henry Comstock. Comstock did not find the gold and silver, but he took credit for finding it.

Mining towns developed near mines. Most people in mining towns were men. However, some women moved to mining towns and ran restaurants and laundries. Others ran boarding houses, or places for miners to eat and sleep. Once all the metal from these mines was removed, people often left. Busy mining towns turned into empty towns called "ghost towns."

Raising Cattle on the Great Plains

Early Spanish settlers were the first to raise cattle in the American Southwest. The Spanish taught the Mexicans how to raise cattle. After the United States won control of the Mexican Cession, American cowboys, or cowhands, learned their skills from Mexican cowboys called vaqueros. Many cowhands were Mexican Americans or African Americans.

The longhorn cattle raised by the Spanish now lived in large herds in Mexico and in Texas. Texas became the cattle-raising center of the United States. Much of the land in Texas and other parts of the Great Plains was called the **open range**. The open range was grassy land that belonged to the federal government. Cattle were allowed to graze, or feed, freely on this land.

Each spring the cowhands would begin the long drive, or trip, to move their cattle to Abilene, Kansas. It would take two months of hard work for the cowhands, riding horses, to move thousands of cattle from Texas to Abilene. In Abilene the cattle were shipped to Chicago, Illinois, by railroad. Chicago became the meat-packing center of the United States.

As more farmers settled on the Great Plains, there were fights between farmers and ranchers, or cattle raisers. Farmers did not want cattle moving freely through their crops and destroying their farms.

The open range came to an end with the invention of **barbed wire** in 1873. Barbed wire made it easy to put fences around large areas of land. Farmers used barbed wire to keep cattle off their farms. Ranchers had to raise cattle on their own land instead of on the open range. Since cattle could no longer eat free grass on the open range, ranchers had to buy corn, hay, and grain from the farmers to feed the cattle.

Indians of the Great Plains

Before the Civil War, the federal government had said that the West would belong to the Indians "as long as the rivers shall run and the grass shall grow." This promise was broken many times when whites tried to take control of Indian lands.

Indians of the Great Plains depended on buffalo to survive. Before 1860 there were about 12 million buffalo on the Great Plains. The Plains Indians ate buffalo meat and made clothes and homes from buffalo skins. They moved from place to place to follow the herds of buffalo.

It was almost impossible for white settlers and Indians to live together on the Great Plains. Indians wanted to move from place to place as they hunted buffalo. White settlers wanted the land to be free of buffalo so it could be used for farming and ranching. Settlers killed millions of buffalo. By 1903 there were only 34 buffalo left in the entire country. As the buffalo disappeared, Indians often starved and died.

From 1850 to 1890, the United States Army fought against the Plains Indians. During these wars thousands of Indians were killed. As a result of the wars, Indians were forced to move onto **reservations,** land set aside for Indians. These reservations usually had such poor-quality land that settlers did not want to live there. As early as 1854, an important Indian leader in the Northwest, Chief Seattle, warned his people that they would be forced to live and suffer on reservations:

Cowboys, or cowhands, first learned their skills from Mexican cowhands called vaqueros. American cowboys even wore clothing similar to that worn by vaqueros.

"Day and night cannot dwell together. The Red Man [the Indian] has ever fled the approach of the White Man.... It matters little where we pass the remnant of our days. They will not be many. The Indians' night promises to be dark."

When gold was discovered in Colorado in 1859, people looking for gold settled on land that belonged to the Cheyenne and the Arapaho. After Indians attacked these settlers, Colonel John Chivington attacked a peaceful group of Cheyenne, and about 450 Cheyenne were killed. The Cheyenne and Arapaho were forced to move to reservations in Oklahoma and in the Black Hills of Dakota.

In 1868 the federal government signed a treaty with the Sioux Indians. This treaty gave the Sioux a reservation that included all the land in what is now South Dakota west of the Missouri River. The Black Hills were part of the land promised to the Indians. After gold was found in the Black Hills of South Dakota in 1874, the army ordered the Sioux to stay on a reservation. The Sioux leaders Sitting Bull and Crazy Horse refused. So in 1876 General George Custer led about 200 soldiers in an attack against the Sioux at the Battle of Little Bighorn. Thousands of Sioux led by Sitting Bull and Crazy Horse defeated Custer. Custer and all of his soldiers were killed,

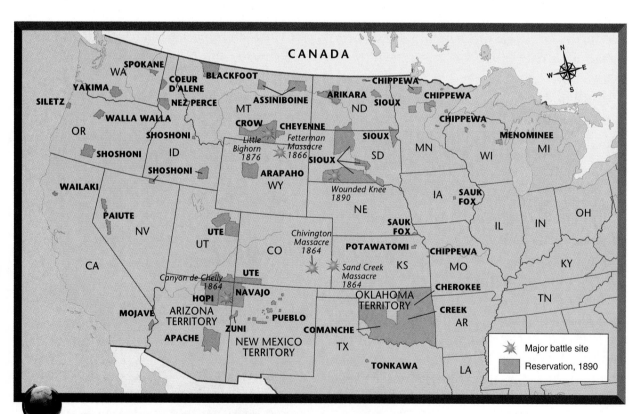

Indian Reservations in 1890 *There were many Indian reservations west of the Mississippi River in 1890. There were also many battles fought for control of the land in the West. What battle took place in Montana in 1876?*

242

and the battle became known as "Custer's Last Stand." It was one of the greatest Indian victories. Although the Sioux won this battle, they lost other battles to the army. In 1881 Sitting Bull and his followers surrendered.

Chief Joseph, the leader of the peaceful Nez Percé tribe, wanted to save his people from being forced onto a reservation. He tried to escape to Canada with tribe members. They had almost reached Canada when they were captured by the army. Eventually Joseph agreed to move to a reservation. In his surrender speech, Chief Joseph said "I am tired of fighting.... It is cold and we have no blankets. The little children are freezing to death.... I am tired; my heart is sick and sad. From where the sun now stands, I will fight no more forever." The Nez Percé were sent to a reservation in Oklahoma. Joseph was separated from his people and forced to move to a reservation in the state of Washington.

Helen Hunt Jackson wrote a book, *A Century of Dishonor*, that told Americans how unfair the government had been. Many members of Congress read Jackson's book, and they also criticized the government's treatment of the Indians. To improve the government's treatment of Indians, Congress passed the Dawes Act in 1887. For the first time, Indians were allowed to become American citizens. The Dawes Act encouraged Indians to become farmers. This law broke up land owned by Indian tribes into small sections. Indian families could receive 40 to 160 acres of their own land. But the land was not good for farming, and the Indians did not have the skills or the tools to be farmers. Many

Chief Joseph was one of the leaders of the Nez Percé. From June to October 1877, they were pursued by the army through the Idaho, Wyoming, and Montana territories.

Indians sold their land, but then they had no way to earn a living. **Poverty** became a serious problem. The Dawes Act failed to help the Indians.

The last battle between the Indians and the United States Army happened in 1890 at Wounded Knee, South Dakota. Indians there were doing religious dances called Ghost Dances. Soldiers killed more than 200 Sioux men, women, and children. After the Wounded Knee Massacre, most Indians agreed to live on reservations.

By the 1890s the Great Plains had been settled by white people. Most Indians had been forced to move to reservations. Farms, railroads, and mining towns were being built across the West. Each year more Americans would continue to make the Great Plains their home.

Crazy Horse 1842-1877

Crazy Horse was one of the greatest warriors and chiefs of the Sioux Indians. Crazy Horse was determined to protect Sioux land from settlers who were moving to the Great Plains. From 1866 to 1868 Crazy Horse fought alongside Chief Red Cloud to stop people from traveling west on the Bozeman Trail, which was in Sioux territory. Red Cloud and Crazy Horse attacked United States forts and settlements along the trail in Wyoming. Crazy Horse became famous for tricking and trapping his enemies. In 1868 the government signed a treaty with the Sioux. In that treaty the government gave up its forts along the Bozeman Trail. The Sioux were given the western part of South Dakota, including the Black Hills.

When gold was discovered in the Black Hills in 1874, the federal government broke the treaty. The government wanted to buy the Black Hills, but the Sioux refused to sell their land. So the army sent General George Custer to fight for the land. In 1876 Crazy Horse and Chief Sitting Bull defeated General Custer at the Battle of Little Bighorn.

Crazy Horse and his warriors continued to fight, but in January 1877 they were defeated by General Nelson Miles. On May 6, 1877, Crazy Horse and hundreds of his followers surrendered to the army. A number of months later, Crazy Horse was killed when a soldier tried to force him into a jail cell. Crazy Horse's parents buried their son in a secret grave near Wounded Knee, South Dakota.

In 1948 Korczak Ziolkowski began carving a huge statue of Crazy Horse on one of the mountains in South Dakota's Black Hills. When it is completed, the statue will be more than 500 feet tall. Ziolkowski worked on that statue until he died in 1982. Others are now working to finish the statue. Although it is not yet finished, thousands of people visit the statue each year.

In Your Own Words

In the journal section of your notebook, write a paragraph that tells why Crazy Horse was a great leader.

REVIEW AND APPLY

- The Great Plains is a flat region between the Mississippi River and the Rocky Mountains. It receives little rain and has few forests.

- Congress passed the Homestead Act in 1862 to encourage people to settle on the Great Plains.

- Inventions such as the steel plow and the reaper helped farmers grow crops on the Great Plains.

- In 1869 the first transcontinental railroad was completed, allowing people to travel from New York to California in a week.

- The search for gold and other metals caused mining towns to develop throughout the West.

- As settlers moved onto the Great Plains, Indians were forced onto reservations. Some Indian groups fought for their land.

VOCABULARY

Matching ■ **Match the vocabulary word or phrase in Group B with the definition in Group A. You will not use all the words in Group B.**

Group A	Group B
1. When the railroads were completed, a gold one of these was used to connect the railroads together.	A. spike
2. This means having very little money.	B. technology
3. This machine is used to harvest fields of wheat and corn.	C. barbed wire
4. This is the land where cattle grazed.	D. transcontinental
5. These were the places where Indians were forced to live.	E. reservations
6. This means "across the continent."	F. poverty
7. This invention made it easier to put up fences on the Great Plains.	G. open range
	H. reaper

USING INFORMATION

Writing an Opinion ■ Many people today believe that the white settlers and the American government treated Indians unfairly. Do you agree or disagree? Give two or three reasons for your opinion.

COMPREHENSION CHECK

Who Said It? ■ Read each statement in Group A. Then match the name of the person in Group B who might have said it. There is one name you will not use.

Group A	Group B
1. "I took credit for finding gold and silver in Nevada."	A. Helen Hunt Jackson
	B. Cyrus McCormick
2. "My invention helped farmers harvest crops on the Great Plains."	C. Henry Comstock
3. "I led an attack that killed about 450 peaceful Cheyenne."	D. John Chivington
4. "I drove into the ground the golden spike that completed the transcontinental railroad."	E. Leland Stanford
	F. George Custer
5. "I wrote a book about the unfair treatment of Indians."	

CRITICAL THINKING

Fact or Opinion ■ Write the numbers 1-6 in your social studies notebook. Next to each number, write an **F** if that statement is a fact. Write **O** if the statement is an opinion. If the statement gives both a fact and an opinion, write **FO**. Then write the part of the sentence that is an opinion.

1. The Great Plains were called the Great American Desert, but it should have been called the Great American Farm.

2. The Homestead Act gave settlers 160 acres of free land on the Great Plains.

3. The transcontinental railroad cost too much money to build.

4. Miners in the West should not have given up so easily when they did not find gold at first.

5. By 1903 most of the buffalo in America had been killed.

6. Chief Joseph tried to save his people from being forced to live on a reservation.

246

AMERICAN EOGRAPHY

Region: The Great Plains

A region has places that may share similar climates, landforms, businesses, products, and culture. The Great Plains is a large region of flat plains and low hills stretching from western Texas to northern Canada and from the Mississippi River to the Rocky Mountains. The Great Plains has very hot summers and very cold winters. It has a dry climate with less than 20 inches of rain a year. Tornadoes, thunderstorms, and blizzards are common weather problems in this region.

Read the paragraph above and study the map of the Great Plains. Then write the answers to the questions below in the assignment section of your social studies notebook.

1. Name four states that are part of this region.

2. Which four major rivers run through the Great Plains?

3. What is considered to be the western border of the Great Plains?

4. What is considered to be the eastern border of the Great Plains?

5. What is the climate like in the Great Plains?

6. What are some common weather problems in this region?

7. What are three features shared by places in this region?

8. Why did the region known as the Great American Desert become known as America's breadbasket?

THE GROWTH OF BUSINESS AND INDUSTRY

Alexander Graham Bell's first telephone

People

Henry Bessemer • Granville
T. Woods • Elijah McCoy •
Thomas Edison • Cyrus W.
Field • Alexander Graham
Bell • Cornelius Vanderbilt •
Andrew Carnegie • John D.
Rockefeller • Madam C. J.
Walker • J. P. Morgan

New Vocabulary

capital • natural resources •
capitalism • free
enterprise • competition •
partnership • corporations •
shares • stocks •
monopoly • trust •
refinery • laissez-faire

Focus on Main Ideas

1. Why was the United States able to become an industrial nation?
2. How did new inventions help the growth of industry?
3. How did big business affect the growth of industry?
4. Why did Congress pass laws to control big business?

After the Civil War, the United States became a nation with huge businesses and many different kinds of industries.

The Industrial Revolution Changed America

The Industrial Revolution began in England in the 1700s. This revolution was a change from making products by hand at home to making products by machine in factories. After the Industrial Revolution started in England, it spread to other nations. The Industrial Revolution started in the United States when textile mills were built in New England. After the Civil War, industry grew rapidly throughout the United States. The United States became a great industrial nation between the years 1865 and 1900 for seven reasons.

First, the United States had people with **capital**, or money, to spend on developing industries and businesses.

Second, the United States had important **natural resources** such as iron, coal, and oil. These resources were needed to develop the steel, oil, and railroad industries. From these three industries, hundreds of other industries developed. For example, glass was needed for railroad car windows.

Third, the United States had the energy sources it needed to run railroads and factories. During the early days of the Industrial Revolution, steam and water power were the main types of energy used in factories. By the end of the 1800s, coal provided energy for many railroads and factories. Later, oil and electricity became important sources of energy.

Fourth, the United States was developing a large railroad system. The railroads moved natural resources, such as coal, oil, and iron, to where they were needed.

Fifth, new inventions helped the growth of industry. For example, the inventions of the telegraph and the telephone made it possible to communicate over long distances.

Sixth, the United States had a large population. There were plenty of people to work in factories, build railroads, and make new inventions.

Seventh, the American economy is based on **capitalism**. Under this system, also known as **free enterprise**, people can own businesses and industries and keep the profits that they earn. Each business owner tries to make as much money as possible. Capitalism encourages **competition** between businesses. Businesses try to make the best product to sell to customers.

The growth of industry led to new ways of selling products. Department stores, which sold many different kinds of products in one store, were common. Woolworth's and Macy's opened stores in many parts of the nation. Mail-order companies were started. They allowed people who lived far from stores to order products from catalogs and receive them by mail. Customers could order tools, clothes, and other items.

Ways of Organizing Businesses

For hundreds of years, most businesses had been owned by one person or a family. Sometimes two or more people formed a **partnership** and owned a business together. This system had two problems. One problem was that if the business failed, the owners were personally responsible for paying all of the debts. The second problem was that this system could not raise enough capital, or money, to build very large businesses. For example, one person or a partnership could not raise enough money to build a railroad.

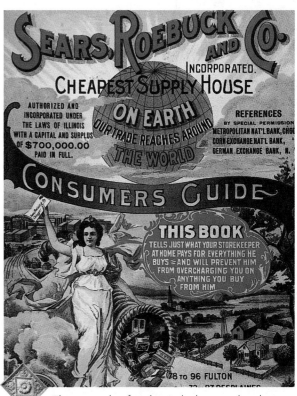

The growth of industry led to mail-order companies that sold products through the mail. Catalogs, such as this one from Sears, Roebuck and Company, advertised many different products.

249

Since the late 1800s, large businesses have been organized as **corporations.** A corporation is a company that can raise large amounts of money by selling **shares** of the company. People own a part of the corporation when they own shares. Shares are also called **stocks.** People who own shares are called shareholders or stockholders. If the corporation fails, shareholders cannot lose more money than they paid for their stock. If the company earns profits, the price of the stock will rise. Then shareholders can sell their stocks for a profit.

New Inventions Helped the Growth of Industry

In 1856 Henry Bessemer, an English inventor, found a fast, cheap way to change iron into steel. Steel is a metal made from iron, which is found in rocks inside the earth. Iron is not a strong metal. It cracks and rusts easily. Steel is much stronger than iron.

The Bessemer process changed American industry. Bridges and machines in factories were made of steel. The invention of steel made it possible to build tall skyscrapers. Railroad companies began to make railroad tracks out of steel.

Besides steel, other inventions helped the growth of the railroad industry. After refrigerator railroad cars were invented, it became possible to ship meat and farm products across the nation. Granville T. Woods, an African American, invented a system that used electric power rather than steam engines to run trains.

In 1872 Elijah McCoy, another African American inventor, made the lubricating cup, which allowed oil to drip slowly onto the moving parts of a train so they would move smoothly. Before this invention every train had to stop frequently to be oiled. Others tried to copy McCoy's invention, but no one made one that worked as well. The owners of the railroads insisted on buying the "real McCoy" for their trains.

One of the most important American inventions was the electric light bulb. Thomas Edison made the first one in 1879. Soon factories, homes, offices, and trains were lit with electric bulbs. To use electric light bulbs, a large supply of electricity was needed. Power plants that produced electricity were invented. Electricity became the most important form of energy for homes and factories. Thomas Edison, one of America's greatest inventors, also made hundreds of other useful inventions.

The invention of the telegraph in 1837 made it possible to send messages across the nation in seconds. In 1866 Cyrus W. Field laid the first telegraph cable across the Atlantic Ocean. This underwater cable made it easy to send messages quickly between the United States and Europe.

The telegraph could send signals, but it could not send sounds made by the human voice. Alexander Graham Bell, a Scottish immigrant and a teacher of deaf children, invented the telephone in 1876. Ten years later thousands of telephones were being used across the nation.

The Growth of Big Business

The corporations that ran the oil, steel, and railroad industries became huge and powerful by the end of the 1800s. These

The Bessemer process, pictured above, made stronger steel. The improved steel brought about changes in many industries. It also changed the look of modern cities. Before the Bessemer process, city buildings were made with iron. New buildings called skyscrapers could be built using steel. The Home Insurance Building in Chicago was one of the first to use this new technology.

companies were called big businesses. A big business controls many other businesses. For example, one company controlled most of the steel industry in America.

To grow bigger, companies tried to gain a **monopoly**. As a monopoly a company controls an entire industry. These monopolies prevented competition from other companies. By controlling competition a monopoly could decide the price of a product everywhere. Several large corporations could become a single monopoly by forming a **trust**. A trust is a group of corporations that is run by a group of people called a board of directors. For example, the board of directors of an oil trust could control most of the oil companies.

Three powerful leaders of big business were Cornelius Vanderbilt, Andrew Carnegie, and John D. Rockefeller. Cornelius Vanderbilt controlled much of the railroad industry. He decided the rates that most people had to pay. By the time Vanderbilt died, he was worth about $100 million.

Andrew Carnegie became even richer than Vanderbilt. Carnegie owned most of America's steel mills. He also owned his own railroads and ships for shipping steel to different places. John D. Rockefeller became rich by controlling the oil industry.

Oil was discovered in Pennsylvania in 1859. After oil was removed from the earth, it had to be cleaned in an oil **refinery** before it could be used. Rockefeller bought his first refinery after the Civil War. He started his own business called the Standard Oil Company.

Rockefeller's goal was to have complete control of the oil business. So he bought his own oil wells. Because he shipped so much oil, Rockefeller convinced railroad owners to charge him lower rates for shipping his oil than they charged other companies.

Because he paid less for shipping, Rockefeller could sell his oil for less money than other companies. Other companies lost money when they tried to sell their oil at the same low price. Then Rockefeller bought all the oil companies that were losing money. Before long he owned almost every oil refinery in America. Rockefeller became the richest man in the nation.

Some people called business leaders like Rockefeller and Carnegie "captains of industry" because they helped industry grow. People also praised these men because they gave away millions of dollars to help others. Rockefeller used his money to build many schools and churches. One of his schools became the University of Chicago.

Other people hated men like Carnegie and Rockefeller and called them "robber barons." People felt that these business leaders were evil because they forced many companies to go out of business. Robber barons also paid very low salaries to most of their workers.

Not all business leaders were men. Madam C. J. Walker was a woman who built a business that made hair care products.

Inventions that Changed America

Inventor	Invention	Importance
Samuel F. B. Morse	telegraph 1837	The telegraph could send messages quickly between places that were far apart.
Elias Howe	sewing machine 1846	Clothing could be made much faster by machine.
Henry Bessemer	Bessemer Process 1856	Steel could be made quickly and cheaply.
George Pullman	railroad sleeping cars 1858	The sleeping car encouraged people to travel long distances by train.
Christopher Sholes	typewriter 1867	The typewriter made it easier to prepare written material.
Elijah McCoy	lubricating cup 1872	The lubricating cup used dripping oil to keep the parts of a train moving smoothly.
Joseph Glidden	barbed wire 1873	Barbed wire made it possible to build fences around large areas.
Alexander Graham Bell	telephone 1876	People could talk with each other over long distances.
Thomas Edison	phonograph 1877	People could hear music and other sounds on records.
Thomas Edison	electric light bulb 1879	Electric light bulbs are used to light homes, schools, offices, and streets.
Jan Matzeliger	shoemaking machine 1882	Shoes are made in factories and sold in stores.
Wilbur and Orville Wright	airplane 1903	The Wright brothers proved that it was possible to build a flying machine.
Henry Ford	moving assembly line 1913	Cars and other items could be made quickly and cheaply.

Walker used part of her profits to create better schools for African Americans.

The Government Tries to Control Big Business

Many Americans believed that the government should not try to control business. This idea is known as **laissez-faire**. However other Americans felt that big businesses had too much power. They wanted Congress to pass laws to control big business.

In 1887 Congress took the first step toward limiting the power of big business. Congress passed the Interstate Commerce Act. Congress said that railroads must charge fair rates on routes between states. Railroad companies had been charging huge companies like the Standard Oil Company lower rates than they charged small companies. To carry out the new law, Congress created the Interstate Commerce Commission, or the ICC.

The new agency found it difficult to force the railroads to charge fair rates. Sometimes the ICC took the railroad companies to court. Sixteen court cases against the railroad companies went to the Supreme Court by 1897. In 15 of those cases, the Court ruled in favor of the railroad companies.

The Sherman Antitrust Act was passed in 1890. The new law made monopolies and trusts illegal. The law's goal was to break up huge companies into smaller companies. Then competition between the smaller companies would force them to lower their prices. Unfortunately, the government found it very difficult to carry

Madam C. J. Walker became a millionaire from her business that made hair care products. Her parents were sharecroppers, and she grew up working on a cotton plantation.

out the Sherman Antitrust Act. The law did not state clearly what businesses could or could not do.

At first, the two laws that Congress passed in 1887 and 1890 did not succeed in limiting the power of big businesses. Now, however, these laws have been changed to allow Congress the power to make decisions about what businesses and industries can and cannot do.

During the years after the Civil War, the United States became an industrial nation. The oil, steel, and railroad industries became rich and powerful. While a small group of business leaders grew wealthy, millions of Americans led very difficult lives. In the next chapter, you will learn how immigrants and factory workers tried to solve their problems.

BIOGRAPHY

Andrew Carnegie 1835–1919

When Andrew Carnegie was a young boy in Scotland, his family was so poor that they had to borrow money to move to America. This poor boy became one of the richest men in the world.

Carnegie's family moved to the United States when he was 12. He went to school for only a short time, but he continued to learn by reading as many library books as he could. Carnegie developed an appreciation for libraries.

Carnegie's first job was working in a cotton mill. He earned only $1.20 a week. By age 24, he had an excellent job and a very good salary with the Pennsylvania Railroad. Carnegie used part of his salary to buy shares in the oil, coal, and iron industries. In less than ten years, he was earning $50,000 a year from those shares.

In 1873 Carnegie used the money he had earned to build his first steel mill. Before long Carnegie's mill was making more steel than any other American steel mill. Carnegie used his profits to buy other steel companies. He also bought railroads and ships to carry his steel. Carnegie's control of the steel industry made him a very rich man.

Many people felt that Carnegie was a cruel robber baron. Most of Carnegie's workers were poor immigrants from Europe. Although Carnegie was rich, he paid his workers very low salaries. Carnegie did not seem to care that the workers did very dangerous jobs but earned little money.

In 1901 Carnegie sold his steel company to J. P. Morgan, a rich banker, for about $500 million. Morgan then renamed the company the United States Steel Corporation. Today it is the largest steel company in the United States.

After Carnegie retired he gave away most of his money. He believed that money should be used to help others help themselves. He spent $60 million to build 3,000 libraries, and he gave millions of dollars to schools and colleges.

In Your Own Words

Write a paragraph in the journal section of your notebook that explains how Carnegie was both a "captain of industry" and a "robber baron."

REVIEW AND APPLY

- The United States became a great industrial nation between the years 1865 and 1900.

- During the late 1800s, most large businesses became corporations which sold shares of the company to the public.

- Inventions helped the growth of industry in the United States.

- In an attempt to grow larger, some companies tried to gain a monopoly by trying to prevent competition from other companies.

- The government tried to control big business by passing the Interstate Commerce Act and the Sherman Antitrust Act.

VOCABULARY

Defining and Using Vocabulary Words ■ Use the glossary to find the meaning of each word or phrase listed below. Write each word's definition in your social studies notebook. Then use each word in a sentence.

competition	free enterprise	monopoly
capital	partnership	trust
natural resources	corporations	laissez-faire
capitalism	stocks	

COMPREHENSION CHECK

Choose the Answer ■ Write the numbers 1–8 in the assignment section of your social studies notebook. Next to each number write the letter of the correct answer.

1. Where did the Industrial Revolution begin?

   a. the United States
   b. England
   c. Russia

2. Who made the first electric light bulb?

   a. Thomas Edison
   b. Alexander Graham Bell
   c. Elijah McCoy

3. What is another name for free enterprise?

   a. capitalism
   b. competition
   c. partnership

4. What are people who own shares in a company called?

   a. borrowers
   b. inventors
   c. stockholders

5. What is capital?

   a. The building where Congress meets.
   b. Natural resources needed for a nation to industrialize.
   c. Money to spend on developing business and industry.

6. Who invented a system that used electric power rather than steam engines to run trains?

   a. Henry Bessemer
   b. Granville Woods
   c. Cyrus Field

7. Who started the Standard Oil Company?

   a. Cornelius Vanderbilt
   b. Andrew Carnegie
   c. John D. Rockefeller

8. Who owned most of America's steel mills in the late 1800s?

   a. Cornelius Vanderbilt
   b. Andrew Carnegie
   c. John D. Rockefeller

USING INFORMATION

Writing an Essay ■ There were many reasons why the United States became a great industrial nation. Identify and explain at least five of these reasons. Start your essay with a topic sentence.

CRITICAL THINKING

Distinguishing Relevant Information ■ Imagine you are telling a friend about the growth of big business in the United States in the late 1800s. Read each sentence below. Decide which sentences are relevant to what you will say. Write the relevant sentences in your social studies notebook. There are four relevant sentences.

1. The United States had important natural resources such as iron and coal.

2. Americans were moving onto the Great Plains.

3. Business owners wanted to be successful.

4. Many new inventions helped businesses.

5. John D. Rockefeller built schools and hospitals.

6. Cornelius Vanderbilt controlled much of the railroad industry.

7. Congress passed laws to try to limit big businesses.

SOCIAL STUDIES SKILLS

Interpreting a Statistics Table

A table is a chart that contains **statistics**, or numbers, that provide information about a topic. The table below gives population statistics from 1850 to 1910. To read this table, first read the name of each heading.

To find information about each heading, read the table from top to bottom. To find information about each year, read the table from left to right.

Growth of City Population 1850–1910

Year	United States Population	Percentage of Population in Cities	Percentage of Population in Rural Areas	Factory and Construction Workers in Cities	Farm Workers
1850	23,191,876	15%	85%	2,140,000	4,982,000
1860	31,443,321	20%	80%	2,940,000	6,208,000
1870	39,818,449	26%	74%	4,560,000	6,850,000
1880	50,155,783	28%	72%	6,120,000	8,585,000
1890	62,947,714	35%	65%	8,860,000	9,938,000
1900	75,994,575	40%	60%	11,530,000	10,712,000
1910	91,972,266	46%	54%	15,601,000	11,340,000

Study the table. Then write the answers to the questions below in the assignment section of your social studies notebook.

1. What was the population of the United States in 1850?

2. In what year did the largest percentage of people live in cities?

3. In what year did the largest percentage of people live in rural areas?

4. How many people were farm workers in 1850?

5. How many people worked in factories in 1860?

6. Did the percentage of people in cities grow larger or smaller between 1850 and 1910?

7. How did the percentage of people in rural areas change between 1850 and 1910?

8. In what years were there more factory workers than farm workers?

Chapter 21

IMMIGRATION AND LABOR MOVEMENTS CHANGE AMERICA

◀ *1870 union poster for eight-hour workday*

National Eight Hour Law

People

Emma Lazarus • Samuel Gompers • Mother Jones • George Pullman • W.E.B. Du Bois

Places

Greece • Austria-Hungary • Japan • Homestead, PA

New Vocabulary

unskilled labor • tenements • ghettos • quota system • management • riot • collective bargaining • arbitration • injunction

Focus on Main Ideas

1. Why did cities grow larger after the Civil War?
2. What problems did immigrants face in the United States?
3. What problems did workers face in the late 1800s?
4. How did unions try to help workers?

In 1911 a terrible fire destroyed a clothing factory where immigrant women were working. While the fire burned throughout the factory, the women working inside the Triangle Shirtwaist Company factory could not escape. The owners had locked the factory doors to force the workers to stay at their jobs. In this tragedy, 146 Jewish and Italian immigrant workers died.

The fire at the Triangle Shirtwaist Company showed that worker safety was a problem. It proved that factory workers needed better working conditions. The fire also showed that immigrants to the United States faced many serious problems.

The Division of Labor in Factories

To make factory products more quickly, a system called the division of labor had developed. Under this system, a factory worker did only one type of job all the time. For example, in a clothing factory, one worker would sew the sleeves onto a shirt. Another worker would sew on the buttons. Still another would sew on the pocket. One worker no longer made an entire product. Division of labor made it faster and cheaper to make many goods in factories. **Unskilled labor**, or workers with few skills, did most of the factory

258

work. Their salaries were low because their jobs were easy to learn.

American Cities Grow Larger

The growth of industry led to the growth of cities. By 1900 almost half of the nation's people lived in cities. New York City, Philadelphia, and Chicago became the nation's largest cities with more than one million people in each city.

Cities developed better transportation that made travel easier. By the late 1800s, many cities had electric streetcars. Boston became the first American city with an underground subway system.

City populations grew as millions of immigrants moved to American cities after the Civil War. Many African Americans also moved to northern cities between 1890 and 1920. African Americans hoped to find better jobs in the North. But most factories would not hire them, so African Americans often took low-paying jobs, such as cleaning, cooking, and sewing.

As the population in cities grew larger, the cities' problems became more serious. There was not enough clean drinking water. Rats became a problem because city workers were not able to remove all the garbage that was produced. There were not enough police officers and firefighters.

In the late 1800s, major cities around the country were growing rapidly. Immigrants filled cities like New York City, Boston, and Philadelphia. African Americans moved north to St. Louis and Chicago from farms in the South. Cities became more modern with taller buildings and public transportation.

Most "new immigrants" to the United States came from southern and eastern Europe. Many of these immigrants were poor people who were looking for new opportunities.

Poor families lived in crowded **tenements**, or apartment houses, because there were not enough homes. Diseases spread quickly in these crowded, unhealthy conditions.

New Immigration After the Civil War

Immigrants started coming to America in the 1600s. Those who had come before the 1880s were called "old immigrants." These immigrants had come from England, Scotland, Ireland, Germany, and other northern and western countries of Europe. Many of these immigrants knew how to read. Most were Protestants. Many spoke English.

Immigrants who came to America after the 1880s were called "new immigrants."

Most of these new immigrants came from countries in southern and eastern Europe, such as Poland, Russia, Greece, Italy, and Austria-Hungary. About one third could not read or write. Most were Catholics, but ten percent were Jews. Most were very poor. Between 1880 and 1914, 22 million new immigrants moved to America.

Why did so many new immigrants come to America? First, many came to escape poverty. Second, they believed that America was a "golden door," or a land of opportunity. Third, people came to America for religious freedom and to escape persecution. For example, in Russia and Poland, Jews were often attacked and killed. Between 1881 and 1914, about 2 million Jews moved to America from Poland and Russia.

The first view of America for most immigrants was the Statue of Liberty. The statue, a gift to America from France, became a symbol of American freedom and opportunity.

Emma Lazarus, a Jewish American, wrote a famous poem about the Statue of Liberty. Lazarus's own family had come to America for religious freedom in the 1700s. Her poem stated that the statue welcomes all immigrants to America. These lines from the poem were placed at the base of the Statue of Liberty:

"Give me your tired, your poor,
 Your huddled masses yearning
  to breathe free,
 The wretched refuse of your
  teeming shore.
 Send these, the homeless, tempest
  tossed, to me,
 I lift my lamp beside the golden door."

Immigrant Life in America

Many immigrants settled in large cities such as New York City, Chicago, and Boston. Most lived in crowded tenements and became factory workers. Because so many immigrants needed jobs, factory owners had a huge supply of cheap labor.

Immigrants usually lived in **ghettos**, or neighborhoods, with people from their own country. For example, in New York City, Italians lived in Little Italy while Jews lived nearby on the Lower East Side.

Many people did not welcome the new immigrants even though most Americans were descendants of immigrants. Because most Americans were Protestants, Catholic and Jewish immigrants met with prejudice. Also, many Americans were angry that immigrants would work for low wages. Factory owners did not want to pay the higher wages that workers had been earning because the factory owners could hire immigrants and pay them less money.

People who feared and disliked the new immigrants wanted the government to stop allowing immigrants to come into the country. Congress began to pass laws to limit immigration. In 1882 the first law of this kind was the Chinese Exclusion Act. This law tried to stop Chinese people from coming to America. In 1907 a "gentlemen's agreement" between Japan and the United States stopped immigration of people from Japan. Starting in 1921 Congress passed laws that created a **quota system**. The quota system limited the number of immigrants who could move to the United States each year from different countries. The quota system favored people from northern and western Europe.

Labor Unions

The number of workers in mines and factories increased as immigrants poured into the nation. These workers were needed as big businesses grew.

Most workers in mines and factories faced many serious problems. First, wages were very low. Few men earned more than $16 a week. Women and children earned much less. Second, people had to work 6 days a week for 14 hours a day. Third, there were no child labor laws to prevent children from working. By 1890 one fifth of all children worked 14 hours a day in mines, factories, and farms. Usually they earned less than $10 a week. Fourth,

People From Many Cultures Helped the United States

Name	Nationality	Contribution
Michael Pupin	Serbian	Developed x-ray pictures
John Holland	Irish	Developed the submarine
Gideon Sundback	Swedish	Invented the zipper
Thomas Nast	German	Drew political cartoons
Albert Michelson	Polish	Developed instruments to measure the eye
Dr. Daniel William Hale	African American	Performed the first heart operation
Dr. Jokichi Takamine	Japanese	Found pure adrenaline in the human body

working conditions were dangerous and unhealthy. Workers who were hurt on the job received no money while they were unable to work. If they could not work, they often lost their jobs.

Many workers believed that they could win better salaries and working conditions by forming unions. To win better salaries and working conditions, union members could go on strike. During a strike, workers stopped working until union leaders reached an agreement with **management**. The chart on the next page shows some of the methods used by labor and management.

The first successful union was the Knights of Labor, which began in 1869. By 1886 more

than 700,000 workers had joined the Knights of Labor. The Knights lost most of their members soon after a **riot** in Chicago's Haymarket Square in 1886. A meeting was held at Haymarket Square to protest the killing of strikers by police. As police tried to end the meeting, a bomb exploded in the crowd. Seven policemen were killed. A riot started. When the police tried to stop the riot, they killed other people in the crowd. The Knights of Labor did not start the riot, but they were blamed for it.

In 1886 Samuel Gompers started another labor union. This new union was the American Federation of Labor, or the AFL. The AFL was made up of several

In the late 1800s, there were few laws in the nation to control child labor. Children could work as many hours as adults. Working conditions for children were often harsh, and injuries were common. In this photograph, children work without shoes or other protective clothing in a textile mill.

Methods Used By Labor and Management

Labor Methods	How it Works	Management Methods	How it Works
strike	Workers stop working.	strikebreakers or "scabs"	Management hires new non-union workers.
collective bargaining	Leaders from both sides find ways to solve problems.	blacklist	Management sends a list of union members to other businesses to prevent them from being hired.
closed shop	Management can hire only union members.	injunction	Management gets a court order to prevent or end a strike.
boycott	The public agrees not to buy products until the union ends the boycott.	yellow-dog contract	To get a job, workers must sign a contract that they will not join a union.
picket line	Union members stop non-union workers from entering a shop or factory.	lockout	Management closes the factory so workers must give in or lose their jobs.

skilled craftworkers' unions such as the shoemakers' union and the printers' union. Since only skilled workers could join these unions, few women, immigrants, and African Americans could become members of the AFL. Still the AFL became the nation's most important union. By 1904 more than one million people had become members of this union. However, most workers were not union members in the early 1900s.

The goals of the AFL were to get better salaries for workers, to win better working conditions, and to have an eight-hour workday. To reach these goals, the AFL used strikes and **collective bargaining** as its weapons. Collective bargaining happens when factory owners and union leaders meet to discuss ways to solve problems. Sometimes the union and the management agree to use **arbitration** as a way to settle a serious problem. In arbitration both the union leaders and the management present their arguments to another person. That person tries to make a decision that is fair for both sides.

Mary Harris Jones, often called Mother Jones, helped unions grow. Mother Jones was an Irish immigrant. In America she worked for laws to end child labor. Mother Jones believed mining work was so dangerous that workers needed unions to protect their rights. So she traveled around the country and helped miners join unions. Mother Jones continued working for unions until she was more than ninety years old.

Striking for Better Conditions

As more people joined unions, workers often went on strike. In 1892 the Homestead Strike began in Homestead, Pennsylvania. Workers at the Carnegie steel plant went on strike because the company had cut their wages. Andrew Carnegie was away on vacation, and management would not discuss the lower wages with the striking workers. Instead the management called in armed guards. A small war was fought between the guards and the union members. Although the strike lasted for months, the union failed to win better salaries. Union members finally returned to work for the lower wages.

Another famous strike, the Pullman Strike, also failed to help union members. George Pullman owned the company that made sleeper cars for railroads. Pullman's workers went on strike in 1894 when their salaries were cut. The American Railway Union, or the ARU, supported the Pullman workers. The ARU refused to handle Pullman cars on any railroads. This action

Many people were injured during the Homestead Strike in 1892. Armed union men are shown here leading away company guards that had surrendered.

stopped railroad traffic throughout the West. It also interfered with the delivery of the United States mail. A federal court issued an **injunction** to end the strike. Finally the government sent troops to force the workers to go back to work. The ARU lost its power and soon fell apart. Most of the striking workers were allowed to return to work at lower salaries. The actions of the federal government during the strike showed that it favored big business over the needs of poor workers.

As more people joined unions, the government began to pass laws to improve working conditions. In the 1900s better laws and stronger unions would help millions of workers achieve better working conditions.

BIOGRAPHY

W.E.B. Du Bois 1868–1963

W.E.B. Du Bois spent his life trying to help African Americans win equal rights. He was born in Massachusetts after the Civil War. Du Bois went to Fisk University in Nashville where he graduated second in his class. Then he became the first African American to earn a Ph.D. at Harvard. Du Bois became a teacher at Atlanta University in Georgia. While living in the South, he realized how unfairly African Americans were treated. He was upset that they were often lynched, or killed, by angry mobs. Du Bois was also angry that most African Americans in the North worked at cooking, cleaning, and sewing jobs. It was difficult for them to join labor unions. Du Bois wrote a book called *The Souls of Black Folk* that explained these problems.

Du Bois strongly disagreed with the ideas of another African American leader, Booker T. Washington. Washington said that African Americans should not demand equal rights. Instead they should improve their lives by working hard and earning good salaries. Du Bois thought African Americans should try to win equal rights immediately.

In 1905 Du Bois started the Niagara Movement. This movement encouraged educated African Americans to demand full voting rights and civil rights for their people.

In 1909 Du Bois joined with African Americans and white people to start the National Association for the Advancement of Colored People, or the NAACP. The NAACP worked to end segregation. Du Bois became the editor of *The Crisis*, the NAACP's magazine. In the magazine Du Bois wrote that African Americans should feel proud of their race and their culture. During elections the NAACP supported candidates who would work for equal rights.

Today the NAACP continues the fight for equal rights. Du Bois is remembered as a leader who worked to end prejudice in the United States.

In Your Own Words

Write a paragraph in the journal section of your notebook that explains the goals and the work of W.E.B. Du Bois.

REVIEW AND APPLY

- American factories in the early 1900s had many problems including unsafe working conditions and unfair treatment of employees.

- By 1900 almost one half of the country's population lived in cities. Chicago, New York City, and Philadelphia each had more than one million people.

- As cities grew larger, problems such as overcrowding and the spread of disease became more serious.

- Most immigrants lived in crowded tenements. Many Americans did not welcome the new immigrants.

- The first successful labor union in the United States was the Knights of Labor. The American Federation of Labor was later started by Samuel Gompers.

- Unions used methods such as strikes and collective bargaining to win better salaries and working conditions.

VOCABULARY

Finish the Sentence ■ Choose one of the words or phrases from the box to complete each sentence. You will not use all the words in the box.

1. In the early 1900s, _____ did most of the work in factories.

2. Many immigrants who came to the United States lived in crowded buildings called _____ .

3. In 1921, Congress passed laws that created a _____ that limited the number of immigrants from different countries.

4. One way that management agreed to settle labor problems was by using _____ .

5. Sometimes federal courts would issue an _____ to end a strike.

> unskilled labor
> collective bargaining
> arbitration
> tenements
> quota system
> injunction

USING INFORMATION

Writing an Opinion ■ In the late 1800s, unions were started to help workers. Write a paragraph in your social studies notebook that tells your own opinion about whether you agree or disagree with the methods used by unions to achieve their goals.

COMPREHENSION CHECK

Understanding Events in History ■ In your social studies notebook, draw a graphic organizer similar to the one shown below. Then complete the graphic organizer with information about immigration or the labor movement.

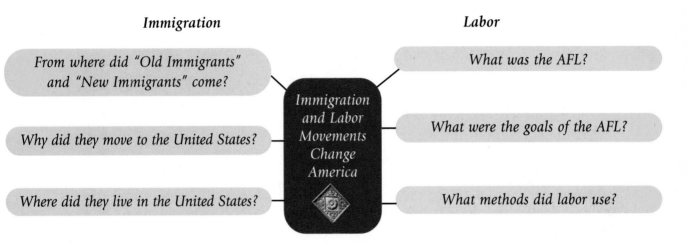

Immigration

From where did "Old Immigrants" and "New Immigrants" come?

Why did they move to the United States?

Where did they live in the United States?

Immigration and Labor Movements Change America

Labor

What was the AFL?

What were the goals of the AFL?

What methods did labor use?

CRITICAL THINKING

Drawing Conclusions ■ Read the paragraph below and the sentences that follow it. In your social studies notebook, write the conclusions that can be drawn from the paragraph. You should find three conclusions.

In the late 1800s, many immigrants came to the United States looking for a better life. Immigrants usually lived in ghettos with other immigrants from the same country. Most immigrants worked in factories. Working conditions in the factories were very bad. The workers were paid low wages and had to work many hours. Some Americans were angry that immigrants would work for lower wages. In 1921 Congress passed laws limiting the number of immigrants that could come into the United States from different countries.

1. Life was not always easy for immigrants living in the United States.

2. Factories were only found in the Northeastern part of the United States.

3. Fewer immigrants came to the United States after 1921.

4. Immigrants enjoyed living near people from their own countries.

5. Immigrant children could not work in factories.

SOCIAL STUDIES SKILLS

Reading a Bar Graph

The bar graph on this page shows the number of immigrants who came to the United States from five countries between 1860 and 1900. Study the key for the bar graph. Each country is represented by a different color. Using the key, you can compare how immigration to America from one country changed between 1860 and 1900. Or you can compare immigration to America from different countries during the same year.

Immigration to the United States 1860-1900

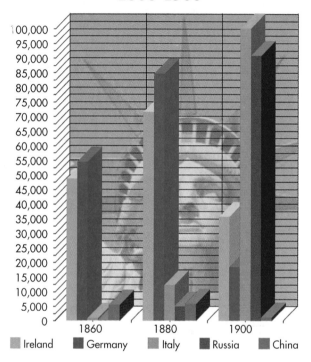

Study the bar graph. Then write the answers to the questions below in the assignment section of your social studies notebook.

1. Which five countries are represented in the bar graph?

2. Which nation sent the most immigrants in 1860?

3. Which nation sent the fewest immigrants in 1860?

4. About how many Chinese immigrants were there in 1860?

5. Which two nations had the most immigrants come to the United States in 1880?

6. About how many Italian immigrants were there in 1880?

7. Which nation sent the most immigrants to the United States in 1900?

8. How did immigration of Germans change between 1860 and 1900?

Reform and the Progressive Movement

◀ *Jacob Riis photograph of Little Katie, 1892*

People

William Jennings Bryan •
William McKinley • William
Tweed • Thomas Nast • Jane
Addams • Lillian Wald •
Jane Edna Hunter • Susan B.
Anthony • Theodore
Roosevelt • Upton Sinclair •
William Howard Taft •
Woodrow Wilson •
Elizabeth Cady Stanton

New Vocabulary

National Grange • gold
standard • inflation •
depression • civil service •
settlement house •
suffrage • muckrakers •
trustbuster •
conservation • third
party

Focus on Main Ideas

1. How did farmers try to solve their debt problems before 1900?
2. How did the Pendleton Act change the civil service?
3. How did Jane Addams help immigrants and workers?
4. What did the American people learn from the muckrakers?

By 1903 baseball had become the most popular sport in the country. Fans were thrilled when Boston's team defeated Pittsburgh's team in the first World Series. While the growth of industry gave middle-class Americans time to enjoy sports, millions of poor workers were struggling to survive. By the end of the 1800s, many reforms, or changes, were needed.

Hard Times for Farmers

Between 1870 and 1900, American farmers grew more food than ever before. However, farmers earned less money because crop prices had dropped. Many farmers were also in debt because they had borrowed money to buy expensive machines like seeders and reapers. They felt that their enemies were the railroad companies that charged farmers very high rates for shipping their crops.

In the 1870s farmers tried to help themselves by joining the **National Grange**. Grange members worked to get laws passed to control railroad rates. Several states passed such laws, which were called Granger laws.

The railroad companies went to court to end these laws. The Supreme Court ruled in favor of the railroads in the 1886 case called *Wabash* v. *Illinois*. The Supreme Court said that only Congress could control railroad rates if the railroad company had routes between states. The next year Congress passed the Interstate Commerce Act to control business between states.

The Populist Party

The Granger laws did not help farmers as much as they had hoped. Farmers looked for another answer. Many farmers believed that they could not earn enough money because all paper money had to be backed by gold. This was called the **gold standard**. Since gold was scarce, the amount of paper money the government could print was limited. Most business leaders wanted to keep the gold standard. Farmers wanted a new law that would allow paper money to be backed by both gold and silver. Since the nation had more silver than gold, the government could print more paper money. Increasing the amount of paper money would cause **inflation**. Farmers wanted inflation to make farm products more expensive so they would earn more money and be able to pay their debts.

In 1892 the farmers formed the Populist party. The main goal of the Populist party

Farmers tried to help themselves by getting new laws passed. This meeting of the Grange in Illinois in 1873 was just one of many meetings where farmers could voice their opinions. By the 1890s, meetings of the Grange led to a new political party, the Populist party.

270

was to end the gold standard, but the new party also supported other important changes. The Populists wanted an income tax that would require the rich to pay more taxes than the poor. They wanted an eight-hour workday. And they wanted to change the law so that the people of each state voted for United States senators, instead of allowing state legislatures to elect them.

The **depression** of 1893 brought hard times to millions of people. Many Americans blamed the gold standard for causing this depression. At the Democratic convention in 1896, Congressman William Jennings Bryan spoke out against the gold standard. He ended his "Cross of Gold" speech with these words: "We will answer their demand for a gold standard by saying to them: You shall not press down upon the brow of labor this crown of thorns, you shall not crucify mankind upon a cross of gold."

Bryan became the presidential candidate for both the Democratic and Populist parties. The Republican candidate, William McKinley, supported the gold standard. Bryan lost the election, and the Populist party soon came to an end.

Reforms in Government

Since the days of Andrew Jackson, people who supported a new President had been rewarded with jobs in the federal government, or **civil service** jobs. The Civil Service Act of 1883, also called the Pendleton Act, reformed the civil service. Under the new law people had to pass tests in order to get civil service jobs. Under this law, people would not lose their jobs when a President left office.

Thomas Nast drew this political cartoon of Boss Tweed as a vulture feeding on the people of New York. Nast's cartoons were seen by many people who would later turn against Tweed.

City governments also needed reform because many were controlled by "bosses." These leaders were not elected to the government. Instead they became powerful by controlling a city's main political party. By controlling the political party, the bosses controlled the elected leaders. Elected leaders needed the support of the bosses and their political party to stay in power.

William Tweed, a New York City boss, had great power in the 1860s and 1870s. He was called Boss Tweed, and he controlled the city's Democratic party. He used his power to steal about $100 million from the government. Thomas Nast drew political cartoons in newspapers that showed Boss Tweed stealing government money. Because of Nast's cartoons, Tweed lost his power and was sent to jail.

The Reform Movement

The growth of American industry brought serious problems to factory workers, immigrants, and the nation's big cities. During the late 1800s, many Americans began to work for change, or reform. One important reformer was Jane Addams. In 1889 Addams started a **settlement house** called Hull House. Hull House was in an immigrant neighborhood in Chicago. Included in its many services were English classes for immigrants, a summer camp for children, and a nursery to care for the children of working mothers. By 1900 about 2,000 people received services from Hull House each day.

Marches were held to bring attention to the women's suffrage movement. The Nineteenth Amendment gave women the right to vote in local, state, and national elections.

Addams did far more than take charge of Hull House. Her work led to the first child labor law in Illinois. She helped win an eight-hour workday for women. She fought for other laws to protect workers. In 1931 Addams became the first American woman to receive the Nobel Peace Prize.

Many people admired Addams for her work at Hull House. About 400 other settlement houses were started across the country. Lillian Wald, a nurse, started the Henry Street Settlement House in New York City. To help sick people who were too poor to visit doctors, Wald started a "visiting nurse" program. This program sent nurses to treat sick people in their homes. Jane Edna Hunter, also a nurse, started the Working Girls' Home Association in Cleveland. She helped African American women find jobs in that city.

While women worked for reform, they also worked for **suffrage**, or the right to vote. They fought for an amendment to the Constitution that would allow women's suffrage. Susan B. Anthony became a leader in the suffrage movement. In 1920 women finally won the right to vote when the Nineteenth Amendment became part of the Constitution.

The Progressive Movement

Between 1890 and 1914, a new reform movement known as the Progressive Movement made possible some of the important changes that the Populist party had wanted. Writers called **muckrakers** were an important part of this movement. These writers were called muckrakers because they raked up the muck, or dirt, in

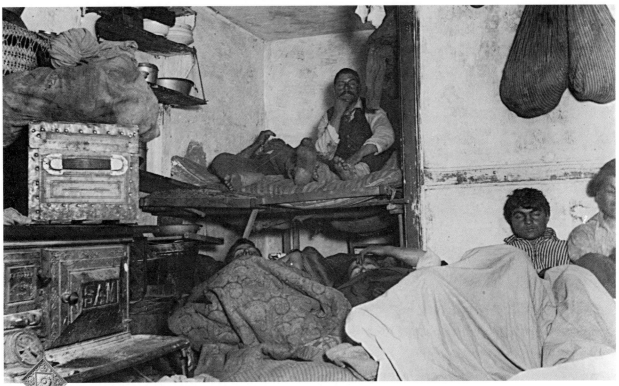

Jacob Riis was a muckraker who wrote about what life was like for poor people living and working in cities. In 1889 Riis took this photograph of an apartment in New York City. Each person paid five cents for a place to sleep in the room.

American life. Americans across the nation read their works and learned about serious problems in business and in society.

Theodore Roosevelt became President in 1901 after President McKinley was assassinated. Roosevelt believed that big business helped the growth of the nation, but he also thought the federal government should have more control over business.

President Roosevelt became known as a **trustbuster**. He used the Sherman Antitrust Act to attack trusts that were harming the country. Huge companies were broken up into smaller companies.

In 1904 Roosevelt was elected to a second term as President. He promised Americans a "Square Deal," a program that would be fair to all. Roosevelt worked to pass more laws that would control trusts. These laws gave more power to the Interstate Commerce Commission. Many more trusts were broken up.

Roosevelt and others learned about problems in the meat-packing industry by reading Upton Sinclair's novel *The Jungle*. Sinclair wrote the book to explain how people had to work under dangerous conditions. But it was his description of how the food was made that got people's attention. Canned meats and sausages often contained meat from sick animals and rats because of poor conditions in the meat-packing plants. In 1906 two laws were passed to protect people from unsafe food. The Pure Food and Drug Act required companies to make only safe foods and medicines. The Meat Inspection Act allowed federal workers to check all meat shipped out of a state.

Roosevelt started **conservation** programs to protect the nation's natural resources. Too many forests were being destroyed. Mining and manufacturing were using up other natural resources. The conservation programs were the first to protect America's forests, animals, and natural resources.

Roosevelt did not run for President a third time. In 1908 William Howard Taft was elected President. Taft continued to break up trusts. However, Roosevelt was not pleased with Taft's work. Roosevelt decided to run for President again in the election of 1912. The Republican party chose Taft as its candidate.

So Roosevelt's supporters started a new **third party**, the Progressive party. It was also called the Bull Moose party. Roosevelt and Taft were defeated by Woodrow Wilson, a Democrat.

Wilson Works for Change

Under Wilson two new amendments were added to the Constitution in 1913. The Sixteenth Amendment allowed Congress to pass income tax laws. The Seventeenth Amendment allowed citizens, instead of lawmakers, to vote for United States senators.

Wilson worked with Congress to pass the Clayton Antitrust Act in 1914. The new law said that companies could not limit competition. Wilson used this law to break up trusts that tried to stop competition. To carry out the laws against trusts, the Federal Trade Commission was started.

Wilson also supported the passing of the nation's first child labor law. Another law gave railroad workers an eight-hour workday. Still another law made it easier for farmers to borrow money.

The growth of big business and the arrival of immigrants brought progress and problems to the growing nation. During the time of the Progressive Movement, Americans began to solve the problems that were created by big business and industry.

Famous Muckrakers

Muckraker	Title of Well-known Work	Why Was the Work Important?
Jacob Riis	*How the Other Half Lives* 1890	Riis used photographs to show the terrible conditions in tenements.
Ida Tarbell	*A History of the Standard Oil Company* 1903	Tarbell wrote about John D. Rockefeller and the oil industry.
Lincoln Steffens	*The Shame of the Cities* 1904	Steffens told about the illegal methods used by city leaders.
Upton Sinclair	*The Jungle* 1906	Sinclair described unhealthy methods and terrible working conditions in the meat-packing industry.
Ray Stannard Baker	*Following the Color Line* 1908	Baker wrote about segregation of African Americans.

274

BIOGRAPHY

Susan B. Anthony 1820–1906

Susan B. Anthony helped women win equal rights. Anthony was born in Massachusetts to a Quaker family. Her parents taught her that men and women of all races should have equal rights. As a child, Anthony saw that women had few opportunities. Often their choices were limited to being wives, factory workers, or teachers.

As a young woman, Anthony became a teacher in Rochester, New York. There she earned only one dollar a week. When she learned that the male teachers were earning better salaries, she became very angry. She wanted to change what was unfair for women.

After 1854 Anthony's goal was to help women win the right to vote. She believed that once women could vote, they would use their voting power to win other rights. Anthony and Elizabeth Cady Stanton became close friends and worked together for women's rights.

Anthony never gave up her goal of women's suffrage. In 1872 she voted in an election for President. Because it was against the law for a woman to vote, Anthony was arrested. A jury trial found Anthony guilty. Her punishment was a $100 fine. Anthony believed that her punishment was unfair, so she never paid the fine. After the trial, Anthony spent the next twenty years traveling across the nation giving speeches about women's rights.

She spoke to senators and other members of Congress about the need for an amendment to the Constitution. Because of her work, people began to understand why women should be allowed to vote. Anthony's efforts helped women win the right to vote in four western states by 1900. Anthony died in 1906 before she reached her goal. Fourteen years later the Nineteenth Amendment to the Constitution was ratified. This amendment gave women the right to vote. The amendment quickly became known as the Susan B. Anthony Amendment.

In Your Own Words

Write a paragraph in the journal section of your notebook that explains how Susan B. Anthony's work has helped American women.

Voices from the Past

The Jungle by Upton Sinclair

Upton Sinclair wrote *The Jungle* to show the terrible working conditions in meat-packing plants. The setting was the Durham meat packing plant in "Packingtown," a part of Chicago. Sinclair showed the unfair hardships that Jurgis, a Lithuanian immigrant, had to deal with in order to earn a living. Jurgis joined the union because he saw how unfair workers were treated. For example, a worker would lose an hour's wage for being one minute late. But Jurgis's problems became much worse after he had an injury.

Jurgis fell into his trap…. At first he hardly noticed it, it was such a slight accident…he turned his ankle…and in the morning his ankle was swollen out nearly double its size, and he could not get his foot into his shoe. Still, even then, he did nothing more than swear a little, and wrapped his foot in old rags…. It chanced to be a rush day at Durham's…by noontime the pain was so great that it made him faint, and…he…had to tell the boss. They sent for the company doctor, and he examined the foot and told Jurgis to go home to bed, adding that he had probably laid himself up for months…. The injury was not one that Durham and Company could be held responsible for…. Jurgis got home some-how, scarcely able to see for the pain, and with an awful terror in his soul….He knew that the family might starve to death….

The latter part of April Jurgis went to see the doctor, and was…told that he might go back to work…. However… he was told by the foreman that it had not been possible to keep his job for him. Jurgis knew that this meant simply that the foreman had found some one else to do the work…. He went out and took his place with the mob of the unemployed.

He must get work, he told himself, fighting the battle with despair every hour of the day….

But there was no work for him. He went to every one he knew, asking for a chance, there or anywhere…. There was not a job anywhere….

There is a place that waits for the lowest man—the fertilizer plant….

The fertilizer works of Durham's lay away from the rest of the plant…. To this part of the yard came all…the waste products of all sorts; here they dried out the bones…. You might see men and women and children…sawing bits of bone into all sorts of shapes, breathing their lungs full of the fine dust, and doomed to die, every one of them, within a certain definite time.... It was to this building that Jurgis came daily...it was his task to shovel this fertilizer into carts.... In five minutes he was, of course, a mass of fertilizer from head to feet; they gave him a sponge to tie over his mouth, so that he could breathe, but the sponge did not prevent his lips and eyelids from caking up with it and his ears from filling solid. He looked like a brown ghost....

Working in his shirt sleeves, and with the thermometer at over a hundred...in five minutes he had a headache, and in fifteen was almost dazed. The blood was pounding in his brain....

At the end of that day of horror, he could scarcely stand.... It was three days before he could keep anything upon his stomach—he might wash his hands, and use a knife and fork, but were not his mouth and throat filled with the poison?

And still Jurgis stuck it out.... And so at the end of the week he was a fertilizer man for life—he was able to eat again, and though his head never stopped aching, it ceased to be so bad that he could not work.

And then one afternoon,...they told him that beginning with the morrow his department...would be closed until further notice!

That was the way they did it! There was not half an hour's warning—the works were closed!...

Jurgis walked home with his pittance [small amount] of pay in his pocket, heartbroken, overwhelmed.

Write Your Answers

Write the answers to these questions in your social studies notebook.

1. How did Jurgis's accident affect his work at Durham?

2. What did the foreman tell Jurgis?

3. What were the dangers of working in the fertilizer plant?

4. How did working at the fertilizer plant affect Jurgis?

5. What would happen to Jurgis and all the people who lost their jobs?

REVIEW AND APPLY

■ One of the reasons the Populist party was formed was to help farmers.

■ During the late 1800s, many Americans began to work to reform child labor laws, living conditions in cities, women's rights, and city governments.

■ Jane Addams started Hull House to help immigrants in Chicago.

■ In 1920 woman gained the right to vote when the Nineteenth Amendment was passed.

■ The Progressive Movement made changes in controlling big business and trusts, improving working conditions, and conserving natural resources.

VOCABULARY

Choose the Meaning ■ In your social studies notebook, write the letter of the word or phrase that best completes each sentence.

1. The **National Grange** was formed to help _____.

   a. immigrants
   b. farmers
   c. politicians

2. The **gold standard** was used to back _____.

   a. paper money
   b. coins
   c. stocks

3. **Suffrage** is _____.

   a. the right to an eight-hour workday
   b. the right to vote
   c. the right to buy gold

4. **Muckrakers** were _____.

   a. writers
   b. politicians
   c. farmers

5. **Conservation** is the protection of _____.

   a. big business
   b. city governments
   c. natural resources

6. President Roosevelt was called a **trustbuster** because he _____.

   a. could not be trusted
   b. attacked harmful trusts
   c. did not want to give women the right to vote

USING INFORMATION

Writing an Essay ■ During the late 1800s and early 1900s, many Americans started to work to change American society. Write a paragraph in your social studies notebook that describes one of these reform movements and the effects it had on the United States.

COMPREHENSION CHECK

Reviewing Important Facts ■ **Match each sentence in Group A with the word or phrase from Group B that the sentence explains. You will not use all the words in Group B.**

Group A

1. The Supreme Court ruled in favor of the railroads in this court case.

2. William Jennings Bryan gave this speech to end the gold standard.

3. This person started the Henry Street Settlement House in New York City.

4. This law reformed the civil service in 1883.

5. He promised Americans a Square Deal.

6. This cartoonist showed that Boss Tweed was stealing from the government.

Group B

A. Lillian Wald

B. *Wabash* v. *Illinois*

C. The Pendleton Act

D. Thomas Nast

E. Jane Addams

F. Cross of Gold

G. Theodore Roosevelt

CRITICAL THINKING

Cause and Effect ■ **Choose a cause or an effect from Group B to complete each sentence in Group A. Group B has one more answer than you need.**

Group A

1. The Supreme Court ruled in favor of the railroads in *Wabash* v. *Illinois,* so _____ .

2. _____ , so the amount of paper money the government could print was limited.

3. Jane Addams fought for laws to protect workers, so she _____ .

4. _____ , so the Pendleton Act was passed to reform the civil service.

5. Upton Sinclair wrote *The Jungle,* so _____ .

Group B

A. Gold was scarce

B. the Federal Reserve Act was passed in 1913

C. Americans learned about the problems in the meat-packing industry

D. won the Nobel Peace Prize

E. Congress passed the Interstate Commerce Act

F. People were given jobs in the federal government even if they could not do the job

Unit 5 Review

Study the time line on this page. You may want to read parts of Unit 5 again. Then use the words and dates in the box to finish the paragraphs. In the assignment section of your notebook, write the numbers 1–14. The box has one possible answer that you will not use.

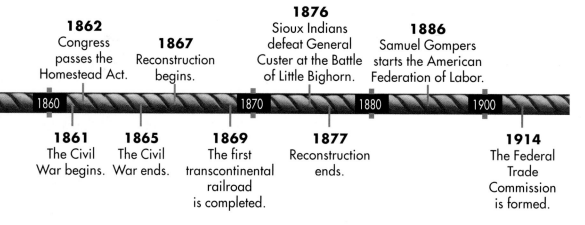

1862 Congress passes the Homestead Act.

1867 Reconstruction begins.

1876 Sioux Indians defeat General Custer at the Battle of Little Bighorn.

1886 Samuel Gompers starts the American Federation of Labor.

1860   1870   1880   1900

1861 The Civil War begins.

1865 The Civil War ends.

1869 The first transcontinental railroad is completed.

1877 Reconstruction ends.

1914 The Federal Trade Commission is formed.

impeach	1869	John D. Rockefeller
industrial	telephone	tenements
1877	Samuel Gompers	trustbuster
reservations	Chinese	gold standard
Homestead Act	Custer	Federal Trade

In 1867 Congress passed the Reconstruction Act, so the South could rejoin the Union. Congress did not like President Andrew Johnson. In 1868 the House of Representatives voted to __1__ President Johnson. The Senate did not have enough votes to find Johnson guilty so he finished his term as President. In __2__ federal troops were removed from the South and Reconstruction ended. After the Civil War, many factories were built, and the United States became an ___3___ nation. Many Americans also moved west because the ___4___ gave settlers 160 acres of free land on the Great Plains. The first transcontinental railroad was completed in ___5___ . As people settled the Great Plains, Indians were forced onto ___6___ . The Sioux defeated General ___7___ at the Battle of Little Bighorn.

The growth of industry was helped by the invention of the ___8___ and the electric light bulb. By the end of the 1800s, ___9___ and Andrew Carnegie were leaders of big business. As millions of immigrants moved to American cities, they lived in crowded ___10___ . Because many factory workers worked under terrible conditions and earned low salaries, ___11___ started the American Federation of Labor.

Farmers blamed hard times on the money system called the ___12___ . Theodore Roosevelt became known as a ___13___ . President Woodrow Wilson helped control big business with the Clayton Antitrust Act and the ___14___ Commission.

Looking Ahead to Unit 6

At the end of the 1800s, the United States won control of Alaska, Hawaii, Puerto Rico, and other territories. The United States began to act as a police officer for Latin America. With American help, England and France won World War I. The years after the war brought some good times to the nation.

As you read Unit 6, think about the ways the United States won control of new land. Find out why World War I began in 1914. Discover how the United States entered World War I and how the nation changed in the years after the war. Read on and learn how the United States became an important world power.

Unit 6

THE UNITED STATES AS A WORLD POWER

In 1898 Theodore Roosevelt led a group of brave Americans against Spanish soldiers in the Battle of San Juan Hill in Cuba. The Rough Riders, as they were called, won the battle, and their success helped the United States win the Spanish-American War. This victory moved the United States one step closer to becoming a world power.

As you read Unit 2, you will learn how the United States became a world leader. Find out how the United States tried to control Latin America. Learn the reasons the United States entered World War I. Discover the many ways the nation changed during the 1920s.

1898
The United States annexes Hawaii.

1850 — 1900

1853
Commodore Matthew Perry visits Japan.

1867
The United States buys Alaska from Russia for $7.2 million.

1898
The United States defeats Spain in the Spanish American War.

1901
President McKinley is assassinated. Teddy Roosevelt becomes President.

THINK ABOUT IT

- Hawaii is a group of islands in the Pacific Ocean. It is 2,000 miles from California. How did Hawaii become part of the United States?

- For more than 100 years, the United States stayed out of Europe's affairs. Then in 1917 American soldiers went to France to fight in World War I. Why did Americans decide to fight in Europe?

- Before World War I, most American women wore long skirts and did not work outside their homes. Why did life change for women between 1917 and 1929?

▲ The Rough Riders capture San Juan Hill.

1914
The Panama
Canal opens.

1918
World War I
ends.

1920
The Nineteenth
Amendment allows
women to vote.

1920

1908
Henry Ford
makes the
Model T.

1914
World War I
begins.

1917
Congress
declares war
against
Germany.

1919
Prohibition
begins.

1927
Charles Lindbergh
flies alone across the
Atlantic Ocean.

283

THE UNITED STATES BECOMES A WORLD POWER

◀ *Campaign button from election of 1900*

People

Matthew C. Perry •
William Henry Seward •
Queen Liliuokalani •
José Martí • George Dewey •
John Hay • Grover
Cleveland • Sanford Dole

Places

Japan • Midway Islands •
Hawaii • Pearl Harbor •
Cuba • Puerto Rico •

Philippines • Guam •
Santiago, Cuba

New Vocabulary

world power •
expansionism • isolationist •
annexed • refuel •
descendants • naval •
yellow journalism •
commonwealth •
spheres of influence • Open
Door Policy

Focus on Main Ideas

1. Why did the United States want to rule colonies?
2. How did the United States win control of Alaska and Hawaii?
3. How did the Spanish-American War help the United States?
4. How did the United States deal with Japan and China?

The growth of industry helped the United States to become a **world power.** By 1900 the United States ruled colonies in the Pacific Ocean as well as in the Caribbean Sea.

Expansionism and Imperialism

Americans had always wanted to increase the size of their nation. This desire to gain more land is called **expansionism**. First, the United States doubled in size with the Louisiana Purchase in 1803. During the 1800s the idea of Manifest Destiny led Americans westward, to the Pacific Ocean.

By the end of the 1800s, some Americans wanted to expand the nation by having colonies outside the United States.

After the Civil War, the United States became an imperialist nation, or a nation that rules colonies. The belief in imperialism spread to the United States from Europe. The Industrial Revolution and the growth of industry helped cause imperialism. European nations did not have many of the raw materials that they needed to make goods in their factories. Colonies would provide raw materials such as oil, rubber, and cotton. Europeans conquered and ruled colonies in Africa and Asia.

Americans also wanted colonies as a source of raw materials for their factories. By ruling colonies the United States hoped to become an important, powerful nation. To conquer and control colonies, the United States had to build up its army and navy.

Some people in the United States believed that imperialism was wrong. They remembered that Americans had been unhappy when they were the colonists of Great Britain. People who were against imperialism thought it was wrong for Americans to take away the freedom and independence of people in other countries.

Trade with Japan

Japan is an island nation in the Pacific Ocean in eastern Asia. During the 1630s Japan ended relations with other nations. It became an **isolationist** nation.

In 1853 the American government sent Commodore Matthew C. Perry to Japan with a group of warships. The United States wanted Japan to end its isolationist policy. Perry had two goals—to develop trade between the two nations and to improve Japan's treatment of American sailors. When American sailors had been shipwrecked off the coast of Japan, the Japanese had treated them badly.

In 1854 Japan's government signed a friendship treaty with the United States. The treaty allowed the United States to trade in two Japanese ports. The Japanese promised to treat American sailors fairly. The 1854 treaty helped Japan become a modern nation. The Japanese began their own Industrial Revolution. They built new factories and a strong army and navy. Soon

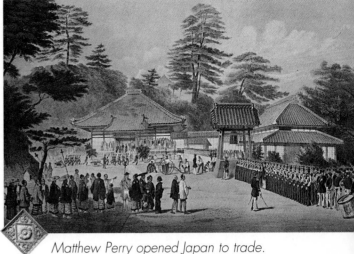

Matthew Perry opened Japan to trade. For more than 200 years, the Japanese had refused to trade with other nations. The 1854 treaty with Japan opened trade in two port cities.

Japan became one of the most powerful nations in Asia.

The Purchase of Alaska

William Henry Seward, the secretary of state under President Andrew Johnson believed in expansionism. Seward wanted the United States to own Alaska, which was then owned by Russia. Most people thought that Alaska was nothing more than a huge northern icebox. In 1867 Russia agreed to sell Alaska to the United States for $7.2 million. People laughed at Seward and called the purchase of Alaska "Seward's Folly." Soon Americans learned that Alaska was rich in natural resources such as oil, forests, and metals. After the gold rush in Alaska, everyone agreed that Alaska was a real bargain. In 1959 Alaska became the forty-ninth state.

In the same year that Seward bought Alaska, the United States **annexed** two small islands in the Pacific Ocean.

285

This check for $7,200,000 was used to buy Alaska from Russia. The United States and Russia had talked about a deal since the 1850s, but they did not agree until 1867.

Altogether the Midway Islands had a very small population, but they were an excellent place for steamships to **refuel** before sailing on to Asia and Australia.

Annexation of Hawaii

Hawaii is a group of islands in the Pacific Ocean about 2,000 miles from California. During the 1800s American missionaries moved to Hawaii to teach Hawaiians to be Protestants. **Descendants** of these missionaries became planters who raised sugar on large plantations. Most of the sugar was sold to the United States, and Americans in Hawaii grew wealthy.

By the late 1800s, Hawaii had become an important place to refuel American ships. In 1887 Hawaii's king allowed the United States navy to use Pearl Harbor as an American **naval** base.

By 1891 the Americans in Hawaii wanted the islands to be part of the United States. But Hawaii's new queen, Queen Liliuokalani, wanted Hawaii to remain an independent nation. In 1893 Americans revolted against the queen. The revolution ended quickly, before anyone was killed. As a result, Queen Liliuokalani had to give up her throne. For a few years, Hawaii was an independent republic. In August 1898 the United States annexed Hawaii. In 1959 Hawaii became the nation's fiftieth state.

The Spanish-American War

Spain had once been a powerful nation that ruled a large empire. By the 1890s Spain had lost most of its colonies. But Spain continued to rule the islands of Cuba and Puerto Rico in the Caribbean Sea and the Philippines and Guam in the Pacific Ocean. In 1898 the United States fought and won a short war against Spain. As a result of that war, Spain lost these four colonies.

The United States went to war against Spain for several reasons. First, the United States wanted to help Cuba, an island near Florida, win its independence. The Cubans had revolted against Spain, but they lost their fight for freedom. José Martí was an important leader in the Cuban struggle against Spain. After ending the Cuban revolt, the Spanish treated the Cubans more cruelly than before.

Americans also wanted to protect their trade with Cuba. Americans owned property and businesses in Cuba that were worth about $50 million.

The *New York Journal* and the *New York World* wrote exciting but often untrue stories about Cuba's revolution. They wrote these types of stories in order to sell more newspapers. The stories were examples of

yellow journalism. They encouraged the United States to go to war against Spain.

In February 1898 an American battleship called the *Maine* exploded in a Cuban harbor, killing most of the sailors onboard. The *Maine* had been sent to Cuba to protect American citizens and their property. The explosion was caused by a problem in the engines of the ship. But at the time no one knew why the *Maine* had exploded. Newspaper stories blamed Spain for the explosion. "Remember the *Maine!*" Americans cried, as they encouraged Congress to declare war against Spain.

President William McKinley tried to avoid war with Spain. But because more and more Americans and members of Congress wanted war, McKinley finally asked Congress to declare war against Spain. In April 1898, the Spanish-American War began.

Winning the Spanish-American War

The first battle of the Spanish-American War was fought in the Philippines, which was a Spanish colony. Theodore Roosevelt, the assistant secretary of the navy, ordered Commodore George Dewey to attack. Dewey and the American navy destroyed the Spanish fleet, quickly giving Americans control of the Philippines.

This artist's version of the explosion on the Maine was painted in 1898. Because of the articles and drawings in newspapers, many people believed that the Spanish were to blame. Today we know that it was not the Spanish. The explosion was caused by a problem in the engines of the ship.

More fighting in the war took place in Cuba. Theodore Roosevelt resigned his job as assistant secretary of the navy to join the fight in Cuba. Roosevelt led a group of men known as the "Rough Riders" to capture San Juan Hill. On July 17, 1898, the Spanish surrendered the city of Santiago, Cuba, in yet another battle.

Next, Americans fought to free the nearby island of Puerto Rico. The fight for Puerto Rico ended quickly with an American victory. In August 1898 the Spanish surrendered. Americans had won the Spanish-American War in less than four months. Secretary of State John Hay said the Spanish-American War was "a splendid little war." About 5,000 Americans died from diseases during this short war. Only a few hundred actually died in battle.

The United States and Spain signed the Treaty of Paris. The Treaty of Paris ended the war and forced Spain to give Cuba, Puerto Rico, Guam, and the Philippines to the United States. Control of these islands and the people living there led to a debate, or argument, in the United States. Should these places be treated as territories? Could they become states? Could the people there become citizens of the United States with the same rights under the Constitution? Eventually the government treated each of these islands differently.

Congress passed the Platt Amendment, which gave Cuba its independence. However, that law also gave the United States the right to interfere in Cuba. Eventually the island of Puerto Rico became a **commonwealth** of the United States, and Guam became a territory.

The Philippines were promised that they would get independence when they were ready. But the people of the Philippines had expected to be independent after the Spanish-American War. When the United States would not give them independence, they revolted against American rule. It took the United States several years to end the revolt.

As time passed, the people of the Philippines were given more power to rule themselves. It was not until 1946 that the United States allowed the Philippines to become independent.

This poster is from the election of 1900. The drawing at lower right shows that control of Cuba, Puerto Rico, and the Philippines was still being debated two years after the war.

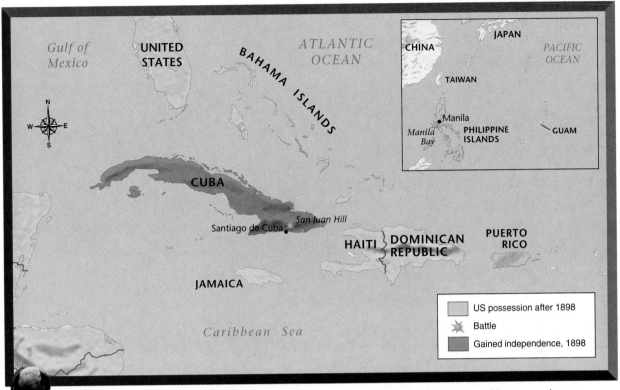

The Spanish-American War 1898 *The Spanish-American War started because the United States wanted to help Cuba. But the war was fought in the Philippines, in Cuba, and in Puerto Rico. Which country gained its independence in 1898?*

China and the Open Door Policy

The United States wanted to trade with China. But it was difficult for Americans to trade with China because China had been divided into **spheres of influence**. A sphere of influence was an area in China that was controlled by a European nation or by Japan. The United States did not have a sphere of influence in China, so it could not trade with China.

The Chinese were unhappy that foreign nations had taken control of their country. In 1900 a large group of Chinese, known as Boxers, decided to force the foreigners to leave China. Their fight was called the Boxer Rebellion. Soldiers from Europe and the United States fought back and defeated the Boxers.

After the Boxer Rebellion, Secretary of State John Hay said that China should have an **Open Door Policy**. He meant that all nations should be allowed to use any of China's ports. There would be no more spheres of influence. With this policy China would remain an independent nation. Although the United States wanted an Open Door Policy in order to improve its own trade with China, the new policy was also good for China.

By the year 1900, the United States had become a world power. It ruled an empire with colonies in the Pacific Ocean and the Caribbean Sea.

BIOGRAPHY

Queen Liliuokalani 1838–1917

Queen Liliuokalani was the last royal leader of Hawaii. Although she loved her country and wanted it to stay independent, she could not prevent Hawaii from becoming a territory of the United States.

When she was a child, Hawaii's last queen was called Lydia Kamekeha. She was the daughter of a Hawaiian chief. Lydia's brother became king of Hawaii. Since he did not have children, he chose Lydia to be the next royal ruler. When her brother died in 1891, Lydia became queen. After that she was known as Queen Liliuokalani.

Queen Liliuokalani's goal was to protect Hawaii's independence so it would not become an American territory. She was not pleased that American business leaders had great power in Hawaii's government. Liliuokalani tried to increase her own royal power so she could limit the power of American planters and business leaders.

In January 1893 Liliuokalani declared that she held all the power in the Hawaiian government. Americans revolted, and American troops prepared to fight. The Queen knew the Hawaiians could not defeat American troops. She did not want anyone to be killed, so she agreed to surrender.

President Grover Cleveland wanted Liliuokalani to rule the Hawaiian Islands. But the Americans who had taken over Hawaii would not give up control of the islands. They made Hawaii an independent republic. Sanford B. Dole, one of the American business leaders, was president of Hawaii until 1898. At that time President McKinley decided to annex Hawaii. The islands became part of the United States.

Liliuokalani had tried unsuccessfully to protect Hawaii's independence. She was loved and respected by her people until her death. Today millions of people visit the royal palace where Hawaii's last queen once lived.

In Your Own Words

Write a paragraph in the journal section of your notebook that tells why Queen Liliuokalani was forced to give up her throne.

REVIEW AND APPLY

- The United States and the countries of Europe wanted to rule colonies. This was known as imperialism.

- In 1854 the United States and Japan signed a friendship treaty that opened trade between the two nations.

- In 1867 the United States bought Alaska from Russia for $7.2 million.

- The United States annexed Hawaii in 1898.

- As a result of the Spanish-American War, Spain gave the United States control of Cuba, Puerto Rico, Guam, and the Philippines.

- The Open Door Policy ended the spheres of influence in China.

VOCABULARY

Finish the Sentence ■ In your social studies notebook, write the correct word or phrase that best completes each sentence. You will not use all the words in the box.

1. During the 1630s, Japan ended its relations with other nations, becoming an _____ nation.

2. Secretary of State John Hay wanted China to have an _____, which would allow all nations to use China's ports.

3. The desire to gain more land is called _____ .

4. It was difficult to trade with China because the country had been divided into _____ .

5. The growth of industry helped the United States become a _____ .

6. In 1898 the United States _____ Hawaii, making it part of the country.

> world power
> expansionism
> isolationist
> annexed
> spheres of influence
> refuel
> Open Door Policy

USING INFORMATION

Writing an Opinion ■ Write a paragraph in your social studies notebook that tells your opinion about whether the United States was right or wrong to keep control of Guam, Puerto Rico, and the Philippines.

COMPREHENSION CHECK

Who Said It? ■ **Read each statement in Group A. Then match the name of the person in Group B who might have said it. Write your answers in your social studies notebook. There is one name you will not use.**

Group A

1. "I was sent to Japan to develop trade between the United States and Japan."

2. "I wanted the United States to buy Alaska from Russia."

3. "I wanted Hawaii to remain an independent country."

4. "I led Cuba's fight for independence from Spain."

5. "I led the Rough Riders up San Juan Hill."

6. "I wanted China to have an Open Door Policy."

Group B

A. William Henry Seward

B. William McKinley

C. José Martí

D. Theodore Roosevelt

E. John Hay

F. Matthew C. Perry

G. Queen Liliuokalani

CRITICAL THINKING

Categories ■ **Read the words in each group. Choose a title for the group from the words in the box. Write the numbers 1–4 in your social studies notebook. Next to each number write the the correct title. There is one title you will not use.**

> Reasons for the Spanish-American War Reasons for Imperialism
> American Expansionism Americans Trade with Japan Hawaii

1. islands in the Pacific Ocean
   Americans owned sugar plantations there
   ruled by Queen Liliuokalani

2. bought Alaska in 1867
   annexed Hawaii in 1898
   gained control of Guam, Puerto Rico, and the Philippines

3. wanted to rule more land
   wanted colonies for raw materials
   wanted larger market for finished products

4. wanted to protect American businesses in Cuba
   wanted to help Cuba gain its independence from Spain
   Americans were angry about the sinking of the *Maine*

292

SOCIAL STUDIES SKILLS

Using Lines of Latitude and Longitude

Lines of latitude and longitude are imaginary lines that form a grid on maps. Lines of latitude run east and west around the earth. Lines of longitude run north and south. Lines of latitude and longitude are identified with a direction and a number that stands for the degrees, or parts of a circle. The latitude of the Equator is 0 degrees, or 0°. To locate a place on a map, find the nearest lines of latitude and longitude.

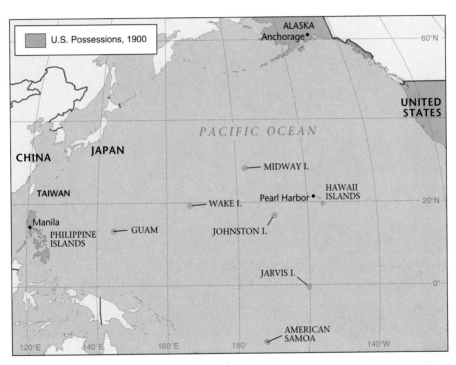

A. Write the latitude for each island.

1. Wake Island

2. Jarvis Island

3. Midway Islands

B. Write the longitude for each island.

1. Wake Island

2. Jarvis Island

3. Midway Islands

C. Match each place with the correct latitude and longitude.

1. Manila, Philippines

2. Anchorage, Alaska

3. Guam

4. Pearl Harbor, Hawaii

a. 21°N/158°W

b. 13°N/145°E

c. 15°N/121°E

d. 61°N/150°W

Chapter 24

THE UNITED STATES AND LATIN AMERICA

◀ Dr. Carlos Finlay

People

Carlos Finlay • William Gorgas • Pancho Villa • John J. Pershing • Herbert Hoover

Places

Chile • Venezuela • British Guiana • Haiti • Guantánamo Bay • Panama • Panama Canal • Colombia • Dominican Republic • Nicaragua

New Vocabulary

Western Hemisphere • stable governments • isthmus • malaria • big stick diplomacy • corollary • dollar diplomacy • Good Neighbor Policy

Focus on Main Ideas

1. Why did the United States become involved in the problems of Chile and Venezuela?
2. How did the United States gain control of the Panama Canal?
3. In what different ways did Presidents Theodore Roosevelt, William Howard Taft, and Woodrow Wilson treat Latin America?

After the Spanish-American War, the United States was a powerful nation. The United States used its power to try to control the countries of Latin America.

United States Interferes in Chile and Venezuela

Most of the nations south of the United States in the **Western Hemisphere** are part of Latin America. Trade developed between the United States and its southern neighbors. American industries bought raw materials from Latin America. They sold their factory products in Latin American countries. Americans who owned land and businesses there wanted **stable governments** in Latin America so that their land and businesses would be protected.

In 1891 the United States interfered in a civil war in Chile. The United States supported the forces that wanted to keep Chile's president in power. However, the forces that opposed Chile's president won the civil war. After the war, Chileans were angry with the United States.

A mob of Chileans attacked a group of American sailors who were visiting Chile. Two sailors were killed, and 16 others were hurt. The United States threatened to go to war unless Chile apologized and paid money to the families of the dead sailors. Chile's government apologized and paid $75,000 to the families. Fortunately, war between the nations was avoided.

In 1895 the United States interfered in Venezuela. The problem began when Great Britain and Venezuela claimed the same piece of land near the colony of British Guiana. According to the Monroe Doctrine, Great Britain could not take control of more land in Latin America. The United States even threatened to go to war against Great Britain if the British would not agree to accept the decision of a committee that did not favor either Great Britain or Venezuela.

The committee decided that most of the land belonged to Great Britain. The United States accepted this decision. But the United States had shown that it was willing to use its power to keep Europe out of Latin America.

Puerto Rico and Cuba After the Spanish-American War

After the Spanish-American War, the island of Puerto Rico belonged to the United States. The United States chose the governor and some members of the government. But the Puerto Rican people were allowed to elect other government leaders.

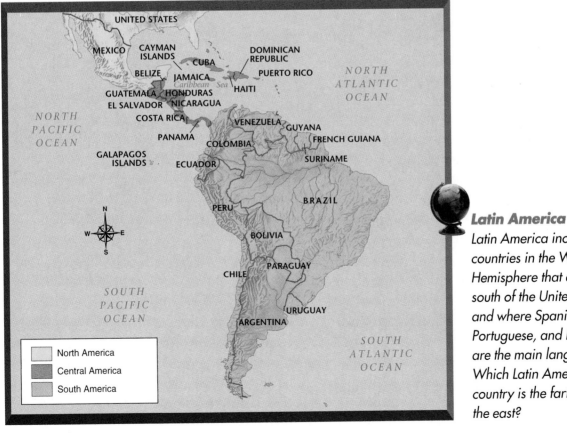

Latin America

Latin America includes countries in the Western Hemisphere that are south of the United States and where Spanish, Portuguese, and French are the main languages. Which Latin American country is the farthest to the east?

295

This woman wants Puerto Rico to remain a commonwealth of the United States. Her sign calls the commonwealth "the best of both worlds."

Since 1917 all Puerto Ricans have been American citizens. In 1952 Puerto Rico became a commonwealth. This means the island belongs to the United States, but the people rule themselves. People who live in Puerto Rico are American citizens, but they do not pay federal taxes and cannot vote in United States presidential elections. Not all Puerto Ricans want their island to be a commonwealth. Some want it to become a state of the United States. Others want Puerto Rico to be an independent nation.

After the Spanish-American War, the United States had military control of Cuba. The United States greatly improved Cuban health conditions while it ruled Cuba. Many Cubans had died every year from a disease called yellow fever. Carlos Finlay, a Cuban doctor, believed a certain type of mosquito spread the disease. The American Army killed the deadly mosquitoes, and yellow fever was no longer a problem.

In 1901 the United States agreed to allow Cuba to rule itself. But first Cuba had to accept a new constitution that included the Platt Amendment. The Platt Amendment gave the United States the right to interfere in Cuba. It also allowed the United States to have naval bases in Cuba. Cuba's Guantánamo Bay became an American naval base.

The American Army left Cuba in 1902, and the Cubans began to rule themselves. However, the American Army returned to Cuba four times when there were problems.

Winning Control of the Panama Canal

In order to reach Asia, ships in the Atlantic Ocean had to sail around South America. After the United States won control of Guam and the Philippines, it needed a faster way to send warships from the Atlantic Ocean to the Pacific Ocean.

The shortest route to the Pacific Ocean would be a canal through the narrowest part of Central America. The narrowest part was in the **Isthmus** of Panama, a narrow strip of land connecting North America and South America.

The United States was not the first country to think of building a canal through Panama. A French company had already tried and failed. The project became too expensive for the French, and too many workers had died of disease. The French company wanted the United States to build the canal because the United States would have to buy the right to build it from their company. The United States decided to build the Panama Canal.

Colombia had ruled Panama since it had become independent from Spain in the early 1800s. The United States offered to pay Colombia for the right to build the canal through Panama. The United States promised to pay rent to Colombia each year. But Colombia wanted more money than the United States was willing to pay. So Colombia refused to allow the United States to build the Canal.

People in Panama did not want to lose the trade that the Canal would bring. In 1903 the people of Panama revolted against Colombia. President Roosevelt sent an American warship to help Panama win its freedom. With American help, Panama won its independence in only three days.

The United States quickly signed a treaty with Panama. The treaty said that the United States would build the Canal and control a ten-mile-wide zone around the Canal. The United States paid $10 million to Panama. The United States would also pay $250,000 a year to rent the Canal zone. In recent years Panama has wanted to control the Canal. The United States has agreed to give control of the Canal to Panama in the year 2000.

The region where the Panama Canal was built had many mosquitoes that carried yellow fever and **malaria**. These diseases

It took more than ten years to build the Panama Canal. This photograph shows the construction of one of the Canal locks. The ship in the inset photograph is the Cristobal, which in 1914 was the first ship to sail through the Panama Canal.

Roosevelt said that his policy was to "walk softly and carry a big stick." In this political cartoon, he is shown walking with a big stick and the United States Navy in the Caribbean.

had killed many of the French company's workers. An American doctor, Colonel William C. Gorgas, worked hard to stop these diseases. It took about two years to cut down the tall grass and to drain the swamps where the mosquitoes laid their eggs. With the mosquitoes gone, people building the Canal no longer died from yellow fever and malaria.

The Panama Canal was a great achievement in engineering. The Canal opened in 1914. Ships from all nations were allowed to use it. The Panama Canal gave the United States the shortcut it needed from the Atlantic Ocean to the Pacific Ocean.

Roosevelt and Big Stick Diplomacy

As President, Teddy Roosevelt changed the meaning of the Monroe Doctrine. To James Monroe, the Doctrine meant that Europe must not start new colonies in Latin America. To Roosevelt, the Monroe Doctrine meant that the United States could interfere in Latin America with military force.

Roosevelt said that the United States would act as a police officer in Latin America by using military force to settle problems. This was known as **big stick diplomacy**. He also stated that European countries would not be allowed to interfere in Latin America. Together these policies were called the Roosevelt **corollary** to the Monroe Doctrine.

Roosevelt used military force in several Latin American nations that had borrowed money from Europe. They did not have enough money to repay what they had borrowed. Instead of allowing Europeans to send ships and troops to force the countries to pay, the United States forced those nations to pay their debts. At different times Roosevelt sent troops to Venezuela, Cuba, and the Dominican Republic. Those nations were forced to pay their debts. But the use of American troops caused many Latin Americans to hate the United States.

Latin American Policies of Presidents Taft and Wilson

William Howard Taft became President after Roosevelt. Taft's policy toward Latin America became known as **dollar diplomacy**. This policy encouraged the growth of large American businesses in Latin America. Through these businesses the United States gained power in Latin America. The United States sent troops to Latin America to protect these businesses. Nicaragua, a country in Central America, was one of the nations into which Taft sent troops. American troops remained in Nicaragua for more than 20 years. Nicaraguans were angry at the United States for interfering.

President Woodrow Wilson also sent troops to Haiti, Cuba, and the Dominican Republic. Wilson wanted Latin American countries to have democratic governments that supported the United States.

After the Mexican Revolution began in 1910, Mexican leaders fought over who would rule the country. President Wilson interfered by supporting Pancho Villa, a Mexican leader. But later Wilson changed his mind and supported Villa's enemy. This decision made Villa so angry that he entered the United States and killed some Americans in 1916. President Wilson then sent General John J. Pershing with thousands of American soldiers into Mexico to find Pancho Villa. Villa was never captured.

Mexicans were furious that American soldiers had invaded their country.

Improving Relations

Big stick diplomacy and dollar diplomacy in Latin America created great anger toward the United States. Presidents Herbert Hoover and Franklin D. Roosevelt worked to improve relations with Latin America. They started a **Good Neighbor Policy** toward Latin America in the 1930s. Both Presidents promised not to use military force there. However, other Presidents since then have found it necessary to send troops to Latin America. The Good Neighbor Policy opened the way for friendship and trade between the United States and its southern neighbors. That friendship has continued to grow between the United States and many parts of Latin America.

Pancho Villa was one of several leaders who tried to control Mexico's government after the Mexican Revolution. Many Mexicans supported him when he was being chased by American troops.

BIOGRAPHY

Theodore Roosevelt 1859–1919

As a child Theodore Roosevelt, nicknamed Teddy, was small, weak, and often very sick. At the age of 12, he began to exercise and lift weights. Through hard work, Roosevelt became a strong, powerful man.

When Roosevelt was 22, he married a beautiful woman named Alice. Alice died soon after giving birth to a daughter, whom he named after his wife. Roosevelt's mother also died on the same day. After the deaths of his wife and his mother, Roosevelt moved west to the Dakota Territory. He owned a cattle ranch and worked as a cowboy. Roosevelt developed a deep love for the American West.

A few years later, Roosevelt married again. Roosevelt and his new wife, Edith, had five children.

Roosevelt was a member of the Republican party, and he helped William McKinley become President in 1896. McKinley appointed Roosevelt to be the assistant secretary of the navy.

When the Spanish-American War began, Roosevelt became famous for leading the Rough Riders. After the war Roosevelt was elected governor of New York.

McKinley chose Roosevelt to run as his Vice President in 1900. McKinley was reelected, and Roosevelt became the new Vice President. Six months after his inauguration, McKinley was killed. Roosevelt then became President.

Teddy Roosevelt was the first President to show support for labor unions. He worked with Congress to pass laws protecting the nation's food, meat, and medicines. Roosevelt passed conservation laws to protect America's land, forests, resources, and wild animals. Roosevelt was given the Nobel Peace Prize because he helped end a war between Russia and Japan. Roosevelt felt that his greatest achievement was the Panama Canal.

Cowboy, soldier, governor, Vice President, and President were all jobs that Theodore Roosevelt did well.

In Your Own Words

Write a paragraph that tells about three of Roosevelt's achievements.

REVIEW AND APPLY

- The United States used its power to try to maintain stable governments in Latin America.

- Puerto Ricans became American citizens in 1917. In 1952 Puerto Rico became a commonwealth of the United States.

- The United States helped the country of Panama gain its independence from Colombia because Americans wanted to build a canal across the Isthmus of Panama that would connect the Atlantic and Pacific oceans.

- The United States built the Panama Canal and controlled a ten-mile-wide zone around the Canal. The Canal opened in 1914.

- President Roosevelt issued his "big stick diplomacy" in Latin America. He stated that the United States would use military power to settle problems in the region. Roosevelt also said that European countries would not be allowed to interfere in Latin America.

- Taft's policy toward Latin America, called dollar diplomacy, encouraged the growth of large American businesses there. Wilson wanted to have democratic governments in Latin America that supported the United States, so he sent troops into Haiti, Cuba, and the Dominican Republic.

- Presidents Herbert Hoover and Franklin D. Roosevelt started a Good Neighbor Policy toward Latin America, which promised that no military force would be used there.

VOCABULARY

Writing with Vocabulary Words ■ Use five or more words below to write a paragraph that describes how different American Presidents treated Latin America.

Western Hemisphere	stable governments	corollary
big stick diplomacy	Good Neighbor Policy	isthmus
dollar diplomacy		

USING INFORMATION

Journal Writing ■ Imagine being on the American warship that helped Panama win its independence from Colombia. How would you feel about helping Panama become an independent nation? Write a paragraph in your journal that describes your feelings. Support your opinions with facts.

COMPREHENSION CHECK

Understanding Events in History ■ In your social studies notebook draw a graphic organizer similar to the one shown below. Then complete the graphic organizer with information about United States involvement in the politics of each Latin American country listed.

CRITICAL THINKING

Cause and Effect ■ Choose a cause or an effect from Group B to complete each sentence in Group A. Write your answers in your social studies notebook. Group B has one more answer than you need.

Group A

1. Two American sailors were killed in Chile, so _____ .

2. The United States needed a shorter route between the Atlantic Ocean and the Pacific Ocean, so _____ .

3. Malaria and yellow fever killed many French workers, so _____ .

4. _____ , so Roosevelt used big stick diplomacy to force them to pay.

5. People in Panama began to revolt against Colombia, so _____ .

6. In 1916, Pancho Villa entered the United States and killed some Americans, _____

Group B

A. Colonel William Gorgas worked to destroy mosquitoes that carried diseases

B. so President Wilson sent American troops into Mexico to look for him.

C. it wanted to build a canal through Panama

D. Roosevelt sent an American warship to help Panama

E. the United States threatened to go to war with Chile

F. In the year 2000, Panama will gain control

G. Some Latin American countries could not pay their debts

AMERICAN GEOGRAPHY

Human/Environmental Interaction: The Panama Canal 1904–1914

Human/Environmental Interaction tells how people can change an area and how an area can change people. By digging the Panama Canal, Americans changed a 50-mile strip of land into a 50-mile water route that joined the Atlantic and Pacific oceans. Before digging the Canal, Americans first built a railroad across the Isthmus. The railroad was used to move workers and supplies to the Canal. Trains carried away tons of dirt.

One big problem in building the Canal was that the land was 85 feet above sea level. To solve this problem, engineers built three pairs of sea elevators called locks. These locks raised and lowered the level of the water to allow ships to pass through. It takes about eight hours for a ship to pass through all three pairs of locks of the Canal. Panama's mountains and jungles were another problem, so workers used dynamite to cut through them.

Study the map of Panama on this page. Use the map and the paragraphs to answer the questions. Write your answers in the assignment section of your social studies notebook.

1. What large lake is part of the Panama Canal?

2. Why did Americans need a railroad in Panama?

3. Which two cities are connected by the railroad?

4. What is the length of the Canal?

5. What were two problems that had to be solved in order to build the Panama Canal?

6. How did Americans solve these two problems?

7. What are the names of the Canal's three pairs of locks?

Chapter 25
THE UNITED STATES IN WORLD WAR I

◄ *Tank used during World War I*

People

Poles • Finns • Allied Powers • Central Powers • Archduke Francis Ferdinand • Czar Nicholas II • Karl Marx • V.I. Lenin • Garrett Morgan • Henry Cabot Lodge • Czechs

Places

Turkey • Serbia • Belgium • Ottoman Empire

New Vocabulary

nationalism • ethnic groups • militarism • alliances • assassin • trench warfare • poison gas • dogfights • submarines • merchant ships • Communists • torpedoes • propaganda

Focus on Main Ideas

1. What were the causes of World War I?
2. How was World War I different from other wars?
3. Why did the United States enter the war?
4. What were the results of the Treaty of Versailles?

Imagine being told not to eat wheat on Wednesdays. From 1917 to 1918, millions of Americans obeyed government rules and did not eat meat and wheat on certain days. The government needed wheat and meat to send to soldiers in Europe who were fighting in World War I.

Causes of World War I

World War I, or the Great War, began in 1914. The causes of World War I developed over a period of many years. First, the growth of **nationalism** led to World War I. Nationalism is pride in one's own people or country. Nationalism made people of different **ethnic groups** want to fight to have their own nations. For example, Poles and Finns wanted their independence from Russia, and the Irish wanted to be free from Great Britain.

Second, imperialism helped lead to war. Great Britain and France had colonies. Austria-Hungary and Germany were willing to fight to win control of colonies, too.

Militarism was a third cause of the war. European nations were building large armies and navies. They had huge supplies of weapons that were more dangerous than weapons that had been used in earlier wars.

Another cause was the growth of **alliances**. Nations had signed secret treaties that said they would fight for each other during a war. Great Britain, France, Russia, and some other nations had formed an alliance. During World War I, they were called the Allied Powers, or the Allies. Germany, Austria-Hungary, Turkey, and some other nations also formed an alliance. During the war these nations were called the Central Powers.

By 1914 Europe was like a bomb that was ready to explode. The spark that started the war happened on June 28, 1914. On that day Archduke Francis Ferdinand of Austria-Hungary and his wife were shot and killed. The **assassin** was a Serbian who was angry that Austria-Hungary was ruling his country. Archduke Ferdinand was supposed to become the next emperor of Austria-Hungary.

Austria-Hungary blamed Serbia for Ferdinand's death. So Austria-Hungary declared war on Serbia. Since Russia, Great Britain, and France had alliances with Serbia, they went to war against Austria-Hungary. Some nations were neutral and did not favor either side. At the start of the war, Italy was neutral. But in 1915 Italy joined the Allies. Germany went to war to protect its ally, Austria-Hungary. World War I had begun.

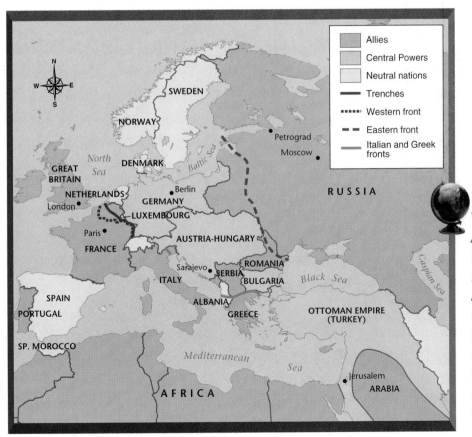

World War I Alliances *Most of the fighting during World War I took place in Europe. Many of the nations of Europe fought for either the Allies or the Central Powers. Some nations remained neutral. Which countries were part of the Central Powers?*

The Early Years of the War

The war in Europe was fought on two fronts. The eastern front was in Russia and in parts of Germany and Austria-Hungary. The western front was in Belgium and northeastern France. Although Belgium wanted to be neutral, Germany invaded that country in order to attack France.

Germany planned to defeat France quickly and then use its army to defeat Russia. To defeat France the Germans had to capture Paris, the French capital. In September 1914 the battle for Paris began. It was called the First Battle of the Marne. The Allied Powers defeated Germany in this battle, but the Great War would continue for four more years.

World War I was fought differently from all earlier wars. At the start of the Great War, the Allies and the Central Powers were about equal in military power. For more than four years, the two sides fought without victory. Soldiers in World War I used **trench warfare**. Trenches were long ditches dug in the earth. Soldiers on both sides hid in hundreds of miles of trenches, which were often separated with barbed wire. They fired machine guns and **poison gas** at the enemy from the trenches.

For the first time, airplanes were used to find the enemy. Airplanes were also used to shoot down other airplanes in battles called **dogfights**. New weapons such as tanks, poison gas, and **submarines** were also used.

For months at a time, soldiers lived in trenches. They hid in the trenches and fired their weapons from the trenches. The trenches were cold, damp, and often filled with rats. Exploding cannon shells destroyed much of the land around the trenches.

The war was also fought in the Middle East and in North Africa. Turkey, one of the Central Powers, controlled much of the Middle East. Great Britain and France fought against Turkey for control of the Middle East.

World War I was also fought at sea. The British blockaded Germany's ports so that Germany could not receive supplies. Germany used submarines to sink ships that were sailing to Britain and France. Americans were furious when German submarines sank their **merchant ships**.

The Russian Revolution and the Russian Surrender to Germany

On the eastern front, the Germans began to defeat the Russians. The Russians did not have enough food, fuel, or weapons for the war. By 1917 almost two million Russians had been killed. The Russian ruler, Czar Nicholas II, refused to surrender.

In March 1917 the angry Russian people started a revolution. The Russians forced Nicholas to resign. The leaders of this revolution started a new government. Russia continued to fight in World War I.

In November 1917 Russia had a second revolution, called the Russian Revolution. In this revolution, **Communists** won control of the government. The ideas of communism had been started back in 1848 by a German named Karl Marx. In a Communist nation, the government owns all businesses. In 1917 the Russians used Marx's ideas to start the first Communist government. In Russia a man named V.I. Lenin became dictator. In 1918 Lenin signed a peace treaty with Germany. As part of that treaty, the

Lenin was the leader of the Russian Revolution. His powerful speeches and writings convinced Russians to revolt and create the world's first Communist country.

Russians surrendered and gave large amounts of land to Germany. The treaty helped Germany. Thousands of German soldiers left the eastern front to fight in France.

America Goes to War

The foreign policy of the United States had always been to stay out of Europe's affairs. When World War I began, President Wilson announced that the United States would remain neutral. But as time passed, the majority of Americans favored the Allies. Americans favored Great Britain and France because they were democracies. However, many Americans supported the Central Powers. Millions of German Americans wanted Germany to win the war. Many Irish Americans were against the Allies because the British refused to allow Ireland to be a free nation.

The United States moved closer to war against Germany in 1915. The *Lusitania*, a British passenger ship, sank after being hit by two **torpedoes** fired from a German submarine. The Germans believed that the *Lusitania* was secretly carrying weapons to Great Britain. Of about 1,200 passengers who died, 128 were Americans. The sinking of the *Lusitania* turned millions of Americans against Germany.

Americans were still hoping to stay out of World War I. In 1916 Woodrow Wilson was reelected. Wilson's campaign slogan had been, "He kept us out of war."

In 1917 the British captured a message that helped push the United States into the war. In the message, called the Zimmermann Note, Germany asked Mexico to go to war against the United States. If Germany won World War I, Mexico could take back the land it had lost to the United States in 1848. Mexico never agreed to this plan. American anger towards Germany grew stronger when the Zimmermann Note was published in American newspapers.

Americans were also angry because Germany had said that its submarines would sink all neutral ships sailing to Great Britain. Germany's goal was to stop the United States and other nations from sending food, weapons, and other supplies to the British.

After German submarines sank several American ships, President Wilson asked Congress to declare war on Germany. In his speech to Congress, Wilson said, "The world must be made safe for democracy." On April 6, 1917, Congress declared war against Germany.

Life in America During the War

Preparing for war was a difficult job for Americans. The nation had to collect money to pay for the war, raise a huge army, grow enough food to feed the Allies, and keep up the spirits of the American people.

Congress raised taxes to collect money for the war. The federal government also sold billions of dollars worth of Liberty Bonds. By buying bonds, Americans were lending money to the government for the war.

To raise an army, Congress passed the Selective Service Act. By 1918 all men ages 18 to 45 were required to register for the draft. About four million served as soldiers during the war.

To raise enough food to feed the American soldiers and the Allies in France, the federal government paid farmers to grow more food. Americans were asked not to eat meat and wheat on certain days of the week. Americans everywhere grew food in small gardens in their backyards.

To build support for the war, the Committee on Public Information created and spread **propaganda**. Propaganda encouraged men to become soldiers and told Americans to buy Liberty Bonds. The government also tried to stop people from speaking and writing against the war. Congress passed laws that limited freedom of speech and freedom of the press. People wrote songs to encourage support of the war. One popular war song, "Over There," had these lines:

> *Over there, over there,*
> *Send the word over there*
> *That the Yanks are coming*
> *And we won't come back till it's over,*
> *Over there.*

Because millions of men were in the armed forces, women worked making tanks, machine guns, and ships. These were jobs that had always been done by men. Women did not serve as soldiers. However, they did dangerous work in Europe as army nurses and ambulance drivers.

Many African American and Mexican American families left the South to work in northern factories. They could get better jobs and better salaries in the North. African American women also became factory workers. However, they often received lower salaries than white women.

FOOD WILL WIN THE WAR
You came here seeking Freedom
You must now help to preserve it
WHEAT is needed for the allies
Waste nothing

Wheat, sugar, and meat were the foods most needed by the Allies. So Americans were asked not to waste these products.

Many Americans began to hate Germany and German culture during the war. Many towns would not allow the German language to be taught in schools.

Americans Help the Allies

General John J. Pershing, the general who had once tried to capture Pancho Villa, led the American Army in Europe. The American forces were called the American Expeditionary Force, or the AEF.

The first American soldiers reached France in June 1917. They arrived at a time when they were really needed. German soldiers were leaving Russia to fight in France. But the AEF made the Allies stronger than the Germans. The turning point of the war was the Second Battle of the Marne in 1918. Americans helped defeat the Germans near the Marne River, not far from Paris. After this battle the Allies won more battles and recaptured land that they had lost earlier in the war. The fighting moved away from Paris. The Allies had saved the capital of France.

Americans of different backgrounds—Polish, Greek, German, Irish, and Italian—fought together against Germany. Thousands of Jewish Americans fought in Europe, and about 6,000 American Indians helped defeat the Germans.

Many African American soldiers won French medals for their courage in battle. Thousands of African Americans fought for the Allies, but they were not allowed to live with or fight in the same units as white soldiers. However, soldiers everywhere owed their lives to an African American inventor, Garrett Morgan. Morgan invented the gas mask.

His invention saved thousands of soldiers from the effects of poison gas.

By November 1918 the Germans knew that the Allies would win. They agreed to stop fighting. At 11:00 A.M. on November 11, 1918, fighting in Europe finally stopped.

The Treaty of Versailles

Before the end of the war, President Wilson had begun to think about creating a fair peace treaty. In January 1918 Wilson presented his ideas for peace to Congress. In a speech called the "Fourteen Points," Wilson said, "What we demand...is that the world be made fit and safe to live in...." In his speech Wilson listed fourteen ways to keep peace between nations. Many of the points addressed the causes of World War I. For example, nations would not form secret alliances. All nations would have freedom of the seas and free trade. Nations would have smaller armies with fewer weapons. Also, people of different ethnic groups would be allowed to form their own nations. Finally, a League of Nations would be started to solve problems between nations. Wilson believed the League would prevent future wars.

In 1919 the Allied leaders met in Paris to write a peace treaty. The treaty was called the Treaty of Versailles. The treaty placed all blame for the war on Germany and forced Germany to pay billions of dollars to the Allies. Germany also lost a large amount of land to the Allies. Woodrow Wilson felt that the Treaty of Versailles was unfair. Wilson did not want to punish Germany and the Central Powers. But the other Allies wanted the Central Powers to pay for the war. Wilson accepted the Treaty of Versailles only because it included his plan for a League of Nations.

Although Wilson signed the treaty, the United States Senate had to ratify, or approve, it. The treaty needed the votes of two thirds of the senators. Senator Henry Cabot Lodge led the fight to defeat the treaty because many Americans did not want to join the League of Nations. They feared that the League would involve Americans in future European wars. The Senate refused to ratify the treaty. As a result the United States did not join the League of Nations.

Results of World War I

World War I caused terrible damage and loss of life. The Allies lost more than five million soldiers. The Central Powers lost more than three million. Americans lost 126,000 soldiers. Millions of soldiers were wounded. Large areas of France were destroyed during the war. The war had cost both sides billions of dollars.

The Treaty of Versailles created a new map of Europe and the Middle East. Austria-Hungary's Empire and Turkey's Ottoman Empire were broken up. New nations were created from those empires. The treaty gave ethnic groups such as Poles, Finns, and Czechs their own countries and the right to rule themselves.

Americans had fought to make the world safe for democracy. But the world was less safe for democracy after the war. The Treaty of Versailles had planted seeds of anger in Germany that would grow and lead to World War II.

BIOGRAPHY

Woodrow Wilson 1856–1924

Woodrow Wilson led the American people through the difficult years of World War I.

Wilson came from a family of ministers. Not only was his father a minister, but both of his grandfathers were ministers. His wife was also the daughter of a minister.

As a child Wilson did not learn to read until he was nine years old. Although he later became an excellent speaker, teacher, and writer, he was never a fast reader. As a young man, Wilson became a college teacher. Later he became famous as the president of Princeton University.

In 1910 Wilson was elected governor of New Jersey. Two years later he was elected President of the United States.

Wilson was a progressive President. Together with Congress he worked to end child labor and to lower tariffs on goods from other nations. He also worked to control the growth of big business.

Wilson led the nation during World War I. Throughout the war Wilson's goal was "to make the world safe for democracy." Wilson's peace plan became the "Fourteen Points." Wilson wanted a fair peace plan. Most of all, Wilson wanted a League of Nations. He believed the League would prevent future wars.

Wilson decided to tour the country to win support for the League from the American people. In 1918 he began traveling west. He made speech after speech in many different cities. The trip exhausted Wilson. He became ill, and he suffered a terrible stroke. He would never be strong and well again.

In 1920 the Senate defeated the treaty. Wilson believed that the League would not succeed in keeping peace without the United States. Wilson feared that the unfair Treaty of Versailles would lead to another world war. All of Wilson's fears would turn out to be true. In 1920 he received the Nobel Peace Prize. Wilson is remembered as a President who led Americans through peace and war.

In Your Own Words

Write a paragraph in your journal that describes Wilson's achievements.

Voices from the Past

On Friday, May 7, 1915, a German submarine torpedoed a British passenger ship, the *Lusitania*. The ship, owned by the Cunard Company, sank near Ireland. This news article was in *The New York Times* the next day. Americans were shocked that Germany had attacked a ship that had so many passengers. On that day no one knew all the details about the disaster. Later people learned that 1,198 people had died, and 128 of those people were Americans.

LONDON, Saturday, May 8.

—The Cunard liner Lusitania, which sailed out of New York last Saturday with 1,918 souls aboard, lies at the bottom of the ocean off the Irish coast.

She was sunk by a German submarine, which sent two torpedoes, crashing into her side, while the passengers, seemingly confident that the great, swift vessel could elude [avoid] the German underwater craft, were having luncheon.

How many of the Lusitania passengers and crew were rescued cannot be told at present….

Probably at least 1,000 persons, including many Americans, have lost their lives.

Sank in Fifteen Minutes.

The stricken vessel went down in less than half an hour, according to all reports. The most definite statement puts fifteen minutes as the time that passed between the fatal blow and the disappearance of the Lusitania beneath the waves.

There were 1,253 passengers from New York on board the steamship, including 200 who were transferred to her from the steamer Cameronia. The crew numbered 665.

No names of the rescued are yet available.

Story of the Attack.

…Describing the experience of the Lusitania, the steward [waiter] said:

"The passengers were at lunch when a submarine came up and fired two torpedoes, which struck the Lusitania on the starboard side, one forward and another in the engine room. They caused terrific explosions.

"Captain Turner immediately ordered the boats out.…

"Ten boats were put into the water, and between 400 and 500 passengers entered them. The boat in which I was, approached the land with three other boats, and we were picked up shortly after 4 o'clock.…

"I fear that few of the officers were saved. They acted bravely.…"

Hit 10 Miles Off Kinsale Head.

This greatest sea tragedy of the war, because of the terrible loss of lives of non-combatants [people who are not soldiers] and citizens of neutral nations, took place about ten miles off the

The New York Times.

EXTRA
5:30 A. M.

VOL. LXIV...NO. 20,923. ★★★★★   NEW YORK, SATURDAY, MAY 8, 1915.—TWENTY-FOUR PAGES.   ONE CENT

LUSITANIA SUNK BY A SUBMARINE, PROBABLY 1,260 DEAD;
TWICE TORPEDOED OFF IRISH COAST; SINKS IN 15 MINUTES;
CAPT. TURNER SAVED, FROHMAN AND VANDERBILT MISSING;
WASHINGTON BELIEVES THAT A GRAVE CRISIS IS AT HAND

SHOCKS THE PRESIDENT

Washington Deeply Stirred by the Loss of American Lives.

BULLETINS AT WHITE HOUSE

Wilson Reads Them Closely, but is Silent on the Nation's Course.

HINTS OF CONGRESS CALL

Loss of Lusitania Recalls Firm Tone of Our First Warning to Germany.

CAPITAL FULL OF RUMORS

Reports That Liner Was to be Sunk Were Heard Before Actual News Came.

SOME DEAD TAKEN ASHORE

Several Hundred Survivors at Queenstown and Kinsale.

STEWARD TELLS OF DISASTER

NOTICE!

TRAVELLERS intending to embark on the Atlantic voyage are reminded that a state of war exists between Germany and her allies and Great Britain and her allies; that the zone of war includes the wat...

Old Head of Kinsale about 2 o'clock in the afternoon.

A dispatch [written note] to the Exchange Telegraph from Liverpool quotes the Cunard Company as stating that "the Lusitania was sunk without warning...."

Flickering Gleam of Hope.

There was a gleam of hope in the general gloom soon after 8 o'clock, when this announcement was made unofficially:

The Cunard Company has definitely ascertained [found to be true] that the lives of the passengers and the crew of the Lusitania have been saved.

This was speedily proved untrue, however, but the more optimistic [hopeful] still refused to credit the early reports of the swift sinking of the big liner [ship]....

Write Your Answers

Write the answers to these questions in your social studies notebook.

1. How did the German submarine sink the *Lusitania*?

2. How long did it take for the ship to sink?

3. What were passengers doing when the ship was attacked?

4. Where was the *Lusitania* when it sank?

5. Why was the sinking of the *Lusitania* a tragedy?

REVIEW AND APPLY

- The four main causes of World War I were nationalism, imperialism, militarism, and the growth of alliances. World War I started when Archduke Francis Ferdinand of Austria-Hungary was assassinated by a Serbian on June 28, 1914.

- World War I was fought differently from earlier wars. Trench warfare lasted for years. New technology, such as airplanes, tanks, and poison gas, was used.

- In 1917 the Russian Revolution created a Communist government in Russia.

- The United States entered World War I in 1917 on the side of the Allies.

- On November 11, 1918, World War I came to an end. The Treaty of Versailles included some of Wilson's "Fourteen Points."

VOCABULARY

Choose the Meaning ■ In your social studies notebook, write the letter of the word or phrase that best completes each sentence.

1. **Militarism** lead to the creation of large _____ .

   a. cities
   b. armies
   c. farms

2. **Nationalism** makes people want their own _____ .

   a. factories
   b. houses
   c. countries

3. Nations in an **alliance** _____ .

   a. protect each other
   b. fight against one another
   c. share the same political leaders

4. **Trench warfare** is fought in _____ .

   a. ditches
   b. ships
   c. planes

5. **Propaganda** tries to influence _____ .

   a. the goods that factories produce
   b. the way people think
   c. the alliances countries make with each other

6. **Communists** believe that all businesses should be _____ .

   a. owned by the military
   b. owned by private citizens
   c. owned by the government

USING INFORMATION

Writing an Essay ■ The United States had to prepare quickly for World War I. Write a paragraph in the assignment section of your notebook in which you list and explain two ways that the United States prepared for war. Start your paragraph with a topic sentence.

Write the Answer ■ In your social studies notebook, write one or more sentences to answer each question.

1. What event in June 1914 led to the start of World War I?

2. What were four causes of World War I?

3. What were the main nations that made up the Central Powers?

4. In what ways was World War I fought differently from all earlier wars?

5. What were two results of the Russian Revolution?

6. Why did the United States enter World War I?

7. What was life like in America during World War I?

8. Why did many World War I soldiers owe their lives to Garrett Morgan?

9. What was the main purpose of President Wilson's Fourteen Points?

10. Why did Woodrow Wilson feel that the Treaty of Versailles was unfair?

11. Why did the United States not join the League of Nations?

12. What were two results of World War I?

CRITICAL THINKING

Sequencing Information ■ In your social studies notebook write the following sentences in their correct order.

The Allies won the First Battle of the Marne.

Austria-Hungary declared war on Serbia after Archduke Francis Ferdinand was assassinated by a Serb.

The Treaty of Versailles was signed.

On November 11, 1918, Germany agreed to stop fighting.

A German submarine sank the *Lusitania,* a British passenger ship.

Comparing Historical Maps

You can learn some of the results of World War I by comparing a map of Europe before World War I with a map of Europe after the Treaty of Versailles was signed. After World War I, the Austria-Hungary Empire and the Ottoman Empire were broken up into new nations. The map of Europe was changed so that some of the large ethnic groups could have their own nations.

Compare the map on page 305 with the map on this page. Then write the answers to the questions below in the assignment section of your social studies notebook.

1. What nations were on Russia's western border before World War I?

2. What country was Russia part of after World War I?

3. What nations were on Russia's western border after World War I?

4. What nations were formed from Austria-Hungary in 1920?

5. Name four nations with borders that did not change because of World War I.

6. What country did Serbia become part of after World War I?

7. How did Romania's borders change?

Chapter 26
AMERICA IN THE 1920s

◀ *A radio from the 1920s*

People

Alice Paul • Carrie Chapman
Catt • Warren G. Harding •
Calvin Coolidge • Marcus
Garvey • Nicola Sacco •
Bartolomeo Vanzetti • Henry
Ford • Ernest Hemingway •
F. Scott Fitzgerald • A. Philip
Randolph • Oscar De Priest •
Octaviano Larrazolo •
Langston Hughes • Countee
Cullen • Bessie Smith •

Louis Armstrong • Duke
Ellington • Babe Ruth •
Charles Lindbergh • Amelia
Earhart • Paul Robeson

New Vocabulary

Prohibition • scandals •
prosperity • Red Scare •
anarchists • nativism •
racism • executed •
assembly line • urban

Focus on Main Ideas

1. How did the Republican Presidents help big business?
2. What were some of the problems in the United States in the 1920s?
3. How did American lives change in the 1920s?
4. Who were some important people involved in the Harlem Renaissance?

In the 1920s, a woman would have shocked people if she came to a party wearing a skirt that was just long enough to cover her knees. Women had always worn long skirts that covered their ankles. Women dared to wear shorter skirts because America changed during the 1920s.

New Amendments to the Constitution

In 1919 the Eighteenth Amendment to the Constitution made it a crime to manufacture, sell, drink, or ship alcoholic beverages anywhere in the United States. The period when alcoholic beverages were illegal was called **Prohibition**. Supporters of Prohibition believed that alcohol caused crime and social problems.

Prohibition was supposed to reduce crime, but it actually caused more crime. Millions of people found illegal ways to manufacture, sell, and use alcohol. By the 1930s most people agreed that Prohibition laws were impossible to carry out. In 1933 the Twenty-first Amendment to the Constitution ended Prohibition.

During World War I, women had worked in factories and on farms across the nation. Women insisted that if they could serve their country in so many ways, they should have the right to vote. Alice Paul and Carrie Chapman Catt became the new leaders in the fight for women's suffrage. In 1920 the Nineteenth Amendment, which allowed women's suffrage, was ratified. Many women voted for the first time in the 1920 presidential election.

Republican Presidents

Republicans controlled the White House from 1921 until 1933. President Warren G. Harding wanted the United States to return to the way it had been before the Progressive Movement and World War I. During Harding's presidency, the United States returned to being isolationist. Americans wanted to stay out of Europe's affairs so that they would not have to fight in future wars.

Many **scandals** occurred during Harding's years as President. The people he appointed to federal jobs stole money from the government. The Teapot Dome Scandal was the worst scandal while Harding was President. The navy owned oil fields in Teapot Dome, Wyoming, and Elk Hills, California. Albert Fall, the secretary of the interior, agreed to rent these oil fields to two oil companies. In return the oil companies gave Fall about $400,000. It was against the law for Fall to rent the oil fields or to take money from the oil

During the years of Prohibition, it was illegal to manufacture, sell, drink, or ship alcoholic beverages. Federal police tried to stop the illegal use of alcoholic beverages. When they found illegal alcohol, they destroyed it and arrested the people who made it.

companies. Fall was later sent to jail for one year, and he paid a fine of $100,000.

Harding died while traveling in the West, and Vice President Calvin Coolidge became the next President. Under Presidents Calvin Coolidge and Herbert Hoover, the government continued to favor big business. Coolidge said, "The business of America is business."

Coolidge was a popular President. He was elected to serve again in 1924 and chose not to run in 1928. In 1928 Herbert Hoover defeated Alfred Smith. Hoover won because businesses had been successful under Republican Presidents. Hoover promised that Americans would continue to enjoy **prosperity**. Hoover also won because Al Smith was a Catholic. Prejudice against Catholics stopped millions of people from voting for Smith.

Threats to American Democracy

In the years after World War I, many Americans were afraid that the democracy they had fought for in the war would be lost. So Americans tried to protect their way of life, but some of their attempts actually became serious threats to democracy.

The fear of communism in 1919 caused a time of panic called the **Red Scare**. Red was a symbol of communism. Americans feared Communists might win control of the United States. Americans were also afraid of **anarchists**, people who did not want any government. The government unfairly arrested thousands of people who might be anarchists or Communists. By 1920 Americans realized that Communists were not going to take control of the country.

Warren G. Harding (left) was upset by the many scandals that occurred while he was President. In 1923 Calvin Coolidge (right) became President when Harding died.

But the government's actions during the Red Scare had been a threat to democracy.

Another threat to democracy was **nativism,** or the fear of foreigners. In 1921 a quota system allowed only a certain number of immigrants to come to the United States from each nation. By 1929 only 150,000 European immigrants were allowed to come to America each year. Other laws stopped immigration to the United States from China and Japan. Asians living in America were not allowed to become citizens. However, immigrants were allowed into the United States from Mexico and other Latin American nations.

Racism threatened democracy because the Constitution was supposed to protect the freedom of all Americans. During the 1920s the Ku Klux Klan spread deep hatred for African Americans, Jews, Catholics, and immigrants. The Klan had about 2 million members. When some members of the Klan murdered African Americans, other members left the Klan. By 1930 the Klan had fewer than 10,000 members. However, racism continued to grow throughout the nation.

Marcus Garvey tried to fight racism. He told African Americans to be proud of their African culture. He encouraged them to leave the United States and move back to Africa. Most African Americans did not want to move, but Garvey helped them feel pride in their culture.

The Sacco and Vanzetti Trial

The fear of foreigners and anarchists led to the Sacco and Vanzetti trial. Nicola Sacco and Bartolomeo Vanzetti were Italian immigrants who were anarchists. In 1920 the two men were arrested for murder and robbery. Both men said that they were not guilty.

There was little evidence to prove that Sacco and Vanzetti were guilty. But the judge was prejudiced against them because they were anarchists and Italian immigrants. The two men were found guilty. Another man later confessed to the murders, but Sacco and Vanzetti were not given a new trial. Instead the two men were **executed** in 1927. To this day no one knows if Sacco and Vanzetti were really guilty. We do know that fear of foreigners and anarchists prevented Sacco and Vanzetti from receiving a fair trial.

Prosperity in the 1920s

During the 1920s prosperity increased among Americans. New jobs were created, and many products were inexpensive.

Henry Ford owned a car factory named the Ford Motor Company. In 1908 Ford made a car called the Model T. Ford's goal was to make his Model T so inexpensive that most Americans could buy one. He invented a moving **assembly line** to produce cars faster and cheaper than ever before. By 1926 there were 23 million Model T cars in America. Each car cost less than $500.

The Model T brought prosperity to America. Making tires, gasoline, and glass windows for cars became new industries. The steel industry grew because cars were made of steel. Motels, restaurants, and gas stations were built to serve Americans as

Marcus Garvey was an immigrant from Jamaica who told African Americans to be proud of their African culture.

they traveled farther from home. All of these industries created many new jobs.

The millions of cars on the roads also created dangerous traffic problems. Garrett Morgan, the inventor of the gas mask, also invented the traffic light, which made American roads safer.

Other new industries made American life easier. Airplane travel became popular. Appliance industries grew larger as more homes had electricity. Americans bought refrigerators, washing machines, and other appliances.

Radio was another industry that grew during the 1920s. Popular radio programs brought music, plays, ball games, and news reports into American homes. Businesses used radio commercials to sell their products to millions of people.

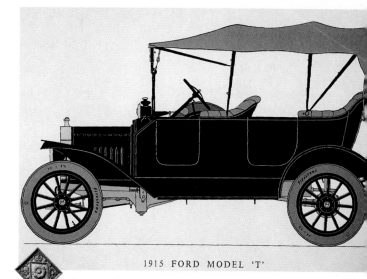

1915 FORD MODEL 'T'

The Ford Motor Company was a success because millions of Model T cars were built on a moving assembly line. The company also had the highest paid workers in the industry—$5 per day.

The Roaring Twenties

The 1920s were called the Roaring Twenties. It was a time when American culture changed in many ways. New fashions, music, literature, and entertainment appeared in the 1920s.

Fashions changed when women said goodbye to long skirts. Instead they wore short skirts, pants, and shorts. They also wore short haircuts and used makeup.

The 1920s were also called the Jazz Age. Jazz was a new type of music that became popular in the 1920s.

Young people wrote literature about life after World War I. Ernest Hemingway later won a Nobel Prize for his novels. F. Scott Fitzgerald wrote *The Great Gatsby*. Hemingway and Fitzgerald questioned the meaning of American life and values.

Movies were a popular kind of entertainment during the 1920s. At first only silent movies were made. Rudolph Valentino and Mary Pickford were two stars of the age of silent movies. By the end of the 1920s, Americans were watching "talkies," or movies with sound. Hollywood, California, became the center of the film industry. In 1928 the artist Walt Disney created a cartoon character named Mickey Mouse.

The Roaring Twenties brought some opportunities for African Americans and Hispanic Americans. A. Philip Randolph started the first labor union for African American railroad workers. In 1928 Oscar De Priest of Chicago became the first African American to be elected to Congress in the north. That same year Octaviano Larrazolo from New Mexico became a United States senator. He had been the first Mexican American governor of New Mexico.

Pictured above are some of the people who were famous during the 1920s. From left to right, they are Charles Lindbergh, first person to fly alone across the Atlantic Ocean; Babe Ruth, baseball player with the New York Yankees; Mary Pickford, movie star; Gertrude Stein, writer; and Louis Armstrong, trumpet player and bandleader.

The Harlem Renaissance

The largest **urban** African American community was in a New York City neighborhood called Harlem. During the 1920s African Americans created new music, art, and literature. This growth of African American culture was called the Harlem Renaissance.

One writer, Langston Hughes, became famous for his poems and novels about his experiences as an African American. Another well-known poet of the Harlem Renaissance was Countee Cullen.

The music of the Harlem Renaissance became famous. Bessie Smith was a popular singer of the African American music called the "blues." Louis Armstrong became the most famous trumpet player in America. Duke Ellington created his own style of music that was loved by people across the nation.

The Age of Heroes

Americans found many people to admire in the 1920s. They loved the famous baseball player Babe Ruth. Ruth was a good pitcher and a great hitter. During his career with the New York Yankees, he hit 714 home runs.

Charles Lindbergh and Amelia Earhart also became popular heroes. In 1927 Lindbergh became the first person to fly alone across the Atlantic Ocean. He landed safely near Paris after flying for about 33½ hours without sleep. In 1928 Amelia Earhart became the first woman to fly across the Atlantic Ocean.

The 1920s were a time of change and prosperity. Millions of people thought that the good times would last forever. In the 1930s the prosperity ended, and the United States faced very difficult years.

322

BIOGRAPHY

Paul Robeson 1898–1976

Paul Robeson was one of the greatest actors and singers of the Harlem Renaissance.

Robeson grew up in New Jersey. Robeson's father, who had been a slave, ran away to freedom when he was 15. He later became a minister. Robeson finished high school at the top of his class. Then he attended Rutgers College in New Jersey where he became a star football player. After four years of college, Robeson graduated at the top of his college class.

After college Robeson attended Columbia University Law School. At that time it was hard for an African American to find work as a lawyer. Robeson found a job with a firm of white lawyers. He was unhappy there and decided to resign.

Robeson began performing as a singer and an actor in Harlem in the early 1920s. In 1927 Robeson moved to London, England, where he became famous for playing the title role in Shakespeare's play *Othello*. Robeson traveled and performed in many parts of Europe, including the Soviet Union. He thought that the Soviet people were less prejudiced towards African Americans.

While in Europe, Robeson spoke out about the need for African colonies to become independent nations. He returned to the United States during the years of World War II.

In the United States, Robeson spoke against racism and prejudice. He praised the Soviet Union for its lack of prejudice toward Africans and African Americans. Before long Paul Robeson was being called a Communist. From 1951 to 1958, he was not allowed to travel outside the United States. In 1958 he was allowed to return to London, where he began singing and acting again.

Robeson was a lawyer, an athlete, a singer, and an actor. He could have used his talents to live an easy, comfortable life. Instead he spent his life helping people of the world win equality.

In Your Own Words

Write a paragraph in the journal section of your notebook explaining how Paul Robeson used his talents to help himself and other people in many parts of the world.

REVIEW AND APPLY

- The Eighteenth Amendment made it illegal to use, buy, or sell alcoholic beverages. The Nineteenth Amendment gave women the right to vote.

- Many scandals, including the Teapot Dome Scandal, occurred during Harding's years as President.

- Republican Presidents Calvin Coolidge and Herbert Hoover favored big business.

- After World War I, fear of communism grew, racism increased, and immigration to the United States was limited.

- Henry Ford's Model T led to new industries and increased prosperity in America.

- The 1920s, called the Roaring Twenties and the Jazz Age, was a period of many cultural changes.

- During the Harlem Renaissance, many African Americans created new art, music, and literature.

VOCABULARY

Matching ■ **Match the vocabulary word or phrase in Group B with the definition from Group A. You will not use all the words in Group B.**

Group A	Group B
1. Fear of communism led to this time of panic.	A. racism
2. This means prejudice towards people because of their race.	B. nativism
3. This is a period when people earn more money and live well.	C. prosperity
4. During this time it was illegal to use alcoholic beverages.	D. Prohibition
5. This fear of foreigners leads to favoring people who were born in the United States and limiting immigration.	E. executed
	F. Red Scare

USING INFORMATION

Journal Writing ■ **In your journal, list and explain what you feel were the most important changes that took place during the 1920s.**

COMPREHENSION CHECK

Finish the Paragraph ■ Use the words, names, and terms in the box to finish the paragraph. In your social studies notebook, write the numbers 1 through 7. Next to each number, write the correct word you choose. There is an extra word, name, or term in the box that you will not use.

Charles Lindbergh		Harlem Renaissance
Republican	immigrants	Model T
Roaring Twenties	anarchists	Red Scare

During the 1920s Americans feared that Communists would take control of the United States. This became known as the ___1___ . Also as a result of the fear of foreigners, Congress passed laws that lowered the number of ___2___ that could enter the United States. During the 1920s the United States had three ___3___ Presidents. The first type of automobile that was bought by millions of Americans was called the ___4___ . The 1920s were called the ___5___ because people enjoyed jazz, new fashions, new literature, and new movies. The ___6___ produced new African American music, art, and literature.

___7___ became an American hero after he became the first person to fly alone across the Atlantic Ocean.

CRITICAL THINKING

Fact or Opinion ■ Write the numbers 1–5 in your social studies notebook. Next to each number, write an F if that statement is a fact. Write O if the statement is an opinion. If the statement gives both a fact and an opinion, write FO. Then write the part of the sentence that is an opinion.

1. The Eighteenth Amendment made it illegal for Americans to drink alcoholic beverages.

2. Women should have been given the right to vote long before 1920.

3. Calvin Coolidge and Herbert Hoover supported big business.

4. Both Sacco and Vanzetti said that they were not guilty.

5. During the Roaring Twenties, fashions changed for women, but women wore nicer clothes at the beginning of the 1900s.

Unit 6 Review

Study the time line on this page. You may want to read parts of Unit 6 again. In the assignment section of your notebook, write the numbers 1–14. Then use the words and dates in the box to finish the paragraphs. The box has one possible answer you will not use.

1900
The United States starts the Open Door Policy with China.

1914
World War I begins.

1917
Russia becomes a Communist nation.

1918
World War I ends.

1920
The Nineteenth Amendment is ratified.

1928
Herbert Hoover is elected President

1900

1898
The United States defeats Spain in the Spanish-American War.

1903
Work begins on the Panama Canal.

1915
A German submarine sinks the *Lusitania*.

1917
The United States enters the war against Germany.

1919
Prohibition begins.

1927
Sacco and Vanzetti are executed.

1898	malaria	Allies
1920s	McKinley	Serbia
Alaska	Hawaii	1917
Latin America	Panama Canal	Prohibition
Open Door Policy	*Lusitania*	Communist

The United States expanded in 1867 when it bought ___1___ from Russia. In
___2___ the United States became an imperialist nation after it defeated Spain in the
Spanish-American War. In that same year, the United States annexed ___3___. The
United States wanted to have trade with China, so in 1900 it announced the ___4___.
Teddy Roosevelt became President after President ___5___ was assassinated in 1901.

Teddy Roosevelt used military force to control events in ___6___ . Roosevelt encouraged Americans to build the ___7___ . Before the Canal could be built, the region had to be made safe from yellow fever and ___8___ .

World War I began after a Serbian killed Archduke Francis Ferdinand of Austria-Hungary. American anger toward Germany grew after more than 100 Americans were killed when a German submarine sank the ___9___ in 1915. During World War I, Russia became a ___10___ nation. After Germany sank several American ships, President Wilson asked Congress to declare war in ___11___ . With American help the ___12___ defeated Germany and the other Central Powers. The Eighteenth Amendment made alcoholic beverages illegal during the time known as ___13___ . During the ___14___ , new fashions, new music, new literature, and movies became popular.

Looking Ahead to Unit 7

The good years of the 1920s came to an end in 1929. In that year the Great Depression began. Millions of people were out of work during the Great Depression. During these difficult years, dictators came to power in Germany, Italy, and Japan. The actions of these dictators led to World War II. From 1941 to 1945, millions of American soldiers fought around the world. After the war Americans tried to prevent a third world war.

As you read Unit 7, think about the ways life changed during the Great Depression. Discover how the United States helped the Allies win World War II. Read on and learn about the difficult challenges Americans faced during the Depression and World War II.

Unit 7

THE GREAT DEPRESSION AND WORLD WAR II

After weeks of deadly fighting on the island of Iwo Jima, six brave marines raised a large American flag on top of Mount Suribachi. About 6,800 Americans died as they fought for victory against the Japanese on Iwo Jima. After capturing the island, Americans continued their fight against Japan during World War II.

As you read Unit 7, you will learn about the difficult years of the Great Depression and World War II. Find out why millions of Americans became very poor during the Great Depression. Discover the ways Americans helped the Allies defeat Germany, Italy, and Japan.

1933
Adolf Hitler becomes dictator of Germany.

1925

1935

1929
The stock market crashes and the Great Depression begins.

1932
Franklin D. Roosevelt is elected President.

1933
The New Deal begins.

1935
Congress passes the Social Security Act.

THINK ABOUT IT

- In the early 1930s, farmers grew plenty of food for the nation. Why did many people need breadlines and soup kitchens to survive?

- During World War II, Germany conquered France in 1940. Why did the Allies wait until 1944 to help France become free?

- Iwo Jima had few people, few natural resources, and poor soil. Why did Americans fight so hard for this island in 1945?

▲ *Statue of Marines raising American flag on Iwo Jima*

1940 France surrenders to Germany.

1941 Congress passes the Lend-Lease Act.

1942 Japanese Americans are sent to internment camps.

1945 Japan surrenders.

1939 World War II in Europe begins when Germany invades Poland.

1941 Japan attacks Pearl Harbor.

1944 Allies invade France on D-Day.

1945

1945 Germany surrenders.

Chapter 27

THE GREAT DEPRESSION

UNEMPLOYED
BUY
APPLES
5¢ EACH

◀ *A sign that was common during the 1930s*

Focus on Main Ideas

1. What caused the stock market to crash in 1929?
2. What were the causes of the Great Depression?
3. How did the Great Depression hurt the United States?
4. How did the federal government try to end the Great Depression?

People

General Douglas MacArthur • Eleanor Roosevelt • Marian Anderson • Frances Perkins • Felix Frankfurter • Matthew Abruzzo • Mary McLeod Bethune

Places

Lincoln Memorial • Warm Springs, GA

New Vocabulary

stock market • invested • Hoovervilles • migrant farm workers • veterans • recovery • insurance • pensions • minority • polio

Many hungry Americans waited in breadlines to receive free bread. Millions of people were so poor that they needed help to survive. During the 1930s Americans lived through the difficult years of the Great Depression.

The Crash of '29

The Great Depression began when the **stock market** crashed in 1929. During the 1920s many Americans had **invested** money in the stock market by buying stocks, or shares, of corporations. You learned about stocks and corporations in Unit 5.

Many people took great risks when they bought stocks during the 1920s. Some people used all their savings to buy stocks. Other people bought stocks with money that they had borrowed from banks. From 1925 to 1929, the price of most stocks went up. So people borrowed more money and bought more stocks.

In October 1929 stock prices began to fall as people tried to sell stocks that no one wanted to buy. On October 29, 1929, the stock market crashed as prices dropped rapidly. People called that day "Black Tuesday." It was the worst day the stock market had ever had.

330

When the stock market crashed, people who had invested all of their savings in stocks became poor overnight. People who had borrowed money from banks to buy stocks were unable to repay their loans. Banks had also invested in stocks. Many banks lost millions of dollars and were forced to close. People who had their savings accounts in those banks lost all their money.

Years of hard economic times followed the stock market crash. This time period is called the Great Depression. This was not America's first depression. But the Great Depression was the longest and most difficult one in American history. This depression lasted more than ten years.

Causes of the Great Depression

The stock market crash started the Great Depression but did not cause it. There were many causes of the Great Depression.

First, the nation's wealth was not shared by everyone during the 1920s. About half of all Americans were poor. Half of the nation's wealth was owned by only 200 businesses.

Second, farmers suffered during the 1920s. During World War I, farmers raised huge amounts of food for the Allies. After the war farmers grew more crops than people could buy. They were forced to sell their crops at very low prices. Many farmers

When the stock market crashed on October 29, 1929, many people lost all of their money. This photograph shows a crowd of people on the street in front of the stock market building on Black Tuesday. In one day the value of the stock market dropped $14 billion.

lost so much money that they were forced to sell their farms.

Third, overproduction caused people to lose their jobs. Factories were producing more than people could buy. When people did not buy the products, the factories closed. About 75,000 people lost their jobs when a Ford Motor Company plant closed.

Fourth, Congress had placed high tariffs on European goods. Then European nations placed high tariffs on American goods. American businesses suffered because Europeans bought fewer American goods.

Fifth, the banking system had many problems. Laws did not require banks to protect money in savings accounts.

Sixth, the government did not pass laws to correct problems in the economy. The three Republican Presidents in the 1920s believed in laissez-faire government. They refused to interfere with business.

Hard Times During the Great Depression

Herbert Hoover was President when the Great Depression began. He was sure that this depression would soon end by itself. Unfortunately the depression grew worse each year. In 1932 Hoover asked Congress to start an agency that would lend money to banks and businesses. Hoover believed that if banks and businesses had more money, they would provide jobs for workers. Hoover's plan failed to help the nation.

By 1933, 13 million people, or 25 percent of Americans, were unemployed. Many people who had jobs were working for lower salaries. People became homeless.

They built shacks out of old boxes and whatever junk they could find. Every city had large areas filled with shacks. People named these areas **Hoovervilles** because they blamed President Hoover for the depression. By 1933, one million people lived in Hoovervilles.

As the depression continued, people throughout the country suffered. Schools closed because towns could not afford to pay their teachers. Hungry people searched for scraps of food in garbage cans. People who lost their jobs had no money to buy food. A loaf of bread cost only five cents, but many people did not even have a nickel for bread. So they waited in breadlines for a loaf of free bread. And they went to soup kitchens to get a free bowl of soup.

Prejudice grew during the depression. Often the first workers to be fired were African Americans or Mexican Americans. It became harder for immigrants to find jobs. Many women were fired so that men could have their jobs.

As the depression continued, farm prices dropped lower because people could not afford to buy the crops. Most farmers could no longer earn a living. Starting in 1931 a seven-year drought destroyed many farms on the Great Plains. After the drought caused soil to dry up and blow away, there were huge dust storms. This area of the nation became known as the Dust Bowl. Thousands of farmers sold their farms and moved west to California. There they became **migrant farm workers** as they moved from place to place looking for work on farms.

John Steinbeck, a famous American writer, wrote a novel about migrant farm

Dorothea Lange took this photograph of a family during the depression. Lange was a famous photographer who captured in her pictures the sad suffering of people during the 1930s.

workers. In that novel, *The Grapes of Wrath*, Steinbeck told how migrants struggled as they moved to California during the depression.

And the migrants streamed in on the highways and their hunger was in their eyes, and their need was in their eyes.... When there was work for a man, ten men fought for it.... If he'll take twenty-five, I'll do it for twenty. No, me, I'm hungry. I'll work for fifteen.... And wages went down.... The fields were fruitful, and starving men moved on the roads.

The Bonus Army

In the summer of 1932, about 20,000 World War I **veterans** went to Washington, D.C., to demand bonus money that the government had promised them. They were supposed to receive the bonuses in 1945, but the hungry veterans did not want to wait. President Herbert Hoover and Congress refused to pay the bonuses, so the veterans camped out in Washington, D.C., in protest. They became known as the Bonus Army.

President Hoover sent General Douglas MacArthur with federal troops to attack the Bonus Army. The troops forced them to leave Washington. Most Americans were angry at Hoover for attacking the veterans.

Roosevelt and the New Deal

By 1932 most Americans wanted a new President. Franklin D. Roosevelt, the Democratic candidate, easily defeated Herbert Hoover in the election of 1932.

333

Roosevelt promised to end the depression. He brought new hope during his campaign when he promised a "New Deal" for the American people. At his inauguration on March 4, 1933, he told the frightened nation, "The only thing we have to fear is fear itself."

Two days after becoming President, Roosevelt closed all of the banks in the nation. The government examined how each bank was handling money. After a few days, safe banks were allowed to reopen. Roosevelt encouraged people to keep their savings in banks again.

Roosevelt spent his first 100 days working with Congress to pass many new programs. His plan to end the Great Depression was called the New Deal.

The WPA was one of the New Deal agencies that put people to work. WPA workers often built or repaired public places.

The New Deal had three main goals. They were relief, **recovery**, and reform. Americans needed relief from poverty and hunger. The nation needed to recover from the depression. And reform, or change, was needed to prevent future depressions.

The New Deal created many agencies to carry out the goals of relief, recovery, and reform. Some agencies gave states money to help the poor. Other agencies helped farmers. Some agencies helped provide jobs for the many people who were unemployed. Once people were earning money, they could buy food, clothing, and other goods. This would help businesses grow stronger.

New Deal agencies created millions of new jobs. The government hired workers to plant trees, build bridges, and clean streets. One New Deal agency, the Tennessee Valley Authority, or TVA, hired thousands of workers to build dams to control floods. The TVA also built power plants that used waterpower to make electricity. See the chart on the next page for names and descriptions of other New Deal agencies.

The New Deal also helped correct problems that had caused the Great Depression. The Federal Deposit Insurance Corporation, or FDIC, provided **insurance** for money in savings accounts. People would no longer lose their savings if a bank failed. Another New Deal agency, the Securities and Exchange Commission, or SEC, made it safer for people to invest in the stock market.

From 1935 to 1936, Roosevelt worked with Congress to pass more laws. Congress passed the Social Security Act, which required all workers to pay a special tax. In return, workers would receive **pensions** when they retired at age 65. The new law also provided money for poor families with children.

Roosevelt's Plan to Pack the Supreme Court

After the Supreme Court found some New Deal agencies unconstitutional, Roosevelt wanted more control over the Supreme Court. So in 1937 he asked Congress to pass a law that would allow him to appoint a new justice to the Supreme Court for every judge who was older than age 70. If the law passed, Roosevelt could appoint six more justices.

Congress defeated Roosevelt's plan to "pack the Supreme Court" with his own judges. It was defeated because the Constitution requires the Supreme Court to be independent from both Congress and the President. However, many justices retired while Roosevelt was President. By 1944 he had appointed seven of the nine justices on the Supreme Court.

Roosevelt Selects His Cabinet

Roosevelt was very popular. He was the first President to be elected more than twice. Eleanor Roosevelt, the President's wife, was also popular. She traveled around the country to help women, workers, and

Important New Deal Agencies

New Deal Agency		What Did the Agency Do?
CCC	Civilian Conservation Corps	It provided conservation jobs for unemployed young men. They planted trees and built dams and roads.
FERA	Federal Emergency Relief Administration	It worked with states to provide relief money to the unemployed or to people hurt by the drought.
FDIC	Federal Deposit Insurance Corporation	It protected the safety of banks. It insured savings deposits so people would not lose money if banks failed.
TVA	Tennessee Valley Authority	It built dams on the Tennessee River to control floods, provide cheap electricity, and improve life in the region.
PWA	Public Works Administration	It created public works jobs. People built bridges, roads, dams, schools, hospitals, and courthouses.
SEC	Securities and Exchange Commission	It controls the stock market so it will not crash again. It tries to protect people from investing in unsafe stocks.
SSB	Social Security Board	It provides workers with pensions and unemployment insurance. It gives aid to poor families with children and to some people with disabilities.
WPA	Works Progress Administration	It employed more than eight million needy people. They built roads, parks, and buildings. The WPA also created jobs for artists, actors, and musicians.

African Americans have equal rights. When a women's group refused to allow Marian Anderson, a famous African American singer, to sing inside its building, Eleanor Roosevelt invited Anderson to sing in front of the Lincoln Memorial. Anderson sang "America" before almost 75,000 people.

President Roosevelt appointed many kinds of Americans to important government jobs. Frances Perkins became the first woman Cabinet member. Roosevelt appointed Felix Frankfurter, a Jewish American, to be a Supreme Court justice. Matthew T. Abruzzo was the first Italian American to be a federal judge.

Roosevelt often met with a group of African American leaders who were called the Black Cabinet. One member of the Black Cabinet was Mary McLeod Bethune. She had started a school for African American girls. Bethune led the Office of

Eleanor Roosevelt was a very active President's wife. She traveled for the President, and she supported many social causes.

Marian Anderson sang at the Lincoln Memorial after a women's group refused to let her sing because she was an African American.

Minority Affairs for President Roosevelt from 1935 to 1944.

Roosevelt made the Democratic party very popular. Most factory workers became Democrats. Most African Americans had been Republicans, but they became Democrats during the New Deal.

Results of the New Deal

The New Deal made the federal government larger and more powerful than ever before. The President became a more powerful leader.

Some people believed that the New Deal hurt the nation. People had to pay more taxes in order to pay for expensive programs. The national debt grew larger because the government borrowed billions of dollars to pay for the New Deal. Many believed the New Deal did not end the depression.

However, the New Deal helped America by providing relief to the poor and hungry. Many of the nation's roads, bridges, dams, and airports were built by New Deal agencies. Some New Deal agencies, such as the Social Security Board and the FDIC, continue to help millions of people.

The New Deal may have protected American democracy. Other nations in the world were also faced with depressions during this time. Some nations turned to dictators to solve their problems, while the United States did not.

The Great Depression finally ended soon after World War II began in Europe in 1939. Americans began to worry more about the terrible events around the world instead of their problems at home.

BIOGRAPHY

Franklin D. Roosevelt 1882–1945

Franklin D. Roosevelt was the only President elected 4 times. He was President for 12 years. Roosevelt was born in New York into a wealthy family. Roosevelt was called FDR by his friends. In 1905 FDR married Eleanor Roosevelt, his distant cousin. Teddy Roosevelt, Eleanor's uncle and President of the United States, came to the wedding and gave away the bride. Franklin and Eleanor would later have 6 children.

Franklin Roosevelt's life changed after he was struck by **polio** in 1921. He spent years trying to learn to walk again, but he could never walk again without leg braces and a cane. Roosevelt went to Warm Springs, Georgia, to swim in a warm pool of mineral water. Roosevelt bought the springs and used his own money to provide low-cost treatment for polio patients.

In 1932 Roosevelt, a Democrat, ran for President of the United States. He had been a state senator and a governor of New York. As President, Roosevelt developed the New Deal program to end the Great Depression.

FDR used the radio to speak to the American people. In talks that he called "fireside chats," he told the nation that the depression would end.

During the 1930s Roosevelt worked at building friendship and trade with Latin America. His policy was called the Good Neighbor Policy.

During World War II, Roosevelt had the nation produce weapons and supplies for the war. The United States sent supplies to its ally, Great Britain.

Soon after Japan attacked the American naval base at Pearl Harbor, the United States went to war against Japan, Germany, and Italy. FDR led the nation through the difficult years of World War II.

FDR died suddenly on April 12, 1945, only months before the United States and the Allies won the war. Roosevelt is remembered as the President who led the nation through 12 hard years of depression and war.

In Your Own Words

Write a paragraph in your journal that tells how FDR helped the United States during his years as President.

REVIEW AND APPLY

- The stock market crash on October 29, 1929 started the Great Depression.

- There were six main causes of the Great Depression: the nation's wealth was not shared by everyone, farmers suffered during the 1920s, overproduction caused people to lose their jobs, Congress placed high tariffs on European goods, banks failed, and the government did not pass laws to correct problems in the economy.

- During the Great Depression, millions of Americans were unemployed. Many people went hungry and homeless.

- Franklin D. Roosevelt promised Americans a "New Deal" that would end the Great Depression. President Roosevelt was reelected three times.

- The New Deal had three main goals: relief, recovery, and reform. Many government agencies were created as part of the New Deal to end the Great Depression and to prevent future depressions.

- Roosevelt tried to "pack the Supreme Court" to protect New Deal agencies.

- The Cabinet selected by President Roosevelt included the first woman Cabinet member.

- The Great Depression ended soon after World War II began.

VOCABULARY

Defining and Using Vocabulary ■ Use the glossary to find the meaning of each word or phrase listed below. Write the definition of each word in your social studies notebook. Then use each word in a sentence.

stock market	Hoovervilles	veterans
recovery	pensions	polio
invested	insurance	minority

USING INFORMATION

Writing an Essay ■ The New Deal had three main goals. Write an essay that lists and explains each goal. Then provide one example of how government agencies tried to reach each New Deal goal. Start your essay with a topic sentence.

COMPREHENSION CHECK

Reviewing Important Facts ■ Match the sentence in Group A with the word or phrase from Group B that the sentence explains. Write the numbers 1–9 in your social studies notebook. Next to each number, write the letter of the correct answer. You will not use all the words in Group B.

Group A

1. The Great Depression began with this event.

2. This was one of the causes of the Great Depression.

3. Veterans of World War I who wanted to receive the money in 1932 that they were supposed to get in 1945 were in this group.

4. This New Deal agency provided retired people with pensions.

5. This President wanted to give Americans a New Deal.

6. She was the first woman Cabinet member.

7. This President felt that the Great Depression would end by itself.

8. She traveled around the country to help women, workers, and African Americans have equal rights.

9. This event led to the end of the Great Depression.

Group B

A. Bonus Army

B. Social Security Board

C. Eleanor Roosevelt

D. Herbert Hoover

E. World War II

F. stock market crash

G. overproduction

H. FDIC

I. Frances Perkins

J. Franklin D. Roosevelt

CRITICAL THINKING

Distinguishing Relevant Information ■ Imagine that you are telling your friend how difficult life was during the Great Depression. Read each sentence below. Decide which sentences are relevant to what you will say. Write the relevant sentences in your social studies notebook. There are four relevant sentences.

1. When the stock market crashed, many people became poor overnight.

2. Starting in 1931, a seven-year drought destroyed many farms on the Great Plains.

3. The country's population grew larger during the Great Depression.

4. Millions of Americans depended on breadlines and soup kitchens for free food.

5. Many new movies were made during the Great Depression.

6. President Roosevelt created New Deal programs to help the poor and the hungry.

AMERICAN GEOGRAPHY

Region: The Dust Bowl

Region tells us the way places in an area are alike. During the 1930s part of the Great Plains became a region called the Dust Bowl.

When farmers planted wheat, they destroyed the prairie grass that held the soil on the Great Plains. Then came seven years of drought in the 1930s. The crops died, and the soil became dry and loose. Wind storms hit the Great Plains and blew dust off of the dry fields. Thick dust buried farms, animals, cars, and houses. Dust storms also damaged other areas of the Great Plains. To prevent another dust bowl, thousands of trees have been planted to hold down the soil and block the wind on the Great Plains.

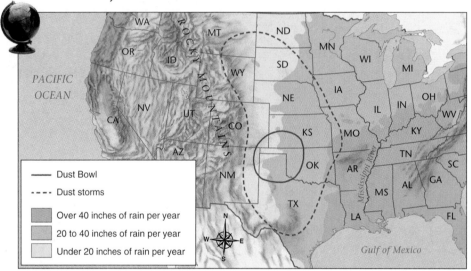

Read the paragraphs and study the map of the Dust Bowl. Write the answers to the questions below in the assignment section of your social studies notebook.

1. What five states were part of the Dust Bowl?

2. What made the Dust Bowl a region?

3. What caused the Dust Bowl?

4. What part of the country was affected by dust storms?

5. What have people in this region done to prevent future dust bowls?

SOCIAL STUDIES SKILLS

Comparing Line Graphs

Line graphs are used to show changes over a period of time. By comparing two line graphs that have different information for the same period, we can draw conclusions. The graph on the left shows how the percentage of people without jobs changed from 1929 to 1940. The graph on the right shows how the amount of money the federal government spent on programs changed from 1929 to 1940.

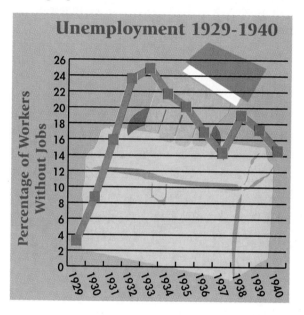

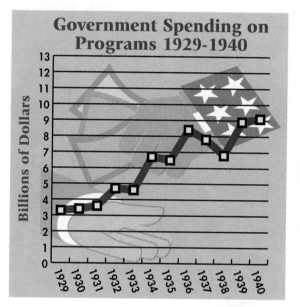

Study the two graphs. Write the answers to the questions below in the assignment section of your social studies notebook.

1. What time period is covered by these two graphs?

2. Which year had the least amount of unemployment?

3. Which year had the least amount of government spending?

4. Which year had the most people unemployed?

5. Which year had the most government spending?

6. What was the amount of government spending in the year with the highest unemployment?

7. How did the lack of government spending in 1938 affect unemployment?

8. How might government spending have changed unemployment between 1933 and 1937?

Chapter 28
THE BEGINNING OF WORLD WAR II

◀ *Winston Churchill*

People

Benito Mussolini • Joseph
Stalin • Adolf Hitler •
Hideki Tojo • Neville
Chamberlain • Winston
Churchill • Jesse Owens

Places

Manchuria • Ethiopia
Austria • Czechoslovakia
Munich • Dunkirk • English
Channel • Moscow •
Pearl Harbor • Berlin

New Vocabulary

totalitarian • Fascist •
Nazi • anti-Semitism •
persecuted • concentration
camps • Axis nations •
aggression • appeasement •
nonaggression pact •
blitzkrieg • civilians •
isolationism • destroyers

Focus on Main Ideas

1. What were the causes of World War II?
2. What did Hitler do after he became dictator of Germany?
3. What happened in Europe during the early years of World War II?
4. Why did the United States enter World War II?

World War II began in Europe in 1939. By the time the war ended in 1945, about 17 million soldiers from many nations had been killed. More Americans died fighting in World War II than in any other war in the twentieth century.

Causes of World War II

World War II had many causes. First, the Treaty of Versailles that ended World War I created new problems. The people of Germany were angry because the treaty punished Germany for its role in World War I. Germany had to pay billions of dollars to France and Great Britain. Also, Germany lost much of its land and was not allowed to rebuild its military. The League of Nations had been created in the treaty to keep peace between nations. However, the League had no power to stop one nation from attacking another.

Second, dictators came to power in Italy, Germany, Japan, and the Soviet Union. People turned to dictators to solve serious economic problems during the Great Depression. Millions of poor people in Europe did not have jobs. These unhappy people wanted leaders who could make their countries strong again.

So dictators won control of the governments of Germany, Italy, and the Soviet Union. These dictators had total power, or **totalitarian** governments.

Third, nationalism and imperialism grew in Germany, Italy, and Japan. Imperialism made those nations want to conquer other countries.

A fourth cause was militarism. Germany, Italy, and Japan built powerful armies, navies, and air forces. Germany built a huge military even though it was not allowed to do so according to the Treaty of Versailles.

Dictators Come to Power

Benito Mussolini became the dictator of Italy in 1922. Mussolini promised to bring order, prosperity, and jobs to the people of Italy. Mussolini became the leader of the **Fascist** party. Fascists wanted to build a powerful army, and they wanted to have a totalitarian government.

Joseph Stalin became the dictator of the Soviet Union in 1929. Unlike Mussolini, Stalin was a Communist. But Stalin also ruled with total power. People who spoke out against him were killed or sent to prison.

Germany also turned to a Fascist dictator, Adolf Hitler, to solve its problems in the 1930s. Hitler was the leader of the **Nazi** party. After becoming dictator in 1933, Hitler immediately began building a huge military. The Nazi party became Germany's only political party.

Nationalism was important to the Nazis. In powerful speeches Hitler told the Germans that they were a "master race." He said that other people, such as Eastern

The rise of dictators led to World War II. Pictured left to right are Benito Mussolini of Italy and Adolf Hitler of Germany. Both were Fascist dictators of their countries. Joseph Stalin was the Communist dictator of the Soviet Union. Hideki Tojo became the military dictator of Japan in 1941.

Adolf Hitler often gave strong speeches to large crowds. Many of his speeches, which inspired German nationalism, were about pride in Germany and the German people.

Europeans, gypsies, blacks, and Jews, were inferior. Hitler promised that Germany would become a powerful empire that would rule the world. He promised jobs and food for the German people.

Hitler blamed some of Germany's problems on the Treaty of Versailles and the country's Communists. But he blamed most problems on Jews. Hitler said that the Jews had caused the defeat of Germany in World War I and the Great Depression. As Hitler repeated lies again and again about the Jews, more and more people believed them. Hatred of Jews, or **anti-Semitism**, spread throughout Germany.

Hitler **persecuted** Germany's Jews. Stores owned by Jews were destroyed.

Jews lost their jobs. Thousands of Jews were arrested and sent to **concentration camps**, where they became prisoners and were often killed. Many Jews tried to escape from Germany. Most countries in Europe did not want them. Strict immigration quotas allowed only a small number of Jews to come to America. The government refused to change the quota laws.

In Japan, military leaders made all important government decisions, although the nation also had an emperor. In 1941 General Hideki Tojo became Japan's military dictator.

Steps Toward World War II

In 1936 Germany and Italy formed an alliance and agreed to fight in wars for each other. They became known as the **Axis nations**. In 1940 Japan also joined the Axis alliance.

During the 1930s Germany, Italy, and Japan used **aggression**, or military force, to attack and conquer other countries. In 1931 Japan conquered Manchuria, a mineral-rich area in northern China. Japan later invaded eastern China and other parts of Asia in order to get raw materials. In 1935 Italy conquered Ethiopia, a country in Africa.

Hitler began building a German empire. Hitler said that all German-speaking people must form one nation. So in 1938 Hitler's army marched into Austria and made Austria part of Germany. Next Hitler said that a German part of Czechoslovakia should be ruled by Germany.

Great Britain and France had an alliance with Czechoslovakia. So in 1938

Hitler met with the leaders of Britain and France in Munich, Germany. Hitler promised that he would not want more territory after he had taken the German region of Czechoslovakia. The British and the French gave in to Hitler, using a policy known as **appeasement**. Britain's leader, Neville Chamberlain, said that by giving in to Hitler's demands he had kept "peace in our time." But six months later, Hitler took control of the rest of Czechoslovakia.

In 1939 Hitler signed a **nonaggression pact** with Joseph Stalin. In the pact, Germany and the Soviet Union agreed not to attack each other during a war.

The Beginning of World War II

On September 1, 1939, Germany invaded Poland. Germany used a new method called **blitzkrieg**, or lightning war, to attack and conquer. Blitzkrieg meant making quick, surprise attacks using tanks and airplanes in many places at the same time. Two days later Poland's allies, Great Britain and France, declared war on Germany. World War II had begun.

As in World War I, Britain and France were called the Allies. The Allied armies were not strong enough to save Poland. Later in September the Soviet Union attacked eastern Poland, and by the end of the month Poland surrendered. Germany controlled western Poland and the Soviet Union controlled the eastern part.

Hitler quickly conquered more nations in Western Europe. By 1940 Denmark, Norway, Belgium, Luxembourg, and the Netherlands were ruled by Germany. Then the battle for France began. Germany

Nazis persecuted Germany's Jews. During the night of November 9, 1938, Nazis destroyed Jewish businesses across Germany in what has been called The Night of Broken Glass.

captured Paris by the end of June, and France surrendered.

The Allied soldiers in France had to escape before Hitler's army surrounded them. They escaped from the French port of Dunkirk and crossed the English Channel in small and large British boats and ships. More than 300,000 French, British, and Belgian soldiers escaped to Great Britain. There they prepared to continue the war against Hitler. Winston Churchill, the new prime minister of Great Britain, inspired the British people after the escape from Dunkirk. "...We shall fight on the fields and in the streets. We shall fight in the hills. We shall never surrender...."

From July 1940 until May 1941, Germany tried to conquer Great Britain with bombs from airplanes. These attacks

During the Battle of Britain, thousands of buildings were destroyed in cities throughout Great Britain.

were called the Battle of Britain. Night after night German planes bombed British air force bases, cities, and towns. The bombs destroyed buildings and caused fires. Thousands of **civilians** were killed. In the city of London, people slept in subway stations in order to be safe. But the British people would not surrender.

Hitler Invades the Soviet Union

Hitler dreamed of conquering the huge Soviet Union. In June 1941 he broke his agreement with Stalin. He invaded the Soviet Union with 3 million soldiers. Hitler wanted to control the Russian wheat and oil fields.

Hitler did not know how difficult it would be for his soldiers to survive Russia's bitterly cold winters. Their trucks and tanks

froze, and thousands of German soldiers froze to death in the cold. The Germans failed to capture the Russian capital of Moscow. Heavy fighting in the Soviet Union continued until 1944.

The United States Helps the Allies

As Hitler grew more powerful and more dangerous, most Americans continued to favor a policy of **isolationism**. In 1935 Congress started passing laws to keep the United States neutral. Although most Americans did not want to fight, they did want the Allies to win. President Roosevelt looked for ways to help the Allies. The Neutrality Act of 1939 allowed nations that were fighting aggression to buy weapons from the United States. This was a "cash and carry" policy because nations had to pay for the weapons with cash and use their own ships to carry them back to their countries.

In 1940, Winston Churchill asked the United States for fifty old **destroyers**, which are small warships that carry weapons. President Roosevelt agreed. In return for the warships, the British allowed the United States to use several British naval and air bases.

In November 1940 Roosevelt became the first President to be reelected to a third term. During the campaign, Roosevelt said that the United States would not fight in World War II. But in January 1941, Roosevelt made his famous "Four Freedoms" speech before Congress. In that speech, Roosevelt said that all people in the world should have freedom of speech and religion. And all people should have

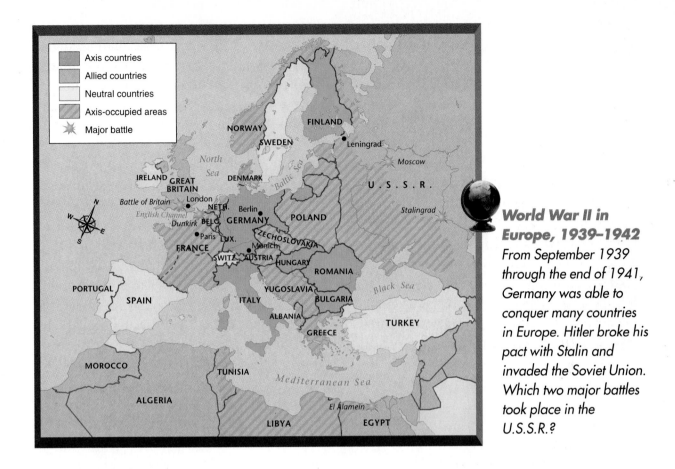

World War II in Europe, 1939–1942
From September 1939 through the end of 1941, Germany was able to conquer many countries in Europe. Hitler broke his pact with Stalin and invaded the Soviet Union. Which two major battles took place in the U.S.S.R.?

freedom from want, or hunger, and freedom from fear.

In March 1941 Congress passed the Lend-Lease Act. This law said that the United States would lend Britain all the weapons and supplies it needed to fight Hitler. Britain would return or replace the supplies after the war. By providing Britain with weapons, Roosevelt said the United States would "become the great arsenal of democracy." After Hitler invaded the Soviet Union, the United States used the Lend-Lease Act to give the Soviets weapons and supplies.

Roosevelt also took steps to prepare America for war. Laws were passed to raise taxes. Tax money was used to build a larger American military. In 1940 Congress passed a law that required all men between the ages of 18 and 35 to register for military service.

Japan Attacks Pearl Harbor

Japan had gone to war against China and had won control of eastern China. Then in 1941 it began attacking France's colony in Indochina in Southeast Asia. Japan wanted this region's supplies of rubber, tin, and rice.

The United States was worried about Japanese aggression. To stop Japanese attacks in Asia, the United States stopped selling scrap iron and oil to Japan. Later the United States stopped all trade with Japan. Japan was furious because it needed these supplies for its industries and its military forces.

In November 1941 Japanese and American leaders met to solve the problems between the two nations. At the same time, Japan secretly made plans to attack American bases in the Pacific if an agreement was not reached. When the two nations did not reach an agreement, Japan decided to carry out its secret attack plans.

Early in the morning on Sunday, December 7, 1941, Japan surprised the United States with an attack. Pearl Harbor, an American naval base in Hawaii, was bombed by 350 Japanese planes. About 2,400 Americans were killed in the attack on Pearl Harbor.

News of the surprise attack on Pearl Harbor spread quickly. Americans were upset and angry. The next day, December 8, President Roosevelt asked Congress to declare war on Japan. Roosevelt said that the attack on Pearl Harbor was "a date which will live in infamy." Congress declared war that day. Three days later Germany and Italy, the other Axis Powers, declared war on the United States. America's isolationism was over.

On the morning of December 7, 1941, Japanese planes attacked the American naval base at Pearl Harbor, Hawaii. Almost 200 American planes were destroyed, and 18 warships were sunk or badly damaged. When it sank, only the top of the U.S.S. Arizona, a large battleship, remained above the water.

BIOGRAPHY

Jesse Owens 1913–1980

Jesse Owens won four gold medals at the 1936 Olympic Games. This great athlete was born in Alabama to a poor family with nine children. His grandfather had been a slave. Owens's father was a sharecropper who struggled to earn enough money for his family. In 1921 Owens's family moved to Ohio.

When Owens was in the fifth grade, the coach at his school asked him to join the track team. After six years of training, Owens became a high school track star.

After high school Owens studied at Ohio State University. Owens attended classes, trained for the track team, and worked at three part-time jobs.

At a track meet in 1935, Owens broke four track records for running and jumping. He was chosen to represent the United States in the 1936 Olympic Games. The Olympics were to be held in Berlin, Germany. In 1936 Adolf Hitler was the dictator of Germany.

Hitler was sure that German athletes would win most of the gold medals at the Olympics. Hitler believed that the Germans were better than other people because the Germans were a "master race." Hitler also believed that black athletes were inferior people. Owens embarrassed and angered Hitler by winning four gold medals at the Olympics.

Hitler left the stadium so that he would not have to give Owens his awards at the medal ceremony. But Owens had proved that no group of people is superior or inferior. He proved that black athletes could be the best in the world.

After the Olympics Owens finished college. He spoke and wrote about ways to help African Americans and whites get along.

Owens is remembered as a great athlete. He showed that Hitler's ideas about race were wrong.

In Your Own Words

Jesse Owens embarrassed Hitler when he won four gold medals at the Olympic Games in 1936. Write a paragraph in your journal that tells why Hitler was embarrassed and what Owens proved to the world.

Review and Apply

- There were several causes of World War II, including problems created by the Treaty of Versailles, rise of dictators, economic problems in Europe, and nationalism, imperialism, and militarism.

- Adolf Hitler became the leader of Germany's Nazi party. Germany formed an alliance with Japan and Italy called the Axis Powers.

- The British and the French tried to contain Hitler and the Germans through a policy called appeasement, but World War II started when Hitler invaded Poland on September 1, 1939.

- The Germans captured many nations in Europe, but they did not defeat Great Britain and the Soviet Union.

- The United States stayed out of World War II until December 7, 1941, when the Japanese attacked the American naval base at Pearl Harbor in Hawaii.

VOCABULARY

Find the Meaning ■ **Write in your social studies notebook the word or phrase that best completes each sentence.**

1. A _____ system of government has full control over its people and allows little individual freedom.

   appeasement   democratic   totalitarian

2. The _____ party in Germany stressed total power by the government and a strong love for Germany.

   Communist   Nazi   Germanic People's

3. A _____ was a quick, powerful attack by the German Army and Air Force.

   blockade   blitzkrieg   boycott

4. The policy of not becoming involved in the affairs of other nations is called _____ .

   militarism   isolationism   appeasement

5. Great Britain and France used a policy of _____ to try to avoid a war with Germany.

   appeasement   anti-Semitism   blitzkrieg

6. _____ is attacking other nations with military force.

   Aggression   Isolationism   Appeasement

COMPREHENSION CHECK

Write a Paragraph ■ Use seven or more words or phrases below to write a paragraph that tells how Germany fought to control Europe from 1939 to 1941.

appeasement	Adolf Hitler	Joseph Stalin
Poland	Great Britain	Winston Churchill
Dunkirk	Allies	Lend-Lease Act
invaded	Battle of Britain	

CRITICAL THINKING

Drawing Conclusions ■ Read the paragraph below and the sentences that follow it. In your social studies notebook, write the conclusions that can be drawn from the paragraph. You should find three conclusions.

In order to have a supply of raw materials, Japan began to conquer other lands in Asia. It conquered Manchuria, eastern China, and French Indochina. In an effort to put an end to Japanese aggression, the United States stopped trading with Japan. This angered the Japanese. They decided to weaken American power in the Pacific by attacking the American naval base at Pearl Harbor, Hawaii. Early on the morning of December 7, 1941, Japanese bombers staged a surprise attack on Pearl Harbor. As a result of this act, the United States entered World War II by declaring war against Japan and Germany.

1. Japan, Germany, and Italy had formed an alliance called the Axis Powers.

2. Japan had a powerful military.

3. Japan did not have enough of its own raw materials.

4. The attack on Pearl Harbor was planned by the Japanese emperor.

5. The United States was not prepared for the Japanese attack on Pearl Harbor.

USING INFORMATION

Writing an Opinion ■ World War II began in 1939, but the United States did not enter the war until 1941. Americans were split over the issue of involvement in the war. Do you think that the United States should have become involved in World War II sooner? Write a paragraph in your social studies notebook that explains your opinion. Start your paragraph with a topic sentence.

Chapter 29

THE FIGHT TO WIN WORLD WAR II

◀ *Rosie the Riveter*

People

Daniel Inouye • Dwight D. Eisenhower • Harry S. Truman • Chester W. Nimitz • Edward R. Murrow • Albert Einstein

Places

Stalingrad • Normandy • Yalta • Auschwitz • Guadalcanal • Solomon Islands • Iwo Jima • Okinawa • Hiroshima •

Nagasaki • Nuremberg • Warsaw

New Vocabulary

defense industries • rationed • recycling • internment camps • barracks • strategy • liberated • Holocaust • gas chambers • aircraft carriers • atomic bomb • Zionism • pacifism

Focus on Main Ideas

1. How did American life change on the home front during World War II?
2. How did the Allies win the war in Europe against the Axis Powers?
3. What happened during the Holocaust?
4. How did the Allies win the war in the Pacific against Japan?

In December 1941 the United States entered World War II. The Americans and the Allies would not defeat the Axis nations until 1945.

Life on the Home Front

American life changed after the United States entered the war. Millions of men served in the armed forces. For the first time, women were allowed to join the armed forces. They did many types of military jobs, but they did not fight directly against the enemy. Because many men were away fighting the war, women worked in factories, building tanks, planes, and battleships. Rosie the Riveter became the symbol of the millions of women who entered the work force during World War II.

World War II helped to end the Great Depression. The war created millions of jobs in **defense industries**. Americans had to produce enormous amounts of weapons and war equipment for the American and Allied armed forces. By 1945 Americans had produced 15 million guns and 300,000 warplanes.

Because the United States was supplying the Allies with food and equipment, many goods became scarce. The government

352

rationed scarce items, such as soap, shoes, gasoline, meat, sugar, and butter, by using coupon books. Once people used up their coupons, they could not buy any more rationed items. **Recycling** of tin, rubber, and other goods was also important.

Prejudice toward Japanese Americans increased after the attack on Pearl Harbor. In 1942 President Roosevelt ordered that all Japanese Americans living on the West Coast, about 112,000 people, move to **internment camps**. About two thirds of these people were American citizens. Each camp contained **barracks** to house families. A high barbed-wire fence and armed guards surrounded each camp.

About 33,000 Japanese Americans fought for the United States. One Japanese American, Daniel Inouye, lost an arm in battle. Inouye later became a senator.

Fighting in Africa and in Europe

After the United States entered the war, Churchill, Roosevelt, and Stalin disagreed on the **strategy,** or plan, for winning the war in Europe. They finally decided to free North Africa from Italy and Germany. Next they would attack the southern part of Europe. Then they would invade and free France. And finally, they would invade Germany.

General Dwight D. Eisenhower became the leader of all the Allied troops. He led the battles in North Africa. In May 1943 the Axis army in North Africa surrendered.

Recycling of goods, such as rubber, tin, and steel, was very important for the effort to win the war. Americans collected these goods, which were later reused in the making of war supplies. For example, rubber and tin were used to make airplanes. Steel was used to make ships and tanks.

From Africa, the Allied armies invaded Italy. The Italian people were tired of war. They forced Mussolini to resign and later killed him. In September 1943 the Italian government surrendered. German soldiers in Italy did not surrender until May 1945.

While the Allies fought in Africa and in Italy, British and American planes bombed Germany. Many factories and railroads in Germany were destroyed. The Soviets continued to fight the Nazis in the Soviet Union. The turning point of the war in the Soviet Union was at the city of Stalingrad in February 1943. The Germans repeatedly failed to capture Stalingrad. After that the Soviets slowly pushed the German Army out of the Soviet Union.

Victory in Europe

The Allies made plans to cross the English Channel and invade France. D-Day, the day of the invasion, was June 6, 1944. Early that morning about 200,000 Allied soldiers and about 4,600 ships landed in Normandy, a region in northern France. It was the largest invasion by sea in world history. Within a month about one million troops arrived in France.

After D-Day Hitler had to send soldiers to fight on three fronts—in the Soviet Union, in Italy, and in France. The Allies freed Paris on August 25, 1944. The Soviets drove the German Army out of Poland, Romania, and Hungary. At the end of 1944,

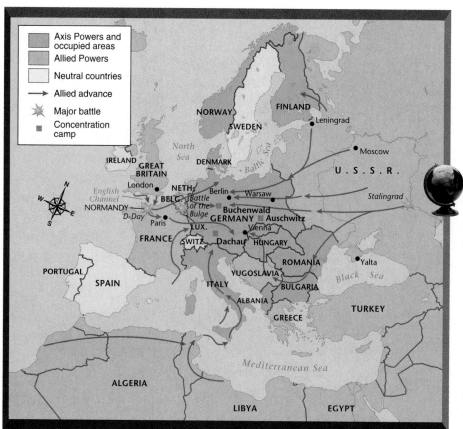

World War II in Europe and in North Africa, 1942–1945

After the invasion of Normandy in 1944, the Germans had to fight on three fronts. Hitler's weakened armies could not withstand the Allied advances. From which direction was Berlin captured?

This survivor of the Holocaust shows the number that had been tattooed into his arm at a concentration camp like the one above.

April 12, 1945. Harry S. Truman became President.

The Soviets captured the city of Berlin in April 1945. On April 30, 1945, Hitler committed suicide. On May 8, 1945, Germany surrendered. Europe had peace at last.

The Holocaust

After the Allies defeated the Axis Powers, prisoners in concentration camps were **liberated**, or set free. People around the world learned that the Nazis had killed six million Jews and several million other people. This mass murder of Jews and other people is called the **Holocaust**.

The Holocaust happened in every country that Hitler captured. Jews were crowded into railroad cars and sent to concentration camps, such as Buchenwald, Dachau, Auschwitz, and Treblinka, in Germany and in Poland. Barbed wire and armed guards made escape from the camps almost impossible.

In the concentration camps, all Jews were forced to have identification numbers tattooed into their arms. They were given only small amounts of food each day, so they slowly starved. People who were strong and healthy when they arrived had to work for the Nazis. Young children, old people, and all people who were sick or weak were killed. Millions were killed in **gas chambers**, rooms filled with poison gas. Then their bodies were burned in huge ovens. Thick black smoke from these ovens filled the sky day after day.

the Soviet Union controlled most of Eastern Europe.

In December 1944 the Germans started the Battle of the Bulge, the last major battle against the Allies. The battle took place in Belgium and in Luxembourg. In January 1945 the Allies won the Battle of the Bulge.

In February 1945 Churchill, Roosevelt, and Stalin met at Yalta in the Soviet Union. They agreed that Great Britain, France, the United States, and the Soviet Union would each control an area in Germany after the war. They also planned a peacekeeping organization called the United Nations. The meeting at Yalta was the last meeting between these leaders. Roosevelt died on

Some people knew what was happening to the Jews, but they did nothing to help. Others risked their lives to help Jews hide or escape. People are still trying to figure out what could have been done to save millions of innocent people from being killed.

Americans at War in Asia

While the Allies were fighting in Europe, they were also at war with Japan. Admiral Chester W. Nimitz became commander of the navy in the Pacific. Nimitz worked closely with General Douglas MacArthur, the commander of the army in the Pacific. Allied soldiers from many countries fought alongside Americans.

After attacking Pearl Harbor, Japan conquered the Philippines. In 1942 Roosevelt ordered General MacArthur to leave the Islands. MacArthur promised the people of the Philippines, "I shall return."

As you can see on the map on the opposite page, the Japanese controlled eastern China, the Philippines, Guam, part of Southeast Asia, and islands near Australia. The Allies knew that it would be difficult to defeat the Japanese.

In June 1942 the Battle of Midway became a turning point in the war in the Pacific. The Japanese attacked the Midway Islands, which are near Hawaii. The Allies sank four of Japan's **aircraft carriers** while winning the battle. The American victory at Midway gave the Allies control of the central Pacific.

After the Battle of Midway, the Allies began a strategy called "island hopping." They planned to capture important islands that would bring them close enough to invade Japan. In August 1942, United States Marines landed on the island of Guadalcanal in the Solomon Islands. After six months of deadly jungle fighting, the Japanese left Guadalcanal.

After capturing Guam and other Pacific islands, General MacArthur returned to the Philippines. He landed there in October 1944. While MacArthur fought on land, Admiral Nimitz used the navy to destroy Japan's fleet of ships in the sea around the Philippines. By February 1945 Americans had won control of the Philippine capital.

In February 1945 Americans won control of Iwo Jima. One of the most famous photographs of World War II was taken on Iwo Jima. It shows marines raising an American flag in victory. In June 1945 they captured Okinawa. The Allies planned to use Iwo Jima and Okinawa as bases to invade Japan and force it to surrender.

The Atomic Bomb and Japan's Defeat

By 1945 the Japanese had lost most of their Asian empire. Most of their navy was destroyed. American planes bombed Japanese cities day and night. However, Japan refused to surrender.

American military leaders told President Truman that one million Americans would probably be killed if the Allies had to invade and conquer Japan. To save the lives of these soldiers, Truman decided to use a powerful new bomb to defeat Japan. The **atomic bomb** was about 2,000 times more powerful than an ordinary bomb. Truman warned Japan to surrender or its cities would be destroyed. Japan still refused to surrender.

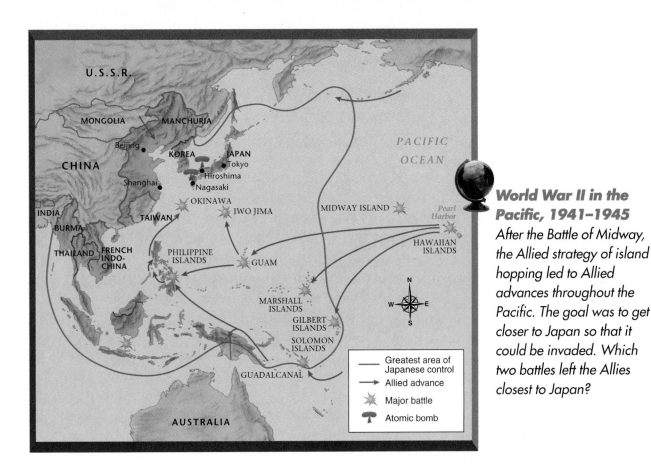

After the Battle of Midway, the Allied strategy of island hopping led to Allied advances throughout the Pacific. The goal was to get closer to Japan so that it could be invaded. Which two battles left the Allies closest to Japan?

Map labels: U.S.S.R. · MONGOLIA · MANCHURIA · Beijing · KOREA · JAPAN · Tokyo · Hiroshima · CHINA · Shanghai · Nagasaki · OKINAWA · IWO JIMA · MIDWAY ISLAND · Pearl Harbor · PACIFIC OCEAN · INDIA · BURMA · TAIWAN · THAILAND · FRENCH INDO-CHINA · PHILIPPINE ISLANDS · GUAM · HAWAIIAN ISLANDS · MARSHALL ISLANDS · GILBERT ISLANDS · SOLOMON ISLANDS · GUADALCANAL · AUSTRALIA

Legend:
Greatest area of Japanese control
Allied advance
Major battle
Atomic bomb

On August 6, 1945, an American plane dropped an atomic bomb on the Japanese city of Hiroshima. In seconds much of the city was destroyed. About 75,000 people were killed and thousands more were injured. But Japan still refused to surrender. On August 9, Americans dropped a second atomic bomb, this time on the city of Nagasaki. The bomb killed about 40,000 people. Japan's emperor told Japan's military leaders to surrender. Japan finally surrendered on September 2, 1945.

The Results of World War II

World War II caused terrible destruction. Much of Europe, Japan, China, North Africa, and the Soviet Union had to be rebuilt. About 50 million people died. Many of these people were soldiers, but large numbers were civilians. About 300,000 American soldiers died in the war.

After the war some Nazi leaders went on trial in Nuremberg, Germany, for their crimes during the Holocaust. Some Nazis were executed for their crimes; others were sent to prison.

The bombing of Hiroshima started the atomic age. Atomic bombs could now be used to destroy cities in only seconds. People were afraid that another world war could end civilization. As a result, in 1945 the United States began to work with other nations to create the United Nations. This organization would work to keep peace among the nations of the world.

VOICES from the PAST

The Radio Broadcasts of Edward R. Murrow

In 1935 Edward R. Murrow, an American reporter, was hired to broadcast news from Europe to the United States. He spent most of World War II reporting from Great Britain. During the Battle of Britain, Murrow spoke about the courage of the British people. The Battle of Britain lasted from July 1940 until about May 1941. Murrow's reports about World War II were heard on the radio throughout the United States.

August 18, 1940

"I spent five hours this afternoon on the outskirts of London. Bombs fell out there today…. But I found that one bombed house looks pretty much like another bombed house. It's about the people I'd like to talk…. To me those people were incredibly brave and calm. They are the unknown heroes of this war…."

December 24, 1940

"Christmas Day began in London nearly an hour ago…. Tonight as on every other night…all along the coast of this island, the observers [listen] for the sound of German planes. The fire fighters and the ambulance drivers are waiting, too…. This is not a merry Christmas in London…. In the underground shelters entire families were celebrating Christmas Eve. Christmas carols are being sung underground…."

December 13, 1942

"Millions of human beings, most of them Jews, are being gathered up…. Let me tell you a little about what's happened in the Warsaw ghetto…. Ten thousand people were rounded up and shipped off. After that, thousands more went each day…. Those who survived the journey were dumped out at one of three camps, where they were killed…. The Jews are being systematically exterminated [killed] throughout all Poland…."

December 27, 1942

"Here in Britain the first year of global war has produced many changes. Civilian consumer goods have gradually disappeared from the shops; more millions of women have gone into industry or into the armed forces; the draft age has been lowered to eighteen…but everyone is working. There is plenty of money, even if there isn't much to spend it on…."

November 26, 1944

"America, in the shape of soldiers on the ground, planes in the sky, ships on the ocean, represents the hope and the fear of an awful lot of little people in Europe….

We now carry—whether we like it or not—the responsibility for what happens to a lot of people other than Americans."

April 15, 1945

"Permit me to tell you of Buchenwald.... It was one of the largest concentration camps in Germany.... They showed me the children, hundreds of them. Some were only six. One rolled up his sleeve, showed me his number. It was tattooed on his arm; D-6030....

I asked to see the kitchen.... The German in charge...showed me the daily ration—one piece of brown bread about as thick as your thumb, on top of it a piece of margarine as big as three sticks of chewing gum. That, and a little stew, was what they received every twenty-four hours....

We proceeded to the small courtyard. There were two rows of [dead] bodies stacked up.... Some had been shot through the head.... Five hundred men and boys lay there in two neat piles...."

May 8, 1945

[Victory Day in Europe after Germany surrendered.]

"As you walk down the street you hear singing that comes from open windows; sometimes it's a chorus, sometimes it's just a single voice raised in song.... Many women are wearing flags in their hats; some are even draped in flags.... London is celebrating today.... The scars of war are all about."

September 2, 1945

[Japan formally surrendered to the Allies.]

"And now there is peace. The papers have been signed. The last enemy has given up...."

Write Your Answers

Answer these questions in the assignment section of your social studies notebook.

1. What happened in London on August 18, 1940?

2. How did the Battle of Britain affect the celebration of Christmas?

3. How did the war change life in England?

4. What was Buchenwald, and what did Murrow see there?

5. What was the mood in London on May 8, 1945?

BIOGRAPHY

Albert Einstein 1879–1955

Albert Einstein was one of the world's greatest scientists. From 1902 to 1909, Einstein developed important scientific theories. His famous theory of relativity changed the way scientists looked at the universe. One part of the theory said that all things are made of atoms. If atoms were split open, they would release huge amounts of energy. This theory was used to develop the atomic bomb.

In 1913 Einstein became the director of the physics department at a university in Berlin, Germany. In 1921 Einstein received the Nobel Prize for his work in physics.

Einstein worked for two other important causes. The first was **Zionism**. Zionism is the belief that Jews should have their own country in Palestine, or present-day Israel. The second cause was **pacifism**, the belief that wars are wrong and that people should work for peace. Einstein spoke out against Germany's actions during World War I.

Einstein's life changed in 1933 when Hitler became the dictator of Germany. Because Einstein was Jewish, the government took away his property, his job, and his right to be a German citizen. Einstein had been traveling in the United States. He stayed and became a professor at Princeton University.

While living in America, Einstein used his own money to help Jews escape from Germany. He visited several foreign countries and spoke about the dangers faced by Jews.

In 1939 Einstein wrote a letter to President Roosevelt. He warned FDR that Germany was probably building an atomic bomb and that the United States should try to build this dangerous weapon first. Because of Einstein's advice, Roosevelt started a secret group, "The Manhattan Project," that built the first atomic bomb.

Einstein was an immigrant who made valuable contributions to the United States. He is remembered as one of the world's greatest scientists.

In Your Own Words

Write a paragraph in the journal section of your notebook that tells how Albert Einstein helped the United States during World War II.

REVIEW AND APPLY

- Millions of American men served in the armed forces during World War II. Women worked in factories, building weapons and supplies for the war.

- Shortages of food and consumer goods led to rationing and recycling.

- About 112,000 Japanese Americans living on the West Coast were ordered to move to internment camps.

- The D-Day invasion started on June 6, 1944. Germany's last major attack against the Allies was the Battle of the Bulge. Germany finally surrendered on May 8, 1945.

- During the Holocaust the Nazis killed six million Jews and millions of other people.

- Japan surrendered on September 2, 1945, after the United States dropped atomic bombs on the Japanese cities of Hiroshima and Nagasaki.

VOCABULARY

Finish the Sentence ■ In your social studies notebook, write the correct word or phrase from the box that best completes each sentence. You will not use all the words in the box.

1. _____ built warplanes, tanks, and other equipment for World War II.

2. During the war about 112,000 Japanese Americans were forced to live as prisoners in _____ .

3. During the _____ the Nazis killed six million Jews and millions of other people.

4. The Allies _____ , or set free, people who had been held as prisoners in concentration camps.

5. During the war items such as soap, shoes, gasoline, and meat were limited, or _____ , in the United States.

> rationed
> defense industries
> Holocaust
> liberated
> internment camps
> aircraft carriers

USING INFORMATION

Writing an Opinion ■ Some people risked their lives to help Jews hide or escape from the Nazis. Write a paragraph that explains what you would have done if you had been living in Europe during World War II.

COMPREHENSION CHECK

Create an Information Chart ■ In your social studies notebook, copy and then complete the chart below about important battles that were fought during World War II. Part of the chart has already been done for you.

Name of Battle	Year Fought	Location of Battle	Significance of Battle
Battles in North Africa	1943	North Africa	Axis armies in North Africa surrendered
D-Day			
Battle of Stalingrad			
Battle of Midway			
Iwo Jima			
Hiroshima and Nagasaki			

CRITICAL THINKING

Making Predictions ■ Read the paragraph below and the sentences that follow it. Write in your social studies notebook three sentences that predict what will happen after the war.

After years of fighting, World War II finally came to an end. The war that started with the German attack on Poland on September 1, 1939, ended with the surrender of Japan on September 2, 1945. About 50 million people died during the war, and many cities in Europe and Asia were destroyed. During the time they had ruled Germany, the Nazis had killed millions of Jews and other people whom the Nazis had held as prisoners in concentration camps. The end of World War II also brought about the beginning of the atomic age.

1. European countries would rebuild their cities.

2. A peace treaty would be signed by the Axis Powers and the Allies.

3. Germans would continue to persecute the Jewish people.

4. Nazi officers would stand trial for their acts during the war.

5. Germany would be allowed to keep its powerful military.

6. More countries would try to make atomic bombs.

362

Comparing Circle Graphs

A circle graph, or pie graph, is a circle that has been divided into sections. Each section looks like a piece of pie. Often a circle graph shows percent or part of 100. All the sections make up the whole circle or add up to 100 percent. The 2 circle graphs on this page compare the types of workers in the work force in 1940 and in 1944. These two different time periods show workers before and after the United States went to war.

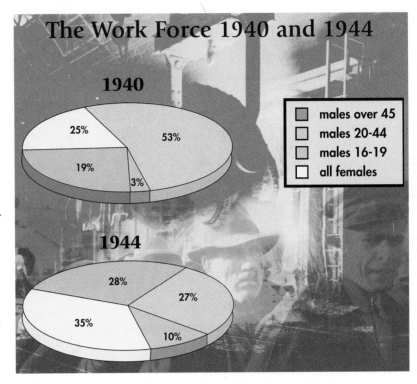

The Work Force 1940 and 1944

1940

25%   53%
19%
3%

males over 45
males 20-44
males 16-19
all females

1944

28%   27%
35%
10%

Study the two graphs. Then write the answers to the questions below in the assignment section of your social studies notebook.

1. What percent of the work force was female in 1944?

2. What percent of men ages 20 to 44 were in the work force in 1940?

3. What percent of men ages 20 to 44 were in the work force in 1944?

4. Which group was 28 percent of the work force in 1944?

5. How did the work force change for women, older men, and teenagers from 1940 to 1944?

6. How did the work force change from 1940 to 1944 for men between the ages of 20 and 44? Explain why.

Unit 7 Review

Study the time line on this page. You may want to read parts of Unit 7 again. Then use the words and the dates in the box to finish the paragraphs. In the assignment section of your notebook, write the numbers 1–14. There is one possible answer you will not use.

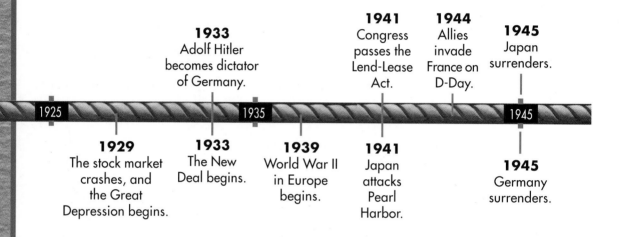

1933
Adolf Hitler becomes dictator of Germany.

1941
Congress passes the Lend-Lease Act.

1944
Allies invade France on D-Day.

1945
Japan surrenders.

1925

1935

1945

1929
The stock market crashes, and the Great Depression begins.

1933
The New Deal begins.

1939
World War II in Europe begins.

1941
Japan attacks Pearl Harbor.

1945
Germany surrenders.

depression	overproduction	Lend-Lease Act
1929	Adolf Hitler	Germany
appeasement	farmers	atomic bombs
Roosevelt	New Deal	D-Day
Czechoslovakia	Social Security Act	Pearl Harbor

The stock market crash in ___1___ was the start of the Great Depression. Some of the causes of the Great Depression were bank failures, ___2___, and difficult years for ___3___ in the 1920s. After Franklin D. ___4___ became President in 1933, he started a program to end the depression called the ___5___. In 1935 Congress passed the ___6___ to give pensions to retired people.

While Americans struggled with the depression at home, there were serious problems in Europe. In 1933 __7__ became the dictator of Germany. In 1938 Hitler took control of Austria and the German region of __8__. Great Britain and France used a policy called __9__ to avoid a war with Germany.

World War II began in Europe when Germany invaded Poland. In 1941 Congress passed the __10__ so the United States could give weapons and supplies to Great Britain. The United States entered World War II after Japan attacked __11__ on December 7, 1941. Thousands of Allied soldiers invaded France on __12__ on June 6, 1944. On May 8, 1945, __13__ surrendered and the war ended in Europe. After the United States dropped two __14__ on Japan, that nation surrendered.

Looking Ahead to Unit 8

The United States and the Soviet Union, the two most powerful nations after World War II, became enemies after the war. The struggle between Communists and non-Communists took place in Eastern Europe, Africa, Asia, and Latin America.

Many changes took place in the United States after World War II. African Americans fought to win equal rights. Americans worried about poverty at home, energy problems, and war in Vietnam.

As you read Unit 8, think about the ways the United States tried to stop the spread of communism. Find out about the work of Martin Luther King, Jr. Explore the reasons why Americans fought in the Vietnam War. Learn about the nation's problems and successes after World War II.

Unit 8

THE YEARS AFTER WORLD WAR II

The civil rights movement in the 1950s and 1960s was a struggle for African Americans to win the rights that belonged to all Americans. Soon after Dr. Martin Luther King, Jr., led 250,000 Americans in the March on Washington, the Civil Rights Act of 1964 was passed.

As you read Unit 8, you will learn how the United States struggled to stop the spread of communism in many parts of the world. Find out how Americans achieved success in space travel. Learn how Americans tried to solve the problems of poverty and prejudice.

1945

1955

1945
The United Nation's begins.

1947
The Marshall Plan is created to contain communism.

1948
The Berlin Airlift saves West Berlin.

1949
Western nations form NATO.

1950
The Korean War begins.

1954
The Supreme Court rules in *Brown* v. *Board of Education* to end school segregation.

THINK ABOUT IT

- Germany and Japan were enemies of the United States during World War II. Why did the United States rebuild those countries after the war?

- Vietnam is a poor Asian country with few natural resources. Why did more than 58,000 Americans die fighting in a war in that far-off nation?

- President Richard Nixon ended the Vietnam War for Americans, and he created better relations with the Soviet Union and China. Why did he become the only President to resign?

▲ Norman Rockwell's painting about school integration.

1962
The Cuban Missile Crisis occurs.

1963
President John F. Kennedy is assassinated.

1964
Congress passes the Tonkin Gulf Resolution.

1973
A cease-fire begins in Vietnam.

1965

1958
The United States sends its first satellite into space.

1963
Dr. Martin Luther King, Jr., leads the March on Washington.

1969
Neil Armstrong is the first person on the moon.

1974
President Nixon resigns.

Chapter 30

THE COLD WAR BEGINS

◀ The flag of the United Nations

People

George C. Marshall • Mao Zedong • Chiang Kai-shek • Alger Hiss • Joseph McCarthy • Margaret Chase Smith • Fidel Castro

Places

San Francisco • Taiwan • Korea

New Vocabulary

Cold War • superpowers • iron curtain • containment • Berlin Airlift • arms race • truce • McCarthyism • satellite

Focus on Main Ideas

1. How did the Cold War develop between the United States and the Soviet Union?
2. How did Senator McCarthy affect the United States?
3. How did the Cold War affect Europe, Asia, Africa, and Latin America?

In 1945 a new type of war, the **Cold War**, began between the United States and the Soviet Union, two of the world's most powerful nations. These two **superpowers** struggled over the spread of communism. Although the United States and the Soviet Union did not directly fight each other, the Cold War brought fear and fighting to many parts of the world.

The United Nations Begins

At the end of World War II, the Allies started an organization called the United Nations, or UN. Its goal was to solve problems peacefully between nations. Representatives from 50 nations met for the first time in April 1945 in San Francisco, California. Since 1952 the home for the United Nations has been in New York City. Today 185 nations are members of the UN.

All nations of the UN meet at least once a year in the General Assembly. Fifteen nations meet in the UN's Security Council. Ten nations are selected at random, and the United States, Russia, France, Great Britain, and China are the Security Council's five permanent members. The UN's Security Council can send UN soldiers to keep peace in troubled regions. Each permanent member can use a veto to vote to stop a Security Council action.

Why Did the Cold War Begin?

The Cold War developed because the two superpowers wanted to spread different political and economic systems throughout the world. The United States wanted to spread its democratic form of government and its capitalist economy. Under capitalism, all people can own property and businesses to earn profits. By spreading capitalism to other countries, the United States could have more trading partners and earn more money.

The Soviet economic system was based on communism. Under communism, the government owned all businesses and property. The government decided what factories could produce, what farmers could grow, and what salaries people could earn. The Soviets had a totalitarian government led by a powerful dictator. Most people in the Soviet Union had little freedom.

Towards the end of World War II, Churchill, Roosevelt, and Stalin met at Yalta. During the meeting Stalin agreed to allow free elections in countries captured by the Soviet Union in Eastern Europe. Stalin broke this promise.

After World War II, the Soviet Union controlled the countries of Eastern Europe. The Soviets often used their military to maintain control. In this photograph, tanks and soldiers from the Soviet Army are in Prague, the capital of Czechoslovakia.

President Truman developed a policy against communism. George C. Marshall, at right, helped carry out that policy.

The Cold War began when the Soviet Union supported Communist governments in Poland and in other Eastern European countries. The Soviets said they needed to control Poland so other nations would not march through Poland to attack the Soviet Union. But Soviet troops remained in other countries in Eastern Europe, not just in Poland. The United States was angry that the Soviet Union was spreading communism into the countries of Eastern Europe.

Soon after the Cold War began, Winston Churchill called the Soviet Union's control over Eastern Europe an **iron curtain**. The term described the tough, invisible wall that surrounded the Communist countries. The iron curtain kept the people of the Communist countries separated from the rest of Europe.

President Truman and Communism

Harry S. Truman was President at the start of the Cold War. In order to stop communism from spreading from Eastern Europe to other areas, Truman developed a policy of **containment**. He stated that the United States must support nations that were fighting to remain free from communism. His ideas were called the Truman Doctrine. Truman used this doctrine for the first time with Greece and Turkey. Americans believed Communist rebels were trying to take control of those countries. To prevent this, Truman asked Congress to give aid to Greece and Turkey. Congress voted to give these countries $400 million to fight Communist rebels. As a result, Greece and Turkey remained free from communism.

To carry out the Truman Doctrine, Secretary of State George C. Marshall devised a plan. Under the Marshall Plan, the United States agreed to rebuild the war-damaged nations of Europe. All European nations, including the Soviet Union, could receive American aid. By helping these nations build strong economies, Marshall and Truman believed the nations would not turn to communism. The nations of Western Europe accepted American aid. The United States gave billions of dollars to Germany and other nations in Western Europe. These nations became democracies with capitalist economies.

The United States also helped rebuild Japan. American troops, led by General Douglas MacArthur, controlled Japan after the war. MacArthur helped the Japanese write a democratic constitution. Japan built a strong capitalist economy and became a democracy.

A Divided Germany and the Berlin Airlift

After World War II ended, the four allies agreed to divide Germany into four zones, or areas. The United States, Great Britain, and France controlled the western part of Germany, while the Soviet Union controlled the eastern part. The German capital, Berlin, was in the Soviet zone. Berlin was also divided into four zones controlled by the same four countries.

In 1948 the United States, Britain, and France united their three zones to form an independent nation called the Republic of West Germany. The Soviets had lost 20 million people during the war, and they were angry that West Germany was becoming a strong, united nation. They decided to force the Allies to give up control of West Berlin.

Trains and trucks from West Germany had been bringing food and supplies through the Soviet zone into West Berlin. The Soviet Union started a blockade. All highways and railroads that carried supplies were closed. To save West Berlin, Truman ordered American planes to fly supplies into the city. The British Air Force also

When Soviet troops stopped supplies from reaching West Berlin, President Truman ordered the American Air Force to fly them into the city. Every day for almost a year, planes landed with supplies about every 90 seconds.

helped. Together they carried out the **Berlin Airlift** that began in June 1948. In May 1949 Stalin ended the blockade. The Soviet zone in Germany became the Communist country of East Germany. West Berlin remained a free city inside East Germany.

The United States and NATO

An **arms race**, or a race to build the largest military forces, began between the United States and the Soviet Union. The Soviet Union tested its first atomic bomb in 1949. After that test, each nation tried to build more powerful weapons and atomic bombs.

President Truman believed Western Europe needed a strong army in order to contain communism. So the United States and Canada formed a military alliance with ten nations in Western Europe. The alliance was called the North Atlantic Treaty Organization (NATO). NATO members agreed to protect any member that was attacked. In 1955 the Soviet Union started a military alliance with Eastern European nations. That military alliance was called the Warsaw Pact.

China Becomes a Communist Nation

During World War II, China fought with the Allies against Japan. After the war the

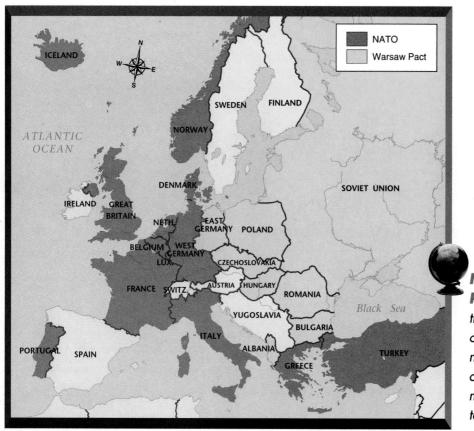

NATO and Warsaw Pact Countries During the Cold War, most of the countries of Europe were members of either NATO or the Warsaw Pact. How many countries belonged to the Warsaw Pact?

Chinese continued to fight in a civil war. During the Chinese civil war, Mao Zedong led the Communists and tried to take control of the government. Mao received help from the Soviet Union. The Communists fought against the Chinese Nationalists. A dictator named Chiang Kai-shek led the Nationalists. The United States helped Chiang Kai-shek and the Nationalists because they were against communism.

Millions of poor people in China helped the Communists win the civil war in 1949. Chiang Kai-shek and the Nationalists escaped to the small island of Taiwan. The nation was called Nationalist China. Communist China was called the People's Republic of China, or Red China. Mao Zedong became the dictator of Red China. Red China became a Soviet ally and also worked to spread communism. The United States refused to recognize, or deal with, Red China's government until 1978.

The Korean War

The Cold War became a "hot" war in the east Asian country of Korea. In 1945 the Allies divided Korea at the 38th parallel. North Korea became a Communist country. The Korean War began when soldiers from North Korea invaded South Korea in 1950. The North Koreans wanted to unite the entire nation under one Communist government. In three days, North Korea won control of most of South Korea.

The United States called for an emergency meeting of the UN Security Council. The Security Council voted to send UN troops to help South Korea. More than half of the UN soldiers were Americans.

Truman asked General MacArthur to lead the UN troops in Korea. MacArthur forced the North Koreans to leave from most of South Korea. Then he captured most of North Korea. However, about 200,000 soldiers from China helped North Korea. Once again Communists won control of North Korea.

General MacArthur wanted to attack Communist China. President Truman refused to allow MacArthur to attack China. When MacArthur continued to criticize the President, Truman fired him.

The Korean War ended when a **truce**, or an agreement to stop fighting, was reached in 1953. By that time Dwight D. Eisenhower was President of the United States. About 34,000 American soldiers had died during the Korean War. Korea is still divided at the 38th parallel. American and UN troops protect the dividing line between the two Koreas to this day.

The Red Scare and McCarthyism

The fear of communism was strong in the United States in the early 1920s and again after World War II. Because of the fear of communism, Truman had the loyalty of three million federal workers checked. Freedom of speech and freedom of the press were in danger of being lost.

The House of Representatives formed the House Committee on Un-American Activities (HUAC) to find Communists in the government. In 1948 the Committee investigated Alger Hiss, an important person in the State Department. Hiss was accused of being a Communist spy. Hiss said he was innocent. The HUAC did not

Senator Joseph McCarthy of Wisconsin accused many members of the government of being Communists.

prove that Hiss was guilty of spying, but he was found guilty of lying during his trial.

Senator Joseph McCarthy spread the fear of communism to every part of the nation. In 1950 McCarthy made a speech in which he said he had the names of 205 Communists in the State Department. McCarthy never named the people on his list nor did he prove they were guilty. But he continued to accuse many Americans of being Communists, and he ruined many of their careers. Even Presidents Truman and Eisenhower were called traitors. Most senators and representatives were afraid to speak out against McCarthy. They feared that they, too, would be accused of being Communists. However, Senator Margaret Chase Smith and six other senators did have the courage to speak out against McCarthy. Edward R. Murrow made television shows that reported how McCarthy had falsely accused people.

In 1954 McCarthy lost his power after he attacked the army for being filled with Communists. The Senate took action and made a statement against McCarthy. The fear of communism remained strong through the 1980s. **McCarthyism** now means the policy of falsely accusing people of working against the government.

The Cold War Around the World

During the 1950s, 24 African colonies became independent nations. These nations were poor because they lacked industry, education, good farming methods, and modern transportation. The Soviet Union and the United States gave millions of dollars in foreign aid to win African nations to their sides.

The Cold War also came to Latin America. In 1959 Fidel Castro took control of Cuba's government. Cuba became a Communist country and a Soviet ally. The United States ended its relations and trade with Cuba. Americans worried that Castro would spread communism and revolutions to other Latin American nations. To prevent the spread of communism, President Eisenhower agreed to give $500 million in foreign aid to Latin America. However, Communist revolutions spread through parts of Central America.

The "space race" became part of the Cold War in 1957 when the Soviet Union sent *Sputnik*, the world's first **satellite**, into space. Not until 1958 did Americans send their first satellite into space.

The Cold War would continue to cause tension between the United States and the Soviet Union for more than forty years.

374

BIOGRAPHY

Harry S. Truman 1884–1972

Harry S. Truman was President during the early years of the Cold War. He grew up in Missouri, and learned to read at an early age. Although he was an excellent student, his family was too poor to send him to college. He spent 13 years working on his family's farm. During World War I, he served as an army captain in France.

In 1934 Truman was elected to the United States Senate. He soon had a reputation for being very honest and hardworking. During World War II, Senator Truman led a committee that checked whether defense money was being wasted. Due to Truman's efforts, $15 billion of defense money was saved for the nation.

During the election for President in 1944, Roosevelt chose Truman to run as Vice President. The two men were elected easily. Truman had been Vice President for less than three months when Roosevelt died and Truman became President.

One of President Truman's first decisions was to use atomic bombs on Japan. Truman's goals were to save the lives of American soldiers and to end the war with Japan quickly.

After the war Truman made other difficult decisions. Truman helped create the Marshall Plan and NATO in order to contain communism. He joined all three branches of the armed forces together under one secretary of defense. He also ended segregation in the armed forces.

When North Korea invaded South Korea, Truman decided to send American troops to South Korea. His decision to send troops to fight with UN forces saved South Korea.

Truman did not run for reelection in 1952. Instead he campaigned for Adlai Stevenson. The popular Republican general, Dwight D. Eisenhower, won the election.

Harry Truman is remembered as a President who made tough decisions during World War II and the Cold War.

In Your Own Words

President Truman made several difficult decisions. Write a paragraph that tells which Truman decision you think was most important.

REVIEW AND APPLY

- During the Cold War, the United States and the Soviet Union struggled over the spread of communism.

- The United Nations was formed to solve problems peacefully between nations.

- The Truman Doctrine supported nations that were trying to remain free from communism. Under the Marshall Plan, the United States agreed to rebuild the war-damaged nations of Europe.

- In 1949 China became a Communist country.

- The Korean War was fought between 1950 and 1953. The United States and UN troops helped South Korea fight Communist North Korea.

- The Cold War spread to Africa, Latin America, and even into a space race.

VOCABULARY

Matching ■ **Match the vocabulary word or phrase in Group B with a definition in Group A. Write the letter of the correct answer in your social studies notebook. You will not use all the words in Group B.**

Group A	Group B
1. falsely accusing people of working against the government	A. superpowers
2. an agreement to stop fighting	B. satellite
3. *Sputnik* was the first one to be sent into space	C. McCarthyism
4. a policy to stop the spread of communism	D. containment
5. a build-up of military forces between the United States and the Soviet Union	E. truce
	F. arms race

USING INFORMATION

Writing an Opinion ■ **In 1950 Senator Joseph McCarthy accused many people of being Communists. At the time, many senators and representatives were afraid to speak out against McCarthy. Imagine that you were living in 1950. In your social studies notebook, write a letter to your state's representatives in Congress urging them to take a stand against Senator McCarthy. Your letter should follow the rules of good letter writing.**

COMPREHENSION CHECK

Choose the Answer ■ In your social studies notebook, write the letter of the word or phrase that best answers each question.

1. Who first used the term "iron curtain"?

   a. Harry Truman
   b. Joseph Stalin
   c. Winston Churchill

2. What was the purpose of NATO?

   a. to provide members with trading partners
   b. to stop communism in China
   c. to protect members that were attacked

3. What line of latitude divides the countries of North and South Korea?

   a. the 38th parallel
   b. the 17th parallel
   c. the equator

4. Who was the Communist leader that came to power in Cuba in 1959?

   a. Alger Hiss
   b. Fidel Castro
   c. Mao Zedong

CRITICAL THINKING

Comparing and Contrasting ■ In this chapter, you read about the differences between the United States and the Soviet Union that led to the Cold War. Compare and contrast the United States and the Soviet Union by copying and completing the chart below.

	United States	Soviet Union
Economic system		
Type of government		
Relationship with Germany		
Relationship with Cuba		
The Space Race		

Chapter 31

THE CIVIL RIGHTS MOVEMENT

◀ Linda Brown

People

Linda Brown • Thurgood Marshall • Earl Warren • Rosa Parks • Dr. Martin Luther King, Jr. • John F. Kennedy • James Meredith • Lyndon B. Johnson • Mohandas Gandhi • Malcolm X

Places

Little Rock • Montgomery • Birmingham • Los Angeles • Newark • Detroit

New Vocabulary

civil rights movement • facilities • discrimination • integration • nonviolent resistance • civil disobedience • sit-ins • affirmative action • race riots

Focus on Main Ideas

1. How did the Supreme Court's decision in *Brown v. Board of Education of Topeka, Kansas* help end segregation?
2. What laws were passed in the 1960s to protect the civil rights of African Americans?
3. What events in the civil rights movement helped African Americans end segregation?

The **civil rights movement** took place during the 1950s and 1960s. During this time African Americans and other minorities struggled to win the equal rights that were guaranteed in the Constitution and in the Bill of Rights.

Segregation

After the Civil War, African Americans who had been slaves were freed. The Thirteenth, Fourteenth, and Fifteenth Amendments ended slavery and gave African Americans equal rights. The Constitution and the Bill of Rights had been written to protect the rights of all Americans. But after Reconstruction ended, southern states passed segregation laws, or Jim Crow laws, to keep African American and white people apart in public places. These state laws took away the rights of African Americans. For almost 100 years, African Americans in the South had to use separate schools, water fountains, hospitals, restaurants, and beaches.

In 1896 the Supreme Court's decision in the case of *Plessy* v. *Ferguson* protected segregation. That decision said there could be segregation as long as places for African Americans were "separate but equal" to those for whites. In fact most of the **facilities** for whites were better than those for African Americans.

Throughout the nation African Americans faced **discrimination**, or unfair treatment, because of the color of their skin. They had fewer opportunities to get good jobs, and they earned lower salaries. Although there were no Jim Crow laws in the North, most African Americans still faced discrimination there. Often they could not live in white neighborhoods because homes would not be sold to them. In many northern cities, African American children went to neighborhood schools that did not have white children.

Goals of the Civil Rights Movement

One of the goals of the civil rights movement that began in the 1950s was to end segregation. To end segregation, people called for the **integration** of public places. First, Jim Crow laws would have to be repealed. Then, new laws would have to be passed to protect the civil rights of all Americans. However, the people who struggled for civil rights knew that economic changes were also needed. African Americans needed the opportunity to have better jobs and to go to better schools.

During the 1950s and 1960s, segregation ended because of Supreme Court decisions,

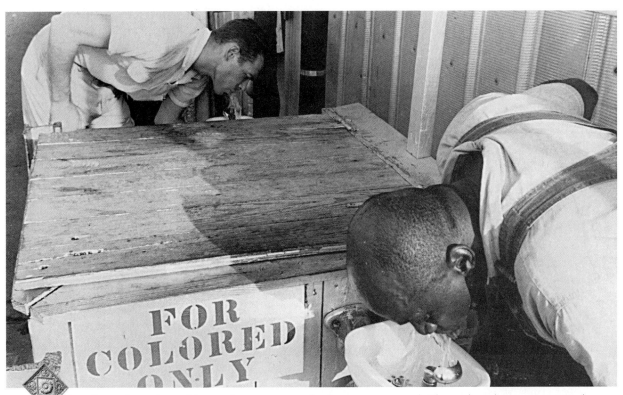

Jim Crow laws kept African Americans and whites segregated. The policy that was created by Supreme Court decisions was that facilities could be "separate but equal." Signs identified which facilities, such as water fountains, rest rooms, restaurants, and schools, could be used.

Thurgood Marshall, center, was the NAACP lawyer who argued that schools should not be segregated.

actions of Presidents, and laws passed by Congress. Some states refused to follow these federal laws and Supreme Court decisions. This led to new arguments about how to share power between state governments and the federal government. What actions would be taken by the federal government if states refused to carry out federal laws and Supreme Court decisions?

Brown v. Board of Education

In 1954 the Supreme Court made a decision to end school segregation. The decision was based on a case called *Brown* v. *Board of Education of Topeka, Kansas.* The case began when Linda Brown's father wanted her to attend the white elementary school that was near their home. The school refused to accept Linda

because she was black. The National Association for the Advancement of Colored People, or the NAACP, took Brown's case to the Supreme Court. Thurgood Marshall, an NAACP lawyer, handled the case. Marshall later became a Supreme Court justice.

In 1954 the Supreme Court ruled in favor of Brown. Chief Justice Earl Warren wrote the decision:

"Does segregation of children in public schools solely on the basis of race...deprive the children of the minority group of equal educational opportunities? We believe that it does.... We conclude in the field of public education the doctrine [idea] of separate but equal has no place...."

The *Brown* decision overturned the decision of *Plessy* v. *Ferguson.* Now all public schools had to end segregation because of the *Brown* decision. The Supreme Court had ruled to end segregation, but state governments had to carry out plans to end it. Southerners were furious and refused to integrate their schools.

Integration at Central High School

Central High School in Little Rock, Arkansas, became a battleground for integration in 1957. The battle began when nine African American students tried to start school at the all-white high school. The governor of Arkansas refused to integrate the school although President Eisenhower had ordered him to do so. The governor said that the Constitution gave states the power to make education laws. Therefore, as governor he had the right to protect segregation of the schools in his state. The governor sent guards to prevent the African American students from entering Central High School. Angry crowds of white people surrounded the school and threatened to attack the nine students.

President Eisenhower believed that states must obey Supreme Court decisions. He sent 1,000 soldiers to Little Rock to protect the African American students. On September 25, 1957, the black students entered the high school for the first time.

For the entire school year, the African American students needed guards to protect them. They were attacked daily by many white students. The following year, Central High School closed for the year in order to prevent integration.

School segregation ended slowly. However, most schools eventually were integrated. The nine brave students who attended Central High School had a reunion thirty years later in 1987. By that time an African American was president of Central High's student organization.

The Montgomery Bus Boycott

In December 1955 Rosa Parks, an African American woman, sat down in the front of a bus in Montgomery, Alabama.

In 1957 Central High School in Little Rock, Arkansas, was a battleground in the fight to end school segregation. Arkansas's governor sent guards to the school so that nine African American children could not enter. President Eisenhower then sent troops so that the children could attend the school.

Rosa Parks started a protest when she was arrested because she would not move to the back of a bus.

She was arrested when she refused to give her seat to a white man. The law required African Americans to sit in the back of public buses. Parks was arrested because she broke the law.

The African American community in Montgomery grew angry about the arrest of Rosa Parks. Led by a minister, Dr. Martin Luther King, Jr., they began to boycott, or stop using, the city's buses. They wanted the unfair law changed. Dr. King believed that **nonviolent resistance** was the best way to end segregation.

During the boycott African Americans refused to ride on the city's buses. Many people walked to work even in cold, rainy weather. The boycott lasted almost a year. The bus company lost money because before the boycott more than half of the bus riders had been African Americans.

In November 1956 the Supreme Court declared that segregation on public transportation was illegal. African Americans were allowed to sit anywhere on buses. The bus boycott ended. The boycott made Dr. King the most famous African American leader in the nation.

More Battles for Civil Rights

In the early 1960s, **civil disobedience**, or disobeying unfair laws, became a weapon against segregation. African Americans and white people began **sit-ins** at lunch counters in the South. Although waiters refused to serve them, the protesters remained at the lunch counters until the restaurants closed. Sit-ins also took place in parks, libraries, and other public places. Often protesters were arrested and sent to jail. But many public places began to integrate.

In 1960 John F. Kennedy was elected President. During his campaign he had promised to help African Americans win equal rights.

In 1962 James Meredith, an African American, ended segregation at the University of Mississippi. The governor of Mississippi refused to allow Meredith to attend the university. President Kennedy sent federal troops to protect Meredith so he could attend school. Meredith became the first African American to graduate from the University of Mississippi.

In April 1963 Dr. King led protest marches to end segregation in Birmingham, Alabama. The city's police violently attacked the marchers. They arrested Dr. King and sent him to jail. Many Americans watched the violence in Birmingham on television. People in many states were convinced that segregation was wrong.

Many civil rights protests occurred during the early Cold War years. People in other nations wondered how Americans could work for democracy in other countries when they did not allow equal rights for African Americans in the United States.

The March on Washington

In June 1963 President Kennedy sent a civil rights bill to Congress. Congress had to pass the bill for it to become a law. To win support for the civil rights bill, in August 1963, Dr. King led 250,000 people in a March on Washington, D.C. African Americans and whites stood together in front of the Lincoln Memorial. Millions of Americans watched the event on television and listened to Dr. King give his now-famous "I Have a Dream" speech.

"...I have a dream that one day...little black boys and black girls will be able to join hands with little white boys and white girls as sisters and brothers....

"With this faith we will be able to work together...to stand up for freedom together, knowing that we will be free one day...."

New Laws Help Civil Rights

President Kennedy was assassinated in November 1963 before the civil rights

Dr. Martin Luther King, Jr., led more than 250,000 people in the March on Washington. Leaders of many civil rights groups were present and gave speeches that day. But the speech given by Dr. King is among the greatest speeches in American history.

Malcolm X was a strong speaker who believed that African Americans and whites should be separated.

law was passed. After he died, Congress passed the Civil Rights Act of 1964. President Lyndon B. Johnson signed the bill and it became law. The new law made segregation and job discrimination because of race, sex, or religion against the law. To carry out the law, Congress created the Equal Employment Opportunity Commission.

In 1964 the Twenty-fourth Amendment was ratified. It ended poll taxes in the South. These taxes had prevented many African Americans from voting.

The next year the Voting Rights Act of 1965 was passed. This law said it was illegal to require people to pass literacy tests in order to vote. Many more African Americans were able to vote in elections. Voting rights gave African Americans more power in the government.

In 1965 President Johnson created **affirmative action** programs to give African Americans equal opportunities in education and jobs. Affirmative action required colleges and businesses to set aside places for African Americans. Affirmative action also helped women and other minority groups to have more opportunities. The Supreme Court later ruled that affirmative action programs cannot discriminate against whites in order to help minorities.

Changes in the Civil Rights Movement

During the 1960s other civil rights leaders began to move away from Dr. King's ideas of nonviolence and integration. They stressed the need for "black power." People who believed in black power said African Americans should defend themselves if they were attacked. They wanted more rights and more power immediately. They also stressed learning about their African heritage. Some African Americans wore African-style clothing and hairstyles and changed their names to African names.

Many African Americans became frustrated that change was not taking place fast enough. That frustration led to **race riots** in large cities such as Los Angeles, California; Newark, New Jersey; and Detroit, Michigan. Then in April 1968, Dr. King was assassinated. Riots spread to more than 100 cities across the country. Millions of dollars worth of property was destroyed.

By 1970 the civil rights movement had ended all Jim Crow laws and had helped Congress pass new civil rights laws. These laws would continue to help many Americans win equal rights.

BIOGRAPHY

Dr. Martin Luther King, Jr. 1929–1968

Dr. Martin Luther King, Jr., was a minister who became the civil rights movement's greatest leader.

King was born in Atlanta, Georgia. His grandfather and his father were ministers. To earn money while he was in college, King picked tobacco during the summer in Connecticut. As he watched African Americans and whites work together in the tobacco fields, King started to believe that the two races could live and work together everywhere.

King studied in Pennsylvania to become a minister. After earning his Ph.D. at Boston University, he was called Dr. King.

King studied the work of Mohandas Gandhi, the Indian leader who helped India win independence from Great Britain. Gandhi used nonviolent resistance to defeat the British. King decided to use nonviolent resistance to end segregation. Dr. King would continue to use nonviolence even when he became a victim of violence when bombs were thrown at his home.

King was working as a minister in Montgomery, Alabama, when Rosa Parks was arrested. He became the leader of the boycott to end segregation on buses. The success of the boycott made Dr. King famous.

In 1964, the new Civil Rights Act was passed, and Dr. King received the Nobel Peace Prize.

Dr. King continued working for equal rights and better economic opportunities for African Americans. He stressed the importance of peace between all Americans.

In 1968 Dr. King was assassinated, and millions of Americans, mourned for him. King's birthday became a national holiday.

Dr. Martin Luther King, Jr., is remembered as a great civil rights leader who wanted freedom for all Americans. The last lines from King's "I Have a Dream" speech were written on his tombstone: "Free at last! Free at last! Thank God Almighty, we are free at last."

In Your Own Words

Write a paragraph in your journal that tells two ways that Dr. King worked to win equal rights.

Voices *from the* Past

Warriors Don't Cry by Melba Pattillo Beals

Melba Pattillo Beals was 15 years old when she became one of the nine students to integrate Central High School in Little Rock, Arkansas. The governor of Arkansas, Orval Faubus, was determined to keep the school segregated. Pattillo wrote about the difficulties she faced as she went to school with hostile white students. While attending Central High School, Pattillo kept a diary in which she wrote about her experiences. She included sections from her diary in her book, *Warriors Don't Cry*.

On our first day at Central High, Governor Faubus dispatched [sent] gun-toting Arkansas National Guard soldiers to prevent us from entering. Three weeks later, having won a federal court order, we black children maneuvered our way past an angry mob to enter the side door of Central High. But by eleven that morning, hundreds of people outside were running wild, crashing through police barriers to get us out of school…. A few…brave members of the Little Rock police force saved our lives by spiriting us past the mob to safety.

To uphold the law and protect lives, President Eisenhower sent soldiers of the 101st Airborne Division, the elite "Screaming Eagles"—Korean War heroes.

On my third trip to Central High, I rode with the 101st in an army station wagon…. With the protection of our 101st bodyguards, we black students walked through the front door of the school and completed a full day of classes.

But I quickly learned from those who opposed integration that the soldiers' presence meant a declaration of war…. It transformed us into warriors who dared not cry even when we suffered….

Would I integrate Central if I had it to do over again? My answer is yes….

[After Melba and the other eight students failed to get into Central High School on the first day of school, the NAACP took the students to a news conference.]

Cameras flashed, bright lights stung my eyes, and reporters asked lots of questions….

"Miss Pattillo, how do you feel about going back to Central High?…"

It was the first time anybody white had ever called me Miss. They cared what I thought. I struggled to find a suitable answer.

"We have a right to go to that school, and I'm certain our governor, who was elected to govern all the people, will decide to do what is just." The white reporters wrote my words down and behaved as if what I said was very important....

For the first time, I knew that working for integration was the right thing for me to be doing....

That night I wrote in my diary:

Today is the first time in my life I felt equal to white people. I want more of that feeling. I'll do whatever I have to do to keep feeling equal all the time.

[Melba Pattillo finally entered Central High School with army troops on September 24.]

"...I picked up my diary and started to write:

It's Thursday, September 26, 1957. Now I have a bodyguard. I know very well that the President didn't send those soldiers just to protect me but to show support for an idea—the idea that a governor can't ignore federal laws. Still, I feel specially cared about because the guard is there. If he wasn't there, I'd hear more of the voices of those people who say...that I'm not valuable, that I have no right to be alive.

The school days that followed were noted in my diary....

February 18, 1958

A red-haired, freckle-faced girl... keeps trailing me in the hallway between classes. Today she spit on me, then slapped me. Later in the day as I came around a corner, she tripped me so that I fell down a flight of stairs. I picked myself up to face a group of boys who then chased me up the stairs.... I told a school official about it.... He asked me what did I expect when I came to a place where I knew I wasn't welcome.

Write Your Answers

Answer these questions in the assignment section of your notebook.

1. What happened on Melba Pattillo's first day at Central High School?

2. What action did President Eisenhower take to integrate Central High School?

3. Why did Miss Pattillo feel happy after speaking with reporters at a news conference?

4. How did Miss Pattillo feel about having a bodyguard?

5. How did white students treat Melba Pattillo?

REVIEW AND APPLY

- During the civil rights movement, African Americans struggled to win equal rights, better jobs, and educational opportunities.

- In 1954 the Supreme Court ruled that school segregation was illegal in the case of *Brown* v. *Board of Education of Topeka, Kansas.*

- President Eisenhower sent soldiers to Little Rock, Arkansas, to protect nine African American students who began to attend Central High School.

- Rosa Parks, an African American woman, sparked a bus boycott in Montgomery, Alabama, when she was arrested for refusing to give her bus seat to a white man.

- The civil rights movement, led by Martin Luther King, Jr., used different methods to achieve their goals including boycotts, nonviolent resistance, civil disobedience, marches, and sit-ins.

- The Civil Rights Act of 1964 made segregation and job discrimination illegal. The Twenty-Fourth Amendment made poll taxes illegal.

- Martin Luther King, Jr., was assassinated in April 1968. As a result, race riots occurred in more than 100 cities across the United States.

VOCABULARY

Writing With Vocabulary Words ■ **Use six or more vocabulary terms below to write a paragraph that tells about the methods used in the civil rights movement. Write your paragraph in your social studies notebook.**

civil rights movement	discrimination
nonviolent resistance	integration
sit-ins	civil disobedience
race riots	affirmative action

USING INFORMATION

Writing an Essay ■ **Choose two events that you feel best describe the goals of the civil rights movement in the 1950s and 1960s. Write a paragraph in the assignment section of your social studies notebook that describes each event. Start your paragraph with a topic sentence.**

COMPREHENSION CHECK

Creating an Information Chart ■ In your social studies notebook, copy and complete the chart below about the civil rights movement.

Event	When It Happened	Why It Was Important
Brown v. Bd. of Education, Topeka, Kansas		
Central High School		
Montgomery Bus Boycott		*Ended segregation of city buses*
March on Washington, D.C.		
Civil Rights Act of 1964	*1964*	

CRITICAL THINKING

Drawing Conclusions ■ Read the paragraph below and the sentences that follow it. In your social studies notebook, write the conclusions that can be drawn from the paragraph. You should find three conclusions.

In a court case called *Brown* v. *Board of Education of Topeka, Kansas,* the Supreme Court ruled that separate schools for African Americans were illegal and ordered schools to become integrated. In 1957, the governor of Arkansas refused to allow nine African American students to attend classes at Central High School in Little Rock. The governor felt that the Constitution gave states the power to make laws about education. He also believed that segregation should continue. President Eisenhower sent troops to Little Rock to protect the African American students.

1. Martin Luther King, Jr., was an important civil rights leader.

2. The *Brown* v. *Board of Education of Topeka, Kansas* case would be used to end school segregation in the South.

3. President Eisenhower wanted to prove that states must obey federal laws.

4. The *Brown* decision helped James Meredith integrate the University of Mississippi.

5. Rosa Parks was arrested for refusing to give up her bus seat to a white man.

AMERICAN GEOGRAPHY

Place: Washington, D.C.

Landforms, climate, people, culture, and work in an area tell us what makes a place special. Washington, D.C., is the center of the federal government. Most people who work in Washington work for the federal government. Because so many important decisions are made in Washington, it is the place for many important rallies like the 1963 Civil Rights March on Washington.

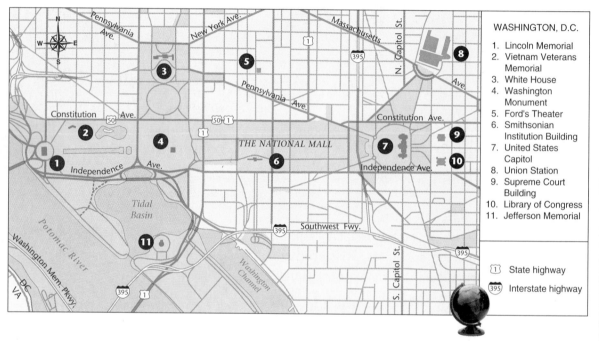

WASHINGTON, D.C.

1. Lincoln Memorial
2. Vietnam Veterans Memorial
3. White House
4. Washington Monument
5. Ford's Theater
6. Smithsonian Institution Building
7. United States Capitol
8. Union Station
9. Supreme Court Building
10. Library of Congress
11. Jefferson Memorial

State highway
Interstate highway

Read the paragraph and study the map of Washington, D.C. Write the answers to the questions below in the assignment section of your social studies notebook.

1. Name three bodies of water in Washington, D.C.

2. Which two buildings are near the United States Capitol?

3. Which building is located on the National Mall?

4. Name two memorials in Washington, D.C.

5. Which avenue would you travel to go from the White House to the Capitol?

6. Why are many protests and rallies held in Washington?

Chapter 32

AMERICANS FIGHT A WAR IN VIETNAM

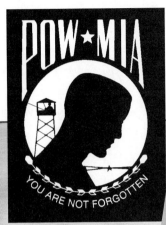

◄ POW/MIA emblem

People

Ho Chi Minh • Vietminh • Viet Cong • Robert F. Kennedy • Richard Nixon • Henry Kissinger • Maya Lin • Everett Alvarez, Jr.

Places

Vietnam • Indochina • North Vietnam • South Vietnam • Gulf of Tonkin • Cambodia • Kent State University • Saigon

New Vocabulary

Buddhism • domino theory • escalate • casualties • guerrilla war • Vietnamization • withdrawal • negotiated • cease-fire • embassy

Focus on Main Ideas

1. Why did war begin in Vietnam?
2. Why did the United States become more involved in Vietnam?
3. How did the Vietnam War end?
4. How did the United States change because of the Vietnam War?

Vietnam is a small country in Southeast Asia. For about twenty years, from the mid-1950s to 1975, the United States was involved in a war there. More than 58,000 Americans died in the Vietnam War. Today people continue to debate whether or not Americans should have fought and died in Vietnam.

Vietnam Under French Rule

Vietnam had been part of a French colony called Indochina. The people of Vietnam wanted their independence. Ho Chi Minh led the fight for Vietnam's independence from France. From 1945 to 1954, Ho led the Vietminh, or Vietnamese Communists, in a war against the French.

Vietnam's northern neighbor, China, had become a Communist nation in 1949. To stop communism from spreading throughout Southeast Asia, the United States gave war supplies to the French in Vietnam. In 1954 the Vietminh defeated the French. Vietnam became independent.

Vietnam Is Divided and War Begins

In 1954 Vietnam was divided at the 17th parallel. Ho Chi Minh became the leader

391

Ho Chi Minh was the Communist leader who defeated the French in 1954. Then he became the leader of North Vietnam.

of a Communist government in North Vietnam. South Vietnam did not have a Communist government, but its government was not popular because it was dishonest. The president of South Vietnam ruled as a dictator.

In 1956 the North Vietnamese wanted to hold elections so people could vote to unite Vietnam under one government. South Vietnam's president refused to have elections. He said Communists would use the elections to control the entire country.

In order to unite all of Vietnam, Communists in the North sent weapons and additional soldiers to help the Viet Cong, the Communists living in the South. Many poor peasants in the South joined the Viet Cong. They joined because they were angry with South Vietnam's government, which did not help the nation's poor people.

The government also took away religious freedom from people who followed **Buddhism**, South Vietnam's main religion.

The Vietnam War began in 1957 when the Viet Cong revolted against South Vietnam's government. The Vietnam War began as a struggle between Communists and non-Communists for control of South Vietnam. North Vietnam and the Viet Cong wanted one united Communist nation. The non-Communist government in South Vietnam wanted to remain an independent nation.

The United States Becomes Involved with Vietnam

President Eisenhower agreed with the Truman Doctrine of containing communism. Eisenhower also believed in the **domino theory**. He compared countries to dominoes. All the dominoes in a row fall when the first one is knocked down. According to the domino theory, if one nation in Southeast Asia fell to communism, all the others would fall, too. So Eisenhower sent money and weapons to South Vietnam.

President John F. Kennedy continued Eisenhower's policies. However, the United States gave greater amounts of weapons and money than before. Kennedy also sent many advisers to South Vietnam.

Vice President Lyndon B. Johnson became President when Kennedy was assassinated in November 1963. At first, Johnson continued Kennedy's policy and sent money, weapons, and advisers to South Vietnam. Johnson was worried because in 1963 and 1964 North Vietnam sent its own soldiers to South Vietnam to win control of the country. By the end of 1964, the Viet Cong controlled about three quarters of South Vietnam's people.

President Johnson believed in the domino theory, and he wanted to save South Vietnam. He did not want to be known as the President who lost South Vietnam to the Communists.

In August 1964, President Johnson said North Vietnam's ships had attacked two American ships in North Vietnam's Gulf of Tonkin. Johnson asked Congress for power to take all necessary military action against North Vietnam. Congress quickly passed the Tonkin Gulf Resolution, which gave Johnson the power to go to war against North Vietnam.

After the Tonkin Gulf Resolution of 1964, the United States was at war with North Vietnam. However, Congress never declared war as the Constitution requires.

President Johnson and the Vietnam War

After winning the election in November 1964, Johnson began to **escalate**, or increase, America's war effort. To stop the North Vietnamese from sending soldiers and supplies to the Viet Cong, American planes bombed North Vietnam's supply routes. In 1965 the first American soldiers and marines were sent to fight in the South.

Each year more American soldiers were sent to Vietnam. In 1965 almost 200,000 troops were there. By 1968 there were more than 500,000 Americans there. The number of **casualties**, people killed or injured, increased as thousands of Americans were killed or wounded each year.

The Vietnam War *The war in Vietnam spread to Laos and Cambodia. What did the Americans attack in those countries?*

To defeat the Communists, the United States bombed North Vietnam. The American Air Force dropped more bombs during the Vietnam War than it had dropped in World War II.

Helicopters were important in the war. Helicopters were used to carry away wounded soldiers for treatment. They were used during "search and destroy" missions. During these missions, Americans in helicopters searched for Viet Cong soldiers who were hiding in villages, jungles, and mountains. Then Americans destroyed their hiding places.

Americans used a chemical called Agent Orange to destroy plants and trees in

Helicopters were used in "search and destroy" missions, and they were used to carry wounded soldiers away from the battlefield.

jungles and on mountains, so the Viet Cong had fewer places to hide. Agent Orange made many American soldiers very sick.

The Tet Offensive

Early in January 1968, Americans were told they were winning the war in Vietnam. So on January 30, 1968, Americans were shocked when the North Vietnamese army and the Viet Cong began to attack cities throughout South Vietnam. These attacks were called the Tet Offensive because they began during the Tet holiday. During this holiday the Vietnamese celebrate the New Year. American and South Vietnamese forces fought back. They recaptured the cities, but they lost many soldiers.

The Tet Offensive upset Americans at home. Americans had sent their best

soldiers and weapons to Vietnam. But after two years of fighting, the Communists still had the power to attack the South. It was clear that many people in South Vietnam supported the Communists. They admired Ho Chi Minh, and they did not like South Vietnam's dishonest government.

Many Americans began to believe that the United States would not be able to defeat the Communists in Vietnam. The Communists fought a dangerous **guerrilla war**. In a guerrilla war, soldiers do not wear uniforms or fight openly. So the Viet Cong soldiers hid in villages and jungles. They would use sneak attacks on American and South Vietnamese forces. It was impossible to know which people in a village were Viet Cong soldiers. Also, Americans were not used to the land and the climate. Much of South Vietnam was covered with mountains and hot, rainy jungles.

In March 1968 President Johnson announced that he would start peace talks to end the war. He also surprised the nation when he said he would not run for President again. Peace talks with North Vietnam began in May, but they failed to end the war.

The Protest Movement

Many Americans supported the war in Vietnam. People who supported the war were called "hawks." Many hawks wanted the United States to declare war against North Vietnam and then destroy the enemy. They did not agree with Johnson's limited efforts to defeat the Communists.

After the Tet Offensive, large numbers of Americans became "doves," or people who wanted to end the Vietnam War. Hundreds of thousands of people across the nation held protest marches. Their goal was to pressure the United States government to leave Vietnam. Many protests turned into violent riots.

Many important leaders became doves. Robert F. Kennedy, President Kennedy's brother, spoke out against the war. Martin Luther King, Jr., also criticized the war. He said the United States was spending billions of dollars on a war that had nothing to do with our nation. He wanted the United States to spend that money on programs to help African Americans and other minority groups.

The protest movement against the war grew stronger each year. It divided Americans against each other. Thousands of men moved to Canada in order to avoid serving in Vietnam.

American soldiers in Vietnam learned about the war protests. It was painful for them to fight in a war that so many Americans did not support.

President Nixon and the Vietnam War

In 1968 Richard Nixon, a Republican, won the election for President. During his campaign, he promised "peace with honor" to end the Vietnam War.

President Nixon began a program called **Vietnamization**. Its goal was to train South Vietnam's soldiers to fight the Communists by themselves. As the South Vietnamese army grew stronger, the American army started a **withdrawal**, leaving Vietnam and returning home. In July 1969, American soldiers began

returning home. The peace talks continued in Paris, but they failed to end the war.

In April 1970 Nixon ordered the air force to bomb Vietnam's western neighbor, Cambodia. The Viet Cong had weapons and bases in Cambodia that they used for attacking South Vietnam. Americans were furious that the war was spreading to Cambodia. There were protests and riots in hundreds of universities across the nation.

Kent State University had one of the worst riots. Students destroyed property to show their anger about the war. The National Guard was called to stop the riots. Four students were shot to death as the National Guard tried to end the riots.

At last Congress took action to end the war. In December 1970 Congress

Vietnamese try to escape the fighting in Saigon during the Tet Offensive. The Vietnam War created thousands of refugees.

395

Four students were killed when National Guard troops tried to stop a Vietnam War protest at Kent State University in Ohio.

Americans left the American embassy in Saigon by helicopter as North Vietnamese troops captured the city.

repealed the Tonkin Gulf Resolution. The President no longer had full power to fight a war in Vietnam.

The United States continued to withdraw American soldiers from Vietnam. After many Americans left, North Vietnamese soldiers invaded the South in 1972. Nixon tried to stop the invasion by bombing North Vietnam.

The End of the Vietnam War

In 1969 President Nixon had sent Henry Kissinger, his security adviser, to lead secret peace talks with North Vietnam. Kissinger, a Jewish American, was born in Germany. He had come to America at age 15 to escape the Holocaust.

Kissinger **negotiated** secretly with North Vietnamese leaders for several years. At last, in January 1973, a **cease-fire** agreement was signed in Paris. The agreement required all American forces to leave Vietnam in two months. The warring nations agreed to return all prisoners of war, or POWs. Two months later, all American soldiers had returned home.

The Vietnam War started again soon after the American forces left. North Vietnam's troops invaded South Vietnam. The South Vietnamese could not stop the North Vietnamese forces. Saigon, the capital of South Vietnam, was captured by the North Vietnamese. The last Americans left the American **embassy** by helicopter. Finally on April 30, 1975, South Vietnam surrendered to North Vietnam. All of Vietnam became one Communist nation.

Many non-Communists were afraid to remain in Vietnam after 1975. More than one million Vietnamese people fled from their country. Thousands escaped in small boats and became known as boat people. Many boat people have settled in the United States.

Results of the Vietnam War

The Vietnam War became the first war the United States ever lost. Almost three million Americans served in the war. More than 58,000 died. The war cost $150 billion.

North Vietnam returned hundreds of POWs to the United States. Many of them had lived through years of cruel treatment in North Vietnamese prisons. But about 4,000 soldiers never returned from Vietnam. Since there was no proof that they were dead, they were listed as "missing in action," or MIA.

The war changed the United States. The nation moved closer to its old policy of isolationism. Americans no longer felt they had to protect all nations in the world from communism.

In 1973 Congress passed a law called the War Powers Act, which limits a President's power to make war. A President must now have permission from Congress to send troops into battles that are expected to last more than a few months.

Americans learned important lessons because of the war in Vietnam. One lesson was that the domino theory was wrong. Communists did not win control of all of Southeast Asia. Another lesson was that when we fight in a war, we must really believe in the cause for which we are fighting. Then all Americans must unite and do everything possible to win.

The Vietnam Veterans Memorial

Many Americans felt the nation needed a memorial to honor the men and women who died in the Vietnam War. Maya Lin, a Chinese American, designed the memorial. Money to build the memorial was contributed by Americans from every part of the nation.

The Vietnam Veterans Memorial is in Washington, D.C. On its two long, black walls are the names of more than 58,000 soldiers who died in the war. It also has the names of people who are still missing in action. In 1993 the Vietnam Women's Memorial was built nearby to honor thousands of women who served in the war. Millions of Americans have visited the memorials. Honoring the people who served in Vietnam has helped heal the anger from this long, bitter war.

The names of more than 58,000 soldiers killed or missing in action during the Vietnam War are listed on this memorial.

BIOGRAPHY

Everett Alvarez, Jr. 1937–

Everett Alvarez, Jr., became the first American pilot to be shot down while flying over North Vietnam. He spent more time as a prisoner of war than any other American.

Alvarez was born in California to a Mexican American family. He became the first person in his family to graduate from college. After college he joined the navy. He became a fighter pilot and was sent to Vietnam. In August 1964, Alvarez's plane was shot down over North Vietnam. He was captured and he became a prisoner of war, or POW.

For more than eight years, Alvarez suffered terribly in a filthy North Vietnamese prison. He was beaten and tortured. He was given very little to eat, and the food that he was given was often full of bugs. Alvarez's hardest time in prison was when he learned that his wife had divorced him and had married another man.

The North Vietnamese wanted Alvarez to publicly criticize the United States. However, the loyal pilot refused to speak out against America, even when he was tortured.

After the cease-fire in 1973, Alvarez was returned to the United States. Upon landing, he spoke on television to the nation: "For years and years we dreamed of this day and we kept the faith.... We have come home. God bless the President and God bless you Mr. and Mrs. America. You did not forget us."

Alvarez rebuilt his life. He became a lawyer, married again, and had two sons. After the Vietnam Veterans Memorial was completed, Alvarez spoke at its dedication ceremony in Washington, D.C.

In California there is a high school that is named for Everett Alvarez. From Alvarez's story students learn the importance of hard work, a good education, and loyalty to the United States.

In Your Own Words

Everett Alvarez spent more time as a POW in North Vietnam than any other American. Write a paragraph in your journal that describes what happened to Alvarez after he became a POW in 1964.

REVIEW AND APPLY

- In 1954 the country of Vietnam won its independence from France. Communist leader Ho Chi Minh led this fight for independence. After it became independent, Vietnam was divided at the 17th parallel.

- Communist North Vietnam attacked South Vietnam in hopes of making the entire country a Communist nation.

- At first the United States sent money and supplies to aid the South Vietnamese. By 1964 the United States was sending soldiers to fight there.

- By 1968 more than 500,000 American troops were in Vietnam, but the guerrilla warfare tactics of the Viet Cong made it difficult to defeat the Communists.

- Thousands of Americans protested against the Vietnam War.

- In 1975 American troops finally left Vietnam. A short time later, South Vietnam surrendered, and Vietnam became a united Communist country.

VOCABULARY

Find the Meaning ■ **Write in your social studies notebook the word or phrase that best completes each sentence.**

1. Soldiers do not wear uniforms or fight in the open in a _____ .
   civil war   world war   guerrilla war

2. An agreement is _____ when two or more parties discuss a settlement.
   boycotted   negotiated   protested

3. An agreement to stop fighting during a war is called a _____ .
   contract   debate   cease-fire

4. The belief that one country after another will become Communist if the spread of communism is not stopped is known as (the) _____ .
   escalation   Vietnamization   domino theory

5. The main religion in Vietnam is _____ .

   Buddhism   Judaism   Islam

6. President Johnson began to _____ , or increase, America's involvement in the war in 1964.
   escalate   negotiate   involve

Write the Answer ■ **Write one or more sentences in your social studies notebook to answer each question.**

1. How did Vietnam gain its independence from France?

2. Why did North Vietnam attack South Vietnam in 1957?

3. Who were the Viet Cong, and what did they want?

4. How did the domino theory lead to the United States becoming involved in Vietnam?

5. What was the importance of the Tonkin Gulf Resolution?

6. What was result of the Tet Offensive?

7. Why did Americans protest against the Vietnam War?

8. How did American involvement in the Vietnam War come to an end?

9. What was the War Powers Act?

10. What lessons did Americans learn from the Vietnam War?

CRITICAL THINKING

Sequencing Information ■ **In your social studies notebook write the following sentences in their correct order.**

Communists attack cities in South Vietnam during the Tet Offensive.

A cease-fire is signed and all American troops leave Vietnam.

Ho Chi Minh helps the Vietnamese gain their independence from the French.

South Vietnam surrenders to North Vietnam, and Vietnam becomes a united, Communist country.

Vietnam is divided at the 17th parallel.

President Nixon starts his plan of Vietnamization.

USING INFORMATION

Writing an Opinion ■ **The United States fought for nine years in Vietnam, and over 58,000 Americans died there. Write a paragraph in your social studies notebook in which you describe how you would thank a Vietnam veteran for his or her efforts during the war. Start your paragraph with a topic sentence.**

SOCIAL STUDIES SKILLS

Applying a Statistics Table

The **statistics table** on this page provides information about the number of soldiers who were killed or wounded in the Vietnam War. The table shows us that after the Tonkin Gulf Resolution in 1964, the number of casualties, people killed or injured, greatly increased. It also shows us that casualties began to decrease during the period of Vietnamization that began after 1969.

American Casualties in the Vietnam War 1960-1973

Year	Number of American Troops	Combat Deaths	Wounded
1960	900	—	—
1961	3,200	—	14
1962	11,000	14	95
1963	16,500	76	413
1964	23,000	140	1,138
1965	180,000	1,350	5,300
1966	280,000	5,008	30,093
1967	500,000	9,353	99,742
1968	500,000	14,592	100,000
1969	479,000	9,414	60,000
1970	280,000	4,204	9,000
1971	159,000	1,386	2,000
1972	24,000	4,300	5,800
1973	last troops withdrawn	12	21

Study the table. Then write the answers to the questions below in the assignment section of your social studies notebook.

1. In which year were there no casualties?

2. Which two years had the most casualties?

3. Which two years had the most troops?

4. Why did the number of casualties increase from 1960 to 1968?

5. Which two years had the smallest number of wounded men?

6. Which year between 1968 and 1973 had the fewest casualties?

7. How many combat deaths took place in 1972?

8. When the number of troops increased, how did casualty figures change?

SUCCESSES AND TROUBLES IN THE 1960s AND 1970s

◄ *Peace Symbol*

People

John Glenn • Betty Friedan • César Chávez • Dolores Huerta • Neil Armstrong • Buzz Aldrin • Gerald Ford • Jimmy Carter • Rachel Carson

Places

Bay of Pigs • Dallas, TX • Egypt • Syria • Israel

New Vocabulary

Bicentennial • Peace Corps • NASA • Central Intelligence Agency • refugees • missile • Medicare • counterculture • hippies • détente • energy crisis • investigation • pardoned • stagflation

Focus on Main Ideas

1. What were some of the nation's successes in the 1960s and 1970s?
2. What problems troubled the nation in the 1960s and 1970s?
3. What was the Watergate scandal?

On July 4, 1976, Americans celebrated the nation's **Bicentennial** with great pride. But they were also troubled about serious problems facing the nation on its 200th birthday. The 1960s and 1970s were years of troubles and successes.

John F. Kennedy Becomes President

In 1960 John F. Kennedy ran for President and defeated Richard Nixon, a Republican. Kennedy was the first Catholic to become President.

Kennedy inspired Americans to feel that they could improve their country.

In his inaugural speech he said, "...And so, my fellow Americans: ask not what your country can do for you—ask what you can do for your country."

Kennedy's program for the nation was called the New Frontier. The program included plans for a strong civil rights law as well as laws to help the poor, improve the nation's schools, and improve health care. Congress did not pass most of Kennedy's programs. Kennedy did create the **Peace Corps**. Peace Corps volunteers went to Asia, Africa, and Latin America to work with people in different countries to improve health care, farming, and education.

The space race first began in 1957 when the Soviet Union sent *Sputnik* into space. To win the space race, Kennedy promised that the United States would land people on the moon by 1970. To accomplish this goal, Congress created the space agency called **NASA**. In 1962 Americans were thrilled when John Glenn became the first American astronaut to circle Earth.

Kennedy and the Cold War

Like Truman and Eisenhower, Kennedy tried to stop the spread of communism. Kennedy worried that Fidel Castro, Cuba's dictator, would spread communism throughout Latin America. Because of this concern, Kennedy allowed the **Central Intelligence Agency**, or CIA, to secretly train about 1,000 Cuban **refugees** to attack Cuba and capture Castro. In April 1961 the Cuban refugees invaded Cuba. The invasion occurred at the Bay of Pigs, in southern Cuba. Castro's army quickly attacked, and most of the invaders were captured or killed. Americans learned about the attack after it had failed. Many people criticized Kennedy for the Bay of Pigs invasion.

In October 1962 the United States learned that the Soviet Union had built **missile** bases in Cuba. The Soviets had given Cuba missiles armed with nuclear

When President Kennedy learned that the Soviets had placed missiles in Cuba that could attack the United States, he demanded that the missiles be removed. Americans feared that nuclear war would begin. After three tense days, the Soviets agreed to remove the missiles.

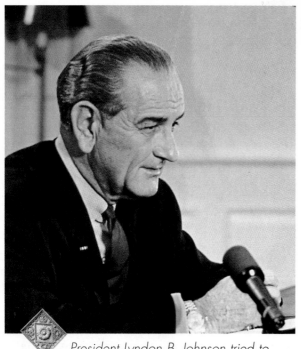
President Lyndon B. Johnson tried to help the nation's poor by launching the War on Poverty to end hunger and poverty in America.

weapons. If those missiles were fired at the United States, they could quickly destroy American cities. Kennedy decided that the Soviet Union must remove the missiles, but he wanted to avoid a war. On October 22, 1962, he announced that American ships would blockade Cuba and stop Soviet ships from delivering more missiles. Kennedy told the Soviet Union to destroy the Cuban missile bases and to remove all missiles that were already there.

For three days Americans lived in fear that a war would start. Finally, the Soviets agreed to destroy the bases and to remove all the missiles. In return, the United States promised not to invade Cuba. President Kennedy became a hero for solving the crisis without a war.

In Europe thousands of East Germans escaped from communism by moving to the free city of West Berlin. To stop people from moving there, the Soviets built the Berlin Wall in 1961 to separate East and West Berlin. East German police shot people who tried to climb over the wall. President Kennedy visited West Berlin in 1963. He told the cheering crowd of Germans, "I am a Berliner." With those words Kennedy showed the Germans that he admired their struggle against communism. The wall divided Berlin until 1989.

Johnson's Great Society

On November 22, 1963, President Kennedy was shot and killed during a visit to Dallas, Texas. Vice President Lyndon B. Johnson immediately became President.

President Johnson's program for the nation was called the Great Society. His goal was to improve life for all Americans.

Johnson had been a member of Congress for almost 25 years, so he knew how to work with Congress to get laws passed. Many laws that Kennedy had wanted were passed soon after Johnson became President. Congress passed the Civil Rights Act of 1964. New laws increased federal aid to the nation's schools. **Medicare**, a health care program for older Americans, was created.

Johnson started the "War on Poverty" to end hunger and poverty. About one fourth of the nation was living in poverty. Johnson's program included job training and food stamps to help poor people have a healthy diet. By 1969 there was much less poverty in America.

While President Johnson planned the Great Society, he needed millions of dollars to pay for the war in Vietnam. To get money for the war, Johnson took money away from Great Society programs. Because of the Vietnam War, the Great Society did not have as much success as Johnson wanted.

The Revolt Against American Culture

During the 1960s and 1970s, many young adults were angry that their government was sending some of them off to fight in Vietnam. Angry young adults did not want to live like their parents. They did not want to think about getting married, having a career, and working to earn a lot of money. They spoke about a new society based on peace, love, and total freedom. To protest against their parents' way of life, they formed their own culture, which became known as the **counterculture**. Many members of the counterculture became **hippies** who dressed in old clothes. They created their own form of music.

The counterculture slowly ended at the end of the 1970s. Many hippies began to get married, wear regular clothes, and start families and careers.

Working for Equal Rights

The civil rights movement encouraged women and minority groups to work for equal rights and equal opportunities. The Civil Rights Act of 1964 and the affirmative action programs helped these groups.

At this time few women were doctors, lawyers, or other kinds of professionals. Most women earned far less money than men. Betty Friedan wrote about these problems in her book, *The Feminine Mystique*. She also worked with other women to start the National Organization for Women, or NOW. NOW worked with Congress to pass laws that gave women equal job and educational opportunities. One law required equal pay for men and women doing the same job.

Minority groups also worked for equal rights. Many Mexican Americans worked as migrant farm workers. They received very low salaries and were not protected by job contracts. César Chávez started a union called the United Farm Workers (UFW) to help migrant workers. Dolores Huerta worked as Chávez's assistant. Chávez used strikes and boycotts to peacefully help migrant workers. By 1970 the UFW had won its first important victory. The grape growers agreed to give grape pickers their first contracts. Today migrant workers continue to have low salaries.

César Chávez led the United Farm Workers, which helped migrant farm workers win better working conditions.

On July 20, 1969, astronauts Neil Armstrong and Buzz Aldrin became the first people to walk on the moon.

American Indians also demanded equal rights and more control over their reservations. Indians faced poverty because their reservations did not have good schools, transportation, or places to work. Most reservations had poor soil for farming. In 1968 Indians started the American Indian Movement, or AIM. The Indians succeeded in winning more control over their reservations. They also wanted the government to return Indian lands that had been taken in broken promises. They had success in Maine when a federal court agreed to pay two Indian tribes $25 billion for land that was unfairly taken from them.

The Nixon Years

Richard Nixon became President in 1969. Nixon succeeded in improving American relations with China and the Soviet Union. He hated communism, but he became the first President to visit Communist China. He also visited Moscow, the Soviet capital. Nixon worked with the Soviets for a peaceful relationship that was called **détente**. Since the Soviets did not have enough food, Nixon agreed to sell American wheat to them.

In 1973 the nation faced an **energy crisis**. During the energy crisis, the nation did not have enough oil for its needs. The United States depended on oil from the Middle East. The energy crisis began because of a war in the Middle East. The war began when two Arab nations, Egypt and Syria, attacked Israel. Because Israel was America's ally, the United States sent large amounts of weapons to help defend Israel. Israel won the war. Several Arab nations started an oil embargo against the United States and other countries that had helped Israel.

As less oil was available, the energy crisis became worse. Americans needed oil to make electricity, to heat their homes, and to make gasoline for cars, trucks, and planes. Nixon encouraged Americans to use less electricity and heat. Many people saved energy by using public transportation instead of driving their cars. In some areas nuclear power plants were built to make electricity. After several accidents in nuclear power plants, Americans stopped building them.

Watergate

In 1972 President Nixon was running for reelection. Most people believed Nixon would easily win the election. However, some people took illegal actions to help Nixon win. They decided to steal the Democrats' campaign plans. On June 17, 1972, five men were caught breaking into the Democrats' headquarters in the Watergate building in Washington, D.C.

Members of Congress tried to find out what had happened at Watergate and who had sent the men to steal campaign plans. Several people who worked for President Nixon tried to cover up, or keep secret, what had happened. During the **investigation** they learned that Nixon had recorded all conversations in his office. Congress asked to listen to the tapes about Watergate. Nixon refused to allow Congress to hear the Watergate tapes. The Supreme Court ordered Nixon to give the tapes to Congress. The Supreme Court said a President cannot use his power to cover up crimes.

The Watergate tapes proved that Nixon had helped plan the cover up. He had broken the law. He had lied to Congress, to the courts, and to the American people.

The House of Representatives prepared to impeach Nixon. If the representatives impeached Nixon, he would have to go on trial in the Senate. If the senators found Nixon guilty, he would no longer be President. To avoid the trial, Nixon resigned on August 9, 1974. Vice President Gerald Ford immediately became the nation's President.

A few weeks later, Ford **pardoned**, or forgave, Nixon for any crimes he might have committed. Nixon was never punished. Many other people who were involved with Watergate spent time in jail. Watergate proved that all Americans, including the President, must obey the nation's laws.

Presidents Ford and Carter

Inflation and unemployment were serious problems when Ford became President. He could not solve these problems in two years, and he lost the 1976 election to Jimmy Carter, a Democrat.

Inflation and unemployment continued to be serious problems. The problem was called **stagflation**. Carter worked with Congress to create jobs. Unemployment began to drop, but inflation grew worse as oil became more expensive. As the 1970s came to an end, Americans hoped that the next decade would bring better times to a troubled nation.

On August 9, 1974, President Richard Nixon resigned because of the Watergate cover up. Nixon is the only President to have resigned from office.

BIOGRAPHY

Rachel Carson 1907–1964

Rachel Carson was one of the first people to make Americans aware of the dangers of pollution.

As a college student, Carson discovered that she loved studying science and biology. She was especially interested in ocean life. Carson studied for a Master of Arts degree in marine zoology, the study of animal life in the sea.

The United States Fish and Wildlife Service hired Carson to write radio programs about marine life. Carson's work quickly became popular. She was promoted to an important position in the Fish and Wildlife Service. Few women at that time held such important jobs. She worked for this agency for most of her life.

In 1951 she wrote *The Sea Around Us*. In her book Carson explained how all living things depended on each other to survive. She taught the importance of taking care of the environment. The book became a best seller and Carson became famous.

In 1962 Carson wrote *Silent Spring*. In *Silent Spring* Carson wrote about the dangers of pesticides, powerful chemicals that are used to kill insects. Farmers depended on pesticides to kill the insect population so they could grow food. Carson explained that pesticides were a danger to plant and animal life. They could also cause cancer in humans. Carson explained other methods that could be used to control the insect population. She wanted pesticides to be used less often and more carefully. President Kennedy started a committee to study the effects of pesticides. The committee found that Carson's work was correct. Efforts were made to limit the use of pesticides.

Rachel Carson proved that women could make important contributions in science. She helped Americans learn to protect their air, land, and water.

In Your Own Words

Through her work as a scientist and a writer, Rachel Carson helped the United States. Write a paragraph in the journal section of your social studies notebook that explains how Carson's work helped the nation.

REVIEW AND APPLY

- John F. Kennedy, who became President in 1960, started a volunteer group called the Peace Corps that taught people in Asia, Africa, and Latin America how to improve their lives.

- President Kennedy used different methods for trying to stop the spread of communism including the Bay of Pigs invasion, the Cuban Missile Crisis, and his visit to West Berlin in 1963.

- Lyndon B. Johnson became President when President Kennedy was assassinated on November 22, 1963.

- President Johnson's program to improve the life of all Americans was called the Great Society.

- During the 1960s and 1970s, many young adults rejected the values of their parents and started a counterculture.

- In 1973, Americans faced an energy crisis because Arab nations started an oil embargo against the United States and other countries.

- President Nixon resigned from office on August 9, 1974, as a result of the Watergate scandal.

- Under Presidents Ford and Carter, inflation and unemployment were serious problems.

VOCABULARY

Defining and Using Vocabulary ■ Use the glossary to find the meaning of each word or phrase listed below. Write each word's definition in your social studies notebook. Then use each word in a sentence.

missile	energy crisis
Medicare	pardon
hippies	stagflation
détente	

USING INFORMATION

Journal Writing ■ Imagine if you lived through the energy crisis in the early 1970s. What would you have done about long gas lines? What would you have done to save energy? Write a paragraph in your social studies notebook that tells what you would have done during this time in our country's history. Start your paragraph with a topic sentence.

COMPREHENSION CHECK

Biography Cards ■ In your social studies notebook, copy and complete the index cards by explaining what problem each person faced and one or two ways he or she tried to solve the problem.

Name *President Lyndon B. Johnson*

Problem:

Solution:

Name *César Chávez*

Problem:

Solution:

Name *Betty Friedan*

Problem:

Solution:

Name *President Jimmy Carter*

Problem:

Solution:

CRITICAL THINKING

Fact or Opinion ■ Write the numbers 1–5 in your social studies notebook. Next to each number, write an F if that statement is a fact. Write O if the statement is an opinion. If the statement gives both a fact and an opinion, write FO. Then write the part of the sentence that is an opinion.

1. The United States had great success in its space program, but the money used for *Apollo 11* should have been used to help the poor.

2. The Soviet Union built missile bases in Cuba.

3. President Kennedy should have sent American soldiers to destroy the Berlin Wall.

4. The United States should have built more nuclear power plants.

5. President Ford pardoned Richard Nixon for his Watergate crimes, but Nixon should have spent time in jail for his actions.

SOCIAL STUDIES SKILLS

Interpreting a Political Cartoon

Political cartoons are drawn by artists to express opinions about events. The cartoons below were drawn by two different artists. They both believed the United States should continue to help Berlin after the Soviets built the Berlin Wall. The legs in Cartoon A represent the United States. In Cartoon B, there is a pile of bricks with the letters *NK* on them. The letters *NK* are the initials of Nikita Kruschev, the Soviet leader who ordered the East Germans to build the Berlin Wall.

CARTOON A

CARTOON B

Study the cartoons. Then write in your social studies notebook the answers to the following questions.

1. In Cartoon A, how does the artist show that the United States is a powerful nation?

2. In Cartoon A, how does the artist show that Berlin is less powerful than the United States?

3. In Cartoon B, what is the United States doing to stop the building of the Berlin Wall?

4. In Cartoon B, how do we know that the Soviet Union wants to build the Berlin Wall?

5. How do both cartoons use different pictures to show the same opinion?

Unit 8 Review

Study the time line on this page. You may want to read parts of Unit 8 again. Then use the words and dates in the box to finish the paragraphs. In the assignment section of your notebook, write the numbers 1–14. The box has one possible answer you will not use.

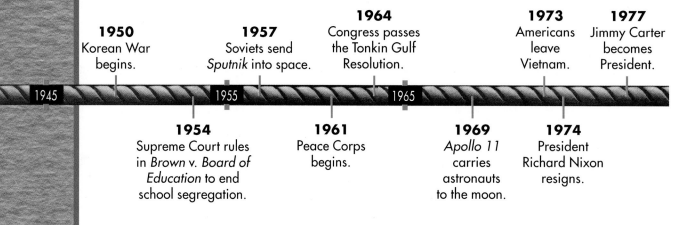

1950
Korean War begins.

1954
Supreme Court rules in *Brown* v. *Board of Education* to end school segregation.

1957
Soviets send *Sputnik* into space.

1961
Peace Corps begins.

1964
Congress passes the Tonkin Gulf Resolution.

1969
Apollo 11 carries astronauts to the moon.

1973
Americans leave Vietnam.

1974
President Richard Nixon resigns.

1977
Jimmy Carter becomes President.

1945 · 1955 · 1965

Joseph McCarthy	Berlin Airlift	iron curtain
missiles	stagflation	Martin Luther King, Jr.
Vietnam	segregation	1964
1954	1950	*Sputnik*
Apollo 11	Watergate	1974

After Communists took control of Eastern Europe, Winston Churchill said there was a wall like an ___1___ around that region. During the Soviet Union's blockade of West Berlin, the United States and Great Britain saved the city with the ___2___. The Cold War became a hot war in Korea in ___3___. The space race became part of the Cold War after the Soviets sent the ___4___ satellite into space in 1957. The

United States won the space race in 1969 when ___5___ carried American astronauts to the moon. The Cold War almost became a hot war when the Soviet Union sent ___6___ to Cuba in 1962. After Congress passed the Tonkin Gulf Resolution in ___7___, thousands of American troops were sent to fight in ___8___.

In the early 1950s, ___9___ falsely accused many Americans of being Communists. In ___10___ the Supreme Court decided in the case called *Brown* v. *Board of Education of Topeka, Kansas*, that school segregation was illegal. After Rosa Parks was arrested for sitting in the front of a bus, ___11___ led the Montgomery bus boycott. The boycott ended in 1956 after the Supreme Court ruled that ___12___ on public transportation was against the law.

Richard Nixon helped plan the ___13___ cover up, and he became the first President to resign. While Jimmy Carter was President, unemployment and inflation led to ___14___.

Looking Ahead to Unit 9

At the end of the 1980s, the nations of Eastern Europe moved away from communism. The Berlin Wall was torn down, and the Soviet Union broke apart. The Cold War ended, and the United States became the world's most powerful nation.

Americans continued to face many problems at home, such as poverty, discrimination, and pollution. As technology improves, Americans will have new tools for solving these problems.

As you read Unit 9, think about how the United States has worked for peace. Find out what Americans are doing to protect the environment. Read on to learn how Americans are building a brighter future at home and around the world.

Unit 9

THE UNITED STATES TODAY AND TOMORROW

For more than 200 years, many kinds of Americans have worked together to create a strong democracy. As the United States prepares for the next century, it will use new technology and the talents of millions of people in order to continue to be a rich, powerful nation. Most Americans feel a sense of hope and pride as they plan and work together for the future.

As you read Unit 9, you will learn how the Cold War finally ended. Explore the ways Americans have worked for peace in many parts of the world. Discover what problems Americans must solve at home while working for peace in other nations. Think about the ways technology is preparing the nation for the next century.

1989
The Chinese army attacks protesters in Tiananmen Square.

1975 — 1985

1978
The leaders of Israel and Egypt sign the Camp David Accords.

1979
An Islamic revolution occurs in Iran.

1983
Sally Ride becomes the first American woman in space.

1985
Mikhail Gorbachev becomes the leader of the Soviet Union.

1989
Communism ends in Eastern Europe.

THINK ABOUT IT

- The United States and Iran were bitter enemies in the 1980s. Why did Americans sell weapons to that nation?

- The Soviet Union was a huge, powerful country before 1992. Why does it no longer exist as a nation?

- The United States is the richest nation in the world. If the United States is rich, why does it owe $5 trillion?

- Terrorism continues to be a problem throughout the world. What steps are being taken to prevent terrorism in the future?

▲ Americans celebrate at a parade.

1995
The United States helps Bosnian leaders reach a peace agreement.

1996
Free elections are held in Russia.

1991
The Soviet Union breaks apart.

1993
United States signs NAFTA.

1995

1990
Germany becomes a united nation.

1993
United States army aids Somalia.

1994
The United States helps Israel and Jordan sign a peace treaty.

1995
A federal building in Oklahoma City is bombed.

THE UNITED STATES FACES WORLD PROBLEMS

◀ An American held hostage in Iran

People

Anwar Sadat • Menachem Begin • Ayatollah Khomeini • Ronald Reagan • Daniel Ortega • Mikhail Gorbachev • Lech Walesa

Places

Jordan • Camp David, MD • Afghanistan • Iran • Teheran • El Salvador •

New Vocabulary

Camp David Accords •

human rights • shah • hostages • Sandinistas • contras • terrorism • hijacked • deficit • Strategic Defense Initiative • perestroika • glasnost • Solidarity • supply-side economics

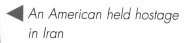

Focus on Main Ideas

1. How did President Carter help Israel and Egypt create a peace treaty?
2. What caused the hostage crisis in Iran and how did it end?
3. What was the Iran-contra scandal, and why did it happen?
4. How did the Cold War end?

During the 1970s and 1980s, the United States continued to fight the spread of communism. The United States also tried to bring peace to troubled areas of the world, such as the Middle East.

President Carter and the Camp David Accords

One of Jimmy Carter's greatest achievements as President was the **Camp David Accords**, a peace treaty between Egypt and Israel. The peace treaty ended 30 years of war between two enemy nations in the Middle East.

Wars between Israel and Arab nations in the Middle East first began in 1948. In that year the United Nations divided the country of Palestine into two nations, Israel and Jordan. Israel was created as a Jewish homeland. The land had been the home of the Jews thousands of years ago when their religion first began.

The Arab nations in the Middle East refused to recognize the Jewish state of Israel. So they fought four wars against Israel in 1948, 1956, 1967, and 1973. After each war Israel remained a free nation. Many Palestinians became refugees when they left Israel during the 1948 war. During the 1967 war, Israel captured lands that had belonged to Egypt, Syria, and Jordan. Some of that captured land is still controlled by Israel.

The United States has been Israel's ally since it became a nation in 1948. The United States gave aid to Israel because that country was a democracy and it was against communism. The Arab nations have also been important to the United States because Americans buy oil from them.

In 1978 President Carter invited Egypt's president, Anwar Sadat, and Israel's prime minister, Menachem Begin, to peace talks in the United States. The three leaders met at the President's vacation home at Camp David, Maryland. After two weeks of hard work, the three leaders reached an agreement. Israel agreed to return land it had captured from Egypt in 1967. In return Egypt agreed to recognize Israel as a nation and to sign a peace treaty with Israel. In 1979 Begin and Sadat signed the Camp David Accords, the first peace treaty between Israel and an Arab nation. The two leaders later received the Nobel Peace Prize. In 1981 President Sadat was assassinated by people in Egypt who opposed the peace treaty. President Carter had played a very important role in creating the Camp David Accords. The peace between Egypt and Israel has lasted since the treaty was signed.

Egypt's President Anwar Sadat, President Jimmy Carter, and Israel's Prime Minister Menachem Begin signed the Camp David Accords. This agreement was the first peace treaty between Israel and an Arab nation. President Carter played a major role in bringing these former enemies together.

417

This protest in Iran was one of many during the Iran hostage crisis. Iranians were angry at the United States for giving the former Shah medical treatment.

Other Foreign Affairs Under Carter

The United States had controlled the Panama Canal since it opened in 1914. President Carter believed Panama should control the Panama Canal. In 1978 the Senate ratified a treaty that said Panama would get complete control of the Canal on December 31, 1999.

Carter also worked to protect **human rights**, the right to personal freedom, in many nations. When the Soviet Union refused to allow Jews to practice their religion, Carter protested strongly.

Carter took action when the Soviet Union invaded the Muslim nation of Afghanistan in 1979. He stopped American wheat sales to the Soviets. Americans did not take part in the 1980 Olympic Games that were held in Moscow, the Soviet capital. The United States Senate did not pass an agreement called SALT II, which required both nations to limit nuclear weapons. The period of détente, or better relations with the Soviets, came to an end.

The Hostage Crisis in Iran

The most difficult problem that President Carter faced in foreign affairs occurred in the Middle East nation of Iran. Iran is a Muslim nation with a large oil supply. In 1953 the CIA helped Mohammed Reza Pahlavi become **shah**, or king, of Iran. The Shah worked to make Iran more like the western nations of the United States and Europe. New industries were started, new schools were built, and women were allowed to vote. Many Iranians were angry with the Shah because he moved the country away from the teachings of Islam. Other Iranians hated the Shah because he was a dictator who allowed very little freedom.

In the late 1970s, a revolution began in Iran. In 1979 the Shah fled from Iran. The Ayatollah Ruhollah Khomeini, a Muslim religious leader, won control of the government. A new government was started that was based on the laws of Islam.

The new government wanted the Shah to return to Iran to be put on trial. When the Shah became ill, he went to the United States for medical treatment. Iranians were furious when President Carter refused to send the Shah back to Iran. On April 4, 1979, angry Iranians took control of the American embassy in Iran's capital, Teheran. For the next 444 days, 52 Americans were held as **hostages** in Iran.

President Carter was not able to win the release of the hostages. To pressure Iran, Carter stopped importing oil from that country. Before long the United States had a new energy crisis.

In April 1980 Carter decided to use military force to free the hostages. Unfortunately, several helicopters crashed, eight members of the rescue team were killed, and the mission failed.

The Shah died in July 1980, but the Iranians refused to release the American hostages. Many Americans were upset that Carter could not get the hostages released. In 1980 Carter lost the presidential election to Ronald Reagan. The Iran hostage crisis was one of several problems that led to Carter's defeat. Finally, on January 20, 1981, the day Reagan became President, Iran released the American hostages.

Civil Wars in Central America

President Ronald Reagan strongly believed that communism was a serious threat to the United States. In 1982 when Communists won control of Grenada, a tiny island located in the Caribbean Sea, Reagan sent American troops to defeat the Communists. A new government was started in Grenada that was friendly to the United States.

The United States also became involved in Nicaragua, a country in Central America. There had been a civil war in Nicaragua. As a result, a group called the **Sandinistas** ruled Nicaragua. The civil war continued because people who opposed the Sandinistas, the **contras**, fought to control Nicaragua. The Soviets sent aid to the Sandinistas to help them fight the contras. In 1981 Congress agreed to send weapons and aid to the contras. Reagan wanted more aid for the contras, but in 1984 Congress passed a law that ended American aid. After years of fighting, the Sandinista leader of Nicaragua, Daniel Ortega, agreed to hold elections. A non-Communist leader was elected president of Nicaragua.

These Sandinista soldiers helped fight the contras in Nicaragua. The United States supported the contra rebels, who continued to fight the Sandinistas after Nicaragua's civil war.

El Salvador, a Central American nation near Nicaragua, also had a civil war. Communist guerrilla fighters tried to win control of the government. Because there was terrible poverty in El Salvador, many people favored the Communists. The Sandinistas in Nicaragua sent aid to the Communist rebels. President Reagan sent aid to the ruling non-Communist government. The war ended and a peace treaty was signed in 1992. Since then El Salvador has elected a non-Communist government.

The Dangers of Terrorism

Since the late 1970s, **terrorism** has been a problem in many parts of the world.

Terrorism is the use of dangerous acts against innocent people to force an enemy to give in to terrorists' demands. Often Palestinians have used terrorism to show the world that they want a homeland in the Middle East. The policy of the United States has been to refuse to give terrorists what they demand.

In 1985 Palestinian terrorists captured a cruise ship and killed a Jewish American passenger. In 1986 a terrorist group **hijacked** an American plane in Athens, killed one passenger, and held the other passengers as hostages.

One of the worst acts of terrorism occurred in 1988. Terrorists placed a bomb in a plane. It exploded as it flew over

In 1988 a terrorist bomb blew up this plane as it flew over Scotland. All of the passengers and crew were killed, including many Americans. Police and government officials looked for clues and eventually charged several terrorists with the crime. They have yet to be captured and brought to trial.

420

Scotland. All 270 passengers, including 38 American students, were killed.

The Iran-Contra Scandal

The Iran-contra scandal developed because President Reagan wanted to find a way to release seven American hostages who were being held by terrorists in Lebanon. He also wanted to help the contras in Nicaragua even though Congress had stopped American aid.

To reach Reagan's goals, members of his staff carried out secret plans. They secretly and illegally sold arms, or weapons, to America's enemy, Iran. In return Iran agreed to work for the release of the seven American hostages. Profits from the arms sale to Iran were sent to the contras in Nicaragua.

Americans were shocked when they learned about the Iran-contra deal. It was against American policy to deal with terrorists and to sell weapons to America's enemies. It was also illegal to help the contras.

Congress investigated the scandal in 1987. Several members of Reagan's staff were found guilty. President Reagan denied that he knew about the secret deals. However, many people criticized the President for not knowing what was happening among his staff members.

President Reagan and the Soviet Union

President Reagan believed that the Soviet Union was a threat to the security of the United States. To protect the United States from the Soviet Union, Reagan spent

President Reagan hated communism, but he developed a good relationship with Mikhail Gorbachev, the leader of the Soviet Union.

billions of dollars building up the military strength of the nation. The increase in military spending helped cause the nation's **deficit**, or shortage of money, to grow larger.

Reagan wanted the nation to build a new defense system called the **Strategic Defense Initiative**. People also called the system Star Wars. The system would have space satellites that would shoot down nuclear missiles that were fired at the United States. However, changing events in the Soviet Union made Star Wars less necessary for the United States.

In 1985 Mikhail Gorbachev became the new leader of the Soviet Union. He decided to try to solve the country's serious economic problems by allowing some private control of business and industry. These changes in the Communist system were given the Russian name **perestroika**.

Gorbachev also allowed more freedoms for the Soviet people. There was more freedom of speech, freedom of the press,

421

Since the time it was built in 1961, the Berlin Wall had become a symbol of the Cold War. In November 1989 Germans celebrated as the Berlin Wall was opened, allowing travel between East and West. Thousands of Germans helped tear down the hated wall.

and freedom of religion. These new freedoms and more openness were given the Russian name **glasnost**.

By 1987 President Reagan believed the Soviet Union was no longer America's most dangerous enemy. In that year Reagan and Gorbachev signed the INF Treaty. In the INF Treaty, both nations agreed to destroy thousands of nuclear missiles.

The End of the Cold War

Since 1945 the nations of Eastern Europe had been controlled by the Soviet Union. The changes Gorbachev made in the Soviet Union quickly spread to Eastern Europe and communism grew weaker.

In 1989 Poland became the first nation in Eastern Europe to hold free elections. Lech Walesa was the leader of the **Solidarity** labor union. He was elected President of a non-Communist Polish government. During the next few months, the other nations of Eastern Europe started non-Communist governments.

As freedom spread through Eastern Europe, East Germans wanted to travel to West Berlin. In November 1989 the Berlin Wall was opened and people could once again travel between East Berlin and West Berlin. Germans on both sides quickly tore down the hated wall. In 1990 all of Berlin became one city again. East Germany and West Germany rejoined and formed a united Germany in 1990.

For more than forty years, Americans had feared the Soviet Union and communism. Once communism was no longer a threat, the Berlin Wall was torn down, and the long years of the Cold War ended.

Ronald Reagan 1911–

Ronald Reagan was one of the most popular Presidents in American history. Reagan grew up in Illinois. Reagan's family was so poor that he wore his brother's old clothes and was often hungry from the lack of food. Reagan became an actor after finishing college. He starred in many movies and several television shows from 1937 to 1965.

Reagan was also interested in politics. In 1966 he was elected governor of California. He served two terms. Then in 1976, and again in 1980, he ran for President. During his campaign against Jimmy Carter in 1980, Reagan promised to cut taxes, lower inflation, and improve the economy. Reagan won the election.

As President, Reagan carried out an idea called **supply-side economics**. The idea was later called Reaganomics. Reagan believed that the economy would improve if the amount of goods produced could increase. Therefore, he cut taxes so that businesses could invest money in hiring workers and producing goods. Once businesses earned larger profits, they would pay more taxes.

Reagan also believed the federal government should be less involved in the lives of the people. So he cut programs for education and welfare. Some people said that these cuts hurt poor Americans, but Reagan insisted that a strong economy would help everyone.

By the end of Reagan's second term, the economy had improved. But the nation had also borrowed large amounts of money to pay for defense spending and social programs.

By 1989, most Americans were happy with the improved economy and the new friendship with the Soviet Union. Even the Iran-contra scandal could not destroy Reagan's popularity. When his second term ended, Reagan was one of the most popular Presidents in American history. Reagan retired to California where he now suffers from Alzheimer's Disease.

In Your Own Words

Write a paragraph that tells why Reagan was a very popular President.

REVIEW AND APPLY

CHAPTER 34 MAIN IDEAS

■ The Camp David Accords, a peace treaty between Egypt and Israel, was one of President Carter's greatest achievements.

■ On April 4, 1979, Iranians took control of the American embassy in Teheran and held 52 Americans hostage for the next 444 days.

■ President Reagan fought the spread of communism in Central America.

■ Terrorist acts throughout the world have killed many innocent people.

■ In 1985 Mikhail Gorbachev became the new leader of the Soviet Union.

■ In 1989 the Berlin Wall was torn down, and the cold war came to an end.

VOCABULARY

Finish the Sentence ■ Choose one of the words or phrases from the box to complete each sentence. Write the correct word or phrase in your social studies notebook. You will not use all the words in the box.

1. The _____ was a peace treaty between the countries of Israel and Egypt.

2. President Carter worked to protect the _____ or personal freedoms, of people around the world.

3. Between 1979 and 1991, American _____ were held captive in Iran.

4. Nicaragua's Communists were called _____ .

5. President Reagan sent aid to the Nicaraguan rebels called _____ .

6. The name of the Polish labor union headed by Lech Walesa was _____ .

> Sandinistas
> Camp David Accords
> Solidarity
> hostages
> human rights
> contras
> shah

USING INFORMATION

Writing an Opinion ■ Both President Carter and President Reagan were successful in foreign affairs. Write a paragraph in your social studies notebook explaining which President you think was more successful in foreign affairs and why. Start your paragraph with a topic sentence.

COMPREHENSION CHECK

Who Said It? ■ Read each statement in Group A. Then look at the names in Group B for the person who might have said it. Write the letter of the correct answer in your social studies notebook. There is one name you will not use.

Group A

1. "I stopped Americans from participating in the 1980 Olympic Games."

2. "I led a new government in Iran that wanted to put the Shah on trial."

3. "I believed that the Soviet Union was a threat to the security of the United States."

4. "I wanted to give the Soviet people more personal freedom."

5. "I was the Egyptian President who signed a peace treaty with Israel."

6. "I was the leader of Nicaragua who agreed to hold elections."

7. "I was elected President of Poland."

Group B

A. Daniel Ortega

B. Ronald Reagan

C. Jimmy Carter

D. Lech Walesa

E. Mikhail Gorbachev

F. Anwar Sadat

G. Ayatollah Khomeini

H. Mohammed Reza Pahlavi

CRITICAL THINKING

Categories ■ Read the words in each group. Use the words and phrases in the box to write a title for each group. Write your answers in your social studies notebook. There is one possible title in the box that you will not use.

Iran-Contra Scandal	End of the Cold War	Terrorist Acts
The Carter Presidency	Sandinistas	

1. could not get Americans freed from Iran
   held meetings with leaders of Egypt and Israel
   stopped American wheat sales to the Soviet Union

2. led by Daniel Ortega
   sent aid to Communists in El Salvador
   given aid by the Soviet Union

3. capturing a cruise ship
   placing a bomb on a plane
   a problem in many parts of the world

4. took place during the Reagan administration
   American weapons were sold to Iran
   Iran agreed to work for the release of American hostages

THE UNITED STATES AS TODAY'S WORLD LEADER

◀ American soldier in the Persian Gulf War

People

Saddam Hussein • George Bush • H. Norman Schwarzkopf • Colin Powell • Boris Yeltsin • F.W. de Klerk • Nelson Mandela • Bill Clinton • Yitzhak Rabin • Yasir Arafat • King Hussein • Ernesto Zedillo

Places

Iraq • Kuwait • Persian Gulf • Saudi Arabia • Somalia •

South Africa • Yugoslavia • Bosnia and Herzegovina • Dayton, OH • Tiananmen Square • Beijing

New Vocabulary

coalition • overthrow • famine • apartheid • sanctions • import • NAFTA • peso • acid rain

Focus on Main Ideas

1. Why did the United States fight in the Persian Gulf War?
2. Why is the Soviet Union no longer a nation?
3. How has the United States worked for peace in the Middle East, Bosnia, and Africa?
4. How has the United States worked with Canada and Mexico?

During the 1990s the United States often used its power to act as a leader and a peacemaker in many of the world's trouble spots.

The Persian Gulf War

In August 1990 Iraq invaded and captured the neighboring nation of Kuwait. Both Kuwait and Iraq are oil-rich nations on the Persian Gulf. Iraq wanted to rule Kuwait in order to control Kuwait's huge oil fields. After winning control of Kuwait, Saddam Hussein, the dictator of Iraq, threatened to attack Saudi Arabia, Kuwait's oil-rich neighbor. Since Americans imported oil from Kuwait and Saudi Arabia, the United States decided to stop Iraq from controlling their oil fields.

President George Bush acted quickly with other UN nations to organize a **coalition** of 28 nations that were willing to use military force against Iraq. The UN started an embargo that stopped trade with Iraq. The UN Security Council told Iraq it would be attacked if it did not leave Kuwait by January 15, 1991. At the same time, Congress allowed President Bush to send more than 500,000 American troops to Saudi Arabia.

War began in the Persian Gulf on January 16, 1991, because Iraq was still controlling Kuwait. The war was called Operation Desert Storm, or the Persian Gulf War. General H. Norman Schwarzkopf and General Colin Powell led American forces during the war. The United States and other coalition members, such as Britain and France, bombed Iraq for five weeks.

Then American soldiers began fighting in Iraq. They also fought Iraq's army in Kuwait. After four days of ground fighting, Kuwait became a free nation. The fighting continued until February 28, 1991. About 85,000 Iraqis and 146 Americans were killed during the war.

The quick victory in Kuwait made President Bush very popular after the war. However, Saddam Hussein remained Iraq's dictator. Americans criticized President Bush for allowing Hussein to remain in power.

American forces stopped Iraqi forces that were trying to leave Kuwait. Thousands of Iraqi trucks were destroyed on this highway.

The Soviet Union Falls Apart

During the forty years after World War II, Americans feared the power of the Soviet Union. No one dreamed that by 1992 the Soviet Union would no longer exist as a nation.

After becoming the leader of the Soviet Union in 1985, Mikhail Gorbachev made important changes. He ended communism in Eastern Europe and the Cold War. He also encouraged peace and friendship with the United States. In 1991 Gorbachev and President Bush signed START, the Strategic Arms Reduction Treaty, a treaty to limit nuclear weapons.

Gorbachev also brought more freedom to the Soviet Union than any Soviet leader

The land battle lasted only four days during the Persian Gulf War. Troops from 28 nations, including the United States, defeated the Iraqi forces.

had ever allowed before. This freedom encouraged nationalism to grow in the 15 republics that made up the Soviet Union. The republics wanted to be independent nations like they had been before the Soviet Union began in 1922.

By 1991 many people in the Soviet Union were unhappy with Gorbachev. Some did not like the changes he had made in the government. Millions of people were upset because there were shortages of all types of food and goods. Even soap was hard to find in Soviet stores. In August 1991 Gorbachev's enemies tried to **overthrow** him. Gorbachev remained in power, but he could not hold the Soviet

Union together. On December 25, 1991, Gorbachev resigned, and the Soviet Union was no longer a nation. The 15 republics became independent countries.

Russia was the largest republic in the former Soviet Union. Russia and 11 republics from the former Soviet Union formed an organization called the Commonwealth of Independent States, or CIS. The CIS tries to keep peace between the republics. It also helps them control their nuclear weapons, and it encourages trade.

In 1996 the first free elections for president were held in Russia. Boris Yeltsin, a non-Communist, defeated a Communist

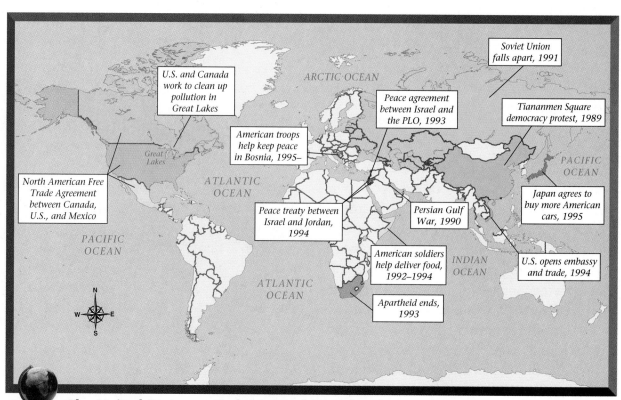

The United States as Today's World Leader *The United States is a world leader because it participates in events around the world. The United States supports peace talks and human rights efforts. During what years did the United States help deliver food in Somalia in Africa?*

candidate to win the election. The election proved that most Russians no longer wanted a Communist government.

Yeltsin has tried to help Russia become more democratic. However, many Russians have been unhappy because Russia has many problems. Millions of people are poor. Crime and unemployment rates are higher than ever before. There are shortages of food and medicine everywhere.

The United States has given Russia more than $5 billion in aid to help as it tries to become a democracy. The fall of the Soviet Union made the United States the most powerful nation in the world. There is no longer a Soviet Union to support revolutions, and communism is no longer a serious threat to world peace.

The United States and Africa

In 1992 President Bush used American money and soldiers to help the East African nation of Somalia. Due to a civil war and a long drought, the nation had a **famine**, or a severe food shortage. To save more than one million people from starving, American troops went to Somalia in 1992. They helped the UN deliver food and supplies to starving Somalians. About 28,000 American soldiers served in Somalia. In March 1994 all American soldiers returned home.

The United States has also tried to help South Africa. For many years **apartheid** laws kept different racial groups apart in all public places in South Africa. Although black people made up 75 percent of South Africa's population, white South Africans controlled the country until 1993. The United States pressured South Africa to end apartheid. Along with European nations, the United States placed **sanctions** on certain kinds of trade with South Africa. Many American companies stopped all business with South Africa.

In 1993 under South Africa's president, F.W. de Klerk, South Africans wrote a new constitution. It gave all racial groups equal rights. In April 1994 national elections were held, and for the first time, all South African adults could vote. Nelson Mandela was elected president, the nation's first black person to hold that office. Both de Klerk and Mandela won the Nobel Peace Prize for their work in South Africa.

The United States and the Middle East

For years the Palestine Liberation Organization, or PLO, had said its goal was to destroy Israel and create a Palestinian state instead. In 1993 President Bill Clinton helped Israel reach an agreement with the PLO. The agreement stated that some of the land Israel had captured in 1967 would be controlled by the PLO. The PLO agreed to recognize Israel's right to exist as a nation and to stop terrorism against Israel. On September 13, 1993, Israel's prime minister, Yitzhak Rabin, and the leader of the PLO, Yasir Arafat, signed the peace agreement at the White House.

Clinton also encouraged Israel's eastern neighbor, Jordan, to sign a peace treaty. In October 1994 Jordan's King Hussein and Israel's Yitzhak Rabin signed a peace treaty. It was the second peace treaty between an Arab nation and Israel.

In 1995 Yitzhak Rabin was assassinated by an Israeli. Also, terrorism by Arabs against the people of Israel increased. Terrorism may cause problems for the peace process in the near future.

Terrorism has been a problem in other parts of the Middle East. In 1996 terrorists bombed an apartment building in Saudi Arabia. The building housed American military people. Hundreds of Americans were injured and 19 were killed. Many Americans fear that there will be more terrorist attacks in the Persian Gulf region.

The United States and Bosnia

Like the Soviet Union, Yugoslavia broke up into separate independent nations when communism ended in that country. Civil war broke out in some of these new nations. The worst fighting has been in one country, Bosnia and Herzegovina, which is often called Bosnia.

In 1992 a civil war began among three ethnic groups in Bosnia. Those groups—Muslims, Croats, and Serbs—have fought for control of the nation. Serbs captured about two thirds of the country. Then they began killing thousands of Muslims in order to remove them from the region the Serbs controlled. The killing of innocent Muslims reminded the world of the World War II Holocaust against the Jews.

In September 1995 American leaders met in Dayton, Ohio, with the leaders of Bosnia's ethnic groups. The goal of their

Like other wars, the war in Bosnia has affected the lives of many people. Thousands of people have become refugees because their homes were destroyed by the fighting. Many others have had to flee to avoid the troops who were killing civilians.

meeting was to end the war and to stop the killing of innocent people. The United States helped create a peace plan. Under that plan Bosnia would be a nation with two states. The Serbs would control one state and the Muslims and the Croats would control the other state. NATO troops, including 20,000 Americans, were sent to Bosnia to carry out the plan and prevent a new civil war.

The United States and Asia

After World War II, the United States helped the Japanese rebuild their nation. Today Japan is the second largest trading partner of the United States. Americans **import** large numbers of cars, cameras, and electronic equipment from Japan. But Japan limits the amount it imports from the United States. The United States has threatened to buy fewer cars from Japan unless that country imports more American cars and products. In 1995 Japan agreed to buy more American cars.

China is another major Asian trading partner with the United States. Unlike the Soviet Union, China has remained a powerful Communist nation. In 1989 thousands of Chinese students began to protest that they wanted more freedom and democracy. They gathered in a place called Tiananmen Square in the capital city of Beijing. The protests spread to more than twenty Chinese cities.

The world watched and waited to see if China's government would allow more freedom. The government's answer came on June 3, 1989. It sent army troops and tanks to attack the protesting students.

In 1989 thousands of Chinese protested in Tiananmen Square in Beijing. They were protesting for more freedom and democracy in Communist China.

At least 5,000 protesters were killed. Thousands were sent to prison. The United States criticized China's actions but did not try to punish China. China continues to be a major trading partner with the United States. There is little freedom in Communist China today.

One of the United States' newest trading partners in Asia is Vietnam. After the Vietnam War, the United States ended all trade and relations with Vietnam. After 19 years President Clinton has allowed trade to start again between the two nations. The United States once again has an ambassador and an embassy in Vietnam. Vietnam has an embassy with government representatives in the United States.

The United States, Mexico, and Canada

The United States trades with many nations around the world. To improve trade with Canada and Mexico, the United States signed **NAFTA**, or the North American Free Trade Agreement. By the year 2005, NAFTA will end most tariffs on products traded between the United States and its neighbors. It will be easier for one nation to start businesses and industries in the other nations. Workers from one nation will find it easier to get jobs in the other nations.

Many members of Congress did not want to vote for NAFTA because they thought it would cause unemployment in the United States. They feared that American businesses would move to Mexico where they could pay lower salaries to Mexican workers. However, Congress passed the agreement in 1993.

Mexico has large supplies of mineral resources such as silver, gold, copper, iron, and petroleum. Mexico is the third largest trading partner of the United States.

Although Mexico is working to become a modern industrial nation, it has many problems. One third of the population is very poor, and its cities are very crowded. Unemployment and inflation rates are high. Its biggest problems are a huge national debt and an enormous deficit.

At the end of 1994, Mexico faced an economic crisis. It had an enormous deficit because it had imported far more goods than it had sold to other countries. Mexico owed other nations huge amounts of money. Mexican money, the **peso**, lost its value. To save Mexico's economy, President Clinton agreed to lend $20 billion to that nation. Mexico's president, Ernesto de Zedillo, created a six-year plan to improve the economy. By 1996 Mexico had repaid some of its debt to the United States, and its economy was improving.

Each year many Mexicans move to the United States. Although most move legally, many arrive illegally, without permission from the United States. The United States wants Mexico to do more to stop illegal immigrants from entering the United States. The United States also wants Mexico to stop the flow of illegal drugs through Mexico into the United States.

The United States and Canada share the world's longest unguarded border. Although Canada is much larger in size, its population is much smaller. The United States has more trade with Canada than it has with any other nation.

Pollution has been a problem between the United States and Canada. Winds blow American air pollution into Canada where it mixes with rain or snow and becomes **acid rain**. Acid rain has damaged plants, forests, lakes, and animal life in both nations. To reduce the problem of pollution and acid rain, Congress passed the Clean Air Act. The law requires cars and factories to send less pollution into the air.

Both nations have also worked together to clean up pollution in the Great Lakes. The two nations share four of the five Great Lakes. By working together, the water in these lakes has become cleaner. However, it is still not safe to eat certain fish from the Great Lakes.

The United States will continue to be a world leader as it moves closer to the year 2000.

BIOGRAPHY

Colin Powell 1937–

Colin Powell became a popular war hero during the Persian Gulf War.

Powell grew up in the South Bronx of New York City. Powell's parents were immigrants from the Caribbean island of Jamaica. His parents stressed the importance of a college education, so after high school he attended City College in New York City. There he joined the Reserve Officers Training Corps, or ROTC. The ROTC prepares students to become army officers. After graduating from college in 1958, Powell began his military career in the United States Army at Fort Benning, Georgia.

Powell won a medal for courage while serving in the Vietnam War from 1968 to 1969. He was in a helicopter that crashed. Powell escaped and returned to the burning helicopter to rescue the other soldiers.

While Ronald Reagan was President, Powell became a four-star general. President George Bush appointed Powell to be chairman of the Joint Chiefs of Staff. The Joint Chiefs of Staff are the leaders of the army, the air force, the marines, and the navy. As chairman, Powell was in charge of all the branches of the military. He was America's highest officer. Powell was the first African American to hold this position.

As chairman of the Joint Chiefs of Staff, he made battle plans during the Persian Gulf War. Due to his excellent plans and the work of General H. Norman Schwarzkopf, Iraq was defeated, with a low number of American casualties.

After the war ended, Powell retired from the military. In 1995 many Americans encouraged Powell to become a candidate for President, but he decided not to run in the election.

Powell wrote a book, his autobiography, called *My American Journey*. By reading his book, you can learn how a New York City boy became one of the nation's great military leaders.

In Your Own Words

Write in the journal section of your social studies notebook a paragraph that tells about Powell's success in the army.

REVIEW AND APPLY

- The Persian Gulf War started after Iraq invaded the country of Kuwait. The United States, along with other UN nations, brought a quick end to the war. The fighting ended on February 28, 1991.

- On December 25, 1991, Mikhail Gorbachev resigned as leader of the Soviet Union, and the country divided into 15 independent countries. Russia was the largest of these independent countries, and Boris Yeltsin became Russia's president.

- President Bush sent money and soldiers to help the East African nation of Somalia, which was suffering through severe drought and famine.

- The United States pressured South Africa to end its policy of apartheid.

- In 1993 President Bill Clinton helped Israel and the PLO reach a peace agreement.

- In September 1995 American leaders helped the leaders of Bosnia's ethnic groups to stop the war in that country.

- The NAFTA treaty was signed to help increase trade and reduce tariffs between the United States, Canada, and Mexico.

VOCABULARY

Defining and Using Vocabulary ■ In the assignment section of your social studies notebook, write the meaning of each word. Then write a sentence for each word.

coalition	NAFTA	overthrow
apartheid	acid rain	import
sanctions	famine	peso

USING INFORMATION

Writing an Opinion ■ In what region of the world do you think the United States had the most impact as a world leader? Write in your social studies notebook a paragraph that uses facts from the text to support your opinion. Start your paragraph with a topic sentence.

COMPREHENSION CHECK

Understanding Events in History ■ Copy and complete the graphic organizer below with information about the United States' role as a world leader.

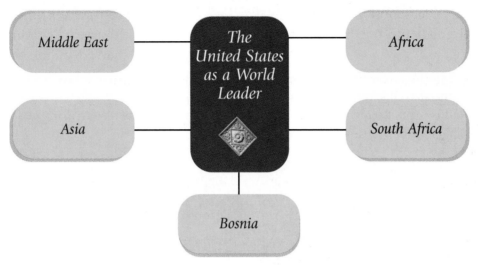

CRITICAL THINKING

Cause and Effect ■ Choose a cause or an effect from Group B to complete each sentence in Group A. Write the letter of the correct answer in your social studies notebook. Group B has one more answer than you need.

Group A

1. _____ , so Iraq wanted to rule Kuwait to control Kuwait's oil fields.

2. Many people in the Soviet Union were unhappy with the leadership of Mikhail Gorbachev, so _____

3. In 1994, all South Africans could vote in a national election, so _____

4. _____ , so today Japan is the second largest trading partner of the United States.

5. In 1994 Mexico's peso lost its value, so _____

6. Acid rain has destroyed plants, forests, and animal life in Canada and the United States, so _____

Group B

A. the United States Congress passed the Clean Air Act to reduce the problem of pollution.

B. After World War II, the United States helped the Japanese rebuild their nation

C. Kuwait is an oil-rich country

D. apartheid came to an end.

E. Gorbachev resigned on December 25, 1991.

F. President Clinton agreed to lend Mexico $20 billion.

G. the country elected its first black president, Nelson Mandela.

AMERICAN GEOGRAPHY

Movement: Foreign Oil to the United States

Movement tells how people, resources, ideas, and goods move from one place to another.

The United States imports oil, or petroleum, from many nations in order to meet its energy needs. Oil is measured in barrels. A barrel contains 42 gallons. In 1994, 51 percent of the oil Americans used was imported from other nations. That year the United States imported more than 2.5 billion barrels of oil. Eighty-five percent of this foreign oil came from nine nations. The map below shows how many barrels were imported from those nine nations.

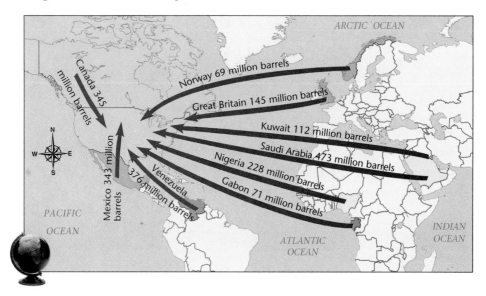

Study the map. Then write in the assignment section of your social studies notebook the answers to the following questions.

1. From which nation did the United States buy the most oil?

2. How much oil did the United States buy from Kuwait?

3. Name two nations in Europe that export oil to the United States.

4. Name two Latin American nations that sell oil to the United States.

5. How much oil did the United States buy from Mexico?

6. How much oil did the United States import from Nigeria?

SOCIAL STUDIES SKILLS

Interpreting a Political Cartoon

Political cartoons are drawn by an artist to express an opinion about an event. The political cartoon on this page shows the changes that were taking place in the Soviet Union in September 1991. Three Soviet republics—Latvia, Lithuania, and Estonia—had declared their independence. Those three republics started the breakup of the Soviet Union. At the time no one knew that by 1992 the Soviet Union would no longer exist.

Read pages 421–422 and pages 427–429 again and study the political cartoon. Then write in your social studies notebook the answers to the following questions.

1. How did the Soviet Union shrink in September 1991?

2. How did the artist show the cause of the shrinking of the Soviet Union?

3. Who, do you think, is the person drawn in the political cartoon?

4. What, do you think, was the artist's opinion of the change in the Soviet Union?

5. What kind of cartoon about the Soviet Union would this artist draw after December 1991?

Chapter 36 CHALLENGES FACING AMERICAN SOCIETY

◀ *Tracking the national debt*

People

Newt Gingrich • Ricardo Murillo • Clara Hale

Places

World Trade Center • Oklahoma City

New Vocabulary

multicultural • poverty line • addicted • drug abuse • AIDS • HIV virus •

vaccine • budget • balanced budget • privatization • illegal alien

Focus on Main Ideas

1. How is American society changing?
2. How is immigration to the United States changing?
3. What are some ways that Americans are dealing with the difficult problems of poverty, crimes, drugs, and terrorism in the United States?
4. How can the United States solve its problems?

Americans have solved many difficult problems since the nation first began in 1776. The United States must continue to solve new problems as the nation changes and moves into the twenty-first century.

Changes in American Society

American society is quickly changing in many ways. First, the nation's African American, Asian, and Hispanic populations are growing faster than the white population. For example, today less than half of the students in California schools are white. Because immigrants are coming to the United States from many nations and cultures, the society is becoming more **multicultural**. America's schools must teach children who come from many different cultures and speak many languages other than English.

Second, the American family is changing. Today almost one fifth of all children come from homes with only one parent. Most of the time that single parent is the mother.

Third, Americans have more education than ever before. About 80 percent of all Americans finish high school, and more students attend college. People with more education usually earn higher salaries.

438

Fourth, more women are working at jobs outside of their homes. Women are working in many jobs that in the past were only done by men.

Fifth, American society has more elderly people than ever before. More than 33 million people are over the age of 65. The elderly population continues to grow larger each year. Many older citizens depend on Social Security pensions and health care through Medicare. But some government leaders believe the Social Security system will not have enough money to care for the growing population of older citizens. New ways must be found to provide money for the Social Security system.

Sixth, more Americans are now settling in the South and the West. California now has the largest population, and Texas has the second largest population. As states gain or lose population, they also gain or lose representatives in Congress. In 1994 Texas had four more representatives than it had in 1984. Those extra representatives gave Texas more power in Congress. Also, since 1964, every President except Gerald Ford has come from the South or the West.

Changes in Immigration

The United States has always been a nation of immigrants. Yet immigration has

The nation's work force continues to change as more women work at jobs outside their homes. Many women are working at jobs that had once been done only by men. More women today are working as construction workers, doctors, lawyers, and military officers than ever before.

439

been a debated issue throughout the nation's history. Some people in the United States criticize immigrants for taking jobs away from other Americans. Others complain that immigrants use government benefits that only citizens should receive.

Most immigrants today still come to the United States for better opportunities. They work hard at low-paying jobs that most American citizens do not want. They earn money and pay their share of taxes. Some immigrants are refugees who have escaped from danger and wars.

Until 1965 immigration laws favored people from northern and western Europe. Immigration laws since 1965 have favored people from Asia and Latin America. A new immigration law passed in 1990 made it easier for people who have special skills to move to America. The law also helped people with families living in this country to become immigrants. Since 1995, 675,000 people have been allowed to settle in the United States each year.

The Problems of Poverty, Crime, and Drugs

The nation has almost 40 million poor people. Many of the poor are immigrants. Often people have become poor because

Many of the nation's poor are homeless. They often live in public parks or on city streets. No one knows how many people are homeless, but the number may be as high as seven million. There are many private and public organizations that try to help homeless people.

the factories where they worked went out of business. Many of the poor are children. Because they often attend lower quality schools, these children will have fewer opportunities for a better future. Without good jobs as adults, their poverty problems will continue.

The federal government measures how much poverty exists in the nation by creating a **poverty line**. People who have incomes that fall below the line are considered poor. The poverty line changes every few years. Since 1993 the poverty line for a family with four people has been $14,800. A family with four people who earned less than $14,800 was counted as poor. To end poverty, more job training programs are needed. New job opportunities must be created. More housing is also needed for people with low incomes.

The nation's homeless population is another problem. Many of the nation's poor often live in bus and train stations or on city streets. To solve this problem, city and state governments are trying to create more low-income housing as well as emergency shelters.

Crime is a serious American problem. There are far more murders in the United States than in other nations such as Canada or Japan. Crime is sometimes caused by unemployment and a lack of education. Violent television shows and movies may also encourage crime. Because handguns are often used to commit crimes, stricter gun control laws may help solve the crime problem.

Much of the nation's crime is caused by the sale and use of illegal drugs. People who use illegal drugs, such as marijuana,

Many illegal drugs are smuggled into the country. Federal agencies work to stop illegal drugs from entering the United States.

cocaine, and heroin, become **addicted** to them. These drug addicts must have the drugs in order to feel normal. Drug addicts often commit crimes to get money to buy more drugs.

The federal government has fought "a War on Drugs" to end the problem of **drug abuse**. Drug abuse means using a drug in a way that is not correct. The War on Drugs costs the nation $10 billion each year. Despite the money that has been spent, the War on Drugs has failed to solve the drug problem.

The AIDS Epidemic

Americans first learned about the disease called **AIDS**, acquired immune deficiency syndrome, in 1981. In 1996, about 500,000 Americans had the disease. But

In 1993 terrorists exploded a large bomb in the garage under New York City's World Trade Center. Six people were killed and more than 1,000 were hurt.

In April 1995, 168 people were killed when a terrorist bomb blew up a federal building in Oklahoma City. Most of the building was destroyed by the bomb blast.

many more carry the **HIV virus** that causes the disease. People can carry and spread the virus for 10 years before becoming sick with AIDS. There are medicines to slow the progress of the disease, but there is no cure. People who have AIDS die after periods of terrible illnesses. Pregnant women with AIDS can give the HIV virus to their babies. Those babies will become sick and die.

AIDS is a serious problem because it is spreading so rapidly. Although millions of dollars have been spent on AIDS research around the world, no cure has yet been found. So far scientists have tried, but failed, to create a **vaccine** to prevent the disease.

The Problem of Terrorism

If you had visited the United States Capitol in 1986, you would have simply entered and toured the building. If you made that same visit in 1996, you would have been stopped at the door by a security guard. That guard would have checked to make sure you were not carrying a weapon or a bomb. Security guards are needed because of the threat of terrorism.

Terrorism is a growing threat in the United States. In 1993 terrorists bombed the garage under New York City's World Trade Center. In April 1995 terrorists blew up a federal building in Oklahoma City. And at the 1996 Olympic Games in Atlanta, Georgia, a terrorist bomb exploded, killing 1 person and injuring more than 100. Government agencies such as the FBI and the CIA are looking for new and better ways to end terrorism.

Budget Problems and the National Debt

Every year the President must plan the nation's **budget**. The budget is the plan for how the government will spend tax money to pay for government programs. The budget includes money for defense, Social Security programs, the War on Drugs, and all other expenses of the federal government. The President's budget cannot be put into action until it is passed by Congress.

For many years our nation has not had a **balanced budget**. In a balanced budget, there is enough money from taxes to pay for all government expenses. Instead there has been a budget deficit, or shortage of money, so the government borrows money to pay for its many programs. To borrow money the government sells bonds. The national debt, the money that the federal government has borrowed and must repay, grows larger each year. In 1996 the national debt was about $5 trillion. The government used one fifth of its budget just to repay the interest on the national debt. That money could be used for many other programs.

Many members of Congress want to pass a Balanced Budget Amendment and have it become part of the Constitution. They say a balanced budget will limit the growth of the national debt. However, other members of Congress oppose the Balanced Budget Amendment. They believe there are times when the government must borrow money in order to prevent a depression or to pay for a larger army during a war.

Since the days when the New Deal tried to end the Great Depression, Americans have depended on the federal government to solve many problems. The federal government now plays a larger role in the lives of Americans than it did before the New Deal. President Reagan tried to reduce the size of the federal government. He believed problems should be solved by state and local governments and by private businesses.

President Clinton and Republican Speaker of the House Newt Gingrich, the leader of the House of Representatives, did not agree on the nation's budget for 1996. Gingrich wanted to lower taxes and to slow increases in spending for education, welfare, and Medicare. His goal was to balance the budget by the year 2002. Clinton argued that Gingrich's budget cuts would hurt too many people. Clinton wanted a balanced budget by the year 2005. After many debates and arguments, a large part of the budget was finally passed.

Today Americans continue to argue about who should solve the nation's problems. Some believe the federal government should create new programs to end poverty, terrorism, drug abuse, and crime. Other people want state and local governments to solve these problems. Still other people feel these problems may be solved by individuals and by private businesses. Some states have started **privatization** by allowing private companies to run government programs such as issuing driver's licenses. If privatization succeeds, other state governments will have private companies take control of public schools, public hospitals, and public transportation.

As the United States grows and changes, it will continue to try different ways to solve old and new problems.

An immigrant's Experience

Ricardo Murillo and his brother escaped from dangerous revolutions in El Salvador and came to the United States in 1982. Murillo left his family in El Salvador. He planned to earn enough money in the United States to bring his family to live with him. He entered the United States as an illegal alien. In the United States, he worked as a migrant farm worker. In an interview, Murillo spoke about the dangers he faced in moving to the United States. He also spoke about his experience as an immigrant.

My brother, José Dimas, and I left [El Salvador] in the predawn darkness on January 15, [1982,] leaving everyone and everything behind. I worked in the army headquarters…in the northern zone of the country. I was not a soldier, but…a bricklayer, one who builds houses.…

The reason I left was because…it kept getting more and more dangerous every day.… Every day we encountered danger in the streets, either with the *guerrilleros*—the rebels—or the government soldiers.…

You couldn't trust anyone. That's when José Dimas and I decided to leave the country. I told my wife and my mother, "I think that God wills it. The road will be difficult, but with the help of God we will continue.…" We hardened our hearts because it is almost unbearable to leave your parents, your wife, your children.…

We went as tourists. We got our passports and tourist visas in El Salvador to enter Guatemala and Mexico. It was all legal to Mexico. We worked in Guadalajara for several months and made good friends there. Those first months, we…were exhausted from worrying about our families who we had left behind. We wrote them letters every day, but had no idea if they were getting through or not.

But we had to keep on to achieve our goal…and that was to get to the United States. To Idaho, really, because my cousin was working there, and it was he who had been sending us money ever since we left El Salvador.… We had to pay the *coyote* $700 each to cross us from Tijuana [Mexico] to Los Angeles.

Crossing was dangerous business.… Our only objective was to arrive, just to arrive. Dead on our feet, we arrived about 6 A.M. in San Diego. At 9 A.M. a car came and put six of us in the trunk. Six people!… And it was a small trunk. Well that is how we got from San Diego to Los Angeles.… We arrived stiff and sore, exhausted, and nearly starving.…

We stayed in Los Angeles for three days waiting for my cousin to send us our plane tickets [to get to Idaho].…

We stayed [in Idaho] until October, working in the fields, irrigating, planting,

harvesting sugar beets, wheat, beans, everything.... After the growing season was over, we were trying to decide what to do and there was this...family that was going to Florida. They took us there for $600.

We arrived in Wahneta [Florida].... I worked first in oranges; I was an orange picker. I wanted to do other jobs that I was qualified for, such as being a mason, but the problem was our immigration papers. We still didn't have them. The next year we got them on June 27, 1983.

If I have to choose which country I love more, of course, I have to say my country. But there I could not be free.... Here [the United States] at least I am free, I can go to the movies or anywhere I want. But there you can't do that even at three in the afternoon much less at seven in the

evening, because of the violence....

Meanwhile, my wife Rosa was still in El Salvador. This was 1983. She arrived here November 8, 1984, two years after José Dimas and myself....

I have applied for permission for my parents to come here, but I haven't heard anything yet.... That's the hard part for me, to know that they're getting older, and maybe God will take them away before I can see them again.

We decided that we needed to do everything possible for our children. I told my wife that we must make the effort for them. My *papá* knew the day that my wife and kids left to join me that I would never return, and he was right. But I told him that we are looking to our kids' future, and I do not regret it....

We have much to be grateful for....

Write Your Answers

Answer these questions in the assignment section of your notebook.

1. Why did Ricardo Murillo want to leave El Salvador?

2. Through which countries did Murillo travel to reach the United States?

3. What dangers did Murillo face in coming to the United States?

4. What types of work has Murillo done in El Salvador and in the United States?

5. How does Murillo feel about the countries he has lived in?

Clara McBride Hale 1905-1992

Clara McBride Hale started Hale House, the first home in the nation for babies addicted to drugs or alcohol. These babies were born to mothers who had abused drugs and alcohol. Because of her work with these children, Mrs. Hale became known as Mother Hale.

Mrs. Hale's husband died when she was only 27. To earn money for her family, she cleaned theaters at night and did child care work during the day.

One day in 1969, Mrs. Hale's daughter, Lorraine, found a drug-addicted mother and her baby on a sidewalk. She sent the woman with a note for help to Mrs. Hale. Mrs. Hale didn't know the woman, but she recognized her daughter's handwriting. Mrs. Hale cared for the baby while its mother received treatment for her drug problem.

Within 2 months, Mother Hale was caring for 22 drug-addicted babies in her Harlem apartment. She helped each baby go through the difficult period of withdrawing from drugs.

To care for the many babies that were brought to her, Mother Hale moved to a five-story house in Harlem that became Hale House. There she lived with her workers and the drug-addicted babies. Mother Hale cared for the sickest babies in her own bedroom. Race and religion were not important to Hale; she wanted all children to get well.

After AIDS became a serious problem, Hale House began a program to care for babies with HIV, the virus that causes AIDS.

In 1985 President Reagan invited Mother Hale to sit with Mrs. Reagan while he gave his State of the Union address. During his speech Reagan called Hale "a true American hero." Everyone in the audience stood up and clapped for her.

Mrs. Hale died in 1992 when she was 87. She had loved and cared for more than 1,000 drug-addicted babies. She had shown that one person can improve a community. Dr. Lorraine Hale, now the Hale House president, continues the work that her mother began.

In Your Own Words

Write a paragraph in your journal that explains why Mother Hale was "a true American hero."

REVIEW AND APPLY

- American society is quickly changing in many ways.

- Three major problems facing the United States in the 1990s are poverty, crime, and drugs.

- AIDS is a serious health problem in the United States because it is spreading so rapidly and no cure has yet been found for this disease.

- Terrorist acts are a growing threat to the United States.

- There is disagreement among our leaders in Washington about the best way to reduce the national debt.

VOCABULARY

Find the Meaning ■ Write in your social studies notebook the word or phrase that best completes each sentence.

1. As more people come to the United States from many different countries, American society is becoming more _____ .
   privatized   multicultural   addicted

2. People whose income falls below the _____ are considered poor.
   budget   depression   poverty line

3. Using drugs in a way that is not correct is known as _____ .
   drug abuse   addiction   disease

4. The _____ causes the AIDS disease.
   crack cocaine   HIV virus   drug abuse

5. The _____ is a plan for how the government will spend tax money to pay for government programs.
   budget   balanced budget   national debt

6. _____ allows private companies to run government programs.
   Monopolies   Budget cuts   Privatization

7. Scientists are trying to create a _____ to prevent AIDS.
   virus   vaccine   security

USING INFORMATION

Writing an Essay ■ There are six reasons why American society is changing so quickly. List and explain four of these reasons. Start your essay with a topic sentence.

COMPREHENSION CHECK

Choose the Answer ■ Write in your social studies notebook, the letter of the word or phrase that best answers each question.

1. In what way is the American family changing?

   a. Families are becoming larger.
   b. There are more one-parent families.
   c. All children are more educated.

2. In what way is American society changing?

   a. American society is becoming more multicultural.
   b. American society is becoming more wealthy.
   c. American society has fewer elderly people.

3. What is the government's "War on Drugs" trying to accomplish?

   a. to legalize marijuana
   b. to stop illegal drugs from entering the country
   c. to sell drugs in stores

4. What must happen before a President's budget can be put into action?

   a. It must be approved by Congress.
   b. It must be balanced.
   c. It must be voted on by the people.

CRITICAL THINKING

Distinguishing Relevant Information ■ Imagine that you are telling your friend about the difficult challenges facing American society today. Read each sentence below. Decide which sentences are relevant to what you will say. Write in your social studies notebook the relevant sentences. There are four relevant sentences.

1. More women are working at jobs that in the past were done only by men.

2. Many Americans criticize immigrants.

3. There are more murders in the United States than in other nations.

4. Bill Clinton was elected President in 1992.

5. Some Americans want a Balanced Budget Amendment.

6. Terrorism is a growing threat in the United States.

448

ENTERING THE NEXT CENTURY

◀ *A computer chip*

Focus on Main Ideas

1. What progress has been made in the field of equal rights and opportunities?
2. How has technology improved life in America?
3. How have Americans harmed their environment and resources?
4. How can Americans help their nation's future?

People

Mae Carol Jemison • Ellen Ochoa • David Duke • Rodney King • Ben Nighthorse Campbell • Carol Moseley Braun • Sally Ride • Guion Bluford, Jr. • Christa McAuliffe

New Vocabulary

disabilities • environmental pollution • emissions • global warming • renewable resources • nonrenewable resources • solar energy • microchip • microsurgery • lasers • fiber-optic cables • Internet • electronic mail

In 1992 Mae Carol Jemison became the first African American woman in space. The next year Ellen Ochoa, the first Hispanic woman in space, took part in a ten-day space mission. Progress in technology made these exciting space flights possible. The space flights also showed that women and minorities were winning equal rights and opportunities.

Equal Rights and Opportunities

Despite the kinds of achievements described above, racism and prejudice are still problems in the United States. This became clear in 1991 when David Duke became a candidate for governor in Louisiana. At one time Duke had been a Ku Klux Klan leader and a member of the American Nazi party. Duke lost the election. However, millions of Americans were upset because Duke had supported hate and racism but was still able to win a large number of votes.

Prejudice was also part of the Rodney King case. After a car chase, King, an African American, was caught and then badly beaten by four white Los Angeles police officers. A jury of white men and women decided that the officers were not guilty. In

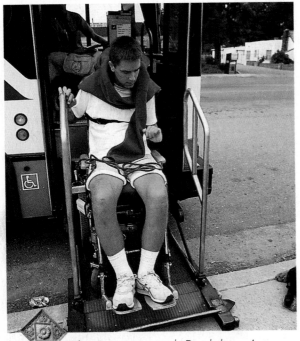

The Americans with Disabilities Act requires that public transportation, businesses, and other public facilities be designed so that all people can use them.

The fight for civil rights has also helped Americans with **disabilities.** In the past, they were unable to use public transportation, and they faced discrimination when they applied for jobs. The Civil Rights Act of 1964 was the first law to help people with disabilities. In 1975 the law called Education for All Handicapped Children was passed. It required all states to provide free education for students with disabilities. Then in 1990 Congress passed the Americans with Disabilities Act, which is often called the ADA. This law makes it illegal to discriminate when a person with a disability applies for a job. It requires public transportation and public places to be designed so that all people can use them.

Progress in Space

After *Apollo 11* went to the moon in 1969, there were other *Apollo* space missions to the moon. New technology made further space exploration possible. Before 1981, each spaceship could be used for one space mission. In 1981 the first reusable spaceship, the space shuttle, was sent into space. Two years later Sally Ride traveled in the space shuttle when she became America's first woman astronaut. The next year Guion Bluford, Jr., became the first African American astronaut.

In January 1986 Americans were shocked when the *Challenger* space shuttle exploded after takeoff. All seven crew members died, including a teacher named Christa McAuliffe. She was the first civilian to travel in space. All space shuttle missions were stopped for two years while the safety of the space shuttle was improved.

response some African Americans started a riot in Los Angeles. Later the Rodney King case went on trial in a federal court. Two of the officers were found guilty.

Although prejudice and racism still exist in the United States, great progress has been made in allowing equal rights and opportunities for all Americans. In 1993 Ben Nighthorse Campbell became the first Native American to be elected to the United States Senate. That same year Carol Moseley Braun became the first African American woman in the Senate. During the mid-1990s, about forty African Americans were elected to the House of Representatives. After Bill Clinton became President, he formed a cabinet with three women, two Hispanic Americans, four African Americans, and seven white men.

By 1986 space travel had become almost routine. The explosion of the space shuttle *Challenger in 1986 shocked the nation. The Challenger had been into space nine times before the disaster and was considered to be very safe. All seven crew members died in the accident.*

In 1995 an American space shuttle docked with the Russian space station *Mir*. American and Russian astronauts worked together in space for more than three months. That same year the unmanned spaceship *Galileo* reached the planet Jupiter after traveling millions of miles from Earth. It sent information about Jupiter back to the United States.

Protecting Our Environment and Resources

Cars, airplanes, and modern factories are some of the modern inventions that have created **environmental pollution**.

Environmental pollution occurs when human activities harm the environment. Factory smoke, car **emissions**, traffic noise, and crop pesticides are some of the things that damage Earth's air, soil, and water.

Some scientists believe that air pollution is causing **global warming**, or a rise in the earth's temperature. Global warming is said to be caused by the burning of oil, gasoline, and coal in order to make energy. To prevent global warming, scientists will need to find cleaner ways to burn fuels.

The United States is fortunate to have many kinds of resources. America has some **renewable resources,** such as trees and animals, which can be replaced.

451

Conservation helps us save our renewable resources. To save America's forests, new trees must be planted when forests are chopped down.

Nonrenewable resources, such as coal, and oil, can never be replaced if they are used up. As we use up America's supply of oil and natural gas, we become more dependent on other nations to meet our energy needs. This dependence may lead to another energy crisis. Our nonrenewable resources can be saved for tomorrow by our using less energy today.

Scientists are also inventing new ways to produce energy. In California, wind farms now produce some of that state's electricity. **Solar energy**, or energy from the sun, is producing electricity, heating homes, and making hot water.

Recycling is one of the best ways to protect our natural resources. Recycling means reusing old products to create new ones. Glass, newspapers, plastic, and metal products can be recycled and made into new products. Many communities now have facilities or collection places for recycling.

Technology Improves the Nation

Modern technology can help us care for our nation's environment and resources. Technology has also improved the nation

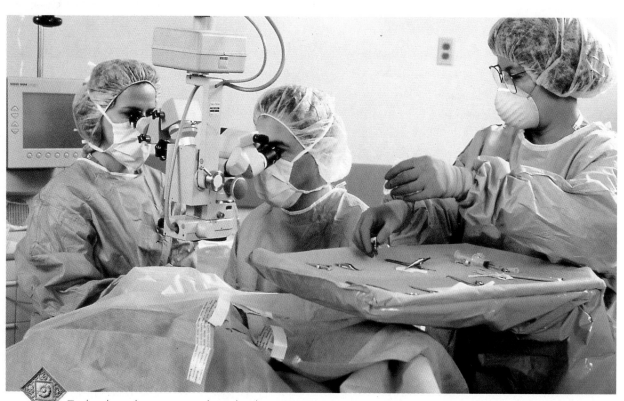

Technology has improved medical care. Many operations that in the past were difficult or impossible to do have become easier. Powerful microscopes allow doctors to see in great detail and to use tiny instruments in surgery. Technology has also helped find medicines that make surgery unnecessary.

in other ways. Computers are now used in almost every school, business, airport, and hospital. The invention of the **microchip** made it possible to build smaller, cheaper, and more powerful computers.

Today, computers, rather than people, operate many machines in factories. Many factory workers have lost their jobs to computers. However, new jobs have been created in the computer industry.

Technology has improved medical care. Doctors have learned to perform operations by using **microsurgery**, surgery done with microscopes and special tiny instruments. Many types of operations are now done with powerful beams of light called **lasers**. The lasers can cut without causing damage to surrounding areas.

Technology has also changed the way we communicate. The invention of **fiber-optic cables** has improved telephone communications. Better computers and fiber-optic cables have allowed millions of people to use the **Internet**. The Internet is a system that links millions of computers to each other. The Internet allows people to gather information from other computers around the world. Computer users can also communicate with each other through **electronic mail**. One computer user can send messages to other computers anywhere in the world in only a few seconds.

Fiber-optic cables use light to send information. This technology has improved communication by telephone and by computer.

Democracy for the Next Century

After winning their independence, Americans started a democracy that has lasted more than 200 years. Our democratic government has allowed the United States to become the strongest, richest, and most powerful nation in the world today. Unfortunately the right to vote is less important to many Americans today than it was long ago. Less than half of all citizens voted in the most recent presidential elections. To make sure the United States continues to be a government by the people, more citizens must vote for their nation's leaders.

As you approach the next century, you can help the United States continue to be a land of liberty. By reading newspapers and listening to news reports, you can form wise opinions about what actions our government leaders should take. You can influence members of Congress and the President by sending your opinion to them. Of most importance, you will have a voice in American democracy by using your right to vote. As you work for America's future, you will be part of the next chapter of America's history.

$\mathcal{B}$IOGRAPHY

Bill Gates 1955–

Bill Gates created Microsoft, the world's largest computer software company. When Gates was a boy, computers were not yet being used in homes and classrooms. He used a computer for the first time at age 12.

After finishing high school, Gates went to Harvard University to study law. Gates liked working with computers more than studying law, so he dropped out of Harvard.

In 1975 Gates and his close friend, Paul Allen, started a company called Microsoft. Their goal was to create computer software for the popular new PCs, or personal computers, that were beginning to be sold. A computer needs different kinds of software in order to do jobs such as typing a report, writing a check, storing information, or making a poster. Gates and Allen began creating software for large computer companies such as Apple and Radio Shack.

In 1980 IBM, an important computer company, asked Gates to create a new operating system, or operating directions, for all of its PC computers. Gates created a new system called the Microsoft Disc Operating System, or MS-DOS. All IBM

PCs needed MS-DOS to run other software programs. Many computer companies built similar PCs that also used DOS. Because 85 percent of America's PCs now use MS-DOS, they can also use other Microsoft software. Soon the Microsoft company was earning millions of dollars.

In 1985 Microsoft introduced a new software program called Windows. Windows makes it possible to do several jobs on a computer at the same time. Millions of copies of Windows were sold, and Microsoft grew richer.

Microsoft programs are now being used by millions of people around the world. Bill Gates, now a billionaire, works six days a week so that Microsoft will continue to develop new programs.

Bill Gates was able to build a giant company because of his own talents and willingness to work very hard.

In Your Own Words

Write a paragraph in your social studies journal that tells how Bill Gates has helped computer technology.

REVIEW AND APPLY

CHAPTER 37 MAIN IDEAS

- Although prejudice and racism still exist in the United States, great progress has been made in allowing equal rights and opportunities for all Americans.

- The United States continues to make progress in space.

- Technology such as the computer, microsurgery, lasers, and fiber optics have improved the nation.

- Environmental pollution caused by factory smoke, car emissions, traffic noise, and crop pesticides is damaging the environment.

- Technology, new inventions, and recycling are ways that are helping Americans care for the environment and for natural resources.

- More American citizens must vote if the United States is going to continue to be a government by the people.

VOCABULARY

Finish the Sentence ■ Choose one of the words or phrases from the box to complete each sentence. Write the correct word or phrase in your social studies notebook. You will not use all the words in the box.

1. The Education for All Handicapped Children law helped people with _____ .

2. The _____ made it possible to build smaller, cheaper, and more powerful computers.

3. The _____ is a system that links millions of computers to each other.

4. _____ allows computer owners to use their computers to communicate with each other.

5. _____ occurs when human activities harm the environment.

6. _____ is a rise in the earth's temperature.

7. _____ are things that can be replaced, like forests.

8. _____ uses the power of the sun.

> electronic mail
> solar energy
> fiber-optic cables
> global warming
> microchip
> renewable resources
> Internet
> disabilities
> environmental pollution

COMPREHENSION CHECK

Create an Information Chart ■ Copy and complete the chart below by listing at least two ways that Americans are preparing for the next century.

Area	How Americans Are Preparing for the Next Century
Equal Rights	
Technology	
Environment	
Democracy	

CRITICAL THINKING

Making Predictions ■ Read the paragraph below and the sentences that follow it. Write in your social studies notebook three sentences that predict what will happen in the twenty-first century.

As Americans prepare themselves for the twenty-first century, many changes are taking place in American society. More American women and minorities are gaining equal rights. These Americans are working as doctors, lawyers, and military officers. Technology is also changing the ways Americans live. Personal computers are becoming a part of many Americans' lives. Also more Americans are becoming concerned about saving Earth's environment and natural resources.

1. All the best jobs in the twenty-first century will be held by women.

2. More Americans in the twenty-first century will use computers.

3. Recycling will mean more natural resources will be available in the twenty-first century.

4. New technology will continue to change the lives of Americans.

5. New voting laws will be passed in the twenty-first century.

USING INFORMATION

Writing an Opinion ■ Your text concludes by discussing the importance of voting in America. Write a paragraph in your social studies notebook that explains why you think voting is so important in a democracy. What do you think will happen if Americans continue to choose not to vote for their political leaders?

456

SOCIAL STUDIES SKILLS

Reading a Flow Chart

A flow chart is used to show a sequence of events. One event follows another on a flow chart.

The flow chart on this page shows the steps that are needed to recycle newspapers and turn them into new paper products. Notice that there are seven events or steps in this flow chart. The steps are numbered, and Step 1 is in the upper left-hand corner of the flow chart.

The Process of Recycling Newspaper

1. Newspaper is separated from garbage.

2. Newspaper is sent to a recycling plant.

3. Cardboard and magazine paper is removed.

4. Newspapers are chopped and mixed with water and chemicals to make pulp.

5. Ink is removed from pulp.

6. Pulp is spread over a moving wire screen. Water drips out, leaving paper fibers. Rollers press fibers into a thin layer that becomes paper.

7. **RECYCLED PRODUCTS**
Recycled paper is made into new products such as newspapers, paper towels, and egg cartons.

Study the flow chart. Then write in your social studies notebook the answers to the following questions.

1. What happens in the first recycling step?

2. What happens when newspaper reaches a recycling plant?

3. In which step do rollers press fibers into a thin layer?

4. What kinds of products are made from recycled newspapers?

5. How does recycling newspaper protect the environment and conserve our resources?

Unit 9 Review

Study the time line on this page. You may want to read parts of Unit 9 again. Then use the words and dates in the box to finish the paragraphs. In the assignment section of your notebook, write the numbers 1–15.

1979 Iranians take 52 Americans as hostages.

1986 The *Challenger* space shuttle explodes.

1990 Germany becomes a united nation.

1991 The United States defeats Iraq in the Persian Gulf War.

1993 The United States signs NAFTA.

1996 Free elections take place in Russia.

1975 · · · 1985 · · · 1995

1981 The United States sends the first space shuttle into space.

1985 Mikhail Gorbachev becomes the leader of the Soviet Union.

1989 The Berlin Wall is torn down.

1990 Americans with Disabilities Act is passed.

1991 The Soviet Union breaks apart.

1995 Bosnian leaders create a peace agreement in Dayton, Ohio.

Mikhail Gorbachev	hostages	space shuttles
Egypt	1981	1991
Soviet Union	medical care	republics
nuclear weapons	Bosnia	glasnost
NAFTA	Camp David Accords	Berlin Wall

President Jimmy Carter helped Israel and ___1___ sign the first peace treaty between Israel and an Arab nation. The treaty, signed in 1979, was called the ___2___ . That same year, 52 Americans were taken as ___3___ in Iran. The Americans were not freed until Ronald Reagan became President in January ___4___ . In 1985, ___5___ became the leader of the Soviet Union.

He began to allow more freedom, or ___6___ , in his country. Gorbachev and Reagan signed the INF Treaty in 1987 to eliminate many ___7___ . In 1989 the ___8___ was torn down, and the Cold War ended.

An army from Iraq invaded Kuwait. During the Persian Gulf War in ___9___ , the United States forced the Iraqi army to leave Kuwait.

At the end of that year, Mikhail Gorbachev resigned, and the ___10___ fell apart. It became 15 independent ___11___ .

To improve trade with Canada and Mexico, the United States signed ___12___ in 1993. The United States helped leaders from ___13___ write a peace agreement in Dayton, Ohio.

American technology led to the invention of reusable spaceships called ___14___ . Technology has also improved computers, communication, and ___15___ .

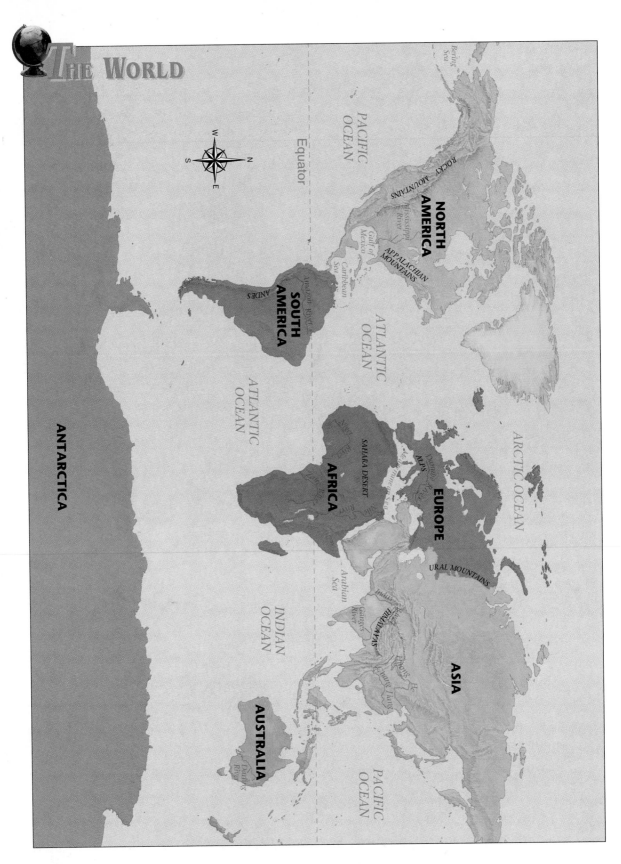

THE WORLD

PACIFIC OCEAN

Equator

NORTH AMERICA

ROCKY MOUNTAINS

Mississippi River

Gulf of Mexico

Caribbean Sea

APPALACHIAN MOUNTAINS

ATLANTIC OCEAN

SOUTH AMERICA

ANDES

Amazon River

ATLANTIC OCEAN

ANTARCTICA

AFRICA

SAHARA DESERT

Niger River

Congo River

ALPS

Danube River

EUROPE

ARCTIC OCEAN

URAL MOUNTAINS

Arabian Sea

INDIAN OCEAN

Ganges River

Indus River

HIMALAYAS

ASIA

Huang He

Chang Jiang

AUSTRALIA

Darling River

PACIFIC OCEAN

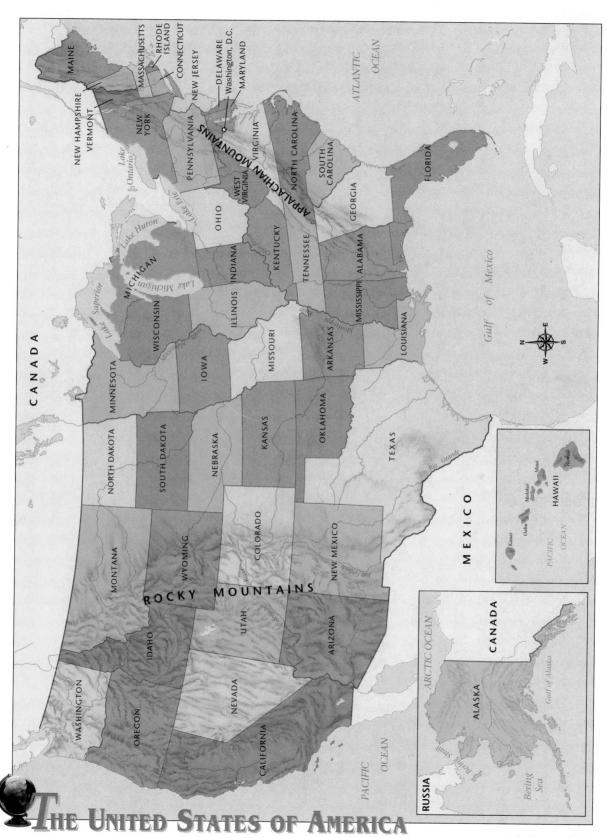

MAINE

MASSACHUSETTS
RHODE ISLAND
CONNECTICUT
NEW JERSEY
DELAWARE
Washington, D.C.
MARYLAND

NEW HAMPSHIRE
VERMONT

NEW YORK

ATLANTIC
OCEAN

Lake Ontario

Lake Erie

PENNSYLVANIA

VIRGINIA

APPALACHIAN MOUNTAINS

NORTH CAROLINA

SOUTH CAROLINA

GEORGIA

WEST VIRGINIA

OHIO

Ohio River

KENTUCKY

TENNESSEE

ALABAMA

FLORIDA

CANADA

Lake Superior

Lake Huron

Lake Michigan

MICHIGAN

WISCONSIN

Mississippi River

MINNESOTA

IOWA

ILLINOIS

INDIANA

MISSOURI

Mississippi

ARKANSAS

MISSISSIPPI

LOUISIANA

Gulf of Mexico

N
E
S
W

NORTH DAKOTA

SOUTH DAKOTA

NEBRASKA

KANSAS

OKLAHOMA

TEXAS

Rio Grande

MEXICO

COLORADO

NEW MEXICO

ROCKY MOUNTAINS

MONTANA

WYOMING

UTAH

ARIZONA

IDAHO

Rio Grande

NEVADA

WASHINGTON

OREGON

CALIFORNIA

PACIFIC
OCEAN

Niihau
Maui
Molokai
Oahu
HAWAII
Kauai

PACIFIC
OCEAN

ARCTIC OCEAN

CANADA

ALASKA

Gulf of Alaska

RUSSIA

Bering Strait

Bering
Sea

THE UNITED STATES OF AMERICA

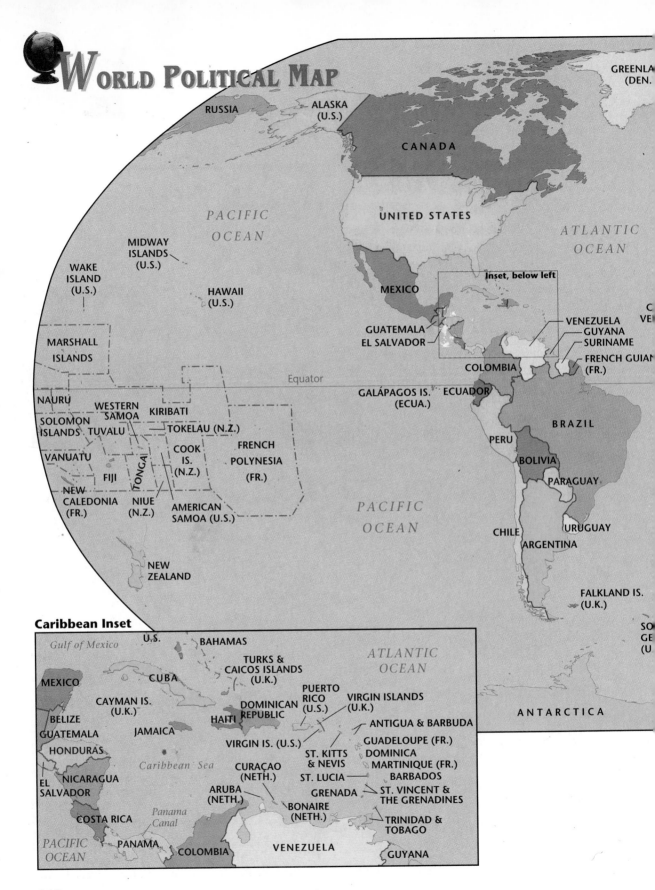

GREENLA
(DEN.

RUSSIA

ALASKA
(U.S.)

CANADA

PACIFIC
OCEAN

UNITED STATES

ATLANTIC
OCEAN

MIDWAY
ISLANDS
(U.S.)

WAKE
ISLAND
(U.S.)

HAWAII
(U.S.)

MEXICO

Inset, below left

GUATEMALA
EL SALVADOR

VENEZUELA
GUYANA
SURINAME

C
VE

MARSHALL
ISLANDS

COLOMBIA

FRENCH GUIAN
(FR.)

Equator

GALÁPAGOS IS.
(ECUA.)

ECUADOR

NAURU

WESTERN
SAMOA

KIRIBATI

PERU

BRAZIL

SOLOMON
ISLANDS

TUVALU

TOKELAU (N.Z.)

BOLIVIA

VANUATU

COOK
IS.
(N.Z.)

FRENCH
POLYNESIA
(FR.)

PARAGUAY

FIJI

TONGA

NEW
CALEDONIA
(FR.)

NIUE
(N.Z.)

AMERICAN
SAMOA (U.S.)

PACIFIC
OCEAN

CHILE

URUGUAY

ARGENTINA

NEW
ZEALAND

FALKLAND IS.
(U.K.)

SO
GE
(U

Caribbean Inset

Gulf of Mexico

U.S.

BAHAMAS

ATLANTIC
OCEAN

TURKS &
CAICOS ISLANDS
(U.K.)

MEXICO

CUBA

CAYMAN IS.
(U.K.)

PUERTO
RICO
(U.S.)

VIRGIN ISLANDS
(U.K.)

DOMINICAN
REPUBLIC

BELIZE

HAITI

ANTARCTICA

GUATEMALA

JAMAICA

VIRGIN IS. (U.S.)

ANTIGUA & BARBUDA

HONDURAS

Caribbean Sea

CURAÇAO
(NETH.)

ST. KITTS
& NEVIS

GUADELOUPE (FR.)
DOMINICA
MARTINIQUE (FR.)

EL
SALVADOR

NICARAGUA

ARUBA
(NETH.)

ST. LUCIA

BARBADOS

GRENADA

ST. VINCENT &
THE GRENADINES

COSTA RICA

Panama
Canal

BONAIRE
(NETH.)

TRINIDAD &
TOBAGO

PACIFIC
OCEAN

PANAMA

COLOMBIA

VENEZUELA

GUYANA

SVALBARD
(NOR.)

ARCTIC OCEAN

D

Inset, below right

RUSSIA

KAZAKSTAN

MONGOLIA

UZBEKISTAN
KYRGYZSTAN
TURKMENISTAN
TAJIKISTAN

NORTH
KOREA

SOUTH
KOREA

JAPAN

CHINA

Mediterranean Sea

CCO

IRAN
AFGHANISTAN

BHUTAN

PACIFIC
OCEAN

NORTHERN
MARIANA
ISLANDS (U.S.)

ALGERIA
LIBYA
EGYPT
KUWAIT
IRAQ

BAHRAIN
QATAR
PAKISTAN

NEPAL

HONG
KONG

ARA
)

SAUDI
ARABIA

UNITED ARAB
EMIRATES

INDIA

MYANMAR

LAOS

MACAO

TAIWAN

TANIA
MALI
NIGER

OMAN

BANGLADESH

THAILAND

VIETNAM

PHILIPPINES

GUAM (U.S.)

CHAD

ERITREA

YEMEN

FEDERATED
STATES
OF MICRONESIA

8

SUDAN

DJIBOUTI

SRI
LANKA

CAMBODIA

PALAU

11
NIGERIA

ETHIOPIA

BRUNEI

7   9
10

12

15

SOMALIA

MALDIVES

MALAYSIA

UATORIAL
GUINEA

13 14
RWANDA

UGANDA

KENYA

SINGAPORE

I N D O N E S I A

PAPUA
NEW
GUINEA

TOMÉ &
PRÍNCIPE

BURUNDI

ZAIRE

TANZANIA

SEYCHELLES

SOLOMON
ISLANDS

CABINDA
(ANG.)

MALAWI

COMOROS

ANGOLA

ZAMBIA

ANTIC

EAN

ZIMBABWE

MADAGASCAR

INDIAN

OCEAN

NAMIBIA

BOTSWANA

MAURITIUS

AUSTRALIA

SENEGAL
GAMBIA
GUINEA-BISSAU
GUINEA
SIERRA LEONE
LIBERIA
CÔTE D'IVOIRE
BURKINA FASO
GHANA
TOGO
BENIN
CAMEROON
GABON
CONGO
CENTRAL AFRICAN
REPUBLIC

SOUTH
AFRICA

MOZAMBIQUE

SWAZILAND

LESOTHO

N
W   E
S

Europe Inset

NORWAY
SWEDEN

ESTONIA

LATVIA

NETHERLANDS

DENMARK

(RUSSIA)

LITHUANIA

RUSSIA

IRELAND

UNITED
KINGDOM

GERMANY

POLAND

BELARUS

BELGIUM

CZECH
REPUBLIC

SLOVAK
REPUBLIC

UKRAINE

ATLANTIC
OCEAN

LUXEMBOURG

LIECH.

SWITZ.

AUSTRIA

HUNGARY

MOLDOVA

FRANCE

SAN
MARINO

SLOVENIA

CROATIA

ROMANIA

ANDORRA

MONACO

ITALY

BOSNIA
AND
HERZ.

YUGO-
SLAVIA

BULGARIA

GEORGIA

PORTUGAL

SPAIN

VATICAN
CITY

ALBANIA

MACEDONIA

GREECE

TURKEY

ARMENIA

AZERBAIJAN

GIBRALTAR
(U.K.)

MALTA

CYPRUS

SYRIA

IRAN

MEDITERRANEAN Sea

LEBANON

IRAQ

MOROCCO

ALGERIA

TUNISIA

ISRAEL

(WEST
BANK)

LIBYA

EGYPT

JORDAN

463

		date of statehood (order)	area in square miles (rank)	1995 pop estimate (rank)	state symbols
Alabama Montgomery		1819 (22nd)	51,718 (29th)	4,252,982 (22nd)	state tree . . . . Southern pine state flower . . . . Camellia state bird . . . . Yellowhammer
Alaska Juneau		1959 (49th)	589,878 (1st)	603,617 (48th)	state tree . . . . Sitka spruce state flower . . . . Forget-me-not state bird . . . . Willow ptarmigan
Arizona Phoenix		1912 (48th)	114,007 (6th)	4,217,940 (23rd)	state tree . . . . Paloverde state flower . . . . Saguaro cactus blossom state bird . . . . Cactus wren
Arkansas Little Rock		1836 (25th)	53,183 (27th)	2,483,769 (33rd)	state tree . . . . Pine tree state flower . . . . Apple blossom state bird . . . . Mockingbird
California Sacramento		1850 (31st)	158,648 (3rd)	31,589,153 (1st)	state tree . . . . California redwood state flower . . . . Golden poppy state bird . . . . California valley quail
Colorado Denver		1876 (38th)	104,091 (8th)	3,746,585 (25th)	state tree . . . . Blue spruce state flower . . . . . Rocky Mountain columbine state bird . . . . Lark bunting
Connecticut Hartford		1788 (5th)	5,006 (48th)	3,274,599 (28th)	state tree . . . . White oak state flower . . . . Mountain laurel state bird . . . . Robin
Delaware Dover		1787 (1st)	2,026 (49th)	710,961 (46th)	state tree . . . . American holly state flower . . . . Peach blossom state bird . . . . Blue hen chicken
Florida Tallahassee		1845 (27th)	58,681 (22nd)	14,165,570 (4th)	state tree . . . . Sabal palmetto palm state flower . . . . Orange blossom state bird . . . . Mockingbird
Georgia Atlanta		1788 (4th)	58,930 (21st)	7,200,882 (10th)	state tree . . . . Live oak state flower . . . . Cherokee rose state bird . . . . Brown thrasher

		date of statehood (order)	area in square miles (rank)	1995 pop estimate (rank)	state symbols
Hawaii Honolulu		1959 (50th)	6,459 (47th)	1,186,815 (40th)	state tree . . . . Kukui state flower . . . . Yellow hibiscus state bird . . . . Nene (Hawaiian goose)
Idaho Boise		1890 (43rd)	83,574 (13th)	1,163,261 (41st)	state tree . . . . White pine state flower . . . . Syringa state bird . . . . Mountain bluebird
Illinois Springfield		1818 (21st)	56,343 (24th)	11,829,940 (6th)	state tree . . . . White oak state flower . . . . Native violet state bird . . . . Cardinal
Indiana Indianapolis		1816 (19th)	36,185 (38th)	5,803,471 (14th)	state tree . . . . Tulip tree state flower . . . . Peony state bird . . . . Cardinal
Iowa Des Moines		1846 (29th)	56,276 (25th)	2,841,764 (30th)	state tree . . . . Oak state flower . . . . Wild rose state bird . . . . Eastern goldfinch
Kansas Topeka		1861 (34th)	82,282 (14th)	2,565,328 (33rd)	state tree . . . . Cottonwood state flower . . . . Sunflower state bird . . . . Western meadowlark
Kentucky Frankfort		1792 (15th)	40,395 (37th)	3,860,219 (24th)	state tree . . . . Kentucky coffee tree state flower . . . . Goldenrod state bird . . . . Kentucky cardinal
Louisiana Baton Rouge		1812 (18th)	47,752 (31st)	4,342,334 (21st)	state tree . . . . Bald cypress state flower . . . . Magnolia state bird . . . . Brown pelican
Maine Augusta		1820 (23rd)	33,128 (39th)	1,241,382 (39th)	state tree . . . . White pine state flower . . . . . . White pine cone & tassel state bird . . . . Chickadee
Maryland Annapolis		1788 (7th)	10,455 (42nd)	5,042,438 (19th)	state tree . . . . White oak state flower . . . . Black-eyed Susan state bird . . . . Baltimore oriole

		date of statehood (order)	area in square miles (rank)	1995 pop estimate (rank)	state symbols
Massachusetts Boston		1788 (6th)	8,257 (45th)	6,073,550 (13th)	state tree . . . . American elm state flower . . . . Mayflower (trailing arbutus) state bird . . . . Chickadee
Michigan Lansing		1837 (26th)	58,513 (23rd)	9,549,353 (8th)	state tree . . . . White pine state flower . . . . Apple blossom state bird . . . . Robin
Minnesota St. Paul		1858 (32nd)	84,397 (12th)	4,609,548 (20th)	state tree . . . . Norway pine state flower . . . . Pink and white lady's slipper state bird . . . . Common loon
Mississippi Jackson		1817 (20th)	47,716 (32nd)	2,697,243 (31st)	state tree . . . . Magnolia state flower . . . . Magnolia state bird . . . . Mockingbird
Missouri Jefferson City		1821 (24th)	69,686 (19th)	5,323,523 (16th)	state tree . . . . Flowering dogwood state flower . . . . Hawthorn state bird . . . . Bluebird
Montana Helena		1889 (41st)	147,047 (4th)	870,281 (44th)	state tree . . . . Ponderosa pine state flower . . . . Bitterroot state bird . . . . Western meadowlark
Nebraska Lincoln		1867 (37th)	77,359 (15th)	1,637,112 (37th)	state tree . . . . Cottonwood state flower . . . . Goldenrod state bird . . . . Western meadowlark
Nevada Carson City		1864 (36th)	110,561 (7th)	1,530,108 (38th)	state tree . . . . Single-leaf piñon & bristlecone pine state flower . . . . Sagebrush state bird . . . . Mountain bluebird
New Hampshire Concord		1788 (9th)	9,283 (44th)	1,148,253 (42nd)	state tree . . . . White birch state flower . . . . Purple lilac state bird . . . . Purple finch
New Jersey Trenton		1787 (3rd)	7,790 (46th)	7,945,298 (9th)	state tree . . . . Red oak state flower . . . . Purple violet state bird . . . . Eastern goldfinch

466

		date of statehood (order)	area in square miles (rank)	1995 pop estimate (rank)	state symbols
New Mexico Santa Fe		1912 (47th)	121,593 (5th)	1,685,401 (36th)	state tree . . . . Piñon state flower . . . . Yucca state bird . . . . Roadrunner
New York Albany		1788 (11th)	49,112 (30th)	18,136,081 (3rd)	state tree . . . . Sugar maple state flower . . . . Rose state bird . . . . Bluebird
North Carolina Raleigh		1789 (12th)	52,672 (28th)	7,195,138 (11th)	state tree . . . . Pine state flower . . . . Flowering dogwood state bird . . . . Cardinal
North Dakota Bismarck		1889 (39th)	70,704 (17th)	641,367 (47th)	state tree . . . . American elm state flower . . . . Wild prairie rose state bird . . . . Western meadowlark
Ohio Columbus		1803 (17th)	41,328 (35th)	11,150,506 (7th)	state tree . . . . Buckeye state flower . . . . Scarlet carnation state bird . . . . Cardinal
Oklahoma Oklahoma City		1907 (46th)	69,919 (18th)	3,277,687 (27th)	state tree . . . . Redbud state flower . . . . Mistletoe state bird . . . . Scissortailed flycatcher
Oregon Salem		1859 (33rd)	97,052 (10th)	3,140,585 (29th)	state tree . . . . Douglas fir state flower . . . . Oregon grape state bird . . . . Western meadowlark
Pennsylvania Harrisburg		1787 (2nd)	45,308 (33rd)	12,071,842 (5th)	state tree . . . . Hemlock state flower . . . . Mountain laurel state bird . . . . Ruffed grouse
Rhode Island Providence		1790 (13th)	1,213 (50th)	989,794 (43rd)	state tree . . . . Red maple state flower . . . . Violet state bird . . . . Rhode Island Red
South Carolina Columbia		1788 (8th)	31,113 (40th)	3,673,287 (26th)	state tree . . . . Palmetto state flower . . . . Yellow jessamine state bird . . . . Carolina wren

		date of statehood (order)	area in square miles (rank)	1995 pop estimate (rank)	state symbols

South Dakota
Pierre

1889 (40th)	77,122 (16th)	729,034 (45th)	state tree.............Black Hills spruce state flower........American pasqueflower state bird..........Ring-necked pheasant

Tennessee
Nashville

1796 (16th)	42,146 (34th)	5,256,051 (17th)	state tree ....Tulip poplar state flower...........................Iris state bird ....Mockingbird

Texas
Austin

1845 (28th)	266,874 (2nd)	18,723,991 (2nd)	state tree ....Pecan state flower.................Bluebonnet state bird ....Mockingbird

Utah
Salt Lake City

1896 (45th)	84,905 (11th)	1,951,408 (34th)	state tree....................Blue spruce state flower ....Sego lily state bird......................Seagull

Vermont
Montpelier

1791 (14th)	9,615 (43rd)	584,771 (49th)	state tree ....Sugar maple state flower ....Red clover state bird ....Hermit thrush

Virginia
Richmond

1788 (10th)	40,598 (36th)	6,618,358 (12th)	state tree ....Flowering dogwood state flower..........Flowering dogwood state bird......................Cardinal

Washington
Olympia

1889 (42nd)	68,126 (20th)	5,430,940 (15th)	state tree...............Western hemlock state flower.........Coast rhododendron state bird...............Willow goldfinch or wild canary

West Virginia
Charleston

1863 (35th)	24,231 (41st)	1,828,140 (35th)	state tree ....Sugar maple state flower ....Rhododendron state bird ....Cardina

Wisconsin
Madison

1848 (30th)	56,145 (26th)	5,122,871 (18th)	state tree ....Sugar maple state flower ....Wood violet state bird ....Robin

Wyoming
Cheyenne

1890 (44th)	97,914 (9th)	480,184 (50th)	state tree....................Cottonwood state flower ....Indian paintbrush state bird ....Western meadowlark

468

TERRITORIES AND POSSESSIONS OF THE UNITED STATES

		status	area in square miles	1990 pop census	symbols
District of Columbia Washington, D.C.		federal district	68	606,900	tree . . . . Scarlet oak lower . . . . American beauty rose bird . . . . Wood thrush
Puerto Rico San Juan		common-wealth	3,515	3,522,037	tree . . . . Ceiba flower . . . . Maga bird . . . . Reinita
American Virgin Islands Charlotte Amalie		territory	151	101,809	tree . . . . n.a. flower . . . . Yellow elder bird . . . . Yellow breast
Guam Agana		territory	209	132,726	tree . . . . Ifit (Intsiabijuga) flower . . . . Puti Tai Nobio (Bougainvillea) bird . . . . Toto (Fruit dove)
Northern Marianas Saipan		common-wealth	184	43,345	tree . . . . n.a. flower . . . . n.a. bird . . . . n.a.
American Samoa Pago Pago		territory	77	50,923	tree . . . . Ava flower . . . . Paogo bird . . . . n.a.

n.a. = not applicable/not available

THE PRESIDENTS
of the United States of America

George Washington
1789–1797
Born: 1732 in
  Westmoreland County,
  Virginia
Died: 1799
Elected from: Virginia
Party: none
Vice President: John Adams

John Adams
1797–1801
Born: 1735 in Braintree
  (now Quincy),
  Massachusetts
Died:1826
Elected from: Massachusetts
Party: Federalist
Vice President: Thomas
  Jefferson

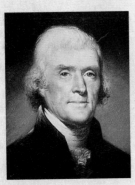

Thomas Jefferson
1801–1809
Born: 1743 in Goochland
  (now Albemarle) County,
  Virginia
Died: 1826
Elected from: Virginia
Party: Democratic-
  Republican
Vice Presidents: Aaron Burr,
  George Clinton

James Madison
1809–1817
Born: 1751 in Port Conway,
  Virginia
Died: 1836
Elected from: Virginia
Party: Democratic-
  Republican
Vice Presidents: George
  Clinton, Elbridge Gerry

James Monroe
1817–1825
Born: 1758 in
  Westmoreland County,
  Virginia
Died: 1831
Elected from: Virginia
Party: Democratic-
  Republican
Vice President: Daniel D.
  Tompkins

John Quincy Adams
1825–1829
Born: 1767 in Braintree
  (now Quincy),
  Masachusetts
Died: 1848
Elected from: Massachusetts
Party: Democratic-
  Republican
Vice President: John C.
  Calhoun

Andrew Jackson
1829–1837
Born: 1767 in Waxhaw, South Carolina
Died: 1845
Elected from: Tennessee
Party: Democratic
Vice Presidents: John C. Calhoun, Martin Van Buren

James K. Polk
1845–1849
Born: 1795 in Mecklenburg County, North Carolina
Died: 1849
Elected from: Tennessee
Party: Democratic
Vice President: George M. Dallas

Martin Van Buren
1837–1841
Born: 1782 in Kinderhook, New York
Died: 1862
Elected from: New York
Party: Democratic
Vice President: Richard M. Johnson

Zachary Taylor
1849–1850
Born: 1784 in Orange County, Virginia
Died: 1850
Elected from: Louisiana
Party: Whig
Vice President: Millard Fillmore

William Henry Harrison
1841
Born: 1773 in Berkeley, Virginia
Died: 1841
Elected from: Ohio
Party: Whig
Vice President: John Tyler

Millard Fillmore
1850–1853
Born: 1800 in Cayuga County, New York
Died: 1874
Elected as V.P. from: New York
Party: Whig
Vice President: None

John Tyler
1841–1845
Born: 1790 in Charles City County, Virginia
Died: 1862
Elected as V.P. from: Virginia
Party: Whig
Vice President: None

Franklin Pierce
1853–1857
Born: 1804 in Hilsboro, New Hampshire
Died: 1869
Elected from: New Hampshire
Party: Democratic
Vice President: William R. King

James Buchanan
1857–1861
Born: 1791 in Stony Batter,
 Pennsylvania
Died: 1868
Elected from: Pennsylvania
Party: Democratic
Vice President: John C.
 Breckinridge

Rutherford B. Hayes
1877–1881
Born: 1822 in Delaware,
 Ohio
Died: 1893
Elected from: Ohio
Party: Republican
Vice President: William A.
 Wheeler

Abraham Lincoln
1861–1865
Born: 1809 near
 Hodgenville, Kentucky
Died: 1865
Elected from: Illinois
Party: Republican
Vice Presidents: Hannibal
 Hamlin, Andrew Johnson

James A. Garfield
1881
Born: 1831 in Orange, Ohio
Died: 1881
Elected from: Ohio
Party: Republican
Vice President: Chester A.
 Arthur

Andrew Johnson
1865–1869
Born: 1808 in Raleigh,
 North Carolina
Died: 1875
Elected as V.P. from:
 Tennessee
Party: Democratic
Vice President: None

Chester A. Arthur
1881–1885
Born: 1830 in Fairfield,
 Vermont
Died: 1886
Elected as V.P. from: New
 York
Party: Republican
Vice President: None

Ulysses S. Grant
1869–1877
Born: 1822 in Point
 Pleasant, Ohio
Died: 1885
Elected from: Illinois
Party: Republican
Vice Presidents: Schuyler
 Colfax, Henry Wilson

Grover Cleveland
1885–1889
Born: 1837 in Caldwell,
 New Jersey
Died: 1908
Elected from: New York
Party: Democratic
Vice President: Thomas A.
 Hendricks

Benjamin Harrison
1889–1893
Born: 1833 in North Bend, Ohio
Died: 1901
Elected from: Indiana
Party: Republican
Vice President: Levi P. Morton

William Howard Taft
1909–1913
Born: 1857 in Cincinnati, Ohio
Died: 1931
Elected from: Ohio
Party: Republican
Vice President: James S. Sherman

Grover Cleveland
1893–1897
Born: 1837 in Caldwell, New Jersey
Died: 1908
Elected from: New York
Party: Democratic
Vice President: Adlai E. Stevenson

Woodrow Wilson
1913–1921
Born: 1856 in Staunton, Virginia
Died: 1924
Elected from: New Jersey
Party: Democratic
Vice President: Thomas R. Marshall

William McKinley
1897–1901
Born: 1843 in Niles, Ohio
Died: 1901
Elected from: Ohio
Party: Republican
Vice Presidents: Garret A. Hobart, Theodore Roosevelt

Warren G. Harding
1921–1923
Born: 1865 in Corsica (now Blooming Grove), Ohio
Died: 1923
Elected from: Ohio
Party: Republican
Vice President: Calvin Coolidge

Theodore Roosevelt
1901–1909
Born: 1858 in New York City, New York
Died: 1919
Elected as V.P. from: New York
Party: Republican
Vice President: Charles W. Fairbanks

Calvin Coolidge
1923–1929
Born: 1872 in Plymouth Notch, Vermont
Died: 1933
Elected as V.P. from: Massachusetts
Party: Republican
Vice President: Charles G. Dawes

Herbert Hoover
1929–1933
Born: 1874 in West Branch,
  Iowa
Died: 1964
Elected from: California
Party: Republican
Vice President: Charles
  Curtis

Dwight D. Eisenhower
1953–1961
Born: 1890 in Denison,
  Texas
Died: 1969
Elected from: New York
Party: Republican
Vice President: Richard M.
  Nixon

Franklin D. Roosevelt
1933–1945
Born: 1882 in Hyde Park,
  New York
Died: 1945
Elected from: New York
Party: Democratic
Vice Presidents: John N.
  Garner, Henry A. Wallace,
  Harry S. Truman

John F. Kennedy
1961–1963
Born: 1917 in Brookline,
  Massachusetts
Died: 1963
Elected from: Massachusetts
Party: Democratic
Vice President: Lyndon B.
  Johnson

Harry S. Truman
1945–1953
Born: 1884 in Lamar,
  Missouri
Died: 1972
Elected as V.P. from:
  Missouri
Party: Democratic
Vice President: Alben W.
  Barkley

Lyndon B. Johnson
1963–1969
Born: 1908 in Stonewall,
  Texas
Died: 1973
Elected from: Texas
Party: Democratic
Vice President: Hubert H.
  Humphrey

Richard M. Nixon
1969–1974
Born: 1913 in Yorba Linda,
  California
Died: 1994
Elected from: New York
Party: Republican
Vice President: Spiro T.
  Agnew, Gerald R. Ford

Ronald Reagan
1981–1989
Born: 1911 in Tampico,
  Illinois *Died: 1994*
Elected from: California
Party: Republican
Vice President: George Bush

Gerald R. Ford
1974–1977
Born: 1913 in Omaha,
  Nebraska
Party: Republican
Vice President: Nelson A.
  Rockefeller

George H.W. Bush
1989–1993
Born: 1924 in Milton,
  Connecticut
Elected from: Texas
Party: Republican
Vice President: J. Danforth
  Quayle

Jimmy Carter
1977–1981
Born: 1924 in Plains,
  Georgia
Elected from: Georgia
Party: Democratic
Vice President: Walter F.
  Mondale

William J. Clinton
1993–~~2001~~
Born: 1946 in Hope,
  Arkansas
Elected from: Arkansas
Party: Democratic
Vice President: Albert
  Gore, Jr.

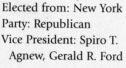

George W. Bush
2001 to present.
Born: 1946 in T
*   Texas.*
Elected from: Texas.
Party: Republican.
Vice President: Dick B.
Cheney.

GLOSSARY

abolition (page 167) Abolition meant ending slavery.

abolitionist (page 167) An abolitionist was a person who worked to end slavery.

acid rain (page 432) Acid rain is rain mixed with air pollution, which causes damage to the environment.

addicted (page 441) To be addicted means to not be able to stop using something.

affirmative action (page 384) Affirmative action programs require colleges and businesses to set aside a certain number of places for minorities.

aggression (page 344) Aggression is the use of military force.

AIDS (page 441) AIDS, or acquired immune deficiency syndrome, is a deadly disease caused by the HIV virus.

aircraft carrier (page 356) An aircraft carrier is a large ship that has a long, flat deck on which planes can land.

alliance (page 305) An alliance is an agreement between two or more nations to work together.

ally (page 70) An ally is a nation that promises to help another nation.

amendment (page 100) A law that is added to the Constitution is called an amendment.

ammunition (page 203) Ammunition is something that can be fired at an enemy. Cannon balls and bullets are kinds of ammunition.

Anaconda Plan (page 205) The Anaconda Plan was the strategy that the Union used to fight the Civil War.

anarchist (page 319) An anarchist is a person who does not believe in any form of government.

annex (page 285) To annex is to add or attach to something larger.

anthem (page 150) An anthem is a song that praises a country. The "Star-Spangled Banner" is the national anthem, or official song, of the United States.

anti-Semitism (page 344) Anti-Semitism is the hatred of Jews.

apartheid (page 429) Apartheid was the system in South Africa that kept different racial groups separated.

appeasement (page 345) Appeasement is the policy of giving into an enemy's demands to maintain peace.

appoint (page 138) To appoint means to choose a person for a job or government office.

apprentice (page 61) An apprentice agrees to work a set amount of time for a person who is skilled at making a product. In return the apprentice learns those skills.

arbitration (page 263) Arbitration is a process that helps two groups come to an agreement.

archaeologist (page 4) An archaeologist looks for bones, tools, and artifacts from people who lived long ago. These objects are studied to find out how people lived then.

arms race (page 372) The arms race is a competition between countries to build the largest military forces.

arsenal (page 196) An arsenal is a place where weapons are stored.

artifact (page 5) An artifact is an object, such as a tool or jewelry, made by a person who lived long ago.

assassin (page 305) An assassin is a person who kills someone for political reasons.

assassinate (page 218) To assassinate means to murder an important leader.

assembly line (page 320) An assembly line is a line of factory workers and machines used to put together a product.

astrolabe (page 15) An astrolabe is an instrument that measures how high in the sky the sun, stars, and planets are. The astrolabe helped sailors locate where they were.

asylum (page 169) An asylum is a hospital that cares for people with mental illnesses who cannot care for themselves.

atomic bomb (page 356) An atomic bomb is an explosive weapon that causes great destruction.

Axis nations (page 344) Germany, Italy, and Japan formed an alliance in the 1930s called the Axis.

balanced budget (page 443) A balanced budget is a budget in which the money taken in is equal to the money spent.

barbed wire (page 241) Barbed wire is twisted strands of wire that has barbs, or sharp points, along it. Barbed wire is used to make fences.

barrack (page 353) A barrack is a building used to house people temporarily.

battlefield (page 214) A battlefield is the place where armies fight a battle.

Berlin Airlift (page 372) The Berlin Airlift was a mission by the United States and Great Britain to deliver supplies to West Berlin by plane when the Soviet Union would not allow supplies to come in by land.

Bicentennial (page 402) The Bicentennial was the 200th birthday of the United States, celebrated on July 4, 1976.

big stick diplomacy (page 298) Big stick diplomacy was President Theodore Roosevelt's foreign policy. It said that the United States would use military force to settle problems.

bind up (page 217) To bind up means to put a bandage on a wound so that the wound will heal.

blend (page 180) To blend means to mix two or more things together.

blitzkrieg (page 345) A blitzkrieg is a quick military attack.

blockade (page 79) Blockade means one nation uses its ships to block an enemy's ports so that the enemy's ships cannot sail in or out.

border state (page 203) A border state was one of the eight states located along the border between the Union and the Confederacy.

boycott (page 72) A boycott is a protest against a group or a nation's actions by not buying goods from that group or nation.

Buddhism (page 392) Buddhism is a religion based on the teachings of Buddha.

budget (page 443) A budget is a plan for spending money.

Cabinet (page 138) The Cabinet is the group of people that advises the President and leads the executive departments of the government.

campaign (page 226) To campaign means to take part in activities to gain support for a cause. The cause might be getting a person elected or keeping a law from being passed.

Camp David Accords (page 416) The Camp David Accords was a peace treaty signed by Israel and Egypt in 1979.

candidate (page 142) A candidate is a person who runs in an election for a government office, such as President.

capital (page 248) Capital is money that is used to earn more money.

capitalism (page 249) Capitalism is a type of economic system that allows people to own businesses and keep the money the businesses earn.

carpetbagger (page 228) Carpetbagger was the name Southerners gave to a person from the North who came to the South during Reconstruction. Many carpetbaggers cared more about becoming rich than about helping the South.

cash crop (page 59) A cash crop is a crop that a farmer grows to make money.

casualty (page 393) A casualty is a person who is injured or killed during a war.

cease-fire (page 396) A cease-fire is an agreement to stop fighting.

central government (page 96) A central government is a government that rules an entire nation.

Central Intelligence Agency (page 403) The Central Intelligence Agency, or CIA, is a government agency that gathers political, economic, and military information about other nations.

charity (page 217) Charity means kindness and love to others.

charter (page 45) A charter is a paper signed by a person in power that gives the owner of the charter certain rights.

checks and balances (page 100) Checks and balances is a system of dividing power among the branches of a government so that no branch has enough power to control the others.

circumnavigate (page 19) Circumnavigate means to sail all the way around.

civil disobedience (page 382) A person commits civil disobedience when he or she peacefully refuses to obey certain laws that are considered unfair.

civilian (page 346) A civilian is a person who is not in the military.

civilization (page 8) A civilization is the way of life of a group of people who have a written language, laws, and a government.

Civil Rights Act (page 226) A Civil Rights Act is a law that protects the rights of people. Civil rights include the right to vote and the right to equal treatment under the law.

civil rights movement (page 378) The civil rights movement was the struggle to win equal rights for African Americans.

civil service (page 271) Civil service jobs are jobs in the federal government.

civil war (page 29) A civil war is a war between people who live in the same nation.

coalition (page 426) A coalition is a temporary alliance.

Cold War (page 368) The Cold War was a political and economic struggle between the United States and the Soviet Union that lasted from 1945 until about 1989.

collective bargaining (page 263) Collective bargaining is a process that helps two groups come to an agreement.

colony (page 17) A colony is a place ruled by another country.

commander in chief (page 78) The commander in chief is the leader in charge of all of a nation's armies.

Committee of Correspondence (page 72) A Committee of Correspondence was one of many protest groups in the 13 colonies that sent information to each other about the actions of the British.

commonwealth (page 288) A commonwealth is a territory, state, or nation that rules itself.

Communist (page 307) A Communist is someone who believes in the system of government called communism.

compass (page 15) A compass is an instrument that shows directions.

competition (page 249) Competition is when two or more businesses try to sell similar goods or services to the same people.

compromise (page 98) A compromise is a way of solving a problem in which each side gives up something they want so that an agreement can be made.

concentration camp (page 344) A concentration camp was a place during World War II where Jews and other people were kept as prisoners by the Nazis. Millions of prisoners were killed in concentration camps.

Confederacy (page 197) The Southern states that seceded at the beginning of the Civil War were called the Confederacy.

Confederate States of America (page 197) The Southern states that seceded at the beginning of the Civil War started a new nation called the Confederate States of America.

confederation (page 7) A confederation is a group of nations that have joined together for a purpose. Five Iroquois nations formed the Iroquois Confederation in order to have peace.

conquistador (page 25) A conquistador was one of the explorers who came from Spain to the Americas in the 1500s to conquer land for Spain.

conservation (page 274) Conservation is the protection and wise use of Earth's natural resources.

containment (page 370) Containment was President Harry Truman's policy to keep communism from spreading.

contra (page 419) The contras were Nicaraguan rebels who opposed the Sandinistas.

contract (page 39) A contract is an agreement between two or more people.

convert (page 36) To convert means to change to a different religion.

corollary (page 298) A corollary is an idea that follows up another idea. The Roosevelt Corollary builds upon the ideas of the Monroe Doctrine.

corporation (page 250) A corporation is a type of business.

cotton gin (page 155) The cotton gin is a machine that separates cotton seeds from cotton fibers.

counterculture (page 405) A counterculture is made up of a group of people that do not agree with the traditional beliefs of their society.

Creole (page 28) Creole was the Spanish name for a person who had Spanish ancestors but was born in the Americas.

criminal (page 169) A criminal is a person who has done a crime.

culture (page 5) Culture is the way of life of a group of people. Clothing, food, beliefs, language, and customs are all part of culture.

dame school (page 61) A dame school was a school for girls that was taught by a woman in her home.

debate (page 194) A debate is a discussion in which people tell why they are for or against an idea.

debtor (page 49) A debtor is a person who owes money.

defense industry (page 352) The defense industry is made up of businesses that produce weapons and other equipment for fighting wars.

defensive war (page 205) A defensive war is a war in which a nation tries to fight off attacks on its own land.

deficit (page 421) A deficit is when a government spends more money than it takes in.

delegate (page 78) A delegate is a person who is chosen to represent others at a meeting.

democracy (page 59) Democracy is government that is run by the people.

depression (page 271) A depression is a time when business activity is slow and many people are unemployed.

descendant (page 286) A descendant is a person that comes from a certain ancestor.

destroyer (page 346) A destroyer is a type of warship.

détente (page 406) Détente was a time of peaceful relationship between the United States and the Soviet Union.

dictator (page 219) A dictator is a leader who has complete power.

disability (page 166) A disability is a condition that makes it hard for part of a person's body or mind to work.

discrimination (page 379) Discrimination is the unfair treatment of a person because he or she belongs to a certain religious or racial group.

diverse (page 182) Diverse means made up of different kinds.

dogfight (page 306) A dogfight is a battle that takes place in the air between enemy planes.

dollar diplomacy (page 298) Dollar diplomacy was President Taft's policy toward Latin America. It encouraged the growth of American businesses there.

domino theory (page 392) The domino theory was the belief that if one country in Southeast Asia became a Communist nation, then all the other nations would become Communist as well.

draft (page 204) A draft is a rule that requires men of certain ages to serve in the armed forces.

drug abuse (page 441) Drug abuse is using a drug in a way that it was not intended to be used.

due process (page 227) Due process is a lawful way to give everyone the same rights and treatment.

elector (page 142) An elector is a person chosen by his or her state to be part of the Electoral College.

electoral college (page 142) The Electoral College is a group of delegates from each state who elect the President and Vice President of the United States.

electronic mail (page 453) Electronic mail, or e-mail, is a type of communication between computers.

emancipate (page 212) To emancipate means to set free.

Emancipation Proclamation (page 212) The Emancipation Proclamation was a paper written by President Abraham Lincoln that said all slaves in Confederate States at war with the Union were free.

Embargo Act (page 148) The Embargo Act of 1807 was a law that stopped Americans from trading with other countries.

embassy (page 396) An embassy is the official home and office of an ambassador to a foreign country.

emissions (page 451) Emissions are substances sent into the air that cause damage to the environment.

empire (page 9) An empire is a large area of land, sometimes including many nations, in which the people are ruled by one leader.

energy crisis (page 406) An energy crisis occurs when a nation does not have enough energy to meet the normal needs of all of its citizens.

Enlightenment (page 80) The Enlightenment was a movement during the 1700s that encouraged new ideas about freedom and government.

environmental pollution (page 451) Environmental pollution is when the earth is harmed through human activities.

Episcopal Church (page 60) In the United States, the Church of England was called the Episcopal Church.

escalate (page 393) To escalate means to increase.

established church (page 44) An established church is one that the government says everyone must belong to and that the people pay taxes to support.

ethnic group (page 304) An ethnic group is a group of people of the same race, of the same religion, or from the same country.

execute (page 320) To execute is to kill a person, by order of the government, as punishment for breaking the law.

execution (page 178) Execution is the killing of a person by a government as punishment for breaking the law.

executive (page 100) Executive means having to do with carrying out the nation's laws. The executive branch of the federal government is led by the President and carries out the laws of Congress.

expansionism (page 284) Expansionism is the desire to gain more land.

facilities (page 379) A facility is a place created to serve a particular purpose, such as a school or a hospital.

famine (page 429) A famine is a severe food shortage.

fare (page 39) A fare is the cost a passenger is charged for a journey on a ship.

Fascist (page 343) A Fascist is a member of the Fascist party. Fascist governments build powerful armies and are led by dictators.

favorable balance of trade (page 62) A favorable balance of trade means that a nation sells more products to other nations than it buys from other nations.

federal (page 99) Federal means having to do with a central, or national, government.

federalism (page 99) Federalism is a type of government in which power is divided between a national government and state governments.

fertile (page 179) Fertile means good for growing crops.

fiber (page 155) A fiber is a thin, threadlike part of a plant that can be spun into yarn.

fiber-optic cables (page 453) Fiber-optic cables are a type of wire that use light to carry a great deal of information.

flexibility (page 100) Flexibility is the quality of being able to change to fit new conditions.

foreign affairs (page 140) Foreign affairs means a nation's relationships with other nations.

foreign minister (page 141) A foreign minister is the person in some governments who handles problems and creates treaties with other countries.

freedman (page 226) A freedman was a slave who was set free.

free enterprise (page 249) Free enterprise is the economic system that allows people to operate businesses in competition with other businesses. It is so called because the businesses generally operate free from government rules.

Free Soiler (page 195) A Free Soiler was a person who believed that slavery should not be allowed in the western territories.

frontier (page 70) The frontier is an area in a country that has not been settled yet.

gas chamber (page 355) A gas chamber was a room that was filled up with poison gas to kill people.

gatherer (page 5) A gatherer was a person from long ago who found and collected foods such as fruit, nuts, and roots. Gatherers did not know how to grow their own food.

Gettysburg Address (page 215) The Gettysburg Address is a short speech given by Abraham Lincoln to dedicate the military cemetery built for the Union soldiers who died at the Battle of Gettysburg during the Civil War.

ghetto (page 261) A ghetto is a neighborhood in a city where people from the same country or of the same religion live because they are discriminated against.

glasnost (page 422) Glasnost was the increase in personal freedoms in the Soviet Union during the 1980s.

global warming (page 451) Global warming is a rise in the earth's temperature.

gold standard (page 270) The gold standard was an economic idea in which all paper money was backed by gold from the United States Treasury.

Good Neighbor Policy (page 299) The Good Neighbor Policy was a policy toward Latin America during the 1930s. It said that the United States would not use military force there.

grammar school (page 61) A grammar school is an elementary school.

grandfather clause (page 230) A grandfather clause is a part of a law that allows someone to be excused from the law.

Great Awakening (page 61) The Great Awakening was a religious movement that started in New England in the early 1700s.

guerrilla war (page 394) A guerrilla war is a war that is fought by soldiers called guerrillas who do not fight openly and make surprise attacks.

hijack (page 420) To hijack is to take control of a vehicle using force.

hippie (page 405) A hippie was a person in the 1960s and 1970s who did not believe in the established culture.

HIV virus (page 442) The HIV virus is the virus that causes AIDS.

Holocaust (page 355) The Holocaust was the mass murder of Jews and other people during World War II.

Hooverville (page 332) A Hooverville was an area of a city where poor, homeless people built shacks to live in during the Great Depression. Hoovervilles were named after President Hoover.

hostage (page 419) A hostage is a person who is held as a prisoner until demands made by the captors are met.

Huguenot (page 29) Huguenot was the name for French Protestants during the 1500s and 1600s.

human rights (page 418) Human rights are the rights to personal freedom and safety.

human sacrifice (page 8) Human sacrifice means killing human beings as a gift to a god. Some ancient peoples believed that their gods needed human sacrifices or the gods would become angry and punish the people.

illegal alien (page 444) An illegal alien is an immigrant who enters a country without permission.

impeach (page 227) To impeach is to charge a government leader with a crime.

import (page 431) To import is to bring in goods from other nations.

impress (page 148) To impress means to force a person to serve in the navy.

income tax (page 205) An income tax is a law saying that people must give a certain amount of the money they earn to the government.

indentured servant (page 39) An indentured servant was a person who agreed to work a set number of years for a person who would pay the cost of the trip to the English colonies.

indigo (page 60) Indigo is a plant that was raised as a cash crop in the 13 colonies. A blue dye can be made from indigo.

Industrial Revolution (page 155) The Industrial Revolution was a change from making products by hand at home to making products by machine in factories.

inflation (page 270) Inflation is a sharp, quick rise in prices.

injunction (page 264) An injunction is an order given by a court that forbids a person from doing something.

insurance (page 334) Insurance is protection against property loss or damage.

integration (page 379) Integration is the act of making something open to people of all races.

Internet (page 453) The Internet is a system that links millions of computers.

internment camp (page 353) An internment camp was a place where Japanese Americans living on the West Coast were sent and held as prisoners by the government during World War II.

Intolerable Acts (page 72) The Intolerable Acts were laws that Parliament passed to punish the American colonists. Intolerable means hard to put up with. The colonists called them the Intolerable Acts because the laws were so unfair.

invest (page 330) To invest is to buy something or to put money into a business in order to make more money.

investigation (page 407) An investigation is the act of looking into a specific subject carefully to get information.

iron curtain (page 370) The iron curtain was a term that described the political division between Eastern and Western Europe during the Cold War.

irrigation canal (page 5) An irrigation canal is a ditch that carries water from a river to a farm to water crops.

Islam (page 36) Islam is a religion based on the teachings of Muhammad. People who follow Islam are called Muslims.

isolationism (page 346) Isolationism is a policy in which a nation avoids getting involved with the economic and political problems of other nations.

isolationist (page 285) An isolationist nation is a nation that avoids economic or political dealings with other countries.

isthmus (page 296) An isthmus is a narrow strip of land that connects two larger pieces of land.

joint stock company (page 45) A joint-stock company is a business that is owned by many people. If the company makes money, all the people who own stock in the company share the money.

journeyman (page 62) A journeyman is a person who has learned enough skills by working for another person to be able to work on his or her own. A person cannot become a journeyman until he or she has been an apprentice for a number of years.

judicial (page 100) Judicial means having to do with judges and courts of law. The judicial branch of the federal government is made up of courts. The judges in these courts use the laws made by Congress to make decisions.

judicial review (page 148) Judicial review is the power of the United States Supreme Court to decide if a state or federal law is unconstitutional, or says something different from the laws in the Constitution.

just (page 217) Just means fair to all.

Ku Klux Klan (page 229) The Ku Klux Klan, or KKK, was a secret organization started by Southerners after the Civil War. The KKK attacked, frightened, and killed African Americans to stop them from using the rights they had won.

labor (page 169) Labor means people who work.

labor union (page 169) A labor union is a group of workers who join together, often to demand better pay and working conditions.

laissez-faire (page 253) Laissez-faire is the idea that the government should not try to control business.

lasers (page 453) Lasers are powerful beams of light.

latitude (page 179) A latitude is an imaginary line circling the globe. Latitudes are used to measure distance north or south of the equator. Lines of latitude are also known as parallels.

lay siege (page 216) To lay siege means to try to conquer an area by surrounding it with an army so that no food, supplies, or people can go in or out.

legislative (page 100) Legislative means having to do with making laws. The legislative branch of the federal government is Congress.

liberate (page 355) To liberate means to set free.

literacy test (page 230) A literacy test was a reading test a voter had to pass in order to vote. Literacy means the ability to read and write.

log (page 20) A log is a journal written by the captain of a ship to record the events that happen on the trip.

Loyalist (page 80) A Loyalist was a colonist who wanted the 13 colonies to remain part of Great Britain.

Magna Carta (page 68) The Magna Carta was the first set of laws in England to limit the king's power.

mainland (page 17) The mainland is the land that is part of a continent.

majority (page 157) A majority is more than half. If 100 people vote, at least 51 votes are needed to make a majority.

malaria (page 297) Malaria is a deadly disease that causes chills, fever, and sweating. People get malaria from the bite of an infected mosquito.

malice (page 217) Malice means wanting to hurt others.

management (page 262) Management is made up of the person or persons who are in charge of a business.

Manifest Destiny (page 179) Manifest Destiny was the belief that the United States should rule all of the land between the Atlantic and the Pacific oceans.

manufacture (page 59) Manufacture means to make products, usually by machine in factories.

McCarthyism (page 374) McCarthyism, named for Senator Joseph McCarthy, is the policy of falsely accusing people of working against the government.

Medicare (page 404) Medicare is a federal health care program that provides medical care for older Americans.

mental illness (page 169) A mental illness is a disease of the mind. A person with a mental illness is sick and needs medicine or special care.

mercantilism (page 62) Mercantilism is the idea that nations become wealthy by selling more goods to other countries than they buy from other countries. Mercantilism was popular in Europe during the 1600s and 1700s.

merchant ship (page 307) A merchant ship is a ship that carries goods.

mestizo (page 28) Mestizo was the Spanish name for a person whose parents were Indian and Spanish.

microchip (page 453) A microchip is a tiny device that stores or processes information in a computer.

microsurgery (page 453) Microsurgery is surgery that is done with microscopes and specially built, small instruments.

Middle Passage (page 37) The Middle Passage was the step in the slave trade when slaves were sent by ship from Africa to America.

migrant farm worker (page 332) A migrant farm worker is a person who goes from farm to farm looking for work.

militarism (page 304) Militarism is the build up of large, powerful armies and navies.

militia (page 73) A militia is a group of people who train themselves to act as soldiers during a war.

minority (page 336) A minority is a group of people that is thought to be different than the larger group it is a part of because of race or religion.

missile (page 403) A missile is a weapon that is shot at a target.

mission (page 28) A mission was a place where Spanish priests taught their religion to Indians.

missionary (page 179) A missionary is a person who tries to teach his or her religion to a group of people who do not yet believe in that religion.

monarch (page 15) A monarch is a king or queen.

monopoly (page 251) A monopoly is when one company controls an entire industry.

morale (page 83) Morale is a feeling of excitement and purpose shared by a group.

muckraker (page 272) A muckraker is a writer who exposes political and social wrongdoings in business and in government. Muckrakers got their name because they raked up the muck, or dirt, in American life.

mulatto (page 28) Mulatto was the Spanish name for a person who had African and Spanish or African and Indian parents.

multicultural (page 438) Multicultural means made up of different cultures.

Muslim (page 35) A Muslim is a person who follows the religion of Islam.

NAFTA (page 432) NAFTA, or the North American Free Trade Agreement, is a trade agreement between the United States, Canada, and Mexico.

NASA (page 403) NASA, the National Aeronautics and Space Administration, is the United States' space agency.

National Grange (page 269) The National Grange is an organization that promotes laws that are helpful to farmers.

nationalism (page 304) Nationalism is a feeling of deep love and loyalty for one's nation.

nativism (page 319) Nativism is a fear of foreigners.

natural resource (page 248) A natural resource is a material found in nature that can be used by people. Iron, coal, water, and trees are natural resources.

naval (page 286) Naval means having to do with a navy.

Navigation Acts (page 62) The Navigation Acts were trade laws that Parliament began to pass in 1651. These laws forced England's colonies to trade only with England using English ships.

Nazi (page 343) A Nazi is a member of the Nazi party. The Nazi party in Germany believed in nationalism and blamed other people, particularly Jews, for their country's problems.

negotiate (page 396) To negotiate is to talk to reach an agreement.

neutral (page 80) Neutral means not taking sides during a war or disagreement.

nominate (page 196) To nominate means to name a person to run for an office as a candidate in an election.

nonaggression pact (page 345) A non-aggression pact is an agreement between two countries to not attack each other during a war.

nonrenewable resources (page 452) Nonrenewable resources are natural resources, such as coal and oil, that cannot be replaced once they are used up.

nonviolent resistance (page 382) Nonviolent resistance uses peaceful methods, such as boycotts, sit-ins, and marches, to end unfair laws.

novel (page 194) A novel is a long story that a writer invented.

nullify (page 159) To nullify means to make a law no longer exist.

oath (page 225) An oath is a promise.

Open Door Policy (page 289) The Open Door Policy was the American idea in the early 1900s that all nations should be allowed to use China's ports.

open range (page 240) The open range was unfenced, grassy land on which cattle grazed, or fed.

oppose (page 195) To oppose means to be against or act against something.

overthrow (page 428) To overthrow is to remove from power.

pacifism (page 360) Pacifism is the belief that wars are wrong and that disputes should be settled peacefully.

pamphlet (page 79) A pamphlet is a short booklet.

parallel (page 179) A parallel is an imaginary line circling the globe. Parallels measure the distance north or south of the equator. Parallels are also known as lines of latitude.

pardon (page 407) To pardon is to forgive a person for crimes he or she may have committed.

Parliament (page 68) Parliament is the group of people who make laws for Great Britain. British people vote for people to represent them in Parliament.

partnership (page 249) A partnership is when two or more people own and run a business together.

pass (page 180) A pass is a way between or through mountains.

Patriot (page 80) A Patriot was an American colonist who wanted independence from Great Britain.

Peace Corps (page 402) The Peace Corps is an organization made up of volunteers who go to developing countries to teach people how to improve health care, farming, and education.

peasant (page 29) In some European countries, a poor person who does farm work is called a peasant.

pension (page 334) A pension is a sum of money paid regularly to a person after he or she has retired from a job.

perestroika (page 421) Perestroika was the opening up of the Soviet economy during the 1980s.

persecuted (page 344) To persecute is to harm someone because of their beliefs.

persecution (page 170) Persecution means causing a person to suffer, often because of his or her race, religion, or ideas.

peso (page 432) The peso is the unit of money used in Mexico.

plantation (page 27) A plantation is a large farm where one or two cash crops are grown.

planter (page 59) A planter is the owner of a plantation.

poison gas (page 306) Poison gas is a deadly chemical used in war.

polio (page 337) Polio is a disease that is caused by a virus. It leads to paralysis and mainly affects children.

political party (page 141) A political party is a group of people who work together to get people elected who agree with their ideas.

political right (page 169) A political right allows a person to be involved with government. Political rights include the right to vote, the right to serve on a jury, and the right to hold a public office.

poll tax (page 230) A poll tax is a tax people pay when they vote.

popular sovereignty (page 194) Popular sovereignty means the vote of the people decides an issue.

poverty (page 243) Poverty means being poor, or having little money.

poverty line (page 441) The poverty line is an amount of money that the federal government uses to determine whether or not a person is poor.

precedent (page 138) A precedent is an action that sets an example for others to follow. George Washington created a precedent when he selected a Cabinet of people to advise him.

prejudice (page 39) Prejudice is an unfair dislike or hatred of a person who belongs to a certain group or looks a certain way.

prey (page 205) Prey is an animal that is hunted for food by another animal.

principle (page 99) A principle is an important idea that shapes and guides people's choices and decisions.

privatization (page 443) Privatization is the act of allowing private companies to run government programs.

proclamation (page 70) A proclamation is an order that is written by a government leader.

Prohibition (page 317) Prohibition was the time period from 1919 until 1933 when it was illegal to manufacture, sell, drink, or ship alcoholic beverages.

propaganda (page 308) Propaganda is ideas or information that is deliberately spread to try to influence how people think and act.

proprietary colony (page 46) A proprietary colony was a colony that was owned and ruled by one person or a small group of people.

proprietor (page 46) A proprietor is an owner of a business or land.

prosperity (page 319) Prosperity is success, wealth, or good fortune in life.

public office (page 169) A public office is an elected or appointed job in the government.

pursuit of happiness (page 80) The pursuit of happiness means the right to earn a living and to own property.

pyramid (page 8) A pyramid is a large stone building made of four triangle-shaped walls that meet at the top in a point.

quota system (page 261) The quota system in the United States limited the number of immigrants from different countries who could move to this country.

race riot (page 384) A race riot is a violent disturbance caused by the frustration that one race feels at being treated unfairly.

racism (page 319) Racism is a person's belief that he or she is better than other people who are not of the same race.

Radical Republican (page 225) A Radical Republican was a member of a group in Congress who wanted to punish the South for starting the Civil War.

ratify (page 96) To ratify means to approve by a vote.

ration (page 353) To ration is to limit the amount of items allowed.

reaper (page 239) A reaper is a machine that harvests crops.

rebel (page 140) A rebel is a person who fights the government and refuses to obey its laws.

rebellion (page 193) A rebellion is a fight against the government or the people in power.

Reconstruction (page 225) Reconstruction was the period after the Civil War when the Southern states became part of the United States again.

recovery (page 334) A recovery is a return to normal conditions.

recycle (page 353) To recycle means to make an item fit to be used again.

Red Scare (page 319) The Red Scare was a panic that occurred in 1919 when Americans feared that Communists might win control of the United States. It is so called because red was a symbol of communism.

refinery (page 252) A refinery is a place where oil is cleaned and turned into other products.

reform (page 165) Reform is a change to improve something.

refuel (page 286) To refuel means to take on a fresh supply of fuel.

refugee (page 403) A refugee is a person who has to leave his or her country to find safety.

rejoin (page 202) To rejoin means to join again.

religious freedom (page 44) Religious freedom is the right to belong to any religion.

renewable resources (page 451) Renewable resources are resources, such as trees and animals, that can be replaced.

repeal (page 146) To repeal means to end or to remove a law.

representation (page 71) Representation means standing in someone's place. Having representation in the government means having people in the government who will fight for the needs of the people who voted for them.

representative (page 45) A representative is a person who is elected to work in the government for the people who voted for him or her.

489

representative government (page 45) In a representative government, people vote for leaders to work for them in the government and make the laws.

reservation (page 241) A reservation is a piece of land set aside by the federal government as a place for Indians.

retreat (page 81) To retreat means to back away from danger.

revolt (page 28) A revolt is a fight in which people turn against the ruling government or the people in power.

riot (page 262) A riot is a violent disturbance created by a large number of people.

royal colony (page 46) A royal colony was a colony owned by a king or a queen.

rum (page 37) Rum is an alcoholic drink that is made from sugar or molasses.

sanctions (page 429) A sanction is a method used by nations to force a country to change.

Sandinista (page 419) A Sandinista is a member of a group of people who ruled Nicaragua.

satellite (page 374) A satellite is an object that orbits a planet.

scalawag (page 228) Scalawag was the name used by Southern Democrats for white Southern Republicans who worked in Reconstruction governments.

scandal (page 318) A scandal occurs when a person does something that leads him or her to be publicly embarrassed.

secede (page 194) To secede means to leave an organization.

sectionalism (page 156) Sectionalism is caring more about one's section of the nation and less about the entire nation.

segregation (page 230) Segregation means separating people because of their race.

self-governing colony (page 47) A self-governing colony was a colony in which people voted for their own leaders.

senator (page 98) A senator is a member of a senate.

separation of powers (page 100) Separation of powers divides power between the branches of government. Giving some power to each branch prevents one part of the government from having too much power.

settlement (page 26) A settlement is a small, new place to live, usually in an area where other people do not live.

settlement house (page 272) A settlement house provides poor people with services such as English classes, summer camp for children, and day care.

shah (page 418) The shah was the name given for the rulers of Iran.

share (page 250) A share is one of the equal parts of ownership into which a business is divided. A share is sold to a specific person or group.

sharecropper (page 229) A sharecropper was a poor farmer who rented farmland from a landowner and paid rent with a share of the crops.

sit-in (page 382) A sit-in is a peaceful way to protest unfair laws. People seat themselves in a place that follows these unfair laws and refuse to leave until their demands are listened to.

slogan (page 179) A slogan is a group of words that expresses an idea. The person who makes up a slogan wants people to hear and remember the idea.

smallpox (page 26) Smallpox is a sickness that causes tiny pocks, or blisters. Smallpox spreads easily from one person to another.

solar energy (page 452) Solar energy is energy from the sun.

Solidarity (page 422) Solidarity was a labor union that helped end communism in Poland.

sphere of influence (page 289) A sphere of influence is an area of a nation that is controlled by a foreign nation.

spike (page 240) A spike is a large, heavy nail that is used to join railroad tracks.

spoils system (page 158) The spoils system is the custom of allowing a President who wins an election to give government jobs to the people who helped him or her.

stable government (page 294) A stable government is a government that does not change frequently.

stagflation (page 407) Stagflation is when inflation combines with unemployment to create a stagnant, or slow, economy.

states' rights (page 159) States' rights is the idea that state governments, not the federal government, should have control over how their state is run.

stock (page 250) A person owns stock when he or she owns one or more shares in a business.

stock market (page 330) A stock market is a place where stocks are traded.

Strategic Defense Initiative (page 421) The Strategic Defensive Initiative was a plan for a defense system that would use satellites to shoot down nuclear missiles fired at the United States. It is also called Star Wars.

strategy (page 353) A strategy is a plan for winning a war.

submarine (page 306) A submarine is a ship that can travel underwater.

suffrage (page 272) Suffrage is the right to vote.

superpower (page 368) A superpower is a powerful nation, such as the United States, whose actions and policies affect many other countries.

supply-side economics (page 423) Supply-side economics is the idea that the economy will improve if the amount of goods produced increases.

surrender (page 70) To surrender means to give up fighting.

survive (page 6) To survive means to stay alive.

tariff (page 156) A tariff is a tax on goods that a nation buys from other nations. Tariffs protect a nation's businesses because tariffs make foreign goods more expensive, so people will buy goods made in their own nation.

taxation (page 71) Taxation is the act of requiring people to pay a certain amount of money to the government.

technology (page 15) Technology is the knowledge that people use to improve their way of life. For example, technology helps people find new ways to travel and to make new foods and medicines.

tenement (page 260) A tenement is an apartment building that is usually run-down and crowded, and which has unhealthy living conditions.

tepee (page 6) A tepee is an Indian tent made of animal skins.

terrace (page 9) A terrace is a flat place made on the side of a hill or mountain to keep rain from washing away plants and soil.

terrorism (page 420) Terrorism is the use of dangerous, violent acts against innocent people to force an enemy to give in to terrorists' demands.

textile mill (page 155) A textile mill is a factory where machines spin thread and make cloth.

third party (page 274) A third party is a political party other than the two major parties.

torpedo (page 308) A torpedo is a missile that is launched from a ship or a submarine and is designed to blow up when it hits its target.

totalitarian (page 343) Totalitarian governments are led by dictators that have total power over the people they rule.

total war (page 216) Total war means destroying everything in the enemy's area in order to force the enemy to surrender.

totem pole (page 6) A totem pole is a wooden post carved and painted with symbols of the owner's family. Some Native American tribes made totem poles.

traitor (page 81) A traitor is a person who works against his or her own nation.

transcendentalist (page 170) A transcendentalist was a person in the 1800s who believed in the importance of each individual and in living close to nature.

transcontinental (page 239) Transcontinental means across a continent. The transcontinental railroad goes from the Atlantic Ocean to the Pacific Ocean.

treaty (page 70) A treaty is an agreement between two or more nations.

trench warfare (page 306) Trench warfare was used to fight World War I. Trenches were long ditches dug in the earth in which soldiers hid and attacked the enemy.

triangular trade route (page 63) A triangular trade route was a trip to three different places on the globe to trade one or two products for another product.

tributary (page 19) A tributary is a river or stream that runs into a larger river or stream.

truce (page 373) A truce is an agreement between enemies to stop fighting.

trust (page 251) A trust is formed when a group of companies join together under the same leadership so that they can control an industry.

trustbuster (page 273) A trustbuster is a person who tries to break up and punish business trusts.

turning point (page 82) A turning point is a time when an important change takes place.

unalienable right (page 80) An unalienable right is a right that belongs to all people and should never be taken away.

unconditional surrender (page 215) Unconditional surrender means giving up completely.

unconstitutional (page 142) A law that says something other than what the laws in the Constitution say is unconstitutional.

Union (page 156) The Union is the United States of America.

unskilled labor (page 258) Unskilled labor means workers who have few skills.

urban (page 322) Urban means having to do with a city.

vaccine (page 442) A vaccine is a medicine given to protect against a disease.

vaquero (page 181) A vaquero is a Mexican cowboy.

veteran (page 333) A veteran is a person who has been in the armed forces.

viceroy (page 28) A viceroy is a governor who rules in the place of a king or queen.

Vietnamization (page 395) Vietnamization was a program to train South Vietnam's soldiers to fight the Communists by themselves.

War Hawk (page 149) A War Hawk was an American who wanted to fight a war.

Western Hemisphere (page 294) The Western Hemisphere is the western half of the earth. It includes North America and South America.

withdrawal (page 395) Withdrawal is the act of removing, as in troops from a battle.

world power (page 284) A world power is a major country whose actions affect other countries of the world.

yellow journalism (page 287) Yellow journalism is exciting but untrue stories printed by a newspaper to attract more readers and sell more papers.

Zionism (page 360) Zionism is the belief that Jews should have their own country in Palestine, or present-day Israel.